HANDBOOK OF
NETWORKING & CONNECTIVITY

HANDBOOK OF
NETWORKING & CONNECTIVITY

Edited by
Gary R. McClain

AP PROFESSIONAL

Boston   San Diego   New York
London   Sydney   Tokyo   Toronto

AP PROFESSIONAL
955 Massachusetts Avenue, Cambridge, MA 02139

An imprint of ACADEMIC PRESS, INC.
A Division of HARCOURT BRACE & COMPANY

United Kingdom Edition published by
ACADEMIC PRESS LIMITED
24–28 Oval Road, London NW1 7DX

ISBN 0-12-482080-8

Printed in the United States of America
94 95 96 97 98 ML 9 8 7 6 5 4 3 2 1

Contents

2   Guide to Digital Communications   61

5   An Overview of the Synchronous Optical Network   139

6   X.25 and Worldwide Networking   167

PART 3   Metropolitan Area Networks   213

7   Metropolitan Area Networks   215

8   An Overview of the Switched Multimegabit Data Service   231

11 Disaster Recovery Planning for Local Area Networks   317

12 Selecting a Tape Backup System   333

PART 5   Data Communications   349

Foreword

The content of the *Handbook of Networking and Connectivity* illustrates the diversity of issues and considerations in this important area of information management. I am grateful to the contributors for taking time out from their hectic schedules to expand the body of knowledge in this subject area and provide valuable reference materials for technical professionals. The chapter contributors are all experts in their own right.

Contributors

Numbers in parentheses indicate the page on which each author's contribution begins.

E. Scott Barielle (61), Irv Shapiro and Associates, Ltd.

Nick Blozan (333), M.T. Network Solutions, Inc.

Fred M. Burg (167), AT&T Bell Laboratories

William Carltock (297), Equinox Systems Inc.

Shaun E. Deedy (73), LXE, Inc.

Mikael Edholm (351), Ericsson Hewlett-Packard Telecommunications, A.B.

John Enck (265), Forest Computer Inc.

Marc Farley (317), Palindrome Corporation

Gary C. Kessler (139, 231), Hill Associates

Thomas A. Maufer (139), NASA Goddard Space Flight Center

Conall Ryan (375), ON Technology Corporation

Matthew N.O. Sadiku (123, 215), Temple University

Kenneth M. Zemrowski (3), TRW Corporation

Introduction

The new era in information management during the 1990s will focus on connectivity, with the technical staff increasingly placed in the role of not only making sure that the hardware and software resources *work*, but work *together* as a unified whole. Attaining this level of connectivity will require an extensive knowledge of both proprietary and international standards as well as an understanding of the technical considerations inherent in choosing one networking strategy over another.

As organizations streamline to compete in the global economy, it is critical that diverse information resources be coordinated and distributed across departmental, national, and even international boundaries. Hardware and software vendors have individually moved toward network management, through local and wide area networks that form a basis for enterprise-wide information sharing.

Network management professionals will be key players in IS departments of the 1990s. Many vendors are building some level of standards compliance into their product offerings. However, the IS staff will be responsible for understanding the nuances of this compliance, discerning the levels of compliance and approach that is correct for their organizations, and making the strategy work.

The overall purpose of the *Handbook of Networking and Connectivity* is to serve as a comprehensive networking and connectivity reference book for MIS networking and systems professionals. The reader will be able to look to this book as a source for understanding the current connectivity standards in use, as well as hardware and software options, and as a guide for solving specific problems that arise in designing and maintaining organizational networks.

P A R T 1

Enterprise-Wide Networks

1

Open Systems Interconnection

Kenneth M. Zemrowski, CDP, CCP
TRW Corporation

PURPOSE OF OSI

The aim of Open Systems Interconnection (OSI) is to allow, with a minimum of technical agreement outside the interconnection standards, the interconnection of computer systems:

- from different manufacturers,
- under different management,
- of different levels of complexity, and
- of different technologies.

The OSI standards were developed to allow computer systems built by different vendors to exchange data; the previous use of proprietary network architectures hampered the development of large, multivendor networks. Even though these computer systems have different operating systems and vary in how data is processed internally, as long as the information that passes between the processors conforms to the OSI international standards, information can be interpreted upon receipt and communication is possible. Openness, in this context, does not necessarily imply that the network is public.

With the growing importance of computer interconnection, there was a need for increasingly sophisticated and powerful communications standards, as well as improved planning to support future growth and produce well-coordinated, timely standards. By the early 1980s, proprietary solutions were causing difficulty in establishing networks, as networks grew more complicated and there was increased demand for multivendor systems. By the 1990s, users demanded open system architectures that would permit the use of new components in a system, whether for purposes of technology insertion or simply to enhance their choice of vendors.

By developing a Reference Model of OSI, the International Organization for Standardization (ISO) expected to provide a common basis for the coordination of standards development for the purpose of systems interconnection, while allowing the existing standards to be placed into perspective within the overall reference model. This was an attempt to provide improved capabilities in the then unstandardized area of process-to-process communications (in contrast to node-to-node) while preserving the investment in existing protocols.

OSI has reached a point where there is arguably a critical mass of software available to begin fulfilling the promises of OSI. There are now production quality implementations for a variety of platforms. Vendors cooperate to verify interoperability, and there are also independent agencies that certify conformance to protocol standards and test interoperability of implementations (see the section on Conformance Testing).

PRINCIPLES OF OSI

OSI involves the exchange of information between open systems, but not the internal functioning of each individual system. (Open systems environments are concerned with the openness of individual systems and the portability of the applications. OSI is primarily concerned with interoperability.) This exchange of information is facilitated by the mutual use of applicable standards and agreement on the use of options and parameters from those standards.

The OSI Reference Model does not provide a protocol (or even selection of protocols). Rather, it provides a conceptual and functional framework that allows international teams of experts to work productively and independently on the development of standards for each layer of OSI. Another consideration was the ability to accommodate existing protocols in the framework. The OSI model has sufficient flexibility to accommodate advances in technology and expansion in user demands. This flexibility is also intended to allow the phased transition from existing implementations to

OSI standards. Besides flexibility to accommodate change, the framework helps support planning.

OSI addresses both the network interconnections and the interworking of applications. Applications may be user-developed or include standard applications such as message handling (using X.400, MHS) or file transfer (file transfer, access, and management [FTAM]). In addition, OSI standards now explicitly address conformance testing, which forms an important step in assuring interoperability.

The important principles are that (1) each layer performs a unique, generic, well-defined function, and (2) layer boundaries are designed so that the amount of information flowing between any two adjacent layers is minimized. A particular layer has to provide a sufficient number of services to the layer immediately above for the latter to perform its functions.

The functions of each of the protocol layers will be explained later in this chapter. The protocols can be connection-oriented or connectionless. In connection-oriented protocols, a user must set up a virtual connection, which is valid for the life of the communications activity, and disappears when the communications activity disappears. The converse of this is connectionless activity, whereby the user does not set up a virtual connection but communicates by transmitting individual "pieces" of information. An example of the former is a telephone conversation; an example of the latter is message delivery by the postal service.

OSI standards have been developed under the aegis of the ISO and International Electrotechnical Committee (IEC), with many of the standards developed collaboratively with the International Telephone and Telegraph Consultative Committee (CCITT). Where the CCITT and JTC1 (ISO/IEC Joint Technical Committee 1) have equivalent specifications, the documents are technically aligned.

BASIC PRINCIPLES OF LAYERING

The first step in OSI standards development was the creation of an OSI Reference Model. This model is divided into seven layers; each layer provides a well-defined set of functions necessary for the effective transmission of data. Each of these layers provides a service to the layer above by carrying on a conversation with the same layer on another processor. The rules and conventions of that conversation are called a protocol. The information that is passed between a layer on one processor and the corresponding layer (or peer entity) on another processor is called a protocol data unit (PDU).

The OSI framework imposes a seven layer model to define the communications processes that occur between systems. The Basic Reference Model (ISO 7498-1:1984) describes seven layers, as well as the relationships between a layer and the layer below it. The reference model, and other standards, define the services necessary to perform the functions. Other standards specify the protocols for how the information is actually communicated. Only protocols are actually implemented; the service definitions describe the structures and functions that are performed, while the protocols describe the detailed formats and dialogs.

Service primitives are special messages that define the services that a layer provides. The details of how the services are implemented are transparent to the service user, which is usually the next upper layer. Communication between layers is via a service access point (SAP), which is a special location through which service primitives pass. Service request and service response information passes between adjacent layers at the service access point. Service definitions are defined primarily for the purpose of developing protocol specifications.

For any layer (N+1), the reference model describes services provided by the next lower layer (N). For example, the Application Layer (Layer 7) uses services provided by the Presentation Layer (Layer 6).

Layers 1 to 6, together with the physical media for OSI, provide a step-by-step enhancement of communication services. The boundary between two layers identifies a stage in this enhancement of services at which an OSI service standard is defined, while the functioning of the layers is governed by OSI protocol standards. In some cases, there are several standards defining services and protocols for a particular layer, especially at the Application Layer.

According to ISO/IEC 7498-1, several principles are used in determining the seven layers in the Reference Model and will also guide future decisions.

1. Do not create so many layers as to make the system engineering task of describing and integrating the layers more difficult than necessary.

2. Create a boundary at a point where the description of services can be small and the number of interactions across the boundary are minimized.

3. Create separate layers to handle functions that are manifestly different in the process performed or the technology involved.

4. Collect similar functions into the same layer.

5. Select boundaries at a point that past experience has demonstrated to be successful.

6. Create a layer of easily localized functions so that the layer could be totally redesigned and its protocols changed in a major way to take advantage of new advances in architectural, hardware, or software technology without changing the services expected from and provided to the adjacent layers.

7. Create a boundary where it may be useful at some point in time to have the corresponding interface standardized.

Within the abstract model, an open system is logically composed of an ordered set of subsystems. Adjacent subsystems communicate through their common boundary. Entities in the same layer are termed *peer entities*.

It is important to note the distinction between the abstract model, which is expressed in ISO 7498-1, and the real model, which is embodied in implementations. The real model does not require discrete separations between the layers, which may reduce the protocol overhead. However, a "glued together" stack might make it more difficult to perform conformance tests, which rely on an exposed stack at various layers. Typically, there will be an exposed interface to the Network Layer, which is necessary if a node is to serve as an intermediate system, and to the Transport Layer. The upper layers are often grouped together without having explicit separations between the software implementing each layer. (See Figure 1.1.)

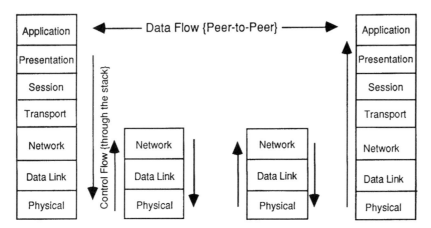

Figure 1.1 Data flow and control flow from end system through intermediate nodes to end system.

As a result of proposed changes to the reference model, it may become easier for applications to directly use the Transport Layer services while maintaining compatibility with existing implementations. Often, this can provide the possibility of improved performance by reducing overhead.

Use of a layered model can help understanding as well as giving a framework for developing standards. The framework gives an organization to the functions that would need to be performed anyway. Consider an analogy with the telephone system, which will be used to introduce the names of the lower layers of the protocol stack.

Layer 1 (Physical): Mechanical, electrical, functional, and procedural aspects of data circuits among network nodes.

> *Analogy*: To connect to the telephone network, we must have the actual wires and connectors and electrical signaling protocols. There are various types of connectors, definitions of voltage levels and signaling rates, and assigned functions to each wire in a cable.

Layer 2 (Data Link): Transfers data frames over the Physical Layer; responsible for reliability.

> *Analogy*: A data link is signaled (to our ears or to a fax or modem) by presence of a dial tone. Hanging up terminates a data link.

Layer 3 (Network): Routes information among source, intermediate, and destination nodes. Establishes and maintains connection, if using connection-oriented exchange.

> *Analogy*: In a telephone system, this activity is similar to dialing the phone number and being processed through the various intermediate exchanges and long distance networks.

Layer 4 (Transport): Manages connections between two end nodes by establishing and releasing end-to-end connections; controlling the size, sequence, and flow of transport packets; and mapping transport and network addresses.

> *Analogy*: This is similar to the ringing and busy signals.

Layer 5 (Session): Manages connections between two cooperating applications by establishing and releasing sessions, synchronizing information transfer over the session, and mapping session-to-transport and session-to-application connections.

Analogy: Establishment and release are similar to the "Hello" and "Good-bye" of a telephone conversation (including the protocol of asking for the desired party); the conversation forms the remainder of the session. This could also be compared to the handshake between two facsimile machines through the completion of the transmission.

Layer 6 (Presentation): Negotiates formats (if not prenegotiated) and transforms information into the appropriate format.

Analogy: Determining screen size or color capabilities when using a terminal. Choosing a common language for a human conversation.

Layer 7 (Application): Responsible for providing services to the actual applications to accomplish information transfer, involving not only the exchanges of data but also security checks, negotiating the exchange mechanisms, and requesting specific application services.

Analogy: The purchase of a theater ticket using a telephone reservation service involves several exchanges of data.

In actual practice, many implementations do not include a full seven-layer stack. In some cases, a "short stack" of the lower three layers (or sometimes up to transport) are used; although this is often done for interoperability with existing systems, it is sometimes used to avoid the cost of implementing and using the upper layers. However, new techniques are being developed that minimize the overhead of using the upper three layers while preserving the OSI architecture.

In some of these approaches, the protocol data for a layer (e.g., Presentation Layer) is minimized, but the Presentation Layer is still present. Some experiments are using a single octet. Other implementations minimize turn-around times by gambling that operations will be successful; if they are, then you gain some time, although if recovery is needed, this will take a little longer. These implementations opt to trade capability for overhead.

Besides the "short stack," some implementors have begun to use a "skinny stack." Full capabilities are preserved for data transfer, but special mechanisms are used to set up and tear down an association (a process that is potentially very time consuming). OSI has matured to the point where there is a better understanding of the legal shortcuts. The basic premise of the skinny stack is that for a particular application, since the requirements are precisely known, it is possible to limit the OSI implementation to support only the features that are needed, without generalizing for all potential

Figure 1.2 The seven-layer stack.

applications. In a more generalized form, a skinny stack profile can be used; such a profile would not be tailored for only a single application, but would restrict the capabilities to an agreed-upon subset.

There are instances in which even a full OSI implementation will require fewer than seven layers. OSI only uses seven layers for end systems (ES). For intermediate systems (e.g., routers), only the lower three layers are involved. In many networks, a node may serve as an intermediate system (IS) but will also be an ES for some applications.

Addressing occurs at many layers. In this discussion, it will be introduced with the Transport Layer. (See Figure 1.2.)

The way an interface will be implemented depends to a certain extent on the way the adjacent protocol layers are implemented, and to a great extent on the operating system environment. Basically, there are two categories: an open or accessible interface and an embedded interface. An embedded interface is "invisible" to program users. The protocols are enmeshed and entangled so that there is no clear boundary between them. In an open interface, there appears to be a clear, well-defined boundary separating two distinct pieces of code. However, even OSI does not require "exposed" service boundaries at the layer boundaries, as long as the interfaces behave according to the OSI protocols.

PROTOCOLS AND SERVICES

Each layer defines data units that are used within the communication between layers. Ultimately, it includes the application data, which is augmented by overhead data to perform the necessary functions for OSI.

For any given layer, the data transferred between entities on behalf of the adjacent upper layer are considered user data. Data used by the Application Layer are considered user data to the Presentation Layer. The principle continues downward through the OSI stack; that is, for example, the data needed by the Session Layer are considered user data to the Transport Layer, even if the Session Layer data only includes protocol control information needed for coordinating their joint operation. As shown in Figure 1.3, protocol-control information (i.e., a "header") is added to each successive data unit as the data pass down the stack; the protocol-control information is used by the corresponding layer at the other end system. The information transferred between entities at adjacent layers to coordinate their joint operation is considered interface-control information. The relevant standards for each layer define the functions performed by the layer and also specify the state changes.

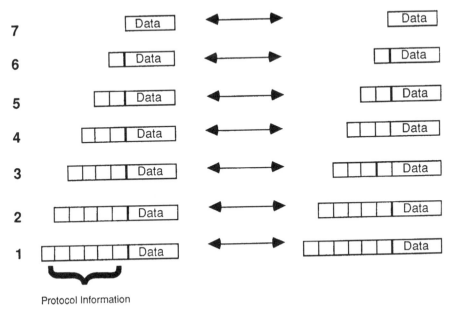

Figure 1.3 Addition of protocol data to perform services.

In the "skinny stack," the knowledge of the specific application requirements makes it possible to "hard-wire" parts of the interface. For example, if the application will always use the same values in some elements of the protocol, invariant octet sequences for PDUs can be encoded for outbound messages. In addition, it might not be necessary to test for all possible values on an incoming message if it is known that only certain values will occur. First, the processor would check against the expected invariant sequences for inbound messages; if the match fails or is inappropriate, minimal additional analysis would be performed. Protocol values that are "not important" for an interface could be ignored. This approach has been shown to improve performance, while still remaining a legal implementation (although some amount of potential connectivity might be sacrificed).

A protocol data unit (PDU) is a unit of data specified in the protocol for a layer, consisting of protocol-control information and, possibly, user data of the adjacent upper layer. Protocol standards will sometimes use abbreviations such as TPDU (Transport PDU), SPDU (Session PDU), etc. (See Figure 1.4.)

The OSI architecture does not limit the size of data units; however, protocol standards for individual layers may impose limitations. In order that efficiency or other considerations do not pose a limit to the PDU size for upper layers, blocking can be used to map several service data units (SDU) in a single PDU. On the other hand, concatenation can be used to map multiple PDUs into a single SDU.

Separate but related standards are developed for protocols and services. Protocol specifications are written in terms of the data that are exchanged between layers, while service definitions describe the types of services provided by the lower of two adjacent layers on behalf of the upper layer. Because it is possible to "see" the PDUs, compliance is specified through the protocols. However, this does not weaken the determination of conformance, because if the services do not work correctly, the protocols, which are actually specified in terms of services, will not work correctly either.

	Control	*Data*	*Combined*
Peer entities	Protocol-control information	User data	Protocol data unit (PDU)
Adjacent layers	Interface-control information	Interface data	Interface data unit

Figure 1.4 The passing of data between layers.

The protocol is used to transfer the service request. The services are actually provided at SAPs, which have several important properties:

- When an entity requests a service from the lower layer, it is done via a SAP, which permits the upper layer entity to interact with the service provider.

- The entities from adjacent layers that are attached to a specific SAP are in the same system.

- The relationship between entities at adjacent layers is not one to one with respect to SAPs. An entity can be concurrently attached to more than one SAP at the lower layer, which could be the same or different entities; similarly, the lower layer entity can be attached through more than one upper layer entity through SAPs. However, any single SAP can only be connected to one entity at the lower and upper layers.

SAPs also become important for programming interfaces. There are efforts underway to standardize application program interfaces (APIs) so that access to the services can be portable at the source code level. In general, an API is not likely to have a one-to-one correspondence with the service definitions in the standard, as the service definitions are intended primarily for use in developing (and understanding) the protocol. APIs are discussed further later on in this chapter.

How Is an Association Established?

When an application process (AP) needs to communicate with another, an association must be established between the source and destination entities. Any given AP is represented to its peer by one or more application entities (AE). The aspects of an AP that need to be taken into account for the purpose of OSI are represented by one or more AEs. An AE represents one and only one AP in the OSI environment.

For purposes of OSI, an application process is defined as an element within a real open system that performs the information processing for a particular application.

Application entities are associated with each other at the top layer, with the associations carrying down through the stack between corresponding layers. AP titles and AE titles may be used so the AEs can be independent of their Presentation Layer addressing. An AE attaches to one or more Presentation Service Access Points (PSAPs), in order to make it addressable.

AEs are joined through "associations," which permit them to exchange information. For information to be exchanged within two or more entities at a specific layer (i.e., [N+1]), an association is established between them in the next lower layer (N) using an N-layer protocol; for example, to exchange information between peer entities at the Presentation Layer, an association is established at the Session Layer using the Session Layer protocol.

Regardless of the method used, establishment of an association requires some knowledge of the lower layers, which comprises:

1. Knowledge of the addresses of the peer entities involved (e.g., corresponding entities in the network-to-network layers for each side of the interface)

2. Knowledge of a protocol agreed upon by the peer entities for use at least to initiate communication

3. Knowledge of the availability for communication of the peer entities

4. Knowledge of the quality of service (QOS) available from the lower layer

At the lower layers, there are also protocols involved with connection establishment. For example, this could include an exchange of version information to ensure that both sides are using the same version of the protocol. A calling entity sends information of all supported versions to a called entity. The called entity examines whether there are any supported versions common to the calling and called entities. If there is more than one common version, the highest common version is selected. If there is no common version, the connection establishment request is refused.

At several layers, especially Network and Transport, QOS can be negotiated at the beginning of an association. For connectionless, there is no negotiation—take it or leave it. If there are minimum standards for establishing a connection (e.g., the connection is not worthwhile unless the QOS criteria can be satisfied), the connection may be rejected.

Quality of service (QOS) is the collective name given to a set of parameters associated with data transmission between (N) service access points. Different parameters can be defined for each layer. QOS parameters may be optionally selectable. The Data Link Layer establishes and maintains a selected QOS for the duration of the data-link connection. The QOS parameters include mean time between detected but unrecoverable errors, residual error rate (where errors may arise from alteration, loss, duplication, disordering, misdelivery of data-link SDU, and other causes), service availability, transit delay, and throughput.

For connection-oriented service, possible parameters include:

- Expected transmission delay
- Probability of corruption
- Probability of loss or duplication
- Probability of wrong delivery
- Cost
- Protection from unauthorized access
- Priority

APPLICATION LAYER

All OSI services needed by the application process are provided by the Application Layer. The generalized interface at the Application Layer is supplied by Association Control Service Element (ACSE). Specialized services, such as FTAM and MHS, also provide commonly needed general functions.

The highest level of abstraction is the AP. All other features of the Application Layer serve to support the AP, and all other layers serve to support the communication between two application entities. An AP represents a set of resources, including processing resources, within a real open system, which may be used to perform a particular information-processing activity. An AP may organize its interactions with other APs in whatever way is necessary to achieve a particular information-processing goal. An AP is an abstract representation of those elements of a real open system that performs information processing for a particular application. It represents a set of resources, including processing resources, within a real open system that may be used to perform a particular information-processing activity.

Any given application process is represented to its peer by one or more application entities, so there can be more than one connection. An application entity is an active element within an application process, embodying a set of capabilities pertinent to OSI and corresponding to a specific application-entity type. The aspects of an AP that need to be taken into account for the purpose of OSI are represented by one or more AEs. An AE represents one and only one AP in the OSI environment, but an AP may be represented by a set of AEs; each AE in this set is of a different AE type. Different APs may be represented by AEs of the same AE type. An AE type is a class of application entities in terms of a set of capabilities defined for the application layer.

The activity of a given AP is represented by one of more AP invocations; cooperation between APs takes place via relationships established among AP invocations. At a particular time, an AP may be represented by none, one, or more AP invocations. An AP invocation is responsible for coordinating its interactions with other AP invocations. An AP invocation is a specific utilization of part or all of the capabilities of a given application process in support of a specific occasion of information processing.

ACSEs provide common association or connection-control services that are needed by a number of applications; it is more efficient to incorporate these services into a common protocol than to reproduce them, perhaps differently, in every application. The ACSE protocol performs essential services for the application, such as connection establishment, connection release, and error notification. An ACSE is an ASE that provides the exclusive means for establishing and terminating all application associations. An AE always includes an ACSE.

The Application Layer contains all functions that imply communication between open systems and those not already performed by the lower layers. These include functions performed by programs as well as functions performed by human beings. The lower layers provide the services through which the AEs cooperate.

The AE contains a set of one of more application-service elements (ASEs) (always including one consistent means to establish all associations and related control functions that coordinate the various ASEs). An ASE is a set of application functions that provides a capability for the interworking of AE invocations for a specific purpose. ASEs may call upon each other and/or upon presentation services to perform their function. The only means by which APs in different systems may communicate is through the exchange of application-protocol data units (APDUs). These APDUs are generated by ASEs. An ASE contains all the functions and corresponding APDUs that are required for a protocol machine that is logically complete and consistent in itself. The capabilities of an individual ASE are defined by the specification of a set of APDUs. This constitutes the application protocol between two ASEs of the same kind.

A service definition conveys the understanding of the function carried out by the ASE. These service definitions for ASEs are conceptual, so do not imply conformance. Service definitions may be used in defining specialized standards at the Application Layer.

Users may have reasons to request that the vendor provide an accessible interface to one or more layers in their implementations. An accessible Transport Layer interface allows a user to write software that uses the services of OSI layers 1–4 to transfer data reliably between different end systems. An accessible interface to the ACSE allows different applications to access the ACSE to perform common application layer services. An accessible interface to the MHS Message Transfer Agent allows users to write their own User Agents that use the services of the Message Transfer System to transfer information to each other. ACSE services are defined in ISO 8649 and the protocol for ACSE is specified in ISO 8650. The Application Layer structure is described in ISO 9545.

The Application Layer differs from the other layers of OSI in several important respects. The internal structure of an AE is recursive: an AE is made up of one or more application service objects (ASOs), each of which is made up of a collection of application service elements and/or application service objects and a control function. These ASEs, ASOs, and control functions are combined in various ways to form various types of ASOs and AEs. The Application Layer, as the highest layer of OSI, does not provide connections within the Application Layer. As a result, relationships formed by the transfer of information between AE invocations in the Application Layer have particular significance.

The File Transfer, Access, and Management (FTAM) Protocol provides a means of communicating about groups of related information, i.e., files. A user can move files, interrogate the properties of files, and manipulate files on a variety of different systems, without knowledge of the characteristics of any particular file system. This is accomplished by means of a common communications model and language, as described in the ISO 8571. Future extensions may make it possible for third-party file transfers in which one process will request a transfer of a file between two other systems; this capability would be useful not only for end users, but also for many specialized OSI applications.

The Message Handling Systems (MHS) application is based on the CCITT X.400 Series of Recommendations. These Recommendations specify a store-and-forward Message Transfer System consisting of individual Message Transfer Agents (MTAs) that cooperate to deliver a message from Interpersonal User Agents (UAs) serving an originator to Interpersonal User Agents serving one or more recipients. The UAs provide the capability for users to read and send mail. MHS is also known as Message Oriented Text Information System (MOTIS); ISO/IEC 10021 is technically equivalent to X.400 despite the different title.

The Transaction Processing (TP) application supports the provision of the ACID properties (Atomicity [the total work is performed or nothing is done], Consistency [work is performed accurately and correctly], Isolation [while the work is being performed inconsistent data is not available to other transactions], and Durability [the work is fault-tolerant]) including the necessary commitment, concurrency, and recovery to support transaction processing. In OSI TP, a transaction is not simply an exchange of messages, but TP provides mechanisms so the exchanges of information form a protected indivisible set. To help understand what a complete transaction might look like, a transaction's conversation might appear as:

Program A	*Program B*
Initialize Conversation	
Allocate	
Send Data (to initiate transaction)	
Receive	{Program is started}
	Accept Conversation
	Receive
	Send Data (to return response)
{Data is received}	Deallocate

The above example shows only the operations that might be used in an application program via an Application Program Interface (API). This shows a high-level interface, which hides some of the details of the underlying communications.

The Remote Operations Services (ROS, sometimes referred to as ROS Element or ROSE) was designed originally to support coordination with processes on a remote system, particularly in an office-processing environment. ROS is used by MHS and is sometimes used by applications in which the implementors want to avoid some of the details of implementation.

PRESENTATION LAYER

The Presentation Layer provides the mechanisms for achieving a machine-independent representation of application data that AEs communicate. This process is related to representation and manipulation of structured data for the benefit of application programs. When networks involve end systems with differing architectures (or possibly unknown architectures), the internal representation of data may differ. Similarly, a new system may require revised structures in order to take advantage of new system capabilities.

The Presentation Layer provides for common representation to be used of the data transferred between AEs. This relieves AEs of any concern with the problem of "common" representation of information; that is, it provides them with system independence. The syntactic independence is provided in the following way:

The AEs can use any syntax and the Presentation Layer provides the transformation between these syntaxes (via an encode/decode capability) and the syntax needed for communication between AEs. This transformation is performed inside the open systems. It is not seen by other open systems and therefore has no impact on the standardization of presentation protocols.

The abstract syntax, which is expressed in a language Abstract Syntax Notation One (ASN.1), is typically compiled off-line into a machine-readable form for the encoder/decoder to interpret while processing a particular PDU. A porting of an application dialog defined using an abstract syntax notation is referred to as an abstract syntax.

ASN.1 is described by ISO 8824. The syntax notation is strongly typed like Pascal or Ada. This allows the Presentation Service to achieve interoperability with a very large base of OSI applications. Strong typing is also useful for detection of programming or unsignaled communication errors.

It is necessary that each side of the transfer understand the content and meaning of what is being transferred. Accordingly, the Presentation Layer will take information from the applications and convert this information into a form and structure that can be recognized and interpreted by the destination OSI end system.

The Presentation Layer covers two complementary aspects of this representation of information:

1. The representation of data to be transferred between AEs
2. The representation of the data structure that AEs refer to in their communication, along with the representations of the set of actions that may be performed on this data structure

Because the Presentation Layer knows the abstract syntaxes that are to be employed by the AEs, the Presentation Layer is responsible for selecting mutually acceptable transfer syntaxes.

The concrete syntax includes those aspects of the rules used in the formal specification of data, which embody a specific representation of that data. The transfer syntax signifies the concrete syntax used in the transfer of data between open systems. Presentation context is an association of an abstract syntax with a transfer of syntax.

The Presentation Layer provides the following facilities:

- Identification of a set of transfer syntaxes
- Selection of transfer syntax
- Access to session services

One of the potential Presentation Layer services is special-purpose transformations, such as data compression, which can be useful in reducing the cost or time of data transmission. Presentation Layer services can also be used for code conversion.

AEs agree on the abstract syntaxes that will be used for their communication. It is necessary that these abstract syntaxes are represented in appropriate transfer syntaxes for communication to take place. The structure of the APDUs of an ASE is specified by at least one named abstract syntax. To transfer these APDUs between AE invocations using the presentation service, it is necessary to establish one or more presentation contexts for each abstract syntax. During an association, occurrences of these APDUs are linked to presentation contexts. Each presentation context specifies a pairing of a particular abstract syntax with a transfer syntax.

There is not a single predetermined transfer syntax for all of OSI. In connection mode, the transfer syntax to be used on a presentation connection is negotiated between the correspondent presentation entities. Thus, a presentation entity must know the syntax of its application entity and the agreed transfer syntax. Only the transfer syntax need be referred to in the Presentation Layer protocols.

In OSI, the syntaxes used by AEs that wish to communicate may be very similar or quite dissimilar. When they are similar, the transformation functions may not be needed at all; however, when they are dissimilar, the Presentation Layer service provides the means to converse and decide where needed transformations will take place.

Negotiation (or selection) of transfer syntax takes place between two presentation entities when an AE provides the name of an abstract syntax for which a transfer syntax is required. In connectionless mode, the transfer syntax is selected, but cannot be negotiated. Syntaxes can be registered. At the highest level, these syntaxes may be registered through standards bodies. They may also be registered by an industry group (e.g., air traffic control) or by a single organization.

Each combination of abstract syntax and transfer syntax is called a presentation context. From the viewpoint of the AE, a presentation context represents a specific distinct use of an abstract syntax.

Presentation Layer Services and Organization

The services of the Presentation Layer are defined in ISO 8822 and the Presentation Layer protocol is specified in ISO 8823. The Presentation Layer deals with generic functions which are needed by many different kinds of applications; specifically, a common means is provided of representing a data structure in transit from one end system to another.

The Presentation Layer is organized in terms of functional units. The kernel functional unit provides: (1) data representation functions (as described above) and (2) connection-oriented functions. Representation deals with the way the actual data is coded or represented during data transfer. Connection functions deal with establishing, preserving, and managing the connection between two applications.

The Presentation Layer has sometimes been criticized for the overhead involved in processing ASN.1. Some applications may wish to forego the benefits of the Presentation Layer, while still retaining compatibility with it. To fully avoid the use of abstract syntax, Unstructured Data Transfer (UDT) can be used so that a prenegotiated format (e.g., a "record layout") can be used. Thus, the Presentation Layer will perform no services, but the cost of performing those services will be eliminated.

In recognition of the sometimes undesirable cost of using the Basic Encoding Rules (BER), Lightweight Encoding Rules (LWER) have been devised. Lightweight encoding rules are useful in applications in which some flexibility is needed, but it is possible for the formats to be prenegotiated (for example, in a well-defined interface) or other limitations are acceptable. Alternative transfer syntaxes make it possible to optimize for central processing unit (CPU) time (less complicated encoding) or PDU length (to minimize the number of bits transferred, particularly in applications with limited bandwidth).

SESSION LAYER

The purpose of the Session Layer is to provide the means necessary for cooperating presentation entities to organize and to synchronize their dialog and to manage their data exchange. To do this, the Session Layer provides services to establish a session connection between two presentation entities, to support orderly data exchange interactions, and to release the connection in an orderly manner. The only purpose of the Session Layer for connectionless-mode communication is to provide a mapping of transport addresses to session addresses.

The Session Layer provides user-oriented services to aid in the orderly and reliable flow of information between users in two different end systems. These services provide for increased efficiency in managing the dialog between applications. The Session Layer protects applications and users from irregularities and problems in the underlying network.

A presentation entity can access another presentation entity by initiating or accepting a session connection. A presentation entity may be associated with several session connections simultaneously in relation to one or more presentation entities.

The initiating presentation entity designates the destination presentation entity by a session address. In general, there is a many-to-one correspondence between the session addresses and transport addresses. This implies that at session-connection establishment time, more than one presentation entity is a potential target of a session-connection establishment request arriving on a given transport connection.

The session-connection establishment service allows the presentation entities cooperatively to determine the unique values of session connection parameters at the time the session connection is established. The Token Management service allows the presentation entities to control explicitly whose turn it is to exercise certain control functions.

There are two types of dialog control. Either end can send data at any time (duplex) or each end can take turns sending data (half-duplex). In the latter case, tokens are used to control the direction of data transfer and to determine which process is authorized to send data. Data may also be expedited, which means that it has a higher transmission priority. Data may be typed, which allows it to be sent even if the sender does not possess the token.

The synchronization services allow the connection to reset to a defined point and agree on a resynchronization point. The Session Layer provides a synchronization facility that allows presentation entities to define and identify synchronization points, to reset a session connection to a predefined state, and to agree on a resynchronization point. The Session Layer does not actually accomplish the recovery, but merely provides the means for negotiating a recovery by the applications. Loss of data is possible.

The activity concept allows session-service users to distinguish logical pieces of work called activities. Each activity consists of one or more dialog units. Only one activity is allowed on a session connection at a time, but there may be several consecutive activities during a session connection. An activity may also span more than one session connection.

At any given instant, there is a one-to-one mapping between a session connection and a transport connection. However, the lifetime of a transport connection and that of a related session connection can be distinguished so that a transport connection supports several consecutive session connections.

When providing the connectionless mode, the Session Layer provides a one-to-one mapping of session connectionless-mode transmission onto transport connectionless-mode transmissions.

The Session Layer protocol is organized in terms of functional units; examples of these functional units are kernel (basic connection and data transfer) and duplex. Also included are half-duplex, expedited data, minor synchronize, major synchronize, typed data, activity management, resynchronize, and exceptions.

The Session Layer service and protocol are specified in ISO/IEC 8326 and 8327, respectively.

TRANSPORT LAYER

The transport service provides transparent transfer of data between session entities and relieves them from any concern with the detailed way in which reliable and cost-effective transfer of data is achieved. That is, the Transport Layer serves to hide the differences between several network concepts (connection oriented versus connectionless), packet size, QOS, and other types of lower-layer differences.

Control of data transportation from source-end open system to destination-end open system (which is not performed in intermediate nodes) is the last function to be performed in order to provide the totality of the transport service. Thus, the upper layer in the transport-service part of the architecture is the Transport Layer. The Transport Layer relieves higher-layer entities from any concern with the transportation of data between them. Correspondingly, the Transport Layer is relieved of any concern with routing and relaying since the network service provides network connections from any transport entity to any other, including the case of tandem subnetworks.

All protocols defined in the Transport Layer have end-to-end significance, where the ends are defined as correspondent transport entities. Therefore, the Transport Layer is OSI end-system oriented and transport protocols operate only between OSI end systems. The Network Layer protocol is the highest protocol at an Intermediate System, performing services on behalf of the Transport Layer.

When providing the connectionless mode, the Transport Layer provides a connectionless-mode service, which maps a request for transmission of transport-service data unit onto a request to the connectionless-mode network service. In connection mode, the transport service provides the means to establish, maintain, and release transport connections. Transport connections provide duplex transmission between a pair of transport addresses.

More than one transport connection can be established between the same pair of transport addresses. A session entity uses transport-connection endpoint identifiers provided by the Transport Layer to distinguish between transport-connection end points.

The Transport Layer has five classes of services defined. These service classes are characterized by combinations of selected values of parameters such as throughput, transit delay, and connection set-up delay and by guaranteed values of parameters such as residual error rate and service availability. These classes are:

Class 0:   Simple class, with basic Teletex capabilities (TP-0).

Class 1:   Basic error recovery class, designed for X.25. Provides minimal error recovery for errors signaled by network and includes sequence numbers so TPDUs can be resequenced (TP-1).

Class 2:   Multiplexing, which enhances Class 0 but assumes a highly reliable network without a need for error recovery. Supports multiplexing of multiple transport connections onto a single network connection (TP-2).

Class 3:   Provides multiplexing and basic error recovery (TP-3 = TP-1 $\cup$ TP-2).

Class 4:   Error detection and recovery, providing the ability to recover from lost or out-of-sequence TPDUs. Provides retransmission, duplicate detection, flow control, connection establishment and termination, and recovery from crashes.

The basic distinction is between connection oriented (CO) and connectionless (CL).

Connection-mode transmission is appropriate in applications that call for relatively long-lived, stream-oriented interactions between entities in stable configurations, for example, Virtual Terminal, FTAM, or Job Transfer.

Connectionless forms of data transmission might be associated with particular forms of data transmission such as LANs or digital radio, and particular types of applications, such as remote sensing and banking.

It is a basic characteristic of connectionless-mode service that no negotiation of parameters for a transmission takes place at the time the service is accessed and no dynamic association is set up between the parties involved. However, considerable freedom of choice can be preserved by allowing most parameter values and options (such as transfer rate, acceptable error rate, etc.) to be specified at the time the service is accessed. In a given implementation, if the local (N) subsystem determines immediately that the requested transmission cannot be performed under the conditions specified, it may abort the transmission, returning an implementation-specific error message. If the same determination is made later, after the service access has been completed, the transmission is abandoned, as the servicing layer is assumed not to have the information necessary to take any other action.

A connection is established by referencing, either explicitly or implicitly, a transport address for the source session entity and an address for each of one or more destination entities.

Multi-end-point connections are connections that have three or more connection end points. Two types of multi-end-point connection are currently defined:

- Centralized
- Decentralized

In the centralized mode, data sent by the entity associated with the central-connection end point is received by the entities associated with all other connection end points. The data sent by an entity associated with any other connection end point is received by the entity associated with the central-connection end point.

A connection requires establishment and release procedures. Some protocols provide for the combining of connection establishment and connection-release protocol exchanges.

The establishment of a connection by peer entities of a layer requires:

- The availability of a connection at the point immediately between the supporting entities
- Both entities be in a state in which they can execute the connection establishment protocol exchange

The process continues downward through the layers until an available connection is found or the physical medium for OSI is encountered. The release of a connection is normally initiated by one of the entities associated in it. Release can also occur as the result of an exception condition in the layer or layers lower than it.

Connection-Oriented Transport Protocol

The basic function of connection-oriented transport is to provide the difference between the quality of service desired by the Transport Layer user and that which is provided by the Network Layer. Messages can be broken into individual packets; the Connection-Oriented Transport Protocol at the other end system reassembles the packets into a message. The protocol provides reliable, orderly end-to-end data transfer. This means that data packets are received uncorrupted and in the correct order by the Transport Layer user.

There are many parameters that are negotiated between two communicating transport entities. These provide for proper flow control, proper sequencing, and proper error detection and retransmission of lost data. The international standard (ISO/IEC 8073:1988) contains provisions for five classes of transport service (Class 0 through Class 4). Class 4 assumes the least about Network Layer services—and provides the most capability.

Connectionless Transport Protocol (CLTP)

The Connectionless Transport Protocol (CLTP) is used to provide the Connectionless Transport Service (CLTS). The CLTP is to be used only as an option among participants with a similar capability. Although there currently are no detailed implementation agreements for connectionless protocols at OSI layers above the Transport Layer, the Connectionless Transport Protocol is included so that non-OSI applications can take advantage of its services or for future applications.

Functions used in Modes of Communication include:

Function	Connection Oriented	Connectionless
Connection establishment and release	X	
Suspend	X	
Resume	X	
Multiplexing and splitting	X	X
Normal data transfer	X	X
During establishment	X	
Expedited	X	
Flow control	X	X
Segmenting	X	X

Function	Connection Oriented	Connectionless
Blocking	X	
Concatenation	X	X
Sequencing	X	X
Acknowledgment	X	X

Error notification may or may not lead to the release of the network connection, according to the specification of a particular network service.

The *expedited* network SDU transfer is optional and provides an additional means of information exchange on a network connection. The transfer of an expedited network SDU is subject to a different set of network service characteristics and to separate flow control.

A transport entity that is receiving at one end of a network connection can cause the network service to stop transferring network SDUs across the service access point. This *flow control* condition may or may not be propagated at the other end of the network connection and thus may be reflected to the transmitting transport entity, according to the specification of a particular network service. Each network entity can dynamically control (up to the agreed maximum) the rate at which it receives data-link SDUs from a data-link connection. This control may be reflected in the rate at which the Data Link Layer accepts data-link SDUs at the correspondent data-link connection end point.

The Network Layer may provide sequenced delivery network SDUs over a given network connection when requested by the transport entities. This function preserves the order of SDUs that were submitted to the layer.

In order to limit protocol complexity, segmentation and reassembly are not provided in layers above the Network Layer. As a consequence, the size of SDUs in layers above the Network Layer is limited by the size of the PDU used in the layer below and by the size of its own protocol-control information.

Connectionless

Connectionless-mode transmission is the transmission of a single unit of data from a source SAP to one or more destination SAPs without establishing a connection (this approach is sometimes called datagrams). A connectionless-mode service allows an entity to initiate such a transmission through a single-service access. A connectionless-mode service does not have a clearly distinguishable lifetime.

The basic connectionless-mode service is not required to exhibit any minimum values of the QOS measures and is not required to exhibit peer flow control.

Because basic connectionless service is not required to maintain the sequence of service data units, there are no requirements to provide sequencing functions. Thus, an entity at a particular layer does not provide the servicing layer any information about the logical relationships between datagrams, other than the source and destination addresses.

Connectionless does not provide any negotiation, although there is QOS or version checking on a take it or leave it basis.

Despite the lack of a requirement to maintain sequencing, the characteristics of the particular medium or subnetwork may provide a high probability of in-sequence delivery. A stack may contain combinations of layers using connection-oriented services and other layers using connectionless services. For example, the lower layers may be connectionless, but the upper layers may use connection-oriented services.

In order to provide these capabilities, OSI uses relay functions.

When the Transport Layer is unable to provide the agreed quality of service and all possible recovery attempts have failed, the transport connection is terminated and the session entities are notified.

The Transport Layer Service and Protocol are defined in ISO 8072 and 8073, respectively.

ADDRESSING

In the OSI Reference Model, reliable data communications occur between two end systems, usually via one or more intermediate systems. End systems are terminus systems where data transfers originate or terminate. Intermediate systems are "transit systems" through which information passes from one end system (source) to the other end system (destination). In many cases the Intermediate System must perform routing to determine the path.

The terms *end system* and *intermediate system* refer to roles in transmittal of data and not to any special configurations. An individual system may be an end system or an intermediate system at different times or with respect to different data streams. Intermediate systems are used to interconnect subnetworks in OSI communications.

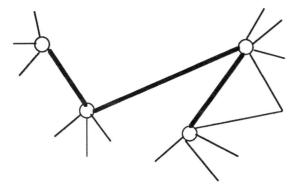

Figure 1.5 An ES may be on two or more subnetworks; subnetworks may be chosen for their differing technology or to provide redundant paths.

Intermediate systems are used to link together subnetworks to provide paths connecting end systems. An end system may be connected to more than one subnetwork; similarly, a subnetwork may have multiple end systems connected to it. The actual physical connections are labeled as subnetwork points of attachment (SNPAs). (See Figure 1.5.)

A service access point is identified by a unique Network Service Access Point (NSAP) address.

An NSAP is an identifier that uniquely distinguishes one end system from another in a network of systems. An intermediate system will "read" the NSAP address and determine where to send the packet (a similar function to that of a post office in reading an address on an envelope). Each NSAP is unique globally in the context of OSI; an NSAP value must be known to all other systems communicating with this system. The NSAPs themselves only have meaning to the communicating entities, such as OSI Network Layer service entities.

The NSAP also identifies a point at which network service is provided to the Transport Layer, which is responsible for the end-to-end transfer of data in the OSI model. There may be any number of NSAPs for an end system. These NSAP values must be known to the "end-to-end" communications software which runs in end systems. NSAPs are encoded as unique strings of characters (or numbers) which may be interpreted reading from left to right using the hierarchical model described previously. Each NSAP value in an end system specifies a different user of the Network Layer service.

Intermediate systems route information based upon selected components of NSAPs received in transit. If the NSAP "matches" the system address, that system is in fact the destination system. If not, then a routing table is used to find the next system along the route to the destination.

The NSAP is the only address in OSI that identifies end systems uniquely; all other OSI addresses identify intermediate systems or end-system processes. Globally unique NSAP addresses are important because increased communication across different subnetworks in a distributed global environment is anticipated. If every end system in all organizations is assigned a unique address, then every end system can potentially communicate with every other end system. NSAPs are the first category of objects which must have registration authorities established to assure assignment of unique addresses for all.

In sum, an OSI network is composed of end systems on different subnetworks interconnected by intermediate systems. NSAPs identify the end points of network communications, or the service access points of the Network Layer. The NSAP selector allows different users of the Network Layer service to be distinguished.

Routing is accomplished by a function within a layer that translates the title of an entity, or the service-access-point address to which the entity is attached, into a path by which the entity can be reached. This sometimes uses a directory (i.e., X.500) which translates global titles of peer entities into the NSAP addresses through which they cooperate. Use of the directory allows an application to dynamically associate with a process to perform a required function, by knowing only the name of the other application, or possibly by using a "yellow pages" feature to find the desired service.

Within a given layer, a hierarchical structure of addresses simplifies address-mapping functions because of the permanent nature of the mapping it presupposes. The model does not impose the hierarchy in all layers in order to allow more flexibility in address mappings and to cover the case where an entity attached to more than one subordinate layer SAP supports only one SAP. The structure of an address is known by the same layer entity that is attached to the identified SAP; however, the superior layer entity does not know this structure.

The connection end-point identifier consists of two parts:

- The address of the SAP, which will be used in conjunction with the connection
- A connection end-point suffix which is unique within the scope of the NSAP

For example, at the Transport Layer, when a session entity requests the Transport Layer to establish a transport connection with another session entity identified by its transport address, the Transport Layer determines the network address identifying the transport entity which serves the correspondent session entity.

Because transport entities support services on an end-to-end basis, no intermediate transport entity is involved as a relay between the end transport entities. Therefore, the Transport Layer maps transport addresses to the network addresses, which identify the end transport entities.

A routing function within a layer enables communication to be relayed by a chain of peer entities. The fact that communication is being routed by intermediate peer entities is known by neither the lower layers nor by the higher layers. Any entity that participates in a routing function may have a routing table.

An entity can be accessed either by its address or by the entity title. In order to establish uniquely identified entities, registration authorities have been established by ISO (and subsequently by ANSI, the U.S. government, etc.) to register unique names within hierarchies. As an analogy, consider postal addressing schemes: The postal service determines zip codes; cities (or other local governments) decide basic address structure; and housing developments might actually name the streets. While 123 Elm Street in Springfield is hardly unique, when used in a hierarchy (below either zip code or state name) the identifier becomes unique. Similar principles apply in OSI. One of the more prominent responsibilities of ISO Registration Authorities is to register organization names, so organizations are uniquely identified.

OSI names and addresses consist of attribute-value pairs which are hierarchical in nature and which combine to uniquely identify or locate an OSI object. Since the relationship between the components of a name or address is hierarchical, it follows that the registration authority for names and addresses should also be hierarchical. A governing organization does not always have sufficient knowledge of organizations lower in the hierarchy to wisely assign values within those organizations. Thus, an approach frequently taken is to delegate registration authority to the lower organizations in the name or address hierarchy.

No one element in the sequence is necessarily unique, but all the elements considered together in the proper order are unique as a group. Also, each element with the same immediate parent is unique at its level. The term "sequence" implies a definite ordering of elements. To create a unique sequence, an ADP system may "pick off" elements in a path down the tree, and append each selected element to the end of the list of previously selected elements. To decode or "parse" a unique sequence, an ADP system will read the elements of the sequence in the order encountered from the beginning of the sequence, and construct a "path" in the hierarchical identification tree.

Registration authorities are created to register names of objects and, in some cases, to advertise these names. For example, the telephone companies assign numbers to subscribers and publish some of the numbers in a telephone directory. In the OSI world, some names are included and registered in the standard.

If applications want to exchange objects not included in the standard, such objects must be registered somewhere, so that no one else will use the same number for a different body part or a different number for the same body part. In the future, when a standard is approved which will require further registration of names, the procedure for registration and the registration authority will be approved at the same time.

Objects are not used only for addressing; the Common Management Information Protocol (CMIP) for system management has many objects defined and other protocols also have defined objects. Because of the hierarchical definition of object identifiers, new protocols can safely add objects without conflicting with existing object identifiers, whether assigned as part of an international standard, an industry standard, or assigned by another registration authority.

The NSAP addressing structure incorporates various numbering schemes or types of addresses to deal with the diverse users of packet data. The NSAP address consists of two major parts, the Initial Domain Part (IDP) and the Domain Specific Part (DSP). The IDP is subdivided into two parts which are specified by ISO 8348/Addendum 2.

The first part, Authority and Format Identifier (AFI), identifies the type of address being used and gives the syntax of the DSP.

The second part, Initial Domain Identifier (IDI), specifies the domain to which the address belongs.

The format of the DSP is not defined by ISO 8348/Addendum 2, but must be established by the registration authority for the 0005 domain. A typical format used is illustrated in Figure 1.6.

It is not necessary for two innterconnected subnetworks to use the same NSAP format. This allows different administrative domains to each use a suitable format. Typically, administrative domains will use the same number of octets, but this is not required.

An administrative domain is defined by ISO as a collection of end systems, intermediate systems, and subnetworks operated by a single organization or

IDP	DSP (Domain Specific Part)

IDP = Initial Domain Part

AFI	IDI	DFI	AAI	RS	RD	AR	ESID	NSEL

AFI = Authority and Format Identifier
IDI = Initial Domain Identifier (allowing different addressing domains)

    DFI = DSP Format Identifier
    AAI = Administrative Authority Identifier
    RS = Reserved
    RD = Routing Domain
    AR = Area (to allow unique routing areas)
    ESID = End System Identifier, which identifies a unique open system
    NSEL = NSAP Selector (identifying a service access point)

Figure 1.6 Typical NSAP format.

administrative authority. These domains may or may not be synonymous with organizational entities.

Within an administrative domain there may be zero, one, or more routing domains. A routing domain is a set of end systems and intermediate systems which operate according to the same routing procedures and which is wholly contained within a single administrative domain. Systems within a routing domain possess the following properties: (1) a high degree of trust in exchanging routing information with other such systems and (2) use of the same routing protocols as other such systems. These properties may not be present in systems outside this routing domain. A routing domain is divided (usually partitioned) into subdomains called areas. A minimal amount of routing information needs to be transferred between adjacent areas in order to determine the most appropriate path to a system within a particular area.

The system ID field identifies a unique system within an area. Once the end system is found, the directional routing stops; now all that remains is to find the appropriate user of the network layer service within that end system. This is done by examining the value of the NSAP selector field. The NSAP selector field identifies the user of the Network Layer service, usually a Transport entity.

A TSAP selector identifies a point within a computer system where information is passed in both directions between the Transport Layer and the

Session Layer. The TSAP selector does not have to be unique globally, but must be unique within an end system; it is appended to the NSAP address (forming a TSAP address) to identify a user of the Transport service. There may be more than one TSAP selector per end system; each identifies a separate user of the Transport service.

The TSAP selector has meaning only within an end system. If a particular TSAP selector of one end system must be known to another end system, that value could be conveyed a priori or by a common directory service.

The Session Service Access Point (SSAP) Selector identifies a point in the system through which information passes in both directions between the Session Layer implementation and the Presentation Layer implementation. The SSAP selector identifies a user of the Session service. There may be more than one SSAP selector per end system; each would identify a different user of the Session service.

Any value may be inserted for the SSAP selector as long as it is the correct type and format, and is correctly interpretable at the other end system. In transmitting information the SSAP selector is appended to the end of the TSAP address (forming an SSAP address). If it is necessary for one end system to know the SSAP selector for another end system, then that information could be conveyed a priori or via a common directory service.

The Presentation Service Access Point (PSAP) Selector identifies a user of the Presentation service in an end system. The PSAP selector does not have to be globally unique. PSAP selectors are encoded in Abstract Syntax Notation (ASN.1) type OCTETSTRING. There may be more than one PSAP selector per end system; each value identifies a different user of the Presentation service.

Any value may be inserted for the PSAP selector as long as it is the correct type and format and is correctly interpretable at the other end system. If it is necessary to identify a PSAP selector on one end system to another end system, a common directory service could be used, as well as an a priori method. A PSAP address consists of the PSAP selector appended to the SSAP address, and is intended to globally identify an application.

NETWORK LAYER

In OSI, some open systems will act as the final destination of data. Some other open systems may act only as intermediate nodes, forwarding data to other systems. This leads to identification of a Network Layer on top of the Data Link Layer. Network-oriented protocols, such as routing, are grouped in this layer. Thus, the Network Layer provides a communication path (network connection) between a pair of transport entities, including the case where intermediate nodes are involved.

The Network Layer provides the functional and procedural means for connectionless-mode or connection-mode transmission among transport entities and, therefore, provides to the transport entities independence of routing and relay considerations associated with connectionless-mode or connection-mode transmission.

Network Layer services provide for the transparent transfer of data between transport entities. This service allows the structure and detailed content of submitted data to be determined exclusively by layers above the Network Layer. The Network Layer contains functions necessary to provide the Transport Layer with a firm Network/Transport Layer boundary which is independent of the underlying communications media in all things other than quality of service. Thus, the Network Layer is able to mask the differences in the characteristics of different transmission and subnetwork technologies into a consistent network service.

The Network Layer provides independence from routing and relay consideration associated with the establishment and operation of a given network connection. This includes the case where several subnetworks are used in tandem or in parallel. The transport entities can ignore underlying resources such as data-link connections used to provide the network connections. This is important in systems formed by two or more subnetworks, for example, when several LANs are involved.

Any relay functions and hop-by-hop service enhancement protocols used to support the network service between the OSI end systems are operating below the Transport Layer, i.e., within the Network Layer.

According to ISO/IEC 7498-1, a "real subnetwork" is a collection of equipment and physical media which forms an autonomous whole and which can be used to interconnect real systems for purposes of data transfer. A subnetwork is a representation of a real network such as a carrier network, a private network, or a LAN. A subnetwork may itself be an open system, but this is not essential to achieve openness at a system level.

The service provided at each end of a network connection is the same even when a network connection spans several subnetworks, each offering dissimilar services. The need to offer different services is one reason for using different subnetworks. Subnetworks may also be needed when different media are involved, such as satellite communications, radio, or LANs.

The QOS is negotiated between the transport entities and the network service at the time of establishment of a network connection. While this QOS may vary from one network connection to another, it will be agreed for a given network connection and be the same at both network-connection end points. QOS at the Network Layer includes security, priority, congestion experienced, and cost.

The Network Layer uniquely identifies each of the end open systems (represented by transport entities) by their network addresses. This may be independent of the addressing needed by the underlying layers.

Network connections are point to point; however, more than one network connection may exist between the same pair of network addresses.

Network connections are provided by network entities in end open systems but may involve intermediate open systems which provide relaying. These intermediate open systems may interconnect subnetwork connections, data-link connections, and data circuits. Routing functions determine an appropriate route between network addresses.

As in the Transport Layer, there are two types of services available from the Network Layer: Connection-Oriented and Connectionless. The function of the Network Layer is to relay and route network service user packets to the correct destination, while at the same time masking the differences in the underlying subnetwork technologies (e.g., X.25 and CSMA/CD). The source and destination network service users may be on the same subnetwork or different, interconnected subnetworks.

Connectionless Network Service (CLNS)

The Connectionless Network Service (CLNS) is provided by the Connectionless Network Protocol (CLNP), which allows different subnetwork technologies to be interconnected. The CLNP masks the differences between these subnetwork technologies and allows these differences to be transparent to the OSI Network Layer user. CLNS can provide higher efficiency because the absence of complex flow-control algorithms in intermediate systems can reduce the CPU cycles needed for these routers. If the Transport Layer is also being operated in connectionless mode, then response time may be shortened when using CLNS.

The services of the existing subnetwork technologies such as LANs must be augmented to provide the OSI Network Layer service; this enhancement is also provided in the CLNP. Since the protocol to provide this service is connectionless, each protocol data unit is routed separately and the header of each protocol data unit contains addressing information as well as information relating to optional services provided by the protocol (e.g., priority and security).

The End System (ES)–Intermediate System (IS) Protocol is a dynamic routing protocol which operates in the network to support CLNP. It operates over either point-to-point links or broadcast subnetworks. Functionally ES–IS (1) enables ISs to dynamically find ESs that are attached to the same subnetwork, (2) enables ESs to dynamically find ISs that are attached to the same subnetwork, (3) enables ESs to locate each other on a single subnetwork, (4) enables ISs to redirect ESs to the IS representing the most efficient route to a given destination when two or more ISs are attached to the same subnetwork, and (5) allows ESs to automatically configure their OSI addresses.

Connection-Oriented Network Service

Use of the CONS can improve efficiency when operating over a single logical connection-oriented subnetwork (e.g., a single X.25 subnetwork or an ISDN). The headers of connection-oriented network protocol packets can be much shorter, since the full address is not required once a connection has been established; the reduction might be significant on slow lines. Use of this service can, under certain circumstances, avoid the overhead associated with the CLNP and may permit interoperability with end systems that do not implement CLNP.

Subnetwork Technologies

Different subnetwork technologies provide for transfer of data packets between adjacent nodes of a network. This corresponds to the lower portion of the Network Layer, the Data Link Layer, and the Physical Layer. The nodes of a wide area network are separated by long distances, whereas local area networks are usually contained within a small geographic area. This difference is responsible for the different technology used in the two types of networks. The functionality required to transfer data packets between "adjacent" nodes of a subnetwork is provided by the Physical Layer and the Data Link Layer.

Because Network Layer functions provide for a wide variety of configurations supporting network connections ranging from point-to-point configurations to network connections supported by complex combinations of subnetworks with different characteristics, it is common to structure network functions into sublayers. This is not generally done when the access protocol to the subnetwork supports the complete functionality of the OSI network service, but may be useful in other cases.

With connection-oriented Network Layer, the three sublayers are (top to bottom):

- Subnetwork-Independent Convergence Protocol (SICP)
- Subnetwork-Dependent Convergence Protocol (SDCP)
- Subnetwork Access Protocol

In a connectionless network, the Network Layer comprises two sublayers:

- Internetwork Protocol (IP)
- Subnetwork Specific Protocol (SSP)

The internal organization of the Network Layer is defined in ISO 8648. The network service and addressing formats are defined in ISO 8348. ISO 8472 and ISO 8473 are the basic references to the Network Layer services and protocol. Separate standards are used for different router relationships. The End System to Intermediate System (ES–IS) routing protocol is specified in ISO/IEC 9542; Intermediate System to Intermediate System (IS–IS) routing protocol is specified in ISO 10589; and the Inter-Domain Routing Protocol (IDRP) is defined in ISO/IEC 10747.

DATA LINK LAYER

The control of interconnection of data circuits (which are in the Physical Layer) from the Network Layer requires interaction between a network entity and a physical entity in the same open system. Because the Reference Model permits direct interaction only between adjacent layers, the network entity cannot interact directly with the physical entity. This interaction is thus described through the Data Link Layer, which intervenes transparently to convey the interaction between the Network Layer and the Physical Layer.

Some physical media (for example, telephone line) require specific techniques to be used in order to transmit data between systems despite a relatively high error rate (i.e., an error rate not acceptable for the great majority of applications). These specific techniques are used in data-link procedures which have been studied and standardized for a number of years. Newer physical communication media (for example, fiber optics) require different data-link control procedures. These procedures are included in the Data Link Layer.

The Data Link Layer takes the raw transmission facility provided by the Physical Layer and transforms it into a link that appears substantially free of transmission errors to the network layer. It performs this function by taking bits and forming them into data frames; these data frames are then transmitted sequentially. The Data Link Layer provides error detection and, optionally, correction (involving two computers directly connected) across a line between nodes of a subnetwork.

The Data Link Layer provides functional and procedural means for connectionless-mode transmission among network entities and establishes, maintains, and releases data-link connections among network entities and transfers data-link SDUs. A data link is built upon one or several physical connections.

The Data Link Layer conveys to network entities the capability of controlling the interconnection of data circuits within the Physical Layer. This function is particularly used when a physical connection is established/released across a circuit-switched subnetwork by relaying within an intermediate system between data circuits that are elements of the end-to-end path under control of a network entity, which makes the appropriate routing decisions as a function of the path requirements derived from the network signaling protocols.

The Data Link Layer checks the number and position of bits received, and performs various calculations to determine if there is an error, for example, if a "1" bit is accidentally received as a "0." Synchronization of sender and receiver is important in this layer. The Data Link Layer emphasizes "box-to-box" communications, that is, management of bits between directly connected computers.

The Data Link Layer provides delimiting and synchronization, sometimes called framing, which provide recognition of a sequence of physical SDUs (i.e., bits) transmitted over the physical connection, as a data-link PDU.

If needed, the Data Link Layer provides data-link end-point identifiers which can be used by a network entity to identify a correspondent network entity.

The portion of the subnetwork technology that resides in the Network Layer is responsible for routing and relaying within the subnetwork, if necessary. For instance, in an X.25 subnetwork, the X.25 Packet Layer Protocol provides for the internal routing (i.e., from switch to switch) of X.25 packets from one X.25 subscriber to another. Alternatively, in "8802" subnetworks (IEEE 802), the Network Layer component is logically empty, since the method of transfer is broadcast and there is no explicit subnetwork routing performed.

The X.25 protocol establishes a virtual circuit between two machines; this is a definite path connecting the two machines through intermediate machines. This path is valid for the lifetime of the connection. Source and destination addresses, as well as other information, are put on a call setup packet; data packets follow.

The X.25 Packet Layer (Layer 3) protocol is concerned with data format and meaning in a frame, as well as subnetwork routing and virtual circuit management. When one system wants to connect to another system, a logical circuit is set up between them; there are a number of parameters which specify various kinds of information. Some functions are reset and clearing a circuit (when a call request cannot be completed).

PHYSICAL LAYER

It is essential that an open architecture permits usage of a realistic variety of physical media for interconnection with different control procedures. This led to the creation of Physical Layer as the lowest layer.

The Physical Layer provides mechanical, electrical, functional, and procedural means to activate, maintain, and deactivate physical connections for a bit transmission between data-link entities. A physical connection may involve intermediate open systems, each relaying bit transmission within the Physical Layer. Physical Layer entities are interconnected by means of a physical medium.

The Physical Layer allows for the correct pin settings and signaling techniques of interfaces to lines so that bits of data may be transmitted from one machine to another machine. Issues here involve the nature of the physical medium and ensuring that proper synchronization is applied for the transfer. There are a large number of Physical Layer specifications, depending on the physical medium employed (e.g., wire, coaxial cable, fiber optics, radio signals, laser signals, microwave signals), but the standards also include connectors, modulation techniques, environmental limits, etc. The mechanical, electromagnetic, and other media-dependent characteristics of physical media connections are defined at the boundary between the Physical Layer and the physical media.

APPLICATION PROGRAM INTERFACES

For many large OSI networks, portability can be almost as important an economic issue as interoperability. Obviously, an absolute consideration is that applications interoperate, regardless of the hardware configurations or operating systems used for each of the nodes. However, in many systems there will be certain common applications which might need to be used in a variety of hardware and operating systems environments. Presumably, the use of OSI will facilitate the interoperability of the applications. However, the user also wants to avoid reprogramming applications because the Application Program Interfaces (APIs) to the communications services are not consistent. As a result, there are a number of efforts by various standards groups to define standard APIs. This increases the possibility that users can find multivendor products with consistent API interfaces. In many cases, an API can also function with non-OSI communications, thus facilitating operation of multiprotocol networks or transition to OSI.

- Same user application programs can operate in a variety of hardware/software environments (possibly facilitating use of "shrink-wrapped" software or COTS).

- Applications can be moved to other platforms in existing or future inventory of the using organization.

- Reuse and development of program libraries is facilitated.

- Knowledge becomes more portable, as programming practices can become more uniform and there is increased likelihood of familiarity with interfaces.

Although most of these benefits can be achieved by adaptation of an organizational standard API, the full benefits of an API cannot be achieved unless the API is supported by many vendors across multiple programming languages and operating systems environments.

There are several efforts underway to standardize APIs. X/Open has published an API for transaction processing, largely based on IBM's Computer Program Interface, Communications (CPI-C). IEEE has undertaken several API projects, including standard APIs for X.400 (MHS) and X.500 (the directory).

SOME OTHER TOPICS

The initial OSI model addressed only the basic framework. As OSI matured, the framework has been expanded to include security (ISO 7498-2) and naming and addressing (7498-3); in addition, the OSI family of standards now includes many additional areas, such as network management (ISO/IEC 7498-4).

OSI Security

The basic framework for OSI security is described in ISO 7498-2. The basic security framework has been divided into an Upper Layers Security Model and Lower Layers Security Model, partly to divide the work among the committees involved in OSI, but also because the security mechanisms for the upper and lower layers are different. (The responsibilities are different, so the vulnerabilities are different.)

The Upper Layers Security Model (ISO/IEC DIS 10745, 1992) describes a basic model:

> The generation and processing of security information are performed by *generic security functions* (GSFs), whose specifications fall outside the scope of OSI but which can be invoked by OSI entities to provide the required security service(s). GSFs generate and process security information exchanged using OSI protocols in the Application and Presentation layers. The logical structure of exchanged security information can be standardized in OSI so it can be represented in OSI protocol exchanges.

> The exchanged security information, generated and processed by GSFs, can be either generic in nature or application-specific. As far as possible, generic security elements should be factored out to carry security information in support of the requirements of a wide range of applications. This is facilitated by the concept of security exchanges and an associated notational framework which can allow security implements specifications to be referenced by any application standard.

The security model defines GSFs including *security transformation functions* to support confidentiality and *security check-value functions* to support integrity. Within the upper layers, these functions can be invoked from within the Application Layer or Presentation Layer. When some mechanisms, such as encryption, are involved, it may be necessary to perform the function at the Presentation Layer, so the encryption is applied to the transfer syntax. Otherwise, both sender and receiver would be required to use the same presentation syntax, which limits the value of the Presentation Layer.

Although the Upper Layers model defers to the Lower Layers model for completion of the description of provision of security services, it briefly discusses the use of Lower Layers services to show how the two models relate.

> Lower Layers security services may be used to provide additional protection beyond that provided in the Upper Layers. In particular, Lower Layers security services may be used to protect protocol-control information of the higher layers and provide a higher degree of traffic flow confidentiality.

Regardless of the layer at which Lower Layers services are provided, the Transport Layer is involved because it provides the QOS parameter, which is the only means by which an application can influence the selection of Lower Layers security services for a particular instance of communication. This is critical for many applications, as the protection requirements vary according to type of message, etc.

The Integrity Framework addresses integrity-protected data, which can be provided though encryption or error-detecting/correcting codes. The WD also discusses the relationship of integrity to party-to-party authentication and access control.

The mappings of services to layers in ISO 7498-2 should only be considered a framework and not a dependable guide to where the services will be defined within other OSI standards or where they should be implemented. Thus, it seems that the Application Layer is generally responsible for mechanisms involving the identity of the sender or receiver and the lower layers are merely responsible for ensuring that all data, including security mechanisms, are transmitted with confidentiality and integrity intact. The Transport Layer seems to be the best candidate, although some services may also be desirable in the lower three layers.

The security services that may be provided by the protocol that performs the subnetwork access functions associated with the provision of the OSI network service are as follows:

1. Peer entity authentication
2. Data origin authentication
3. Access control service
4. Connection confidentiality
5. Connectionless confidentiality
6. Traffic flow confidentiality
7. Connection integrity without recovery
8. Connectionless integrity

Peer-entity authentication (as defined in ISO 7498-2:1988) is a special case of party-to-party authentication, which is defined in CD 10181-2. Note that the "Upper Layers do not provide for authentication of any entities below the Application Layer."

Party-to-party authentication only provides assurance to an identity at an instant of time. To maintain this assurance throughout the duration of an association, connection integrity is required. In some cases it may be necessary to obtain further assurance of the identify of an entity after a period of time through additional authentication exchanges.

Like peer-entity authentication, "Data origin authentication is provided by protocol and identification of the data being authenticated in the *Application Layer*."

The OSI Systems Management standard also contains parts addressing security. The Security Alarm Reporting Function (DIS 10164-7) may soon be approved by JTC1. The security audit trail function (ISO/IEC 10164-8) and "objects and attributes for access control" (CD 10164-9) received many comments during the latest ballot period, but are making significant progress.

System Management

System management includes functions in the Application Layer related to the management of various OSI resources and their status across all layers of the OSI architecture.

Within the OSI architecture, there is a need to recognize the special problems of initiating, terminating, and monitoring activities and assisting in their harmonious operations, as well as handling abnormal conditions.

The management activities that are of concern are those which imply actual exchanges of information between open systems. Only those management activities which imply actual exchanges of information between remote management entities are pertinent to the OSI architecture. Other management activities local to particular open systems are outside its scope. Similarly, not all resources are pertinent to OSI.

Application management is related to the management of OSI application processes. The following is a list of typical activities that fall into this category, but it is not exhaustive:

1. Initialization of parameters representing application processes
2. Initiation, maintenance, and termination of application processes
3. Allocation and deallocation of OSI resources to application processes
4. Detection and prevention of OSI resource interference and deadlock
5. Integrity and commitment control
6. Security control
7. Check pointing and recovery control

Systems management relates to the management of OSI resources and their status across all layers of the OSI architecture. The following list is typical of activities that fall into this category:

1. Activation/deactivation management, which includes:
   a. Activation, maintenance, and termination of OSI resources distributed in open systems, including physical media for OSI

  b. Some program loading functions

  c. Establishment/maintenance/release of connections between management entities

  d. Open systems parameter initialization/modification

 2. Monitoring, which includes:

  a. Reporting status or status changes

  b. Reporting statistics

 3. Error control, which includes:

  a. Error detection and some of the diagnostic functions

  b. Reconfiguration and restart

Layer management includes two aspects. One of these is concerned with layer activities such as activation and error control. This part is implemented by the layer protocol to which it applies.

The other aspect of layer management is a subset of systems management. The protocols for these activities reside within the Application Layer and are handled by systems management–application entities.

The OSI Reference Model and architecture do not dictate any particular fashion of degree of centralization of management functions. This principle calls for a structure in which each open system is allowed to include any collection of systems-management functions and each subsystem is similarly permitted to include any layer-management functions. If necessary, connections between management entities are established when an open system, which has been operating in isolation from other open systems, becomes part of the OSI environment.

Systems management provides mechanisms for the monitoring, control, and coordination of resources within the OSI environment and OSI protocol standards for communicating information pertinent to those resources. In order to describe management operations on resources in the OSI environment, the resources are viewed as managed objects with defined properties. Information required for systems management purposes in any open system may be provided through local input, may result from input from other open systems through systems management (Application Layer) communication, or may be a result of lower layer protocol exchanges.

Systems management is applicable to a wide range of distributed processing and communications environments. These environments range from local area networks interconnecting small systems, to interconnected corporate and national networks on a global scale. Small-scale environments may be managed by appropriate small-scale management systems, consisting of a single manager capable of controlling and coordinating the open communication environment through a number of agents. The standards and concepts are also applicable to large-scale environments supporting multiple managers.

There are three main groupings within the set of systems management standards. They are:

1. A set of standards specifying systems management functions
2. A set of standards related to the specification of managed objects
3. A set of Application Layer service and protocol standards for communicating information relating to management functions

The overview describes models for these groupings. It also describes the conformance requirements.

ISO/IEC 10164-8, IT—OSI—Systems Management—Part 8: Security audit trail function defines the security audit trail function, which is a systems-management function that may be used by an application process in a centralized or decentralized management environment to exchange information and commands for the purpose of systems management, as defined by CCITT Rec X.700 or the equivalent ISO 7498-4.

ISO/IEC 10164-8 defines:

•   A set of notifications for security-related events that are to be sent to a security audit trail log; the contents of the security audit trail log may be used in a security audit

•   A set of service primitives that constitute the security audit trail function

•   The parameters that are passed in each service primitive

•   Any necessary information for the semantic description of each service primitive

•   The conformance requirements to be met by implementations of this specification

CONFORMANCE TESTING

For several years, all projects for development of OSI protocol specifications have also proposed parts dealing with Protocol Implementation Conformance Statements (PICS) proformas and abstract test suites. These abstract test suites form the basis for conformance tests which can be run against any implementation claiming conformance to OSI.

The standards community, including the many major users and producers, has been very active to increase the likelihood that OSI-compliant systems will interoperate. Standards have been published for the seven-layer stack (ISO/IEC 7498-1), as well as for each of the layers, to define the requirements and interfaces for all the layers. However, merely publishing a specification is not enough; how can we demonstrate conformance? ISO/IEC Joint Technical Committee 1 (JTC1) Subcommittee 21, "Information Retrieval, Transfer, and Management for OSI," which is responsible for the upper layers, has mandated that all OSI standards be accompanied by standards for an "Abstract Test Suite," a conformance test suite based on the abstract test suite, and a PICS, which summarizes the options and results, providing a uniform report.

With these documents, not only are we provided a definition, but we also receive details on how to test that an implementation conforms to the specification. Unlike an acceptance test that a typical user might generate, these tests have been designed and reviewed by top international experts in OSI; these are very costly resources which have been provided on a voluntary basis.

Obviously, having a test suite is not enough; who will run the tests? Do you trust your potential vendor? Or would you prefer a third party? Several organizations worldwide have been gearing up to provide conformance testing services and issue recognized certificates that a particular implementation conforms to a given version of a standard. Many of these organizations have already been accredited to issue certificates. It is worth noting that the European community is very strong about certification and mutual recognition of certificates, which is likely to have a very strong influence on vendors interested in selling products worldwide.

With certification, an implementation is tested with a rigorously controlled test suite with official witnesses of the testing organization. Generally, an entire stack (through the seven layers) is tested with testing proceeding from the bottom of the stack upwards through the layers. A conformance test report (in a standard format) is written and a certificate will be issued if the test is successful. Users should accept these certificates as proof of conformance.

Conformance testing verifies that a protocol implementation performs as the standard specifies. Most conformance test scenarios concentrate on single-layer testing. A single layer of the OSI protocol stack is tested using the services of the lower layers which have been tested previously and are, therefore, presumed to work correctly.

Conformance testing alone will not ensure that an OSI protocol suite will work correctly. No conformance test system can ensure that all errors in a protocol implementation will be detected. In addition, single-layer conformance testing is not always possible because some vendors merge the functionality of two or more layers in a protocol implementation. However, conformance testing will increase significantly the probability that a product interoperates with other products.

While conformance testing increases the probability of interoperability, it is not a guarantee. Interoperation testing will still be needed. This could actually include some of the user's own messages to begin testing more than the vendor-supplied software. First, however, additional conformance testing (and specification work) can improve the odds.

Interoperability testing simulates the "real-life" conditions under which the vendor's product will be seen. Since vendors of OSI products are building implementations to operate with implementations developed by other vendors, it is in both the customer's and vendor's interest to duplicate as closely as possible the environment in which the product will be used before product acceptance is completed. In general, interoperability testing detects configuration options that are set in an incompatible manner. Such errors are relatively easy to overcome.

A typical test suite structure (e.g., ACSE, ISO/IEC 10169) incorporates several types of tests (see Figure 1.7).

Test Suite Structure

The three main test groups are:

1. **Capability tests**, which are used to verify that the observable capabilities of the protocol implementations are valid with respect to the static conformance requirements stated in the protocol specification and with respect to the PICS.

2. **Valid behavior tests**, which test the extent to which the implementation meets the dynamic conformance requirements specified in the protocol specification when the tester behaves in a valid manner. These tests provide a detailed evaluation of the features which are claimed to be supported in the PICS.

3. **Invalid behavior tests**, which test the extent to which the implementation meets the dynamic conformance requirements specified in the

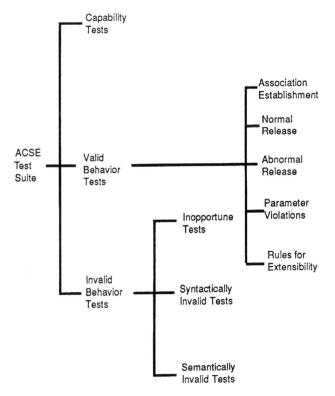

Figure 1.7 ACSE test suite structure (source: ISO/IEC 10169-1:1991).

protocol specification and related documents when the tester sends test events which violate at least one conformance requirement. These include:

a. *Syntactically invalid tests*, where the tester sends test events where the PDU syntax is not permitted by the protocol

b. *Semantically invalid tests*, where the tester sends test events where the semantics are not consistent with those specified by the standard

c. *Inopportune tests*, where the tester generates test events which occur when they are not permitted by the protocol

Interoperability tests are getting much more attention. Many vendors use OSINET for testing interoperability; there are also independent test labs. In addition, some large users have established their own interoperability labs.

This approach has the additional advantage of supporting the additional testing that is needed to ensure that a particular product will work in a user's own environment. The Standards Promotion and Application Group (SPAG) has developed the Program to Support Interoperability (PSI); this suite is possibly the most extensive interoperablity test available. It is used more in Europe than in the United States.

Many international standardized profiles (ISPs) are being developed to actually select various options through all the layers of the stack. Although the Government Open System Interconnection Profile (GOSIP) is one of the more famous profiles (actually it is a collection of profiles), there are many more being developed.

Industry profiles are also being developed; these are harmonized within a particular industry (e.g., aeronautics) but can also be processed as international standardized profiles. Thus, even if a network's requirements are not satisfied by GOSIP, there might be another profile that fits. As with the base protocol, each ISP can be conformance tested; this is not done with new test suites but by using tailoring of the basic test suite. Even without use of the test suite, the form of the ISP is a useful discipline for documenting how the systems of a network will actually use GOSIP. This can greatly help in publishing interface specifications, especially when different groups within an organization have responsibility for various components. One of the great values of the ISP formats is that they are rigorous, well-understood, and required if there is expectation of approval as an ISP.

In some ways, the "skinny stack" might be considered a profile because it sets the optional fields to mandatory. In some ways, all profiles might be considered somewhat skinny. In addition, the practice of conformance testing to a specific profile helps detect implementations that violate the bounds of a profile, thus freeing conformant implementations from the need to handle all cases.

To achieve interoperability, it is beneficial to specify common profiles in procurements rather than requiring adherence to a base standard. This approach provides benefits to vendors because a vendor can build a product, test it once, and then have the test results accepted throughout the world, thus offering the potential of a significant reduction in product development costs. The buyers within an industry (e.g., manufacturers, airlines) must, to the extent possible, agree on a set of procurement specifications, including testing requirements, which are consolidated, giving product vendors a large incentive to build the desired products. In addition, this provides benefits to approval authorities by the availability of well-designed and implemented test suites for the protocols.

COEXISTENCE AND TRANSITION

Most OSI implementations will need to fit into existing networks which may use industry-wide protocols such as TCP/IP or vendor-unique protocols.

Vendors will make suggestions as to how to provide a smooth transition to OSI while preserving capabilities inherent in their particular user interface during the OSI transition process. The vendor whose architecture differs radically from OSI is likely to emphasize the private architecture approach while offering gateways to OSI products. On the other hand, the vendor whose private architecture is close to that of OSI is more likely to effect a smooth transition to a total OSI solution; in this case, private architecture solutions will have a limited life.

Migration requires changes to both the application and the network. Standard applications such as file transfer or mail are likely candidates for transition. For example, if migrating from a TCP/IP environment, it should be relatively easy to convert from SMTP to X.400 or FTP to FTAM. At present, migration from Telnet to Virtual Terminal (VT) may be somewhat more difficult, because there are fewer implementations available in the marketplace.

Applications based on products requiring communications services, such as database products or presentation managers, can often be migrated by using a vendor's OSI-compatible version. Customized applications are likely to require a greater effort; however, use of a common application program interface to the old and new communication protocols can facilitate the conversion (or coexistence) of applications.

For migration of the underlying network, gateways are possibly the most effective approach. However, a network must consider whether to convert when the new protocols are introduced, wait until major changes are needed for the application, or schedule the conversions on a time-available basis. Availability of special features in vendors' implementations is also a major consideration, if you need the features and cannot wait for the standards. At present, it still may not be possible to cut over to a fully compliant implementation because of the need for special features.

Several examples are apparent, in the form of directory service enhancements and network management solutions. In either case, vendors may offer interim solutions as enhancements to OSI products, in the absence of standards supporting these capabilities. Interim specifications may be proposed as a short-term solution. Users may wish to accept these options, and require that the vendor propose a transition path to the standard OSI solutions when they become available in products.

Another example is that of security enhancements to OSI products. Many users have security needs that must be added as options to existing OSI products. Comprehensive security standards are not available currently. Users may accept interim security solutions, if needs exist. These solutions should be moved to OSI solutions in the future, and it is recommended that vendors provide a plan or specific commitment for such a transition.

Vendors may upgrade their products to align with evolving base standards or functional profiles, or they may provide additional functionality beyond that specified in the standard or profiles. In these instances, care should be taken that use of the extensions will not compromise future interoperability, or that there are adequate plans for migrating to the standard once the desired features are standardized.

The transition to open systems is concerned with both implementing OSI and providing interim interoperability with existing protocols until OSI implementation is complete. Interoperability provides a capability for the older protocols on existing networks to interoperate with the open systems protocols being produced. It is necessary to support the existing protocols for the expected life of the systems using them.

Extremely large, diverse networks may choose to use a multifaceted approach to transition, which might include (1) developing a full stack of OSI protocols in a portable operating system environment (e.g., ISODE and POSIX), (2) having both protocols coexist on a particular host (dual-protocol host), (3) converting from one Application Layer protocol to another (Application Layer gateway), and (4) supporting both IP (Internetwork Protocol) and CLNP at the Network Layer (multiprotocol routers).

Multiprotocol Routers

In order for coexistence to occur, it is necessary to provide OSI hosts, on a local area or wide area network, the ability to communicate with other OSI hosts on another non-OSI local area or wide area network. The availability of multiprotocol routers reduces the number of components, and therefore presumably reduces the cost and complexity for LANs, which are composed of a mixture of various protocol hosts, allowing the use of older protocols in areas in which OSI protocols are not yet mature (e.g., internetwork routing and network management).

The IP or CLNP performs the routing functions required to connect nodes on the same network or different networks. A multiprotocol router is a device that will be able to distinguish between the OSI and non-OSI internetwork protocol data units. When a packet arrives at an intermediate system, a Network Layer protocol identification field is checked and then the packet is passed to the appropriate module (either IP or OSI CLNP).

Dual Protocol Hosts

It is also possible to support multiple protocols on a single host. A dual protocol host has the complete OSI and other protocol suites available as part of its networking capabilities.

A dual protocol host can be used directly by applications to communicate to any destination on the network—for both OSI and non-OSI protocols. It can also be used as a staging point for manual interoperation between a host that has only non-OSI protocols and a host that has only OSI protocols by using a dual protocol host as an intermediary. New applications may use OSI, or applications may support both interfaces until the older interface is phased out. Another approach is to use file transfers to move data from one protocol host to another, but this approach is likely to be unsatisfactory for most applications.

Application Layer Gateways

An Application Layer gateway is a dual protocol host which contains a conversion module residing at the Application Layer of each protocol stack. This module performs the semantic, syntax, and service transformation required for the protocol conversion. Gateways could be in use for a period of several years as existing systems are upgraded or replaced. These do have impacts of cost, delays, physical space, etc.

Other concerns for interoperability involve (1) the sharing of hardware resources such as terminals and communication links, (2) support for interoperation of a basic set of application functions, and (3) addressing across multiple subnetworks which might use different formats and mappings for addressing schemes. In addition, there is the need for application-to-application interoperation. An important component of study includes identifying functional layer incompatibilities.

The most comprehensive and simplest interoperability is achieved by implementation of equipment conforming to a single full-function networking architecture. For environments involving multiple-vendor architectures, a compromise may exist between the level of interoperability achieved and the number of vendor environments to be supported.

Terminal protocol converters or emulators provide an inexpensive and effective interoperability capability for single architecture networking environments. Gateways may be optimized for performance but are difficult to extend to support additional protocols if a network involves many vendors' environments.

Vendors whose architectures do not map conveniently to the OSI architecture may decide to provide gateways or protocol converters as a long-term solution, while (1) providing for a gradual transition to OSI or (2) allowing both OSI and the existing native architecture to coexist permanently. It is possible that special user services which exist in the native architecture will be preserved by the vendor; OSI will be available via special hosts or processors. As another approach OSI could be used to permanently interconnect two native architectures.

A processor may need to be upgraded in order to support a dual stack.

Interoperability with "Short Stack" OSI Systems

Many systems are based on OSI's lower-layer protocols, but have not implemented the OSI protocols for Session Layer and above; this approach is sometimes called a *short stack*. Necessary functions of the upper layers are provided by nonstandard software; for example, the application using the short stack will still provide selected functions normally done by the upper layers. This might be done to optimize the application, or to minimize the conversion to use an existing application in conjunction with an OSI network. Use of a short stack has no effect on intermediate systems (which has only the Lower Layers), but a short stack might not work correctly with an OSI end system despite being able to coexist. This may be acceptable if the application using the short stack does not need to interface with all other applications.

In contrast to some other approaches, the Application Layer gateway is architecturally correct and is particularly useful in the relaying of messages between Message Transfer Agents that use Transport Class 0 and the CONS, and those that use Transport Class 4 and the CLNP. In addition, implementations of the Application Layer gateway for this purpose are expected to be widespread. The Application Layer gateway can also be used to implement security services at the Application Layer.

The best means of assuring interoperability across CLNP, CONS, and the most common range of Transport classes is the use of end systems capable of supporting all the required services. Many vendors offer Transport Classes 0, 2, and 4 and also offer both CLNP and CONS. This solution will work well when an end system is connected directly to a wide area network supporting CONS. When end systems are attached to a local area network, where CONS is usually not supported, products containing only Transport Class 4 and CLNP are appropriate.

OSI permits flexibility in addressing schemes. While this allows for greater flexibility in tailoring for a particular network's unique requirements, it also complicates interoperability among networks. Profiles, such as GOSIP, generally standardize the addressing formats. It is necessary for ISs to route to destinations in routing domains that use other addressing formats, such as those specified by ANSI or ECMA (European Computer Manufacturers Association). Such interconnectivity will take place via interdomain routing (e.g., routing domains using GOSIP addressing and routing procedures should not be expected to contain non-GOSIP ESs), as described in ISO/IEC 10737.

For interdomain routing, it is necessary for ISs to be capable of routing PDUs to other domains, based on variable length administration/routing domain identifiers, specified as address prefixes. Similarly, it is necessary that end systems be able to deal with NSAP addresses for remote ESs as variable length octet strings, up to 20 octets in length, whose internal structure, beyond the initial domain identifier (IDI), is not interpreted directly.

Other building blocks are available. At the Application Layer, the Association Control Service Element (ACSE) is designed to provide common Application Layer services, which currently include the management of connections. The ACSE performs all required interactions with the Presentation Layer.

Versions of Protocols and Editions of Standards

Many of the OSI standards are already at a second or third edition of the protocol or related specifications. In many cases, the newer editions incorporate the corrigenda resulting from defect reports or additional features which had been introduced through amendments or addenda to the base standard. Implementors should be aware of the various addenda and corrigenda that have been incorporated in an implementation, and need to consider whether there is a possibility of an incompatibility. Generally, these issues are considered during the ISO/IEC approval process; just as international standards go through several stages of balloting and review prior to approval, any changes to the standard—regardless of the form of the change—must also undergo an approval process.

Protocols themselves may have several different versions. When a new edition of a standard is published, previous editions (and amendments to those editions) are withdrawn; when a new version of a protocol is approved, it is possible that previous versions will still remain in effect. In this case, the standard will generally specify both (or more) versions of the protocol. During establishment negotiation, the two sides of the interface will ensure that both sides can support the necessary version of protocol. For example, any implementation of the Transaction Processing standard (ISO/IEC 10026) requires Version 2 of Session Layer. These mechanisms have been developed in order to ensure forward compatibility and not require existing implementations to upgrade every time a new protocol version is introduced into a network.

REFERENCES

CCITT X.121 (1984), *International Numbering Plan for Public Data Networks.*

CCITT X.21bis(1984), *Use on Public Data Networks of Data Terminal Equipment (DTE) Which is Designed for Interfacing to Synchronous V-Series Modems.*

CCITT X.25 (1984), *Interface between Data Terminal Equipment (DTE) and Data Circuit-Terminating Equipment (DCE) for Terminals Operating in the Packet Mode and Connected to Public Data Networks by Dedicated Circuit.*

CCITT X.28 (1984), *DTE/DCE Interface for a Start–Stop Mode Data Terminal Equipment Accessing the Packet Assembly/Disassembly Facility (PAD) in a Public Data Network Situated in the Same Country.*

CCITT X.3 (1984), *Packet Assembly Disassembly Facility (PAD) in a Public Data Network.*

ISO 6523:1984, *Data Interchange – Structures for the Identification of Organizations.*

ISO 7498:1984, *Information Processing Systems – Open Systems Interconnection – Basic Reference Model.*

ISO 7498:1984/AD1:1987, *Information Processing Systems – Open Systems Interconnection – Basic Reference Model – Addendum 1: Connectionless-Mode Transmission (Now Called ISO 7498-1:1984/AD1:1987).*

ISO 7498-2:1989, *Information Processing Systems – Open Systems Interconnection – Basic Reference Model – Part 2: Security Architecture.*

ISO 7498-3:1989, *Information Processing Systems – Open Systems Interconnection – Basic Reference Model – Part 3: Naming and Addressing.*

ISO 7498-4:1989, *Information Processing Systems – Open Systems Interconnection – Basic Reference Model – Part 4: Management Framework.*

ISO 7776:1986, *Information Processing Systems – Data communication – High-Level Data Link Control Procedures – Description of the X.25 LAPB-Compatible DTE Data Link Procedures.*

ISO 8072:1986, *Information Processing Systems – Open Systems Interconnection – Transport Service Definition.*

ISO/IEC 8073:1988, *Information Processing Systems – Open Systems Interconnection – Connection-Oriented Transport Protocol Specification.*

ISO/IEC 8073:1988/AD2:1989, *Information Processing Systems – Open Systems Interconnection – Connection-Oriented Transport Protocol Specification – Addendum 2: Class Four Operation over Connectionless Network Service.*

ISO 8208:1990, *Information Processing Systems – Data Communications – X.25 Packet Level Protocol for Data Terminal Equipment.*

ISO 8326:1987, *Information Processing Systems – Open Systems Interconnection – Basic Connection-Oriented Session Service Definition.*

ISO 8326:1987/AD2:1988, *Information Processing Systems – Open Systems Interconnection – Basic Connection-Oriented Session Service Definition – Addendum 2: Incorporation of Unlimited User Data.*

ISO 8327:1987, *Information Processing Systems – Open Systems Interconnection – Basic Connection-Oriented Session Protocol Specification.*

ISO 8327:1987/AD2:1988, *Information Processing Systems – Open Systems Interconnection – Basic Connection-Oriented Session Protocol Specification – Addendum 2: Incorporation of Unlimited User Data.*

ISO 8348:1987, *Information Processing Systems – Data Communications – Network Service Definition.*

ISO 8348:1987/AD1:1987, *Information Processing Systems – Data Communications – Network Service Definition – Addendum 1: Connectionless-Mode Transmission.*

ISO 8348:1987/AD2:1988, *Information Processing Systems – Data Communications – Network Service Definition – Addendum 2: Network Layer Addressing.*

ISO 8348:1987/AD3:1988, *Information Processing Systems – Data Communications – Network Service Definition – Addendum 3: Additional Features of the Network Service (1988, 10-15).*

ISO 8473:1988, *Information Processing Systems – Data Communications – Protocol for Providing the Connectionless-Mode Network Service.*

ISO 8473:1988/AD3:1989, *Information Processing Systems – Data Communications – Protocol for Providing the Connectionless-Mode Network Service – Addendum 3: Provision of the Underlying Service Assumed by ISO 8473 over Subnetworks Which Provide the OSI Data Link Service.*

ISO 8648:1988, *Information Processing Systems – Open Systems Interconnection – Internal Organization of the Network Layer.*

ISO 8649:1988, *Information Processing Systems – Open Systems Interconnection – Service Definition for the Association Control Service Element.*

ISO 8650:1988, *Information Processing Systems – Open Systems Interconnection – Protocol Speci-fication for the Association Control Service Element.*

ISO 8802-2:1989, *Information Processing Systems – Local Area Networks – Part 2: Logical Link Control – Amendment 3: PICS Proforma.*

ISO 8802-5:1989, *Information Processing Systems – Local Area Networks – Part 5: Token-Ring Access Method and Physical Layer Specification.*

ISO 8822:1988, *Information Processing Systems – Open Systems Interconnection – Connection-Oriented Presentation Service Definition (1988, 08-15).*

ISO 8823:1988, *Information Processing Systems – Open Systems Interconnection – Connection Oriented Presentation Protocol Specification.*

ISO 8824:1987, *Information Processing Systems – Open Systems Interconnection – Specification of Abstract Syntax Notation One (ASN.1).*

ISO 8825:1987, *Information Processing Systems – Open Systems Interconnection – Specification of Basic Encoding Rules for Abstract Syntax Notation One (ASN.1).*

ISO/IEC 8878-2, *Information Processing Systems – Data Communications – Use of X.25 to Pro-vide the OSI Connection-Mode Network Service – Part 2: Protocol Implementation Confor-mance Statement (PICS).*

ISO/IEC 8878:1987/Amd3:1991, *Information Processing Systems – Data Communications – Use of X.25 to provide the OSI Connection-Mode Network Service – Addendum 3: Confor-mance.*

ISO/IEC 8880-3:1990, *Information Processing Systems – Protocol Combinations to Provide and Support the OSI Network Service – Part 3: Provision and Support of the Connectionless-Mode Network Service.*

ISO/IEC 8882-1:1991, *Information Technology – X.25-DTE Conformance Testing – Part 1: General Principles.*

ISO/IEC 8882-2 (DIS), *Information Technology – X.25-DTE Conformance Testing – Part 2: Data Link Layer Test Suite.*

ISO/IEC 8882-3: 1991, *Information Technology – X.25-DTE Conformance Testing – Part 3: Packet Level Conformance Test Suite.*

ISO/IEC 9542:1988, *Information Technology – Telecommunications and Information Exchange between Systems – End System to Intermediate System Routing Exchange Protocol for Use in Conjunction with the Protocol for Providing the Connectionless-Mode Network Service (ISO 8473).*

ISO/IEC TR 9575:1990, *Information Technology – Telecommunications and Information Ex-change between Systems – Open Systems Interconnection – Routing Framework.*

ISO/IEC 9646-1:1991, *Information Technology – Open Systems Interconnection – Conformance Testing Methodology and Framework – Part 1: General Concepts.*

ISO/IEC 9646-2:1991, *Information Technology – Open Systems Interconnection – Conformance Testing Methodology and Framework – Part 2: Abstract Test Suite Specification.*

ISO/IEC 9646-3:1992, *Information Technology – Open Systems Interconnection – Conformance Testing Methodology and Framework – Part 3: The Tree and Tabular Combined Notation (TTCN).*

ISO/IEC 9646-4:1991, *Information Technology – Open Systems Interconnection – Conformance Testing Methodology and Framework – Part 4: Test Realization.*

ISO/IEC 9646-5:1991, *Information Technology – Open Systems Interconnection – Conformance Testing Methodology and Framework – Part 5: Requirements on Test Laboratories and Clients for the Conformance Assessment Process.*

ISO/IEC 9646-6 (CD), *Information Technology – Open Systems Interconnection – Conformance Testing Methodology and Framework – Part 6: Protocol Profile Test Specification.*

ISO/IEC 9646-7 (WD), *Information Technology – Open Systems Interconnection – Conformance Testing Methodology and Framework – Part 7: Implementation Conformance Statements.*

ISO/IEC 10030: 1990/PART 2, *Information Processing Systems – Data Communications – End System to Intermediate System Routing Exchange Protocol for Use in Conjunction with ISO 8878:1987–Part 2: PICS Proforma.*

ISO/IEC 10589:1992, *Information Technology – Telecommunications and Information Exchange between Systems – Intermediate System to Intermediate System Intra-Domain Routing Exchange Protocol for Use in Conjunction with the Protocol for Providing the Connectionless-Mode Network Service (ISO 8473).*

ISO/IEC CD 10747, *Information Technology – Telecommunications and Information Exchange between Systems – Intermediate System Routing Information Exchange Protocol for Inter-Domain Routing.*

ABOUT THE AUTHOR

Kenneth M. Zemrowski, CDP, CCP, has over twenty years of experience in the information technology field with management, development, and consulting experience in a wide range of technical and application areas. His current assignment for TRW is with the FAA System Engineering and Technical Assistance (SETA) project for the Advanced Automation Program, where he evaluates interoperability issues and serves as a focal point for standardization and standards conformance issues. This program will result in the replacement of the existing Air Traffic Control system.

Previously, Mr. Zemrowski managed the development of operating system and network communications software for the Ocean Surveillance Information System (OSIS) Baseline Upgrade (OBU), a C3I system including message processing, automatic correlation, and report generation. He has managed and developed software to provide operating system support for Pascal compilers, developed communication emulators, tested communication hardware and software, and participated in several studies to evaluate problems in vendor and customer use of communication and transaction processing systems.

Kenneth Zemrowski is actively involved in ANSI and ISO standardization at technical and management levels. He represents the Association of the Institute for Certification of Computer Professionals (AICCP) on Accredited Standards Committee X3 (Information Processing Systems), which manages and approves the development of computer-related ANSI standards, and on the Technical Advisory Group to ANSI for ISO/IEC Joint Technical Committee 1, which develops the United States' position on international standards issues in areas such as programming languages, OSI, microprocessors, applications portability, etc. He is Chair of Technical Committee X3T5, OSI Upper Layers. He also developed standards as Chair of the Joint Pascal Committee, and worked with other language committees to advance applications portability.

TRW's Systems Integration Group provides system development, systems engineering, and integration services, primarily in the civil, federal, and military marketplaces. The FAA SETA project is one of several major TRW projects involving OSI.

2

Guide to Digital Communications

E. Scott Barielle, CDP
Irv Shapiro and Associates, Ltd.

INTRODUCTION

A complete working understanding of data communications and interoperability necessitates a study of Digital Equipment Corporation's (DEC's) approach. Several de facto standards, such as DECnet, have evolved from this company with a long history of connectivity.

Digital Equipment utilizes a multiple protocol approach to communications between platforms. A different protocol "stack," or seven-layer suite of protocols, is used for different types of communications.

After an overview of architectures, each protocol stack and the type of communication it is used for will be examined. Next, the composition of the key integration product PATHWORKS in terms of the protocol stacks used as transports and the interfaces employed will be discussed.

ARCHITECTURES

Rather than examine the detailed workings of these communication facilities, an examination of the architectures, or guidelines for implementation of networks, will give a view from the top down. Digital uses networks of two different architecture families: Digital and supported non-Digital.

Digital Architectures

DNA, Digital Network Architecture, is often confused with DECnet; they are not the same, however. DNA is the architecture, or "master plan" for networking. DECnet is an implementation of that architecture. DNA versions in use in the mid-1990s are DNA Phase IV and DNA Phase V.

The DECnet Phase IV implementations consist of proprietary protocols. Advantage Networks, also known as DECnet Phase V and DECnet/OSI, is an implementation that is compliant with the International Standards Organization's (ISO's) Open Systems Interconnection (OSI) model.

Protocol suites developed by Digital are typically DNA compliant or a derivation of the basic guidelines. Derivations are used to optimize communications of a given type. An example is Local Area Transport (LAT), a terminal input/output (I/O) network optimized for Ethernet communication media.

Non-Digital Architectures

Digital supports IBM's Systems Network Architecture (SNA) with products such as the DECnet/SNA Gateway. The approach taken is to implement the interoperability engine (gateway) as an addressable unit to both networks simultaneously. Thus, a DECnet/SNA Gateway is seen as a DECnet node and an SNA Network Addressable Unit (NAU).

Other non-Digital architectures supported include X.25, TCP/IP, Apple-Talk, and Novell SPX/IPX.

Protocol Stacks

Next, let us overview the implementations of these architectures, the protocol stacks or "networks" DEC uses. The Digital proprietary protocol stacks are:

- **DECnet**
- **LAT:** Local Area Transport
- **MOP:** Maintenance Operations Protocol
- **LAST:** Local Area System Transport or LASTport

As nonproprietary networks, DEC uses:

- **TCP/IP:** Transmission Control Protocol/Internet Protocol
- **X.25:** Value-added network

Protocol stacks proprietary to vendors other than DEC that DEC uses or supports include:

- **AppleTalk** (Apple)
- **SNA** (IBM)
- **SPX/IPX** (Novell)
- **NetBEUI** (Microsoft)

The purpose of each of DEC's protocol stacks is listed below:

- **DECnet** is a host-to-host communications network.
- **LAT** is a terminal-to-host, or terminal I/O network.
- **MOP** is a maintenance protocol, used for down-line loading and control.
- **LAST** is a personal computer network service protocol.

DECnet: HOST-TO-HOST COMMUNICATIONS

An understanding of DECnet is the key to comprehending DEC's other protocol stacks. Digital uses a layered approach to networking, similar to the OSI model. A common misconception is that DECnet (Phase IV) is already very close to OSI. In reality, the approach is similar, but the protocols that implement the layers are very different. A comparison of the DNA Phase IV and OSI layers is illustrated in Figures 2.1 and 2.2.

Each *layer* is expressed by a *concept*, implemented by one or more *protocols*, and configured and monitored by a *component* in the management utility Network Control Program (NCP). Figure 2.2 shows examples of the layers, protocols, and components.

Some layers, such as routing, have only one protocol that implements them; others, such as network application and data link, have several protocols that implement them. A short glossary at the end of this chapter defines the acronyms used in the protocols shown in Figure 2.2.

Layers, So What?

What does the layered approach buy in the real world? It separates form from function, and allows changes to be made to any layer without affecting others. Therefore, as technology changes a DECnet can be changed without having to rewrite the whole shebang. A good example of this is the recent

DNA Phase IV	OSI
User	Application
Network Applications	User
Session	Session
End Communications	Transport
Routing	Network
Data Link	Data Link
Physical Link	Physical

Figure 2.1 Comparison of DNA and OSI.

acceptance of Token Ring as an implementation of Layers 1 and 2; same old DECnet, new data link.

DECnet Summary

There are two main points of functionality that will be summarized in this brief look at the architecture of DECnet: its implementation with peer-to-peer connectivity and functionality of the Network Application Layer.

Peer to Peer

DECnet, as a host-to-host communications network, is designed for and *always involves* a program on one host talking to a program on another host.

Layer	Concept	Protocol	NCP Noun
User	End User	User Written	
Network Applications	Program	DAP	Object
Session	Process	SCP	Node
End Communications	Logical Link	NSP	Link
Routing	Message	DRP	Circuit
Data Link	Frame	DDCMP	Line
Physical Link	Bits	RS232	

Figure 2.2 Layers, protocols, and components in DECnet.

This allows a peer network, in which all nodes are equal. Only *hosts* are *nodes* in DECnet, not all NAUs. Even PCs running PATHWORKS are full-blown DECnet nodes. What this boils down to is that any node can *establish* and *maintain* communications sessions with any other node.

Peer Example

As an example, let us say we have a distributed network between Chicago and New Orleans. A PC in Chicago can copy a file directly to or from a PC in New Orleans without involving a VAX. In PATHWORKS, the client PCs need a VAX server only for the services it provides, such as shared DASD and shared printers. If the VAX is unavailable, the PCs can still use each other's mass storage.

Network Application Functionality

What is so special about DECnet? Digital is about a generation ahead of everyone else in *host-to-host networking*, due to the *functionality* of the *Network Application* Layer. Digital "bundles," or includes with the operating system or PATHWORKS license, several programs which work with the network. These are called network applications, or objects, and implement Layer 6.

Network Application Example

A good example of this is FAL, the File Access Listener object. FAL is the receiver portion involved with DECnet hooking into the native file system of each platform. This allows *any* DECnet node to copy files to and from any other DECnet node. Each platform's implementation of FAL catches the network request for file access and hands off the blocks to the local file system. A standard description format is defined by DAP, or Data Access Protocol. The sender portion of this scheme is built into some operating systems, such as VMS, and included as an additional utility with PATH-WORKS, as in the case of NFT on MS-DOS and NetCopy on Macintosh. Thus, a Macintosh running PATHWORKS can copy a file from an ULTRIX (DEC's BSD UNIX) host. One of the software products, or Access Routines, available in Digital's DECnet/SNA product set is DTF, Data Transfer Facility. DTF implements DAP on the MVS or VM host.

LAT: TERMINAL I/O

The "network" in DEC terms is not used for terminal I/O, in contrast to SNA's origins. This is the origin of the myth that DECnet is slow. When an SNA professional looked at the response time at the terminal of a VAX system (and asynchronous, character-mode terminal), it seemed much slower than the response time to a 327X. DECnet is a lot of overhead just to move keystrokes around a wire. Thus, DEC wrote another network for terminal I/O, LAT or Local Area Transport. LAT has nothing to do with DECnet, but shares the same wire (Ethernet).

LAT is a lean and mean protocol stack whose only purpose in life is to move terminal I/O as fast as possible between hosts and terminals and printers. Several things are given up which are present in DECnet, such as multiple data links and the ability to be routed. In a comparison with DECnet, LAT approximately implements Layers 3, 4, and 5 (see Figure 2.3).

Ethernet Cohabitation

LAT is a nonroutable protocol stack, which can only exist on the Ethernet implementation of Layers 1 and 2. DECnet and LAT coexist on an Ethernet, yet they are different networks. To understand Ethernet cohabitation, think of a group at a party where two pairs of people are conversing in different languages. Corey and Emily are conducting a conversation in English while Blaise and Nadine are speaking in French. Can different carriers using different guidelines for communication access the same channel? Yes, because Ethernet, a set of rules for accessing a channel, does not require that a

DECnet	LAT
User	
Network Applications	
Session	User
End Communications	Slot
Routing	Virtual Circuit
Data Link	Data Link
Physical Link	Physical

Figure 2.3 Comparison of DECnet and LAT.

carrier understand the communications of another carrier, but only that it knows when the channel is in use. Thus, Corey and Emily will not speak while Blaise and Nadine are speaking.

LAT Implementations

LAT is implemented on VAXen, Alpha AXPs, in terminal servers such as DECservers, and in PCs and Macintoshes running PATHWORKS. A PC uses LAT for terminal emulation access to multiuser hosts. It is also used to allow access to a PC's locally attached printer. Hence, if my PC has an expensive PostScript printer hardwired to it, it can be configured to let anyone on the network print to it even while working.

MOP: DOWN-LINE LOADS

Maintenance Operation Protocol (MOP) is sort of like "baby DECnet." It allows a network processor or host to request and accept down-line load service from a host. It is also used for up-line dumps and diagnostics.

MOP Examples

DECserver terminal servers do not have operating software resident, but rather have MOP in firmware. When they power up, they use MOP to trigger an operating software down-line load from a load host. DECnet/SNA gateway bootstrap in the same fashion. MOP is used in the PATHWORKS product to remote boot MS-DOS PCs. Similar to LAT, it implements Layers 3, 4, and 5, or the core protocols (see Figure 2.4).

LAST: FAST PC NETWORK SERVICES

The greatest shortcoming of the early versions (1.0–3.1) of DEC's PATH-WORKS (PCSA) product was performance. To address this, DEC developed the proprietary Local Area System Transport, or LASTport protocol stack. The early version had only DECnet to use for file and print services. The functionality and flexibility of DECnet were simply not needed at many sites. Since there is no free lunch, the DECnet protocol stack is big (memory is precious on PCs) and slow on microcomputers. What they needed was to

DECnet	MOP
User	
Network Applications	
Session	M
End Communications	O
Routing	P
Data Link	Data Link
Physical Link	Physical

Figure 2.4 Comparison of DECnet and MOP.

move certain types of data at high speeds on an Ethernet, so they wrote LAST.

LAST is designed for the PC LAN environment, and can be significantly faster than DECnet (15 to 50 percent). LAST trades the peer connectivity and multiple data link functionality of DECnet for raw performance. In the protocol stack on the MS-DOS PC, for instance, LAST performs one buffer copy from the data link to the user's buffer, where DECnet would perform two.

Role of LAST

The role of LAST is expanding. Originally used only for virtual disks (high-speed read-only), DEC then added LAST transport for traditional PC LAN file and print services. PATHWORKS for DOS uses LASTport to access CD-ROM drives via Microsoft's interface (see Figure 2.5).

DECnet	LAST
User	
Network Applications	L
Session	A
End Communications	S
Routing	T
Data Link	Data Link
Physical Link	Physical

Figure 2.5 Comparison of DECnet and LAST.

PATHWORKS: A MULTIPLE TRANSPORT INTEGRATION PRODUCT

PATHWORKS implements DECnet, LASTport, LAT, and MOP on the MS-DOS platform. Variations of this client use Novell's IPX, NetBEUI, or TCP/IP. Most small sites do not need a fraction of the functionality of PATHWORKS, but rather need only shared files and printers. In contrast to traditional PC LAN products, PATHWORKS' multiple transports, multiple protocols, peer connectivity, and wide area support are sorely needed when the transition from workgroup LANs to Distributed Enterprise Network is made.

An Enterprise PC Network

Because PATHWORKS includes DECnet and the other protocol stacks modeled around it, the underlying design for a large, distributed network can benefit large operations. For example, PATHWORKS supports 64,000 hosts. Servers (VAXen) are scalable from the $4000 VAXstation 4000 VLC to the mainframe VAX 10000 model 440, which sports top-end 3090 processor performance. OS/2, SCO UNIX, Windows NT, and ULTRIX hosts are also available as PATHWORKS servers. MS-DOS, Macintosh, Windows NT, and OS/2 clients are supported. A look at the protocol stacks of an MS-DOS client would resemble Figure 2.6.

PATHWORKS Protocols

Several protocols are implemented in the protocol stacks of pathworks. For example, NetBIOS emulation is provided by the DECnet component at the

DECnet	LAST	LAT	MOP
User			
Network Applications	L		
Session	A	User	M
ECL	S	Slot	O
Routing	T	Virtual Circ	P
Data Link			
Physical Link			

Figure 2.6 PATHWORKS for DOS protocol stacks.

session layer. LAN Manager implements some of the session and network application layers. Digital's Local Area Disk (LAD) provides a virtual disk interface by implementing parts of the session and network application layers on the LAST transport.

Application Programming Interfaces (APIs)

PATHWORKS DOS includes several APIs. Programming support includes:

- DOS File API
- NetBIOS API
- LAN Manager

  —SMB

  —Named pipes

  —Mailslots

- Transparent DECnet

  —TTT

  —TFA

- Non-Transparent DECnet
- LAT Programming Interface
- CTERM Programming Interface

The DECnet "Task-to-Task" interfaces are found on all DECnet platforms. Non-Transparent DECnet is particularly powerful. It is similar in complexity to LU 6.2, yet more mature. For instance, Non-Transparent DECnet is *full* duplex. Here we see DEC's long history (1975) in host-to-host networking pay off.

SUMMARY

DEC's multiprotocol approach to networking underpins Digital's integration products such as PATHWORKS. In large and distributed networks, DEC has become a major force to reckon with. Their role in downsizing strategies can then be fit to the needs of the site, just as the role of the protocol stack and protocol is fit to the application.

GLOSSARY OF ACRONYMS

DAP	Data Access Protocol
DDCMP	Digital Data Communication Messaging Protocol
DNA	Digital Networking Architecture
DRP	Digital Routing Protocol
FAL	File Access Listener
ISO	International Standards Organization
LAST	Local Area System Transport
LAT	Local Area Transport
MOP	Maintenance Operation Protocol
NCP	Network Control Program
NetBEUI	NetBIOS Extended User Interface
NetBIOS	Network Basic Input/Output System
NFT	Network File Transfer
NSP	Network Services Protocol
OSI	Open Systems Interconnection
SCP	Session Control Protocol
SMB	Server Message Block
SPX/IPX	Sequenced Packet eXchange/Internet Packet eXchange
TCP/IP	Transmission Control Protocol/Internet Protocol
TFA	Transparent File Access
TTT	Transparent Task to Task

ABOUT THE AUTHOR

Scott Barielle is a consultant with ISA Consultants, Ltd. in Chicago. Specializing in large network integration, Scott's practice involves him with large organizations throughout North America and Europe. His ten years of data processing experience include heavy experience with DEC as well as microcomputers. He managed system conversions for a number of years, specializing in migration to VMS and LANs. His background includes the development and presentation of dozens of courses in Digital and PC hardware, software, and networking. He is on the steering committee of the Personal Computing Special Interest Group (PC SIG) o f the U.S. chapter of DECUS. An industry recognized expert in Digital's PATHWORKS (PCSA) personal computing integration products, he is contracted by Digital Equipment to instruct advanced PATHWORKS topics such as Iternals and Performance tuning. His current practice includes PATHWORKS configuration auditing, network design, network implementation planning, and technical advisory services. Mr. Barielle's combination of VMS, DOS, Windows, and networking expertise is valued highly by his clientele of large DEC shops with hundreds or thousands of personal computers, and he is quoted extensively by Digital and networking oriented periodicals in North America. Mr. Barielle has earned the credential Certified Data processor (CDP) from the Institute for Certification of Computer Professionals (CCP), an he is a popular lecturer in the United Kingdom.

ISA Consultants, Ltd.

ISA Consultants, Ltd. was established in 1985 to offer professional, value-based consulting services to clients around the world.

3

Implementing TCP/IP in an SNA Environment

Shaun E. Deedy
LXE, Inc.

INTRODUCTION

As networking began to grow, so did the number of communications protocols in use. Each vendor developed its own proprietary protocols, and interconnecting heterogeneous systems was complicated and difficult. In an effort to develop a more open and standardized protocol, several agencies of the U.S. government joined with major universities and corporate researchers to develop what is known as the Transmission Control Protocol/Internet Protocol, or TCP/IP. The TCP/IP protocol provided a relatively simple means to network computers and devices from various vendors. As TCP/IP became established in government and research institutions, the commercial market began to realize the potential benefit of an open communications protocol. While an open communications protocol is desirable, most organizations today have existing proprietary networks in place. One of the first widely used networking protocols is Systems Network Architecture, or SNA, from IBM.

SNA was announced in 1974 as a way to link IBM host computers, communication equipment, and peripheral devices such as terminals and printers into comprehensive, efficient, stable, and secure computer networks. It is often referred to as a hierarchical or host-centric networking architecture.

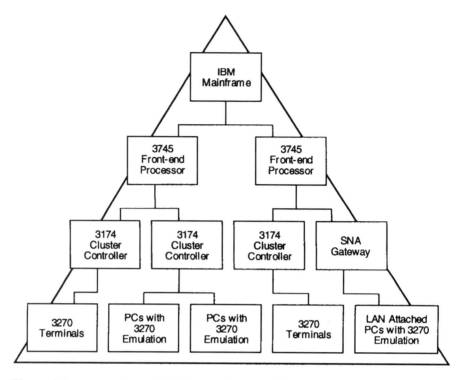

Figure 3.1 The traditional SNA network pyramid.

The entire network is designed for top-to-bottom communication between the IBM mainframe and end-user devices (e.g., terminals and printers). Side-to-side communication between end users is complex to achieve.
Depending on the location of the user one is trying to talk with, the communication path usually runs all the way up to the front-end processor and then
all the way down to the desired target user. Sometimes the path must go all
the way up to the mainframe. If one were to visualize this type of network it
would look like a pyramid with the mainframe at the pinnacle, network
communication devices (e.g., 3745 and 3174) in the center, and access
points (i.e., terminals or PCs emulating terminals) at the base . Figure 3.1
illustrates the hierarchical structure of SNA. At each stage, several lower-
level devices funnel into a higher-level device.

Since its introduction, major companies around the world have invested
hundreds of billions of dollars in SNA hardware and software. With IBM the
undisputed champion of the computer industry and SNA the most sophisticated network architecture available, most major companies designed their
computing infrastructure around SNA networks during the 1970s and
1980s. During the late 1980s and into the 1990s many of these companies

began investigating TCP/IP as a replacement for SNA and are actively moving in that direction. In these times of corporate downsizing and record losses, why would companies consider investing scarce dollars to move away from a safe, robust, proven network architecture like SNA to something relatively unknown in the business world like TCP/IP?

Between the 1970s and the 1990s business became much more competitive on a worldwide basis and every area of technology took dramatic leaps forward. To remain competitive, companies invested heavily in advanced technology like PCs and local area networks. As a result, the nature of business computing and telecommunications changed radically. SNA was based on the centralized computing model, with the following assumptions:

Computing power is expensive and centrally located.

Communication lines are slow, expensive, and offer poor quality.

Communication needs are relatively static and well known in advance.

One technology company can provide all the computing and networking hardware and software to its customers.

The current reality is that computing power is inexpensive and widely distributed to desktops and homes. Communication lines are relatively fast, cheap, and provide excellent quality. The need to communicate is very dynamic and often cannot be predefined. Technology is moving so swiftly and requires such large R&D investments that technology companies must specialize in only one or a few areas if they hope to compete. Customers rebel against being "captive" by one vendor, and the open systems concept is becoming widely accepted.

Try as it might, IBM could not change SNA fast enough to meet the evolving needs of many companies. Like turning a large ship, the direction of SNA could not be quickly changed. During the 1980s IBM announced a new generation of SNA called Advanced Peer-to-Peer Networking, or APPN, to replace the original SNA, which is often called subarea SNA. But APPN is still not complete and many view it as too little, too late. The architecture of TCP/IP, on the other hand, is well suited to meet the computing needs of companies in the 1990s. It takes advantage of desktop computing power to provide robust features and good performance. While it assumes communication lines are of high quality, it is capable of fixing errors when they occur. It is extremely flexible and provides the capability for nearly universal communication on the spur of the moment.

Since many companies have primarily focused on SNA, they often do not have an in-depth knowledge of TCP/IP. This chapter provides general information on TCP/IP, its history, its components, and the technologies it uses.

These topics are followed by a discussion of possible implementation strategies, including integrating TCP/IP with SNA and running both TCP/IP and SNA networks. Next, APPN is compared to TCP/IP. This is followed by a brief discussion of SNMP and NetView. Finally, some questions are presented for those investigating the implementation of TCP/IP. Throughout this chapter a focus on 3270 communication is maintained. It is assumed that the reader has an understanding of traditional SNA networks.

History

In the late 1960s, the Advanced Research Projects Agency of the U.S. Department of Defense (ARPA or DARPA) joined with several universities and corporate researchers to develop open, standard protocols for implementation in a network. This was prompted by a need for agencies to share information and computing resources among a group of physically separated installations. Further complicating the problem was the fact that a number of disparate computing platforms were to be interconnected. In 1969, the first experimental ARPANET network went into operation.

ARPANET was a 56KB packet-switched network that tied together major government, academic, and industrial research computing sites. It allowed users to exchange mail and files and log-on to remote hosts. ARPANET clearly demonstrated the benefits and feasibility of a cross-country network. However, as with most first efforts, there were several problems with ARPANET, including speed, reliability, and inability to interoperate well with other networks. In 1973, DARPA initiated a research program to investigate technologies for linking different types of packet networks. In 1974, two researchers, Vinton Cerf and R. Kahn, published a design for a new set of core protocols to correct these problems. The Cerf/Kahn design was the foundation for Transmission Control Protocol/Internet Protocol (TCP/IP). By 1978–1979, the TCP/IP architecture and protocols achieved their current form. Over the next several years, hosts in the ARPANET were converted to TCP/IP. To facilitate the conversion, TCP/IP was incorporated into Berkeley UNIX and made part of the public domain in 1982. In addition to the basic Internet protocols, Berkeley added several new features, including a set of utility programs with commands similar to familiar UNIX commands and a new concept called the socket, which allowed application programs to access TCP/IP.

In January 1983, the TCP/IP-based network was completed. A TCP/IP network such as this can be thought of as a network of networks. They are often referred to as internetworks, which is usually abbreviated as internets (small i). Internets are discussed in greater detail later in the text. In 1984, the National Science Foundation (NSF) recognized the importance of an open network to link researchers together and to NSF supercomputer sites. Because access to ARPANET was restricted, it could not be used. However, NSF recognized the benefits of TCP/IP and chose to use it as the foundation of its networking efforts. Rather than creating one large network, NSF decided to create an internet. NSF focused its efforts on two areas: creation of a high-speed backbone network called NSFnet to link its supercomputer sites and funding the development of a dozen regional subnetworks to link NSFnet and existing university, government, and industrial research networks.

The overall network created by ARPANET and NSF is referred to as the Internet (capital I) and is the largest network in the world. It is used by over 7.5 million people in the United States and countries on every continent and is growing at a tremendous rate. Some of the major subnetworks in the Internet include:

- ARPANET—DoD unclassified ARPA Network

- NSFnet—National Science Foundation network

- MILNET—An unclassified military network

- University Networks—Virtually all major universities connect to the Internet

- Commercial Research Networks—Many major companies connect to the Internet

- Government Networks—Civilian government agencies connect to the Internet

During the 1980s, TCP/IP became a requirement in many U.S. government bids. This prompted many vendors to add TCP/IP to their products. All this activity, combined with the growth in UNIX and the easy, inexpensive availability of software, caused tremendous growth in TCP/IP. It became the first viable, open, multivendor network standard. Some of the key benefits of moving to TCP/IP were:

- Ability to route data between different networks (subnetworks)

- Independence of technology used for subnetworks (for example, Ethernet, Token Ring, X.25, etc.)

- Independence of host hardware

- Tolerance of high error rates in subnetworks

- Robust recovery from failures

Corporations recognized these benefits, and during the late 1980s TCP/IP gradually expanded from its base in government, university, and engineering environments to the commercial environment. IBM spent many years supporting TCP/IP half-heartedly while steering customers toward SNA and APPN. However, in 1992, market forces became too strong. IBM legitimized TCP/IP in the eyes of many large companies by incorporating it into SAA. With this, TCP/IP became part of IBM's long-term networking strategy.

TCP/IP has flourished in the commercial environment for the following reasons:

Its capabilities are needed.

During the 1970s and 1980s, there was a proliferation of heterogeneous networks using many types of transmission media. Often these were departmental networks. As the need to connect these heterogeneous networks grew, a strong need developed for a hardware independent networking solution. Other alternatives consisted of gateways and protocol converters between platforms. TCP/IP was the best alternative and was widely implemented on routers.

TCP/IP is mature.

It has been well tested in the real world for many years. The maturity of TCP/IP helped make it commercially viable because companies knew that they could rely on it. Refinements have made it relatively easy to install and use. Other peer-based networking schemes (such as OSI and APPN, which will be discussed later in this chapter) are at a disadvantage when compared to TCP/IP, due to a lack of real-world use. Real-world use constitutes third party support and products.

TCP/IP is truly an open environment.

As we'll see in the next section, TCP/IP is truly an open, standards-based environment. Removing the vendor dependency created by proprietary protocols is very appealing. Firms are no longer tied to a specific vendor for all their computing and communications needs.

TCP/IP is ubiquitous.

It is widely supported by a large number of vendors and installed at a large number of companies. This "critical mass" attracts many companies. Products are widely available, trained people can readily be found to install and manage networks, and users can communicate with the large number of other people using TCP/IP.

TCP/IP can save money.

Especially when compared to SNA. TCP/IP is a simpler protocol which means fewer lines of code for vendors of protocol stacks and network devices to maintain. Protocol stack vendors face stiff competition not only from each other, but also from the availability of public domain software.

Vendors of TCP/IP-capable network devices provide low cost, high-performance, bridges, routers, and gateways. These devices stand in contrast to the traditionally expensive SNA network devices. TCP/IP network devices are tailored for specific tasks. This allows them to be smaller and simpler than comparable SNA devices, which must support the complexities of SNA. Intense competition between vendors of TCP/IP network devices ensures continually improving capabilities at competitive prices.

Some companies have chosen to save money by downsizing applications (that is, move them off relatively expensive IBM mainframes to relatively inexpensive platforms such as RISC workstations). TCP/IP facilitates this money-saving migration through its wide availability on the lower-cost platforms. Additionally, some companies have both SNA and TCP/IP networks in place. Since TCP/IP can be used to access IBM mainframes, some companies are reducing costs by reducing or eliminating SNA and using TCP/IP for mainframe access.

One area where SNA usually offers a cost advantage is in line costs. SNA has extensive capabilities that allow it to make maximum use of available bandwidth. TCP/IP, due to its architecture, tends to require more bandwidth. Line costs have been decreasing as competition intensifies in the telecommunications industry, so the cost advantage is lessening. The overall result is that TCP/IP networks can be much less expensive to install and maintain than the SNA networks widely used in corporations today.

Managing TCP/IP through Open Processes

As mentioned previously, the original TCP/IP network has grown into the world's largest network—the Internet. It has become one of the major avenues for communicating and sharing technology between government, universities, and industry. However, while it is used commercially, it is not considered a commercial product. Rather, it is a large, active research project and has become an important part of developing TCP/IP. By 1987, the Internet was growing at a rate of 15 percent per month. Rapid expansion highlighted design and implementation problems. To help manage the Internet, the Internet Activities Board (IAB) was organized by DARPA. The IAB is an autonomous organization with about twelve board members. Each board member heads a task force responsible for investigating issues or problems. The chairman of the IAB is called the Internet architect. The IAB meets several times each year and coordinates with DARPA and NSF. While it generally does not do the work itself, the IAB oversees and controls the process of updating old protocols and creating new protocols. This is handled through a vehicle called Request For Comments (RFC). An RFC can be submitted by anyone. Each RFC is numbered to avoid confusion by the IAB. Users of the Internet are free to implement RFCs. This provides a testing ground for new ideas.

The Department of Defense (DoD) continues to play a key role in the development of TCP/IP. ARPANET and MILNET, mentioned previously, are unclassified parts of the Defense Data Network (DDN). DDN also has other parts that have stringent security. The Defense Information Systems Agency (DISA—formerly the Defense Communications Agency, or DCA) is responsible for defining DDN protocols, architecture, policy guidelines, management, and operation. This agency publishes the *DDN Protocol Handbook,* which is the definitive version of TCP/IP protocols that must be implemented by vendors who wish to supply equipment to the DDN. The DDN protocols are called Military Standards (MIL-STDs) and are often required by other government agencies. Given the size of the DDN and the influence of the DoD, the *DDN Protocol Handbook* is something of a Bible for TCP/IP vendors. It is important to note that all RFCs and TCP/IP protocols are available for free to any interested party.

TCP/IP continues to become more widespread and accepted as a standard. TCP/IP is often associated with the Open Software Foundation's (OSF) Distributed Computing Environment (DCE), which began shipping to vendors late in 1991. DCE is designed to provide true multivendor interoperability. It is an environment for developing and running applications across heterogeneous computer environments, including different operating systems, incompatible communications protocols, dissimilar hardware platforms, and security systems. To do this, DCE focuses on layers 4–7 of the OSI stack. It is designed to sit on top of TCP/IP or OSI. The trial by fire concepts behind the development of TCP/IP contrast sharply with the development of Open Systems Interconnect (OSI) network protocol standards. OSI standards are developed by committees operating under the auspices of the International Standards Organization (ISO). Committee members come from government, industry, and academic institutions from around the world. Proposals are developed, debated, revised, adopted, and published prior to any development activities. While this ensures that the standards are comprehensive, ISO has been criticized for standards that are late; too general in some areas, which leaves them open to interpretation; and poor performers in real-world environments.

THE OSI MODEL

One of ISO's noteworthy accomplishments was the definition of a seven-layer reference model for network protocols, OSI. The model describes the conceptual organization of networking protocols. Many companies have developed OSI protocol stacks based on this model. The U.S. government has adopted a subset of the OSI model as its standard. This is called Government Open Systems Interconnect Profile (GOSIP), and in theory is required in all government networking purchases. The layers of the OSI protocol are commonly used as a standard against which the functionality of other protocols is compared. It is a reference model that provides a common basis for discussion. Figure 3.2 shows the seven-layer OSI model.

Each of the layers described in the following paragraphs builds upon the layer below it. Although each step must be performed in a preset order, there are several processing options within each layer. The bottom three layers, Physical, Data Link, and Network, are concerned with data transmission and routing. The top three layers, Session, Presentation, and Applica-

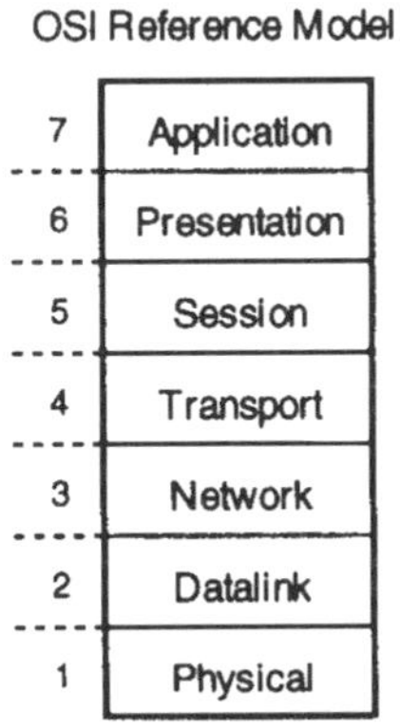

OSI Reference Model

7	Application
6	Presentation
5	Session
4	Transport
3	Network
2	Datalink
1	Physical

Figure 3.2 Protocol layers—OSI reference model.

tion, focus on user applications. The fourth layer, Transport, provides an interface between the top three and bottom three layers.

Layer 1—Physical

Deals with the physical means of sending data over lines. The electrical, mechanical, and functional control of data circuits.

Layer 2—Data Link

Concerned with procedures and protocols for operating the communications lines. Detects and corrects message errors. The Data Link layer is sometimes subdivided into the Media Access Control (MAC) sublayer and the Logical Link Control (LLC) sublayer.

Media Access Control—A media-specific, access-control protocol within IEEE 802 specifications. Currently includes variations for token ring, token bus, and CSMA/CD. This is the lower sublayer.

Logical Link Control—A protocol within the IEEE 802 specifications for data link level transmission control. Includes end-system addressing and error checking. This is the upper sublayer.

Layer 3—Network

Provides the means to establish, maintain, and terminate network connections. It also addresses routing within and between individual networks.

Layer 4—Transport

Provides reliable end-to-end transport of data between communicating users, including error recovery and flow control.

Layer 5—Session

Sets up and manages dialogs, or sessions, between communicating users. Controls the use of the basic communications facilities provided by the Transport layer.

Layer 6—Presentation

Provides the data format translation capability needed in a multivendor environment to mask the differences of varying data formats. It assures that the representation of data is understood by communicating users. Examples are data conversion, data unpacking, encryption, and expansion of graphics commands.

Layer 7—Application

> End-user applications and functions for particular application services such as: file transfer, remote file access, virtual terminals, electronic mail, etc.

While OSI is appealing to many people as a modern, open, standards-based protocol, it is not yet mature. Some ISO standards, such as X.400, have been widely adopted. However, OSI is, in general, falling out of favor, while TCP/IP is gaining favor with users. In practice, the government and most companies interested in OSI are using TCP/IP for the reasons described previously.

TCP/IP PROTOCOLS AND APPLICATIONS

TCP/IP is a protocol suite. It is termed a suite because it is a family of protocols that can be used independent of each other. For instance, TCP and IP do not have to be used together. Figures 3.3 and 3.4 depict TCP/IP and its relationship to OSI, LAN Manager, and NetWare. TCP/IP is not dependent on any particular physical connection. It was designed to connect subnetworks to larger internetworks. Recognizing that the subnetworks could employ a variety of technologies, TCP/IP intentionally does not impose any requirements on the lower layers. Figure 3.5 shows the TCP/IP layers in relation to the seven layer OSI model. While Ethernet is the most popular medium for running TCP/IP, it can run over Token Ring, X.25, and other media. Thus, layer 1 (Physical) and layer 2 (Data Link) of the OSI

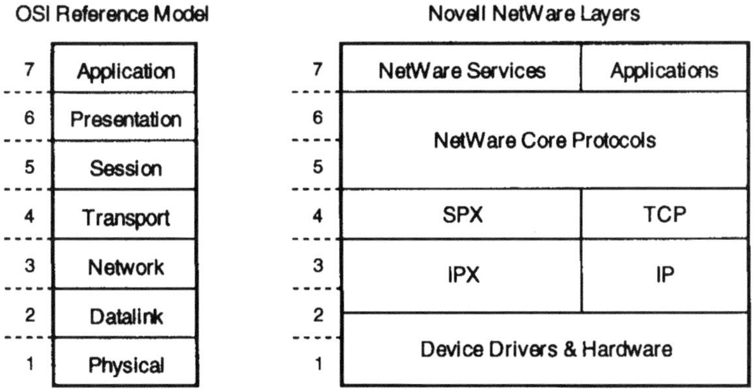

OSI Reference Model		Novell NetWare Layers	
7	Application	7 NetWare Services	Applications
6	Presentation	6 NetWare Core Protocols	
5	Session	5	
4	Transport	4 SPX	TCP
3	Network	3 IPX	IP
2	Datalink	2 Device Drivers & Hardware	
1	Physical	1	

Figure 3.3 Protocol layers—Novell NetWare layers.

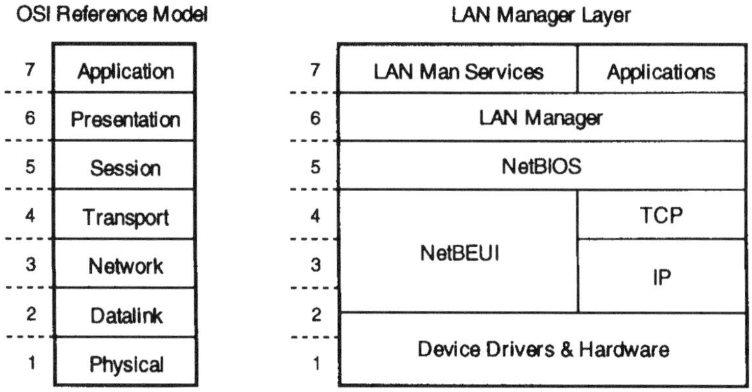

OSI Reference Model

			LAN Manager Layer	

7	Application
6	Presentation
5	Session
4	Transport
3	Network
2	Datalink
1	Physical

7	LAN Man Services	Applications
6	LAN Manager	
5	NetBIOS	
4	NetBEUI	TCP
3		IP
2	Device Drivers & Hardware	
1		

Figure 3.4 Protocol layers—LAN manager layers.

model are not specified as part of TCP/IP. IP resides at layer 3 (Network) of the OSI model and provides a connectionless packet delivery service. It links subnetworks into an internetwork via gateways that route IP datagrams (packets) between the subnetworks. It is connectionless because, unlike a phone call, there is not a dedicated connection between two communicating points in the network. A datagram can reach its destination through any number of paths. A detailed discussion on connection-oriented and connectionless networks occurs later in the chapter under Internets. IP does not provide reliable data transfer. It uses "best efforts" to deliver datagrams, but

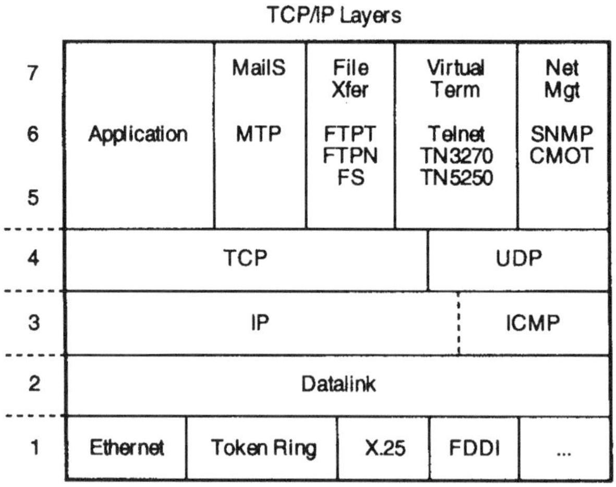

TCP/IP Layers

		MailS	File Xfer	Virtual Term	Net Mgt
7					
6	Application	MTP	FTPT FTPN FS	Telnet TN3270 TN5250	SNMP CMOT
5					
4	TCP			UDP	
3	IP			ICMP	
2	Datalink				
1	Ethernet	Token Ring	X.25	FDDI	...

Figure 3.5 Protocol layers—TCP/IP layers.

it does not guarantee that datagrams will be delivered in order or that they will be delivered at all. Reliability is provided by TCP. However, included as an integral part of IP is the Internet Control Message Protocol (ICMP). ICMP reports errors and problems to the network such as datagrams that cannot be delivered and congestion on the network. It is also used for queries to obtain network information such as to find out if a system is active, estimate round-trip times, and find out a subnetwork's address format.

TCP is a full-duplex, connection-oriented protocol that resides at layer 4 (Transport) of the OSI model. Its primary function is to provide reliable end-to-end communication between entities. TCP sets up and terminates connections, imposes flow control, provides error recovery, and guarantees that data is delivered reliably to the upper-layer user. Reliability is provided by ensuring that the delivery of data is accurate, in sequence, complete, and free of duplicates. Also at layer 4 of the OSI model is a connectionless protocol, the User Datagram Protocol (UDP). UDP plays much the same delivery role as TCP, with certain trade-offs. In return for better performance, UDP does not provide the reliability of TCP. It is often used for transaction-oriented applications and sends small amounts of data where the cost of nondelivery is low. For instance, an application for point-of-sale credit approval might use UDP. If a response is not received within a certain amount of time, the clerk simply resends the transaction, so the cost of nondelivery is low.

Located at layers 5–7 (Session, Presentation, Application) are several applications that help make the TCP/IP environment the mature, robust environment that it is today. These applications use TCP/IP (and UDP) to provide a great deal of functionality to users. These applications include:

File Transfer Protocol (FTP)

FTP does just what its name implies. It is a basic file transfer protocol for moving files among computers. File systems used by computers attached to TCP/IP can vary greatly. Designers of the TCP/IP protocol suite had two options: develop a complicated file transfer protocol to address all possibilities or develop an uncomplicated protocol that all computers could use due to its simplicity. They chose the latter. FTP evolved as a basic system limited in use to a few simple file structures. With a record-structure file structure, the file is made up of sequential records, and FTP preserves the record boundaries. With a file-structure file structure, FTP recognizes no internal boundaries. The file is viewed as a stream of bytes. FTP can transfer ASCII, EBCDIC, and binary data but does not do translations between formats. FTP does have some optional services such as recovery restart. It also provides some limited file management and information services such as rename and delete files, change directory, and list file information.

A second file transfer protocol named Trivial File Transfer Protocol (TFTP) is part of the TCP/IP protocol suite. It is an even simpler file transfer protocol used for such things as the initial downloading of software and configuration files to a diskless workstation.

Network File Service (NFS)

NFS was developed by Sun for users who needed more sophisticated file transfer/access capabilities. While it is not officially a standard, Sun has made it openly available in an RFC and many vendors provide NFS as part of their TCP/IP product set. NFS was designed to be independent of the underlying hardware, operating system, network architecture, and transport protocol. NFS was modeled after the UNIX file system. It makes remote files and directories appear as if they are part of the local directory. This allows end users to access files as if they were local, regardless of the files' locations.

Three protocols are implemented as part of NFS. Mount adds remote server directories to the local directory. Remote Procedure Call (RPC) supports sending file service requests from the client to the server and getting back the results. External Data Representation (XDR) provides a generic way of representing data over a network.

NFS provides optional services to manage files and directories such as access, read, and write files. A user can also find out about the organization and capacity of remote file systems, see attributes of individual files, and perform many other file management tasks. Each NFS service is provided as part of a formatted RPC call.

Telnet

One of the largest areas of incompatibility between computer systems is due to proprietary terminals with unique control and dialog structures that can be used with only a certain type of computer. The Department of Defense wanted its users to be able to connect to any computer system through a single terminal. The result was Telnet. Its purpose is to provide a generic, remote log-in. The primary use of Telnet is to enable a terminal user at one host to log into an application on another host. Secondary uses are terminal-to-terminal and application-to-application communication.

The default mode of operation for Telnet is Network Virtual Terminal (NVT). This is a simple protocol that emulates a half-duplex keyboard and a printer display operating in line-at-a-time mode. The NVT keyboard supports all 128 seven-bit ASCII codes as well as several command codes. The NVT printer is able to represent all 95 ASCII graphics as well as support commands such as Line Feed and Carriage Return. Options to the protocol are available for items such as remote echo of characters, binary transmission of characters, and character-at-a-time transmission. Other Telnet virtual terminal options are available to emulate commonly used terminals such as DEC VT100 and IBM 3270.

Performance is an issue with Telnet. In line-at-a-time mode, the messages sent are short. Header traffic is a large percentage of network traffic. This becomes even worse if a user switches to remote echo and character-at-a-time mode. Then, each character must be sent across the network. Despite these limitations, Telnet is very valuable, especially for terminal activities that are less interactive such as checking e-mail, starting jobs on remote hosts, and viewing output.

TN

TN is a type of NVT developed for specific environments to address some of the Telnet shortcomings. It often operates in block mode and is more efficient than Telnet. TN products are sometimes available as part of TCP/IP, but these often have less functionality than those available for purchase. Popular products are TN3270 and TN5250.

SMTP

E-mail has probably attracted more users to TCP/IP than any other application. The Simple Mail Transfer Protocol (SMTP) was developed either to transfer mail directly between two connecting hosts or to operate in a store-and-forward fashion across multiple networks. A companion protocol often used with SMTP is the Standard for the Format of ARPA Internet Text Messages. This protocol defines the transfer format of the mail content. SMTP does not always have to be used with this protocol, but it is most of the time.

Another part of mail service, the user interface or User Agent (UA), is not standardized. The UA is an interactive interface that allows a user to prepare a message, send mail, view mail, save copies, and so forth. As it is not standardized, it can be adapted easily for any environment, but the quality and sophistication can vary greatly. When sending and receiving mail, the User Agent communicates with a Message Transfer Agent (MTA). The MTA is responsible for queuing mail, setting up communications with remote hosts, and transmitting mail according to the SMTP protocol. X.400 is a similar, but much more powerful, e-mail standard defined by OSI. There is an RFC that maps SMTP to X.400.

SNMP

Recently, emphasis has been placed on network management. The Simple Network Management Protocol (SNMP) was developed to manage TCP/IP networks. SNMP is implemented by each subnetwork. Each has a database of network information called the Management Information Base (MIB), which defines the subnetwork. SNMP applications use this information as they perform functions such as sending out requests for information and configuration settings, receiving responses, and receiving alert (or Trap) messages. Messages are sent between SNMP applications via UDP.

SNMP is currently viewed as an interim solution. The IAB has charted a policy which calls for eventual use of OSI's network management standard, Common Management Information Protocol (CMIP), as a replacement for SNMP. The standard defining the use of CMIP over TCP/IP has the ungainly title of Common Management Information Services and Protocol over TCP/IP (CMOT).

The transition to OSI-based network management will take time. The OSI protocols are not yet complete, and there is little implementation experience with them. Some believe that the transition will never take place. As a result, vendors are currently investing heavily in SNMP-based solutions, and users are implementing them extensively. During 1993, an updated version of SNMP, called SNMP version 2, began to be widely implemented.

Kerberos is a method of distributed network security that is rapidly gaining popularity. While it is not officially part of TCP/IP, it is being implemented at a rapidly growing number of TCP/IP installations. Kerberos was initially developed at MIT as part of Project Athena, a campus-wide network research project funded by IBM and DEC. It has been endorsed by both UI and OSF and has been included as part of OSF's Distributed Computing Environment (DCE). Many vendors, including DEC, have products that use Kerberos.

The two key concepts behind Kerberos are authorization and authentication. Authorization gives users access to those resources they are authorized to use. Authentication verifies that a user requesting access to a resource has the authority to access the resource. To help make it secure, Kerberos is designed so that passwords are not transferred across the network. Instead, a unique ticket, which can be used only once to access a particular resource, is generated by Kerberos. Half of the ticket is sent to the resource, the other half to the user. The technique used is sometimes referred to as the broken poker chip. The server and the user each have half of the chip and they must fit together perfectly for access to be granted.

To access TCP and UDP, and to insulate applications from the network protocols, the applications often use sockets. Sockets evolved from UNIX where they provide a common framework for accessing devices and files. Since network communications are more complicated than file systems, the original UNIX sockets were enhanced at Berkeley to provide a common framework for accessing network protocols. Sockets play a role very similar to NetBIOS. Microsoft recently announced a standard interface for TCP/IP network communications between Windows programs. The standard, called WinSock, was developed in conjunction with DEC, Hewlett-Packard, FTP, Wollongong, Sun, 3Com, and others. WinSock conforms to the standard Berkeley socket, but it is fine-tuned for the Windows environment to provide superior performance. In the past, each vendor supplied a proprietary sockets interface. The new standard will substantially improve interoperability and should spur acceptance of Windows in TCP/IP environments.

INTERNET CONCEPTS

TCP/IP networks are often referred to as internetworks or internets (small i). An internet is essentially a network of networks. The various networks (also called subnetworks or subnets) are linked together via gateways. Each subnetwork is equal in stature (or a peer) to the other subnetworks. Hence, the terms peer-based or peer-to-peer network. Particularly in wide area networks (WANs), a high-performance communication link called a backbone is often used to connect the subnetworks. For those with an SNA orientation, the term gateway implies a device that operates at layers 1 through 7 of the OSI reference model to provide access to services and applications in a dissimilar environment. An example of this is SNA gateways that link IPX, NetBIOS, or Vines LAN environments to SNA environments. For those with an internet orientation, however, the term gateway usually means bridges, routers, and other devices that operate at layers 1 through 3 to connect subnets. Bridges, routers, and other types of internet gateways are discussed under the heading Internet Gateways.

The subnets that are connected to form an internet often use different protocols, hardware, and wiring schemes. As more networks are connected to internets, the trend is increasingly toward heterogeneous networks. Because it is highly functional, designed for the internet environment, and almost universally supported, TCP/IP has become the de facto standard for communicating between the various network environments found on internets.

Internet Gateways

Gateways are a key component of internets. The primary gateway devices are bridges, routers, and brouters. Hubs could be increasingly used in that role in the future. Each is discussed in the following paragraphs.

Bridges operate at layer 2 (Data Link) of the OSI reference model. Usually, they operate at the lower sublayer, the Media Access Control (MAC) layer. Because of this they are often called MAC layer bridges. Bridges link two subnets together so that they look like one extended LAN. They are relatively simple, inexpensive, and provide high performance. A local bridge directly attaches to two local subnets. Note that only one bridge is required. A remote bridge is attached to one local subnet and one remote subnet. A second bridge is required on the remote subnet for the first bridge to connect with. Because bridges operate at layer 2, they are considered protocol independent; that is, since they do not use layers 3–7, it does not matter to the bridge which upper-layer protocols are used. Layer 2 protocol conversion such as Token Ring–Ethernet occurs in bridges. The decision made inside the bridge is essentially binary. Either a packet crosses the bridge to the connected subnet or it doesn't. As simple as this sounds, there are some complexities. Two incompatible bridging methods are used by vendors: source routing and transparent bridging. IBM is a proponent of bridging using the source routing protocol. (Note: source routing is primarily a layer 2 bridging protocol even though the name would lead one to believe that it is a layer 3 routing protocol.) With source routing, the end nodes determine the path for the packet. When a session is established, the source end node broadcasts discovery packets to find the destination end node. When a discovery packet reaches the destination, it contains a record of the route to be traveled. The session is established using this fixed route. Each packet sent as part of the session carries the routing information along with it to tell the bridges where it should be sent. As one might guess, source routing is mostly found on Token Ring-based networks. Ethernet networks have traditionally used transparent bridging. This strategy places more emphasis on the bridges and less on the end nodes. Using their knowledge of the network and the destination address, the bridges decide whether or not to forward a packet. The bridges "learn" about the network (destination locations, congestion, bridges that are down, and so forth) by monitoring traffic on the subnets. Thus, the packets do not carry routing information, and each packet can travel a different path to the destination based on changing network conditions. The spanning tree protocol is used by transparent bridges to prevent packets from looping. Transparent bridging and spanning tree are IEEE 802.1 standards and tend to be used in all but the strongest IBM accounts. The IEEE 802 committee has adopted a standard for bridges, called source routing transparent (SRT), to bring compatibility to bridges. Rather than creating a third unique protocol, the IEEE created a standard for bridges to concurrently operate in both source routing and transparent bridging modes. Essentially, a bit has been added in the packet addressing area to tell bridges which mode to use. Since transparent bridging is the default mode for SRT, older bridges using source routing will have to be upgraded to use SRT.

Routers operate at layer 3 (Network) to connect two or more subnets. Because they operate at layer 3, they are protocol dependent. They must understand IP, OSI, IPX, NetBEUI, SNA, AppleTalk, and so forth in order to read the address information contained in the packet header so they can route the packets. Many routers are multiprotocol routers; that is, they can concurrently support more than one protocol. A router is more complex than a bridge. In addition to performing many of the functions of a bridge, a router must also understand and route multiple protocols, provide network management capabilities (SNMP), and handle differences in the subnets such as different addressing formats, different packet sizes, and different levels of quality (reliability, error recovery, and so forth). The more complex mission of a router has led to higher costs and lower performance as compared to bridges. While bridges will probably always be less expensive, performance issues have been addressed by vendors with techniques such as symmetrical multiprocessing, so that the performance difference is less. The objective, of course, is to route packets to their final destination via the most efficient path. To do this, routers use a process called convergence. This is simply a process of routers teaching each other the network topology. Based on the topology information gathered, each router in the network calculates the optimal path from itself to each destination. It maintains this information in extensive tables used for routing packets. To accomplish all this, complex routing protocols (sometimes called algorithms) are used. In the past, routing vendors used proprietary routing protocols such as Cisco's Interior Gateway Routing Protocol (IGRP). This tied customers to one vendor, which was a serious problem for customers committed to open networks. Industry standard protocols have emerged in recent years and have gradually been implemented. The most prominent routing protocols in

TCP/IP networks are the IAB standards: Routing Information Protocol (RIP) and Open Shortest Path First (OSPF). RIP is older and is gradually being replaced by OSPF. The ISO-supported algorithm is the Intermediate-System-to-Intermediate-System (IS-IS) protocol.

Brouter is a marketing term used to describe devices that combine bridge and router functionality into one device. Brouters usually operate as routers and perform bridging on demand. They can either be routers moving down into layer 2 to bridge packets in a protocol they do not support, or they can be bridges moving up into layer 3 by adding routing capabilities.

Hubs have traditionally been thought of as wiring concentrators operating at layers 1 and 2. However, hub vendors have added intelligence to their products and increased their capabilities to include bridging, routing, network management, LAN servers (such as SNA gateways), and other upper-layer functions.

Distinctions between the network devices described above are quickly disappearing. There is a major trend toward consolidation, into one network device, of the functions and features found in all the devices mentioned above: multiprotocol routing, bridging on demand, wiring concentration, high performance, SNMP network management capabilities, and upper-layer functions such as SNA gateways. While there will probably always be a place for low-cost devices such as local bridges, the future will focus on universal network devices. Leading vendors of gateway devices include Cisco Systems, Wellfleet Communications, 3Com, Network Equipment Technologies (NET), CrossComm, Network Systems (who recently acquired Vitalink Communications), Proteon, DEC, Retix, Ungerman-Bass, Hewlett-Packard, and IBM. Most of these vendors have enjoyed strong growth in recent years due to the rapid expansion of internets.

CONNECTIONLESS VERSUS CONNECTION-ORIENTED NETWORKS

The protocols that form the TCP/IP protocol suite define a connectionless network. This means that each packet is treated as an individual event. Once the communicating parties establish a connection (layer 4), packets are routed along a variety of paths to reach their destination (layer 3). There is not a set path. Routing protocols in routers choose the best path based on conditions on the network at a particular time. As the packets hop from router to router, the devices use their "best efforts" to deliver the packets. However, at the intermediate stops there is no error checking or recovery, and packets are not held awaiting acknowledgments. The router simply receives and forwards the packets. If a router does not know what to do with a packet, it throws the packet away. This means packets can arrive at their destination with errors and out of sequence. Sometimes they do not arrive at all. The TCP layer at the destination is responsible for error and sequence checking. If a packet is missing or damaged, TCP simply has the packet retransmitted. Note: TCP (layer 4) is responsible for maintaining the connection between the two communicating parties. It is sometimes referred to as a connection-oriented protocol. Please do not let this confuse you. TCP/IP and internets are connectionless networks because at the IP layer (layer 3) they route on a connectionless basis.

The primary benefit to a connectionless network is improved utilization of network resources. Fewer resources are required in intermediate nodes and the network is constantly adapting to changing circumstances. The main drawback is some loss of reliability resulting from lost or discarded datagrams. This contrasts sharply with SNA, which is a connection-oriented network. SNA was designed for an era where communication lines were more expensive, less reliable, and slower than today. Within an SNA session, between two communicating end points, all data packets are kept in sequence on a fixed path. In conjunction with intermediate error checking, acknowledgments at each step, and tight timing requirements, errors are quickly discovered and corrected. However, if there is a failure on the fixed path, the session is lost, and the user must log-on again. All paths are predefined by network architects before the network is "brought up."

Note: SNA is often referred to as a nonroutable protocol. What this really means is that SNA is routable only at the session level, not at the packet level (layer 3) as in connectionless internets.

The primary benefits of SNA are improved reliability, more efficient use of bandwidth, and greater control over response time. The drawbacks are some loss of flexibility, increased use of resources in the intermediate nodes, and increased network management overhead. As lines have become faster, more reliable, and less expensive, the value of these benefits has decreased.

The basic philosophy behind each type of network is vividly illustrated above. A TCP/IP internet is designed for universal communication. By definition, this means a user will encounter different types of computers, network hardware, wiring schemes, terminal types, and so forth. Since a user can communicate with a wide variety of devices it is impossible to specifically define beforehand how many aspects of that communication should take place. The only logical solution is to treat each device as an equal and provide each with a common set of rules (protocol) for communicating.

Conversely, SNA is designed to communicate with IBM mainframe computers in an environment where, essentially, there are no unknowns. All devices are known and defined beforehand. Most communication is expected to be transaction oriented between the user and mainframe application programs. The lower-layer data links are expected to be slow and unreliable. Central control allows network managers to fine-tune performance. Processing power is increased throughout the network for error checking, tight control over each packet, and to maximize performance. Maximum performance is usually defined as minimum response times.

ROUTING SNA OVER INTERNETS

As one might gather from the previous discussion, routing SNA over an internet is not an easy task. The lack of layer 3 addressing information, combined with the fact that IBM does not publish its routing specifications, means that no routers can currently route native SNA. Many vendors employ a technique called encapsulation or tunneling to route SNA over an internet. Specific terms used to describe SDLC tunneling over TCP/IP are synchronous passthrough and serial tunneling. It should be noted that tunneling techniques are not limited to routers and SNA over TCP/IP. They can be employed to move any nonsupported protocol across another network. For instance, OpenConnect Systems has products that support both SNA tunneling over TCP/IP and TCP/IP tunneling over SNA. IBM has a function in TCP/IP for MVS and TCP/IP for VM called SNAlink, which routes TCP/IP over SNA LU 0. It is expected that SNAlink will be enhanced to support LU 6.2 in the future. An analogy often used to describe encapsulation is a letter and envelope. The protocol used on a network becomes the envelope. The nonsupported protocol that needs to cross the network becomes the letter. Let's tunnel SNA over TCP/IP as an example:

> An SNA transaction is initiated at an SNA device. It is transported across the SNA network to a TCP/IP gateway. At the gateway, the SNA transaction (letter) is placed inside a TCP/IP packet (envelope) for transport across the TCP/IP network. The TCP/IP packet is delivered to a second gateway that provides an entry point to the second SNA network. In this gateway, the SNA letter is removed from the TCP/IP envelope. It is then placed on the SNA network for delivery to its final destination.

A problem with tunneling 3270 over TCP/IP is time outs. 3270 is a timing-dependent protocol. If TCP/IP takes too much time routing a 3270 packet across the network, acknowledgments are not received in time and the connection is dropped. A technique called spoofing is used to address this issue. Spoofing keeps the connection alive by sending false acknow-ledgments to satisfy timing requirements.

Another option that is growing in popularity is SDLC Conversion. SDLC runs from existing 3x74 controllers to a converter. The converter is gener-ally incorporated into a multiprotocol router. The converter takes the SDLC and converts it into Token Ring (Logical Link Control 2—LLC2). Since many routers bridge LLC2, the converted packets can be transported across multiprotocol internets and delivered to the mainframe via a Token Ring interface coupler (TIC). Thus, the polled, point-to-point SDLC has been changed into a peer protocol. SDLC conversion offers several advantages. The most important are performance and cost. As a general rule, conversion improves performance. SDLC lines running between 9.6 KB/s and 56 KB/s are replaced with 4 MB/s or 16 MB/s Token-Ring links and other high-speed links in the internet. Since the converter controls both the SDLC and LLC2 sides of the link, both can be optimized for performance. SDLC polls are not required across the network which frees bandwidth. From the cost perspective, the investment in existing terminal and controllers is protected. Conversion is also a single-box solution, which can reduce costs. Unlike tunneling, where a partner device is required to remove the SDLC letter from a TCP/IP envelope, the converted SDLC remains LLC2 all the way to the front-end processor (FEP), so no partner device is required.

IBM refers to SDLC conversion as Data Link Switching. They have in-cluded this capability in their 6611 router. Most router vendors have either announced plans to add this functionality or are already shipping it. To protect companies' investments in 3174 controllers and 3270 terminals, IBM has announced RPQ 8Q0935, an enhancement for the 3174 that allows it to attach to a TCP/IP network. Essentially, the 3174 becomes a large Telnet client. The 3270 devices attached to the 3174 (that is, 3270 CUT-mode terminals and ASCII display stations) can communicate to any Telnet server on the network. This includes an IBM mainframe as well as other non-SNA mainframes, minicomputers, servers, and workstations that support TCP/IP and Telnet.

TN3270

TN3270 is essentially a form of 3270 emulation designed to use TCP/IP as the transport. It is an implementation of Telnet that is specially tailored to emulate a 3270 terminal. It covers such things as determining terminal types, binary transmission of data, 3270 function keys, end-of-record options, line mode and block mode, and so forth. There are many different implementa-tions of TN3270 by different vendors. Since it is emulation rather than native

3270, the features available will vary based on the implementation. The RFCs that define TN3270 provide basic 3270 functionality such as 3278/3279 terminal emulation, models 2 through 5. Some vendors have proprietary extensions that provide additional capabilities such as EAB, 3287 printer, graphics, international character sets, and so forth.

For TN3270, both client and server components are required. At the beginning of a TN3270 session, the client and server negotiate the capabilities for the session. During the session each performs several important functions. The client is normally a desktop workstation. TN3270 resides on this machine as an application on top of the TCP/IP protocols. It performs ASCII/EBCDIC translations, creates the data streams, and performs presentation functions. It generally operates in block mode, although it can work in line mode or character mode. The TN3270 data stream is transported across the network in TCP/IP datagrams. There are no LUs or PUs involved with the transport, only an IP address that delivers the packets to a TN3270 server. The server also resides as an application on top of TCP/IP. This can either be on the mainframe, as IBM has implemented it, or off-loaded to another computer or controller, as OpenConnect Systems, McData, Apertus, and others have done. Functions performed by the server can vary. Where the server is not on the mainframe, its primary function is to present an SNA image to the mainframe. In other words, it makes the TCP/IP network look like an SNA device. Essentially, 3174 emulation is being performed. The LU and PU are located here. Like the 3174, other functions can be performed in the server. For example, when nonintelligent desktop terminals are being used, characters can be echoed back to the desktop screen from the server, and ASCII/EBCDIC translations are performed at the server. In IBM's TCP/IP implementation, the TN3270 server already resides on the mainframe, so SNA is not required. Its main function is to interface with the mainframe regions to make sure transactions get to the correct destinations.

An important function not specified in TN3270 is printer support. Native 3270 supports printers (LU 1 and LU 3) in addition to terminals (primarily LU 2). The RFCs describing TN3270 are being updated to add this support, but, as of the end of 1993, this work has not been finalized. Printers can be supported over TCP/IP using another protocol called the Line Printer Daemon Protocol.

Some of the RFCs that impact TN3270 include:

RFC-854   Telnet Protocol Specification

RFC-855   Telnet Option Specifications

RFC-856   Telnet Binary Transmission

RFC-885   Telnet End of Record Option

RFC-930   Telnet Terminal Type

RFC-1041   Telnet 3270 Regime Option

RFC-1060   Assigned Terminal Numbers

RFC-1143   The Q Method of Implementing Telnet Option Negotiation

TCP/IP AND SNA INTEGRATION STRATEGIES

SNA networks have existed in major corporations since the mid-1970s. Their traditional role has been to provide users with access to IBM mainframe-based applications. SNA is a top-down, hierarchical architecture centered around the requirements of the mainframe. It is very effective for linking users to the mainframe, but, as LANs grew in number, it became apparent that SNA was not an effective tool for linking LAN users together. LANs introduced many new protocols to corporations. They also facilitated an explosion of peer communication between users as well as between users and servers. SNA was not equipped to communicate with these protocols or satisfy the peer communication requirements. Internets evolved to meet these needs and link LANs together as equals. Thus began a separate network, independent of the existing SNA network, using a bottom-up approach. Many desktops are nodes on both networks—either the SNA network or the internetwork is used, depending on the destination of the user.

For purposes of this discussion, it's assumed that a company has an existing SNA network in place as its primary corporate network. The company has decided to either implement a new TCP/IP-based internet or expand an existing one. Once the decision is made, there are almost as many ways to implement TCP/IP as there are reasons to implement it. There is no one way to implement TCP/IP that is always right or wrong. Different companies are choosing different techniques. Within a company, more than one method may be used due to differing requirements. There is not one industry trend that can be highlighted as *the* implementation strategy of choice. Often, implementation decisions regarding the TCP/IP internet are driven by the investment in, and architecture of, the existing SNA network. Migration from one network architecture to another can require years to fully implement. Companies must have a technically viable, cost-effective migration strategy for getting from their existing network to their goal network. One key point that must be understood is that SNA and TCP/IP are basically incompatible protocols. A key reason for the incompatibility is that SNA does not have addressing information available at the network layer (layer 3). This makes SNA a nonroutable protocol. Corporations must make key decisions regarding how the two protocols will interact. The primary options are:

Separate Networks—Separate networks are maintained for each protocol. Each has its areas of responsibility (for example, SNA is responsible for communication to the IBM mainframe, TCP/IP for inter-LAN communication), and the two networks have little or no interaction.

Encapsulation/Tunneling—Separate networks are maintained. When a protocol needs to cross a network where it is not supported, it is encapsulated within the protocol that is supported on the network.

Eliminate SNA—One way to eliminate problems with the two protocols working together is to eliminate SNA. TCP/IP can be used for all communications, including communication with the IBM mainframe. Please note that the reverse option is not possible. While the capabilities of APPN are expanding, SNA is not capable of effectively replacing TCP/IP.

TCP/IP–SNA Protocol Conversion—Both protocols operate in their native mode within the sections of the network in which they run. Where areas of responsibility intersect, protocol conversion gateways are implemented to translate each protocol to the other. This option is discussed under SNA within the Data Center.

SDLC Conversion/Data Link Switching—SDLC is converted into Logical Link Control 2—LLC2. Since many routers can bridge LLC2, the converted packets can be routed across multiprotocol internets and delivered to the mainframe via a TIC.

The following are some examples of SNA and TCP/IP implementations. With each example, particular attention is placed on 3270 communications, both in the form of native SNA communications and TN3270.

DUAL SNA AND TCP/IP NETWORKS

Many companies find themselves with dual SNA and TCP/IP networks. As described previously, this is usually due to history—not design. The two networks evolved independently, and now companies are faced with the problem of integrating the two into a coherent network architecture. Maintaining dual networks can be expensive. Compared to one network that handles both SNA and TCP/IP, more lines can be required, additional networking equipment is needed, additional personnel are required, and so forth. Corporations inevitably investigate the possibility of consolidating traffic from both networks onto one physical network with peer characteristics. Dual networks are a viable first step in the migration process to one physical network with TCP/IP as the primary backbone protocol. It is a tactical decision that allows the existing functionality and quality of service provided by SNA to be maintained while the new TCP/IP-based infrastructure is put in place.

Sometimes the answer is that the two networks remain separate as an intermediate or permanent solution. Figure 3.6 illustrates this type of environment. On an intermediate basis, many companies have chosen to maintain the existing SNA network until multiprotocol routers improve their SNA routing capabilities. As described earlier, techniques such as tunneling and data-link switching are necessary to transport SNA across internetworks. Router vendors are working to add routing for SNA in its native mode. Some have announced plans for APPN, LU 6.2, node type 2.1, or partial node type 4. Until these types of support are available, some companies have chosen to continue with their separate SNA network.

Why would a company choose to incur the higher costs of maintaining two networks on a permanent basis? First, there might not be a pressing business need to change. For instance, where users require access to either the SNA network or the internetwork, but not both, dual networks can be a viable option. A second reason is reliability. Many companies have mission-critical applications on the mainframe. Network downtime can cause severe disruptions to business. SNA has been fine-tuned through the years to provide maximum reliability for host-based applications. Related tools such as NetView for network management emphasize this strength. Technology to support routing SNA over TCP/IP is relatively new and is still evolving. This can lead to less reliability and greater difficulty with network management. Since most applications will remain on the mainframe for the foreseeable future, some companies have decided that maintaining two networks is a business requirement, and the added costs are viewed as part of the cost of doing business. A third reason is performance. SNA has been fine-tuned over the years to provide high levels of service as measured by response time. The hierarchical, connection-oriented nature of SNA is the best tool available for providing guaranteed (to the extent any network can guarantee) levels of service for transaction-oriented mainframe-based systems. While TCP/IP can provide excellent service, its peer-based, connectionless orientation cannot guarantee service levels to the extent SNA can. For many companies with mission-critical mainframe applications, the guarantees provided by SNA are critical and are a strong reason for maintaining a separate SNA network.

3270

TN3270 is not a requirement in this environment, as users can continue to use existing 3270 devices over the SNA network. Telnet would be used for terminal access to non-SNA machines. Figure 3.6 shows the classic SNA

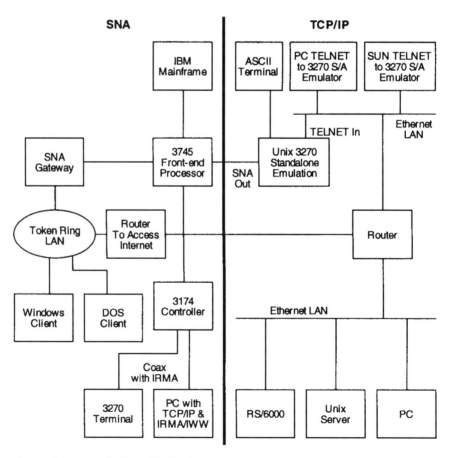

Figure 3.6 Dual SNA and TCP/IP networks.

network with a terminal and workstation connected to a 3174 cluster controller, which is subsequently connected to a 3745 communication controller and the mainframe. The TCP/IP internet is entirely separate. In addition to this, there are other options for connecting devices on the TCP/IP network to the mainframe. These are the Client/Server Communication and Stand-Alone Communication System.

Client/Server Communication

This solution employs the classic client/server architecture that is used in the DCA/Microsoft Select Communications Server, Microsoft's SNA Server for Windows NT, and Novell's NetWare for SAA products. The backbone protocol is SNA, and the LAN protocol is TCP/IP. Communications between the mainframe and workstation are conducted using native 3270. However, for part of the journey, TCP/IP is used as the transport rather than SNA. Essentially, this solution is a tunneling implementation. The client workstation runs 3270 emulation software. The emulation software passes a native 3270 data stream to the TCP transport layer interface (for example, NetBIOS, Named Pipes, Sockets, and so forth), where it is encapsulated in a TCP/IP envelope and routed across the LAN to a 3270 communications server. The 3270 communications server acts as a gateway to SNA. It removes the 3270 data stream from the TCP/IP envelope and places it on the SNA network for delivery to its final destination. All major LAN operating systems (that is, Novell NetWare, Banyan Vines, Microsoft LAN Manager, and IBM LAN Server) now support TCP/IP in addition to their native protocols. TCP/IP can either be the only protocol used on the LAN or it can be one of two protocols run in a dual stack mode.

Stand-Alone Communication System

Again, the backbone protocol is SNA and the LAN protocol is TCP/IP. In this example the server is a UNIX machine (for its multiuser, multitasking capabilities) running dual SNA and TCP/IP stacks. A user workstation on the internet uses Telnet to establish a session over TCP/IP with the UNIX workstation. It starts a 3270 session on the UNIX machine that connects to the mainframe. Telnet echoes the 3270 session back to the user workstation. The difference between the stand-alone system and the client/server system is that in the stand-alone system there is no 3270 activity on the user's workstation. It is attached as a dumb terminal to the UNIX workstation. In the client/server model, a significant portion of the 3270 processing is done on the client workstation. Due to the processing load on the UNIX workstation and response time considerations, this is primarily a departmental solution. It is also particularly appropriate for locations having an installed base of UNIX machines. Examples of available products are AIX 3270 Host Connection Program/6000 and AIX 3278/79 Emulation/6000 from IBM and 3270LINKix from Cleo Communications.

ELIMINATION OF THE SNA BACKBONE

This is the opposite extreme from having two separate networks. As shown in Figure 3.7, with this network architecture SNA no longer exists. The entire network is TCP/IP. TCP/IP resides on the mainframe and all terminal communication to the mainframe is via TN3270 and Telnet. IP addresses are used to route datagrams across the network. There is no need for most IBM communication software and hardware. VTAM and NCP are not needed. LUs and PUs do not exist. 37xx FEPs and 3x74 controllers are not used. The

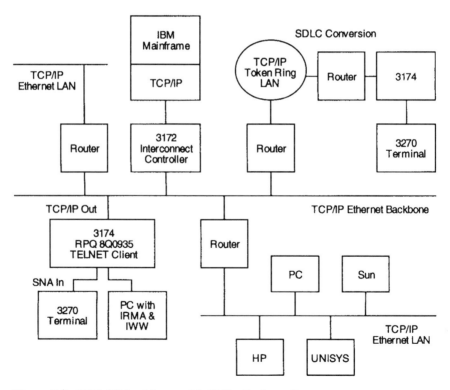

Figure 3.7 TCP/IP backbone with SNA eliminated.

only front-end device used would be an IBM 3172 Interconnect Controller to gain channel connections to the mainframe. To make this solution more efficient, IBM has off-loaded layers 1–4 of the stack from the mainframe to the 3172. There is a socket-type interface between layer 5 on the mainframe and layer 4 on the 3172. This saves up to 50 percent of the host cycles compared to earlier IBM TCP/IP implementations. This solution gives companies one physical network, which should result in significant cost savings once the network is in place. Realistically, however, it is difficult for companies with extensive SNA networks to turn their back on their investments in SNA equipment, software, and personnel. While this is a worthy goal for many companies, movement to this solution requires a great deal of capital and usually can only occur over a long period of time.

All terminal communication with the mainframe is handled via TN3270. A server component of TN3270 resides on the mainframe, and a client component resides in each workstation. To provide companies with protection for their investments in 3270 equipment, IBM has announced enhancements for the 3174 that allow it to attach to a TCP/IP network (RPQ 8Q0935). This allows 3270 terminals to access SNA and non-SNA devices on an internet via Telnet. In June 1992, IBM also announced a new CICS to TCP/IP socket interface. Effectively, this places CICS on top of TCP (layer 4) performing the function of layers 5–7. Using this capability, users access CICS applications via native CICS rather than TN3270. Direct access to CICS from TCP via sockets will improve efficiency compared to TN3270. Unfortunately, this will not help existing applications. Only CICS applications specifically written for sockets will be able to use this functionality.

SNA WITHIN THE DATA CENTER

The data center is the location of IBM mainframes and related peripherals such as front-end processors, disk drives, and printers. This option is a compromise between the two extremes outlined previously and is the network architecture goal for many companies. SNA exists only within the data center, and TCP/IP is the primary protocol for the remainder of the network. Like the first option, previously described, the TCP/IP and SNA networks are separate. However, rather than duplicating each other by maintaining separate networks, TCP/IP and SNA complement each other under this option. From the desktop to the mainframe, most of the network is TCP/IP based. SNA exists in the final step from a front-end processor to the mainframe (within the data center). Note: The term front-end processor is used generically—it does not refer to an IBM 37x5 unless specifically noted. A major benefit to companies implementing this architecture is that TCP/IP does not run on the mainframe. The cost per MIP is much lower on an FEP than a mainframe. By moving TCP/IP off the mainframe, the expensive mainframe MIPS are saved for other tasks such as transaction processing and database management, at which mainframes excel. Another benefit is the money saved by having one TCP/IP-based WAN. A third benefit is elimination of any need to change Legacy systems (older mainframe applications). Occasionally, to access Legacy systems via TCP/IP, there is a need to change or relink the application. Under this scenario, the Legacy systems will be accessed via NCP and VTAM as always, so there is no need for changes.

There are two drawbacks to this scenario. First, as described above, there can be reliability and performance issues when TCP/IP is used as the backbone protocol. Second, network management can become an issue. Since both NetView and SNMP would most likely be used, there can be coordination problems. Products are available to help NetView and SNMP work together, but this is still an evolving market. As illustrated in Figure 3.8, the FEP is a key component of this network. It receives TCP/IP datagrams and converts them into SNA frames. The FEP then passes a normal SNA data stream to the mainframe. This can be accomplished using products from several companies, including:

McData—The LinkMaster 6100 controller is a 3174-type device. However, it combines many of the capabilities of a 3172 and protocol conversion capabilities with standard 3174 functionality.

Apertus—The Datastar controller is a 3174-type device. It also combines standard 3174 functionality with 3172 and protocol conversion capabilities.

OpenConnect Systems—OpenConnect offers a unique product. The OpenConnect Server 2 provides protocol conversion capabilities on RISC workstations. An RS/6000 version and a Sun SPARC version are already shipping. Other RISC platforms will be supported in the future. The major benefits to this product, as compared to the SNA clone controllers, are the flexibility provided by using totally open platforms and excellent price/performance provided by RISC workstations. OpenConnect also offers an OpenConnect Server based on proprietary hardware.

An important player missing from this list is IBM. They currently do not have protocol conversion capabilities included with their SNA products. It is

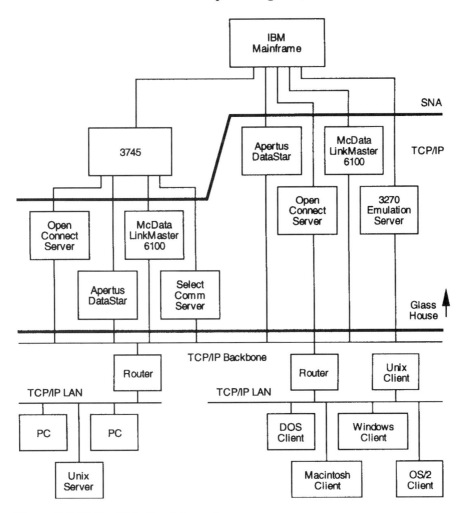

Figure 3.8 SNA within the data center.

expected, however, that IBM and SNA clone manufacturers other than those listed will add these capabilities in the future.

Terminal communication to the mainframe can be handled either using TN3270 or native 3270. TN3270 is handled in much the same way as it is in other environments. The client runs TN3270 over the TCP/IP stack. The TN3270 server resides on the device performing the protocol conversion. This device receives a TN3270 data stream from the client, converts it to a native 3270 data stream, and forwards it to the mainframe for processing. For native 3270 communication, the client/server model described earlier can be used. The difference is that since the backbone is TCP/IP in this scenario, the server is placed close to the mainframe. The 3270 data stream is encapsulated in a TCP/IP datagram and sent across the network to the server. In the server it is removed from the envelope and forwarded to the mainframe for processing.

ADVANCED PEER-TO-PEER NETWORKING (APPN)

Advanced Peer-to-Peer Networking (APPN) is IBM's attempt to change SNA from a hierarchical network into a horizontal peer-based network. Some companies are considering APPN as an alternative to both traditional subarea SNA and TCP/IP. APPN was first introduced in 1986 on the System 36 and AS400 in 1988. Since then, APPN support has slowly expanded to cover a broad range of SNA devices. In 1992 and 1993, IBM made great strides implementing APPN on its equipment to the point that it is, or soon will be, available on most SNA devices. For IBM, 1993 was also a landmark year for convincing vendors of routers and other networking equipment to add APPN support to their products. Many have announced plans to support APPN during 1994. The announcement of APPN support for IBM 3090-class mainframes in March 1992 was a key milestone in the transition from subarea SNA to APPN. It brought APPN into the mainstream of SNA and was the first tangible step in the transition.

Much like TCP/IP, APPN resides at layers 3 and 4 of the OSI model, providing Network and Transport functionality. Its major job functions are to locate resources and dynamically route SNA transactions throughout the SNA network and deliver them to their destination. It does this by using three basic components:

End Node—Where applications reside. Final destinations for transactions. Can be clients or servers. Responsible for initiating sessions. Generally terminals (via the 3174) and OS/2-based workstations. Support for DOS workstations and IBM mainframes was announced in March. Note: A Low Entry Networking (LEN) End Node is a lower-function end node.

Network Node—Locates resources via broadcast messages, sets up session paths, and routes transactions. Network nodes can also be end nodes. OS/2 servers, AS/400 servers, 6611 routers, and 3174 controllers can be network nodes. To allow the mainframe to be a network node IBM created the Composite Network Node (CNN). This was necessary because

APPN network nodes include functionality found in SNA type 4 nodes (3745-NCP) and type 5 nodes (mainframe-VTAM). The CNN runs on the mainframe under VTAM. It combines a single VTAM host and all the NCPs (3745s) within its domain into what looks and acts like a single APPN network node.

Central Directory Servers—Special VTAM hosts that locate resources more quickly and efficiently than network nodes.

Network nodes maintain tables of all resources to which they are directly connected. This includes both physical devices and applications. When an end node is brought up, it is automatically added to the resource tables of the network node that it is connecting to. When an end node needs to access a network resource, it simply contacts its nearest network node. The network node searches its tables to determine the location of the requested resource. If the network node does not know the location, it will use LU 6.2 to broadcast a location request over the network. The network node that the resource is attached to answers back with the location. The network node that originated the request then uses the network topology stored in its tables to determine the path. The session is set up and data can be sent between the two end nodes. To reduce the need for broadcast location requests, Central Directory Servers can be used. Prior to issuing a broadcast, the network node can request a location directly from a VTAM-based Central Directory Server. The Central Directory Server uses location tables to provide the location information. The tables can be built either from VTAM configuration files or from network nodes.

Benefits and Drawbacks of APPN

In addition to gaining a peer-based network capable of supporting the client/server applications of the future, the main benefit gained by users moving to APPN is a significant reduction in the coding effort required to set up an SNA network. Not only does this save time initially, but the simplified nature of the configuration also leads to reduced chances for error and reduced planned outages for updating network configuration information.

There are several problems with APPN from the user's perspective. First, LU 6.2 is the only LU type supported. The current base of LU 6.2 applications is small. Most applications are designed to use 3270 terminals over LU 2, so this is a major limitation for users planning to implement APPN. IBM has announced tunneling capabilities within LU 6.2. That service will take the LU 0, 1, 2, and 3 protocols and place them inside LU 6.2 transactions for transport across the network. APPN can be costly. Users must upgrade operating systems and communications software to the latest releases. APPN capabilities are not supported on non-IBM devices. This lack of competition has allowed IBM to maintain relatively high prices for network devices. Similar to subarea SNA, the design of APPN suggests an assumption that communication lines are slow, unreliable, and expensive. APPN is a connection-oriented protocol that only supports source routing. The network node attached to the end node initiating a session determines the optimal path for transactions to follow to reach their destination. Once this path is set up, it cannot be changed. While this does offer advantages (for example, ensuring packets are delivered in sequence and greater control over response time), the flexibility to react to changing circumstances is missing. If an intermediate node along the path becomes overloaded, delivery is delayed. If it goes down, the session can be lost. Also, APPN performs full error checking and frame recovery at each intermediate routing node. This increases processing requirements throughout the network and is in contrast to industry trends. With communication lines becoming more reliable and speeds increasing, the trend is toward error checking only on an end-to-end basis, which reduces processing requirements in intermediate nodes. IBM has announced connectionless capabilities, but they have not yet been delivered. From a philosophical standpoint, many view APPN as a proprietary solution regardless of IBM's offer to license software to competitors. For companies committed to open systems, this can be a significant drawback.

TCP/IP COMPARISON TO APPN

TCP/IP is conceptually simpler than APPN. It does not have a concept of End Nodes, Network Nodes, LUs, or PUs. A TCP/IP internetwork is simply a number of LANs interconnected by bridges and routers. Every device on the TCP/IP network is equal. Each has an IP address that is used by routers to deliver packets regardless of whether the device is a PC or an IBM mainframe. The relative simplicity of TCP/IP is seen as an advantage by some because it is easier for vendors to maintain, more flexible, and translates into less processing power required in intermediate nodes, which results in lower costs. Another advantage to TCP/IP is that, unlike APPN, it is an open environment that is universally supported. Virtually every vendor of network hardware and software supports TCP/IP. Most consider APPN a proprietary environment. The universal support for TCP/IP has created competitive markets for software and network hardware with low costs and a wide range of choices for users. APPN is currently supported primarily on IBM network equipment, which tends to be expensive. APPN, like SNA, is a connection-oriented protocol. TCP/IP is a connectionless protocol. Connection-oriented and connectionless networks are discussed in greater detail earlier in this chapter. APPN is relatively new. Several of the key components are not yet available; they have only been announced. TCP/IP, on the other hand, has been used for years, has a large installed base, and is battle tested. Also, TCP/IP is much more flexible, running over virtually any layer 1 and 2 data link. APPN, on the other hand, cannot run over many high-speed links such as Frame Relay. The next major version of APPN is referred to as APPN+. Due in the 1994 time frame, it will add support for several high-speed links (for example, ATM, Fiber Channel Standard) with speeds up to 45 Mbps. IBM says that Gigabit APPN will be available the following year.

3270 communication is possible across APPN networks with certain limitations. Currently, APPN only supports LU 6.2, so 3270 must be LU 6.2 based. 3270 over LU 1, 2, or 3 will be supported in the future, but only via tunneling (encapsulation) through LU 6.2. APPN supports native 3270. The only thing changing is the transport method for getting the data stream to the mainframe.

MANAGING INTEGRATED NETWORKS

Network management has long been a major issue for companies. They required tools to help them locate network devices, notify the operator if there are problems on the network, and generate performance statistics. In 1987, IBM shipped NetView, which is a proprietary, mainframe-based, centralized solution for managing SNA networks. Since NetView only supports SNA and views everything as an SNA device, new management tools were required for TCP/IP internets. SNMP became the clear choice because it was functional, easy to use, open, and available. SNMP is also constantly being upgraded to improve functionality and to support new devices. While it is based on standards, vendors add SNMP extensions to improve their products. This can lead to incompatibilities between SNMP-based solutions. SNMP is supported by virtually all vendors of TCP/IP products in the form of agents and Management Information Bases (MIB). Agents run on the managed devices collecting information and communicating with the central manager. MIBs define characteristics of the device and the information (objects) gathered from it. Central managers poll the devices being managed, send instructions to the devices, and present management information to the network administrator. Two leading SNMP-based central managers are Hewlett-Packard (OpenView) and Sun (SunNet).

As companies move toward integrating SNA and TCP/IP networks, network management is a key issue. As one would suspect, due to their differing histories and focuses, NetView and SNMP are incompatible. The result is that NetView cannot see devices on an internet and SNMP cannot see SNA devices. Encapsulation causes another problem—when one protocol is encapsulated within another protocol it cannot be tracked by its network manager. SNA transactions cannot be tracked by NetView when they are being tunneled across a TCP/IP internet. Network managers, obviously not excited about using multiple incompatible management products, have encouraged vendors to provide integrated products. While a great deal of work is underway in this area, few products are available. Many companies have implemented both NetView and SNMP to monitor their SNA and TCP/IP networks, respectively. This places the burden of manually integrating information from the two systems on the network managers. There are some partial solutions that help solve this problem.

SNA Service Point Integration—As illustrated in Figure 3.9, dual NetView and SNMP management systems are put in place. Each system directly controls the devices on its respective network. However, the SNMP manager acts as an SNA service point so it can respond to NetView messages and pass information to NetView. This allows the mainframe to act as a central collection point for management information. The problem with this solution is that there is not a one-to-one correspondence between the information maintained by NetView and SNMP. For instance, there is no data in a MIB that corresponds to SNA resource definitions maintained in VTAM. The result is a limitation on what can be accomplished when NetView and SNMP are mapped to each other. For example, a graphical map of the consolidated networks cannot be prepared, and, if both networks are involved with a failure, it is difficult to diagnose. Products that perform the service point function usually run on a UNIX workstation. They include NetView/6000 (IBM), BrixOpen (Brixton), OneView (Proteon), Lance+ (Lexcel), and Maxm (International TeleManagement).

TCP/IP for MVS—TCP/IP for MVS contains a network management gateway that translates NetView and SNMP messages. Network managers

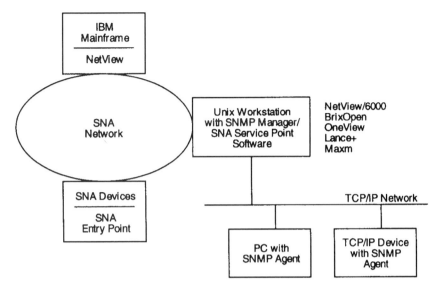

Figure 3.9 SNA service point integration.

can take advantage of this to control TCP/IP-based devices directly from the mainframe. The limitation to this approach is the same as SNA service point integration (described earlier) due to the mapping of the two management protocols to each other.

SNA Agent Integration—As illustrated in Figure 3.10, option three is the inverse of SNA service point integration. It is new and requires specific products. Again, dual networks are in place and they are directly administered by SNMP and NetView, respectively. However, rather than having NetView on the mainframe as the central collection point for management information, H-P OpenView on a UNIX workstation plays that role.

A second required piece of software is OpenSNA Manager from Peregrine Systems. It resides on the IBM mainframe and communicates with OpenView. Benefits of this scenario are that NetView is not required because OpenSNA Manager can manage the SNA network, and, because there is tighter integration of management information, a graphical depiction of the consolidated network is available.

There are longer-term solutions to address the limitations of these solutions. They include better integration of NetView and SNMP, as well as the use of OSI's CMIP as a single management protocol and OSF's Distributed Management Environment (DME). IBM has become pragmatic regarding

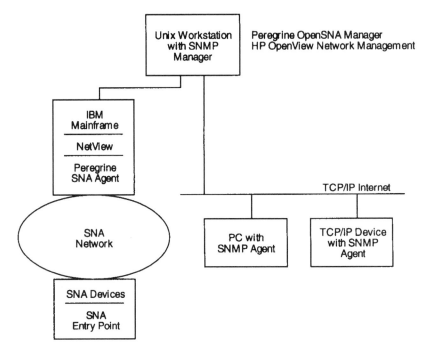

Figure 3.10 SNA agent integration.

network management protocols. They plan to use SNMP, CMIP, and DME based on what is best for a particular situation. However, they still plan to use NetView as the focal point for managing the information gathered by these protocols. Examples of support for the open protocols are:

- SNMP—Currently used in the NetView/6000 network management system. SNMP agents and MIBs are provided for many products including the 6611 router. NetView/6000 is based on OpenView, which has been licensed from Hewlett-Packard.

- CMIP—Will be used to send APPN management information to NetView on the mainframe. Some APPN management will be done with SNMP, but CMIP will be the primary protocol. In the future, CMIP will also be supported with IBM's PC-based LAN Network Manager and AIX/NetView/6000.

- DME—Will be supported in the future on NetView/6000.

Another SNMP-related event is the development of WinSNMP for Windows, which allows SNMP support to be easily built into Windows applications. It is an API that allows the applications to include an SNMP agent so they can be managed by an SNMP central manager. OSI CMIP is not yet complete. While most major vendors (IBM, AT&T , DEC, H-P, and others) have announced support for it, few products are available. As designed, it fixes several limitations identified in SNMP. It is, however, more complex and more expensive than SNMP. Some feel that CMIP will affect higher level managers such as NetView. SNMP agents would still be used, but only for feeding information up to a CMIP manager. OSF DME is a standards-based framework for, and approach to, network, system, and application management. It includes a common GUI, APIs, information storage, management functionality, and object definitions. Most major companies have announced support for DME, and many have begun shipping products based on DME components even though DME is not expected to be generally available until the first quarter of 1993. Since important components of DME are based on H-P's OpenView, Hewlett-Packard is a leader in implementing DME.

INTEGRATION QUESTIONS AND ISSUES TO BE CONSIDERED

There are literally hundreds of questions that must be answered by companies with existing SNA networks who are investigating either installing a TCP/IP-based internet or expanding an existing internet. There is no right or wrong answer to these questions. Within a company, there can be more than one answer to a question. This section does not attempt to provide an exhaustive list of questions. Its goal is to help structure the thought process and identify key issues for making decisions regarding TCP/IP in the corporate network. A short list of issues follows each question. The questions are organized based on the key macro-level steps that should be followed. Each step builds on the previous step.

Define Objectives for the New Network Architecture

What are the key business needs to be supported by the network?

> This could include mission-critical, mainframe-based applications; support mission-critical applications not on the mainframe; peer communication between users; connection to outside networks; etc.

What are the shortcomings of the existing network, how is it not meeting business needs?

> Too expensive, inflexible, slow, unreliable, etc.

In order of priority, what are the corporate objectives for the new network?

Save money, allow applications to be downsized so they reside off the mainframe, easier communication between users, easier implementation of client/server solutions, movement to a nonproprietary architecture, improve performance, etc.

Decide Whether TCP/IP Is Needed to Help Meet Corporate Objectives

What environments will people need to access?

IBM mainframe, minicomputers, UNIX servers, LANs, printers, etc.

Issue: If people need access to more than the IBM SNA environment, they could use TCP/IP to gain access. It may make sense for them to use TCP/IP for IBM access also. Only one protocol would then be required.

Which protocols must be supported to provide the required access?

SNA, TCP/IP, DECnet, OSI, IPX, NetBIOS, NetBEUI, AppleTalk, etc.

Issue: If several non-SNA protocols are used, a peer network based on multiprotocol routers should be in place to facilitate the implementation of TCP/IP.

Is the relatively high cost of SNA and mainframe-based applications a major issue?

Issue: A main reason companies are looking at TCP/IP is to save money. If the cost of maintaining the IBM mainframe and network is not an issue, then a key reason for moving to TCP/IP has been eliminated.

Are open systems being embraced as a strategic direction?

Issue: Some companies have embraced open systems from a philosophical standpoint. For these companies, TCP/IP is a logical choice as both a LAN and a WAN protocol.

Will UNIX play a major server or desktop role in the future?

Issue: TCP/IP is extensively implemented on UNIX machines. If UNIX will be widely used, TCP/IP might be required by default.

Is there movement toward downsizing applications from the IBM mainframe to a distributed client/server architecture?

Downsizing is often accomplished via the use of powerful UNIX servers. The use of UNIX would facilitate the use of TCP/IP. The use of servers would indicate the need for peer networking.

What Role Should TCP/IP Play in the Network?

Are major mission-critical applications IBM mainframe-based with strict response-time requirements? If yes, do plans call for them to remain mainframe based?

Issue: This might indicate the need to maintain a separate SNA network.

Does TN3270 offer the functionality and performance required for users?

Issue: Will TN3270 meet the needs of users? Do certain users require native 3270?

Which LAN protocols are in use? Is there a need for them to communicate across a backbone with non-IBM mainframe applications or other users?

Issue: Will there be a network of multiprotocol routers in place regardless of decisions made regarding SNA?

How will communication between the protocols take place?

No interaction required, dual stacks, protocol conversion, etc.

Issue: Requirements here will impact required equipment and where protocols are implemented.

What, if any, plans are there for implementing APPN?

Issue: If APPN will be the peer-to-peer networking solution, there might not be a need for TCP/IP.

Based on the level of investment in SNA hardware and software, what is the practical time frame for implementing TCP/IP?

Issue: A large investment in SNA hardware and software that has not been fully depreciated could affect management's willingness to invest in a new network.

How Should TCP/IP Be Implemented?

Do the IBM mainframes have enough unused capacity to run TCP/IP?

Issue: Is there enough room for TCP/IP on the mainframe? How does the company feel about investing in yet another series (i.e., 3172) of IBM communication devices?

Should some or all of TCP/IP be off-loaded from the mainframe?

Issue: Companies can leave the entire stack on the mainframe, move part of it off to a 3172, or move all of it off using a clone controller or OCS Server. Many economic and philosophical questions are involved in this decision.

What are corporate feelings toward FEPs and controllers?

Issue: To save money, some companies are trying to minimize the use of 3745-, 3174-, and 3172-type devices. Open solutions such as the OpenConnect Server 2, which runs on an RS/6000 and Sun SPARC, might be of interest in this situation. Others might choose to run TCP/IP entirely on the mainframe to minimize the need for these network devices.

Do any applications require specific LUs?

Issue: With IBM's TCP/IP implementation, applications cannot request specific LUs. With the OpenConnect Server, applications can acquire specific LUs. This can be an important consideration for Legacy systems that have specific LU requirements.

What does the existing network look like?

Issue: Existing resources and architecture will have a strong impact on implementation strategies.

What types of desktop hardware and software are used?

Issue: Do desktops have enough power to run dual stacks or a single stack? How extensive is the use of dumb terminals?

GLOSSARY OF ACRONYMS

APPI	Advanced Peer-to-Peer Internetworking
APPN	Advanced Peer-to-Peer Networking
APPN+	Advanced Peer-to-Peer Networking Plus
ARPA or DARPA	Advanced Research Projects, Agency of the U.S. Department of Defense
ARPANET	ARPA Network
CMIP	Common Management Information Protocol
CMOT	Common Management Information Services and Protocol Over TCP/IP
CNN	Composite Network Node
DCA	Defense Communications Agency
DCA	Digital Communications Associates,Inc.
DCE	Distributed Computing Environment
DDN	Defense Data Network
DME	Distributed Management Environment
FTP	File Transfer Protocol
GOSIP	Government Open Systems Interconnect Profile
IAB	Internet Activities Board
ICMP	Internet Control Message Protocol
IGRP	Internet Gateway Routing Protocol
IP	Internet Protocol
IS-IS	Intermediate System to Intermediate System
ISO	International Standards Organization
LEN	Low Entry Networking End Node
LLC2	Logical Link Control 2
LPD	Line Printer Daemon Protocol

(continued)

MAC Layer	Media Access Control Layer
MIB	Management Information Base
MILNET	An unclassified military network
MIL-STDS	Military Standards
MTA	Message Transfer Agent
NFS	Network File Service
NSF	National Science Foundation
NSFnet	NSF Network
NVT	Network Virtual Terminal
OSF	Open Software Foundation
OSI	Open Systems Interconnect
OSPF	Open Shortest Path First
RFC	Request For Comments
RIP	Routing Information Protocol
RPC	Remote Procedure Call
SMTP	Simple Mail Transfer Protocol
SNMP	Simple Network Management Protocol
SRT	Source Routing Transparent
TCP	Transmission Control Protocol
TFTP	Trivial File Transfer Protocol
UA	User Agent
UDP	User Datagram Protocol
UI	UNIX International
WAN	Wide Area Network
WinSNMP	Windows SNMP
WinSock	Windows Sockets
XDR	External Data Representation

ABOUT THE AUTHOR

Shaun E. Deedy has been a product manager at Digital Communications Associates, Inc. Prior to DCA, Mr. Deedy was director of data processing for Artrac Corporation, Inc. Among other positions, he also served as senior consultant and site coordinator for Financial Application Consulting Services.

Mr. Deedy received an MBA in accounting from Georgia State University and a B.S. in accounting from Berry College. He enjoys running and flying. He and his wife Carmen have three daughters.

P A R T   2

Wide Area Networks

4

Integrated Services Digital Network

Matthew N. O. Sadiku
Department of Electrical Engineering,
Temple University, Philadelphia, Pennsylvania

INTRODUCTION

Voice and data communications have historically been handled by different networks. The reasons for this separation between voice and data are obvious; the two actions are perceived as serving separate purposes. Telephony permits immediate, personal, and interactive contact; data messages allow for more premeditated, formal, and noninteractive communication. In addition, voice is inherently a real-time, analog signal generated by human speakers while most data is machine generated and digital. Interest in integrating voice and data communications has been stimulated recently by the potential benefits of such integration.

Integrating voice and data communications is also motivated by advances in computer and communications technology. The telephone system is gradually converting from analog to an entirely digital network because of decreasing costs, increasing data transmission, and increased capability for integration of services. Prior to 1962, the worldwide telecommunications network was 100 percent analog. In 1962, we started down the digital road with the T1 carrier. From that point, the worldwide network became more and more digital. In the 1970s, the concept of integrated services was born.

Integrated Services Digital Network (ISDN) is the final step in which digital reaches the customer premises, first on copper and later on fiber [1].

ISDN is the first network-based standard for simultaneous integrated voice, data, and image signal transmission. This technology surpasses past networking capabilities by simultaneously transmitting multiple signals over a single pair of wires instead of the separate pairs formerly needed for each service. The long, hard climb up the mountain to ISDN has taken about 30 years. Now, it is here, and it can provide cost-effective pair gain with better performance.

It should be noted that ISDN is not itself a service, but rather an interface to existing and future services. ISDN promotes innovation and the convergence of information technology and telecommunications in open network structures. ISDN is mutually beneficial to the network operator, service provider, the equipment manufacturer, and the end user. First, an all-digital network offers reduced cost, lower power consumption, and easier maintainability. Second, it provides a variety of data communication services over a single subscriber line. Third, high utilization is achieved due to the integration of multiple connection types, services, and applications [2].

ISDN CONCEPT

The keys to understanding the concept of ISDN are in its name. First, its services are integrated. Voice and data, circuit switching, and packet switching are integrated and provided on one line from one source. Whereas today's conventional networks have islands of modern digital apparatus in a sea of analog technology, ISDN is completely digital, except, of course, for certain parts of the telephone, such as the microphone, speaker, and tone pad [3].

The ISDN concept is an all-digital communication network that provides a broad range of services on a switched basis. It is a convergence of communications and computers that integrates networks, customer premises equipment, and distributed intelligence in a common system that can be expanded and upgraded easily. ISDN will be the realization of a completely digital network in which all forms of communication will be transferred using digital methods. Voice, video, data, facsimile, and record traffic will be transmitted over a system that is fundamentally digital. Thus, ISDN is the replacement of the current analog plant using standardized access to permit the user to transmit voice and/or data over a worldwide network to any other user on a demand basis [4]. The ISDN concept is illustrated in Figure 4.1.

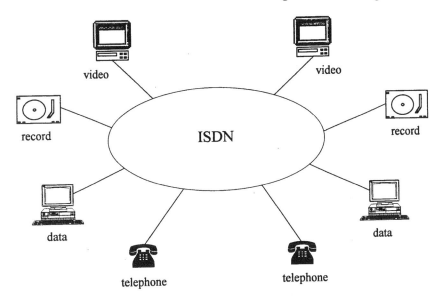

Figure 4.1 ISDN services.

In terms of technologies, rapid progress in the areas of fiber optics, electronics, and information processing now give a sound basis for economically feasible implementations of ISDN. Fiber optics make large bandwidths available at modest cost. This abundant bandwidth, combined with increased network capabilities, is a driving force in implementing ISDN.

KEY ISSUES

There are a number of important issues that must be resolved for the smooth transition from the current telecommunication networks to ISDN.

Billions of dollars worth of electronic equipment, including modems and T1 multiplexers, are currently needed to cajole today's antiquated analog telephone systems into carrying digital information, as their equipment will soon become obsolete. The additional services made available by ISDN will create a demand for new equipment that combines voice and digital communication functions. For these reasons, many semiconductor industries see ISDN-related equipment as the next big market for electronic products [5].

Engineers might think that technology alone is sufficient to interest customers. The hard reality is that the typical user is in business to make money;

his or her interest is based on economic benefits rather than pure technology.

The idea of ISDN is judged by the market standard of what it will do for the user. The great promise of digital technology is cost savings. The ISDN is meant to solve specific user problems, increase user productivity, and allow users to manage costs and changes more efficiently. As an all-digital network, ISDN offers increased clarity, accuracy, and speed. ISDN allows users to achieve convenience, flexibility, and economy [6].

Six end-user needs that are rapidly becoming absolute demands are [7]:

- **Integration:** Delivering more service to each workstation

- **Connection:** Ensuring the most direct access to information without new equipment and systems

- **Sharing:** Moving information from terminal to terminal or machine to machine

- **Phasing:** Implementing flexible, modular systems that are affordable and do not limit potential growth

- **Reliability:** Supporting products and protecting the customer's investment through good design and service

- **Availability:** Meeting demands quickly

Because the ISDN technology works equally well with existing copper telephone lines or with fiber optic systems, a customer does not need to worry about early obsolescence.

However, customer demand is not the main reason why telecommunications industries are pushing for ISDN. The main reason is the high cost of operating the world telecommunication network. The global network—an installed base of copper wiring that girdles the planet—is worth an estimated $300 billion [5]. Because this network provides a variety of services, the telecommunications companies spend a lot of money in planning, installing, and maintaining the existing telecommunications system. Conversion to ISDN will reduce the network's overall operating cost drastically while improving its ability to carry voice and digital traffic.

International compatibility is another issue ISDN has to deal with. As each company has a unique telecommunication history, international compatibility will be difficult to achieve, but nevertheless some basic compatibility is essential [8]. The compatibility problem is being solved by international standard bodies.

BASIC STRUCTURE

In ISDN, all information is digitally encoded before transmission. With an all-digital network, voices will be transmitted at the same speed with improved sound quality, and data will move about seven times faster.

The basic ISDN-operating scheme, or interface, involves two types of channels:

1. The B channel (the in-band, or B for bearer, channel) carries the user's message. This is a 64-Kbps channel like the pulse-code modulation transmission system in existing telephone networks. A B channel can carry voice, data, or video.

2. The D channel (the out-of-band, or D for data, channel) carries primarily network-signaling or control information. It sets up calls, disconnects them, and properly routes data on the B channels through the network.

Fundamental to ISDN are two concepts [9]: distributed processing and out-of-band signaling. Distributed processing permits equipment to perform data processing at remote locations. This, of course, necessitates security measures to prevent unauthorized use. *Signaling* is the name given to the procedures of ISDN for creating and clearing down connections, while *out-of-band* refers to the signaling procedures to indicate that these are carried on a separate channel from voice or data [10]. Out-of-band signaling occurring on the D channel means that the channels carrying user messages are separated from channels carrying signals for controlling the network. This puts message-routing control in the hands of the customer rather than in the hands of the communications provider.

Two such interfaces differing mainly in their carrying capacity are currently defined [9, 11]. These interfaces are illustrated in Figure 4.2. The *Basic Rate Interface* consists of two 64-Kbps B channels and one 16-Kbps D channel. The higher-capacity *Primary Rate Interface* has 23 64-Kbps B chan-

Figure 4.2 Two major interfaces defined for ISDN.

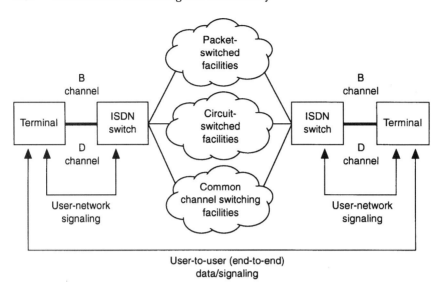

Figure 4.3 ISDN architecture.

nels and one 64-Kbps D channel (i.e., 23B + D). In Europe, the *Primary Rate Interface* consists of 30 64-Kbps B channels with two D channels (i.e., 30B + 2D).

Terminal adapters (TAs) allow the continued use of Customer Premises Equipment (CPE) by providing interface and protocol conversions to ISDN. There are two kinds of TAs [12]: those that plug into a personal computer (PC) in-slot and those that stand alone. The PC in-slot TA fits into a PC expansion slot and meets the IBM-compatible form factor. The stand-alone TA is a self-contained unit that allows computers, data communication switches, cluster controllers, and terminals to interface with ISDN.

A generic architecture for the customer premises end of an ISDN interface is shown in Figure 4.3. Details of this architecture are discussed in Aldermeshian, 1986 [13].

STANDARDS

ISDN is a result of a dozen of years of effort by communications experts all over the world to bring the world into a new age of information by integrating all current and future communications technologies into a single, worldwide network. It is an international push to upgrade business and home communications, with all the convenience, capability, and economy that the current and foreseeable state-of-the-art technologies permit.

Just as electric power standardization allows any electrical appliance to be plugged into any outlet, ISDN standardization will allow a telephone, computer terminal, facsimile machine, video display unit, or alarm system to be plugged into a single interface, for instant access to any form of information [14].

Standards that enable construction of a worldwide integrated network are currently being actively worked out in various international standards bodies such as the International Telephone and Telegraph Consultative Committee (CCITT), the International Standards Organization (ISO), and the Institute of Electrical and Electronics Engineers (IEEE).

ISDN was conceived by the CCITT; problems related to ISDN were handled by CCITT's Study Groups 17 and 11. The United States was an active participant in this standard-setting process as a member nation, represented by a number of telecommunications companies and a Joint Working Party (JWP) sponsored by the State Department [13, 15]. The first standards were issued in the Red Book in 1984. The Red Book recommendations covered the basic architecture, interface functions, and signaling structure. Unfortunately, these are not sufficient to design interoperable ISDNs. The current state of further effort in standardization is contained in the Blue Book, published in 1988.

The responsibility for coordinating the diverse telecommunication standards among the various European nations has fallen to the European Telecommunications Standards Institute (ETSI), whose members hail from 21 European countries. Established in 1988, ETSI is responsible for telecommunications standards for all of Europe. It is meant to coordinate the implementation of such advanced services as ISDN and the Pan-European Digital Cellular System [16].

The ISDN is based on the well-known Open Systems Interconnection (OSI) reference model of the International Organization for Standardization, which defines a seven-layer architecture for communications functions. Layer 1, the Physical Layer, includes the definitions of the R, S, and T interfaces in CCITT recommendations. Layer 3, the Network Layer and the top of the ISDN model, defines call-setup and clear-down procedures. The user's terminal equipment and software must supply the upper OSI layers as needed. For example, when a B channel is used for an end-to-end circuit-switched connection, the ISDN node provides only an OSI Layer 1 (Physical Layer) interface to the terminal; all the protocol layers above

Layer 1 are defined for that channel by the user. On the other hand, when a B channel is used to carry data over multiple virtual circuits to many terminals on the user's premises, the ISDN node provides an interface to each terminal for the functions defined by OSI Layers 2 (Data Link Layer) and 3 (Network Layer) as well.

PROSPECTS FOR ISDN

For the past couple of years, the ISDN concept has been on trial in many countries, including Belgium, Canada, France, Great Britain, Italy, Japan, the United States, and West Germany. These trial efforts are necessary to generate feedback for further work at CCITT and to develop practical applications, determine the cost of full-scale implementation, ascertain the willingness of businesses and residential customers to patronize the services, and stimulate the development of ISDN-related technologies [14].

Japan was the first nation to begin trials in 1984; the services should be available nationwide by 1995. In Europe, ISDN services are commercially available today within at least five nations. British Telecom rolled out its ISDN offering in April 1990. Belgium, the Netherlands, and West Germany have their own services. France Telecom has already supplied ISDN access to half of that country's businesses [16]. In the United States, the first ISDN trial was started in 1986 by Mountain Bell. Today, each regional Bell operating company has held successful ISDN trials, and local ISDN service is available in many areas. Three to five million basic rate ISDN (2B+D) lines were expected to be in service by 1993 [17].

As is well known, competition always drives technological innovation. ISDN is becoming a strategic weapon in global communications. In 1990, NTT (Nippon Telegraph and Telephone), AT&T, Pacific Bell, and Kokusai Denshin Denwa (Japan's overseas carrier) jointly announced an international ISDN link between Tokyo and California [18].

Perhaps one of the most important benefits of ISDN is that the technology provides a platform for application development, a platform that nurtures computer telephony and advances information systems within small and corporate business [19]. Besides providing telephone services, ISDN has the potential to provide LAN-like services to a large, multisite organization. ISDN offers the potential for greatly assisting companies to tie their widely separated organizations together, reduce their cycle times, expand their markets, and improve their ability to interact with and satisfy their customers. In other words, ISDN is an enabler for enterprise integration in that it enables a business to organize its resources so that it improves its ability to respond quickly, coherently, and consistently to customers, and therefore be more competitive in worldwide markets [20]. By making effective use of ISDN, a large business should be able to respond and perform as well as a small business.

APPLICATIONS OF ISDN

ISDN is no longer an idea whose time is yet to come or a technology looking for applications. The skepticism surrounding ISDN has been dismissed by the success of the various trial efforts. As of 1990, over 100 cities benefit from ISDN services [21]. During 1987 and 1988, several studies investigated ISDN applications related to business, education, manufacturing, telemarketing, financial services, health care, utilities, the hospital industry, government operations, security, and others [7, 17, 18, 22].

Office workers today rely on electronic communication devices more than ever before. Two major devices that have gained popularity are the fax machine and the PC. The fax machine and PC have made their greatest strides with capabilities allowing them to be linked by local area networks (LANs). New advancement in microelectronics and software design have significantly reduced the costs of these devices while improving productivity and ease of use. Besides providing faster transmission of documents through fax machines, ISDN technology provides many other functional benefits. The benefits include more professional answering; the receptionist often knows who is calling by recognizing the number. He or she does not have to ask people to leave their numbers because they are right on the display. The efficiency improvements translated into a savings of one hour daily, which is reinvested in handling other tasks. Another ISDN benefit for office workers is the linking of otherwise incompatible systems. With conventional procedures, system administrators must provide separate lines for voice and data transmissions. The high cost of duplication can be reduced by converting the communications system to ISDN technology.

Higher education is a significant and growing market for communications services of all types. The density of computers to people is higher on college and university campuses than anywhere in modern society. Some colleges require the ability to use a PC as a prerequisite for admission. Estimates are that many institutions of higher learning budget 1 percent or more for telecommunications, and 3 percent for computing, producing an annual market for computer-communication services of more than $5 billion. For this reason, progress is being made to ensure ISDN a place in the international community of scholars and scientists [23].

Communication systems are vital for U.S. manufacturers to remain competitive in an increasing global marketplace. A manufacturer can use ISDN capabilities to provide easy growth with little initial investment or planning. Customer services at different locations can be gained by simply placing an order with the local telephone company.

Communication is a critical factor for hospitals which need to link their facilities to physicians' offices, medical centers, laboratories, pharmacies, and research facilities. As electronic digital imaging systems gain more use in the medical field, the high-speed, high-quality transfers of digitized images from radiology, sonograms, nuclear magnetic resonance, CAT scans, and even color photographs can be carried by the telecommunications system.

Banking can benefit from the value of ISDN in view of the fact that the bank's largest single cost item is telecommunication. The U.S. bank experience with ISDN supports the conclusion that many ISDN applications deliver real business value through meeting end-user needs [24]. Some of the benefits are direct savings associated with replacement or better utilization of existing technologies. Other benefits are in the form of enhanced productivity, service quality, and competitive advantage within the banking industry. ISDN provides the flexibility to create services to meet a banking need. It also ensures that the bank's investment in technologies will not need to be replaced in a few years.

Several governmental and industrial agencies have actively identified, designed, and developed specific ISDN applications and their supporting capabilities. Since these applications are end-to-end solutions, they are frequently developed in conjunction with third-party vendors. Working relationships have been established with such third-party vendors as DEC, IBM, Wang, Teleos, Progressive Computing, Fujitsu, Baxter Healthcare, and many others. These vendors have modified their hardware and software products to take advantage of ISDN capabilities, resulting in new product prototypes and Customer Premises Equipment (CPE) products [22].

The list of innovations and applications of ISDN will grow in direct proportion to the growth of ISDN implementation in total and interstate networks, and to the customer's creativity in applying these innovations in its operation. Network vendors and users alike have learned that services based on ISDN make everyday tasks simpler and easier.

BROADBAND ISDN

ISDN is quickly evolving. There are now extensive trial experiences with narrowband ISDN (NISDN). The modes of information transfer implemented by NISDN are subject to limits which soon or later will make it necessary to add a broadband transfer infrastructure. In the not too distant future the user will require transmission speeds higher than those currently offered in NISDN.Higher speeds are needed to match the increasing speed of the PCs, workstations, and terminals that rely on LANs for interconnection to file servers [25]. The requirement for high speeds will be needed to realize LAN–LAN interconnection, Metropolitan Area Network (MAN), High Definition Network (HDTV) distribution, and so on. Today's LANs are on the edge of broadband speeds (e.g., 10-Mbps Ethernets and 4-Mbps Token Rings), and new LAN proposals call for higher speeds (16-Mbps Token Rings and 100-Mbps Fiber Distributed Data Interface). Ultimately, a network providing maximum data-transmission speeds of 150 Mbps or more will be needed.

In addition to higher speeds, there will be a need for higher bandwidths, which the broadband ISDN (BISDN) will accommodate. Besides this, broadband data communications are immune to twisted-wire problems such as the difficulty of relocating equipment and susceptibility to electromagnetic interference (EMI). Another favorable aspect of broadband technology was that a single piece of 1/2-inch coaxial cable was comparable to over 50,000 twisted pairs of wires in terms of capacity [26]. Thus, BISDN is conceived as a true ISDN in that it can carry traffic for all types of applications in a flexible and cost-effective manner.

The cost of constructing a broadband network is enormous compared to that of a narrowband network. However, rapid progress in the areas of fiber optics, photonics, electronics, and information processing now give a sound basis for economically feasible implementation of BISDN.

Asynchoronous Transfer Mode (ATM) has been accepted as the basis for the transfer of information within broadband network. ATM is fundamental for BISDN because ATM provides higher bandwidth, low-delay, packet-like switching, and multiplex for various service types [27–29]. ATM is defined by small cells, containing 32 to 64 bytes of information and 3 to 5 bytes of header [30]. While ATM can be supported by any digital transmission hierarchy, ATM cells within the SONET payload are optimum. With SONET and ATM agreed to by CCITT Study Group 18, substantial progress has been made toward achieving worldwide BISDN standard enabling end-to-end

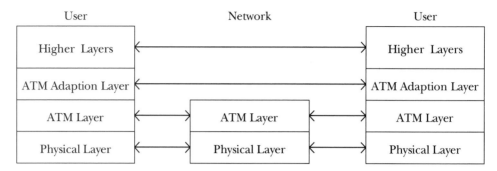

Figure 4.4 BISDN protocol structure.

broadband services. With this consensus, the realization of the all-fiber–digital broadband network is only a few years away.

Broadband ISDN protocol model is shown in Figure 4.4. The current Layer 1 is subdivided into three layers: Physical Layer, ATM Layer, and ATM Adaptation Layer (ALL). The Physical Layer provides transmission payload which carries ATM cell stream. The ATM Layer provides the minimum functions necessary for cell transport. The ALL is a layer between the ATM Layer and the Service-User Layer in the user, control, and management planes [31].

The major forces shaping broadband network evolution are market influence, existing and planned narrowband networks, network intelligence and control, transmission infrastructure, and local loop [32]. Customer requirements for broadband services vary widely, as do the customers. The large investment in narrowband infrastructure would create problems for the penetration of broadband networks. An optical local loop is essential for BISDN and its introduction will precede the introduction of BISDN.

CONCLUSION

ISDN is based on the digital telephone network, which is the backbone for business and private communications. Driven by evolving customer needs, technological progress, and networking, the years ahead will be years of challenge and change for the telecommunications industry. The future of telecommunications will be decisively shaped by ISDN. With ISDN, it is possible to offer services available today, as well as new, enhanced services in one network. Thus, ISDN promotes innovation and the convergence of information technology and telecommunications in open network structures. Because ISDN comprises a set of internationally accepted standards, compatibility of equipment is ensured.

Manufacturers of ISDN products claim that ISDN is still in its infancy and that it is too early to offer a cost-effective, single-chip, S-interface controller. However, it is not the chip cost but the development cost that is the greatest concern for customers. Advanced digital voice and data services using ISDN capabilities provide revenue opportunities for service providers as well as significant cost savings for customers. Through planned evolution, customers can introduce ISDN capabilities with minimum initial investment and expand into more sophisticated features as needed.

Communication over the ISDN will soon become as simple as picking up the phone. Unlike the conventional telephony, however, ISDN telephones digitize the voice directly at the telephone and send both voice and control signals to the switch digitally [33]. ISDN eliminates the need for separate networks and special equipment like modems to send computer or fax messages and makes it possible to talk on the phone about messages as they are being sent.

Applications of ISDN-based technology are expanding rapidly. As with the evolution of PC use, what appears revolutionary today becomes an indispensable tool tomorrow. The first tentative commercial offerings of ISDN are already in place. ISDN lines should be available in most places by the mid-1990s. However, technical, financial, and political problems may slow its progress.

REFERENCES

1. R. G. DeWitt, "ISDN Symposia: A Historical Overview," *IEEE Communications Magazine*, vol. 28, no. 4, 1990, pp. 10–11.

2. H. J. Helgert, *Integrated Service Digital Networks: Architecture, Protocols, Standards.* Reading, MA: Addison-Wesley, 1991, pp. 8–9.

3. J. Duncanson and J. Chew, "The Ultimate Link?" *Byte*, July 1988, pp. 278–286.

4. "The Integrated Services Digital Network and the Fixed-Satellite Service," *Telecommunication Journal*, vol. 54, December 1987, pp. 824–827.

5. S. H. Leibson, "Integrated Service Digital Network," *EDN*, November 12, 1987, pp. 118–128.

6. T. M. Chen and D. G. Messerschmitt, "Integrated Voice/Data Switching," *IEEE Communications Magazine*, vol. 26, no. 6, 1988, pp. 16–26.

7. N. S. Favre and J. L. Johnson, "AT&T's 5ESS Switch Makes ISDN Work," *AT&T Technology*, vol. 4, no. 3, 1989, pp. 12–19.

8. R. Liebscher, "Strategies for the Successful Introduction of ISDN," *Electrical Communication*, vol. 64, no. 1, 1990, pp. 4–14.

9. E. E. Summer, "ISDN: The Telephone of Tomorrow," *Radio Electronics*, October 1988, pp. 41–50.

10. J. W. Burren, "High-Speed Communications—A Tutorial on the Jargon and Technologies," *Computer Networks and ISDN Systems*, vol. 23, 1991, pp. 119–124.

11. R. T. Roca, "ISDN Architecture," *AT&T Technical Journal*, vol. 65, no. 1, 1986, pp. 5–17.

12. D. L. Eigen "Narrowband and Broadband ISDN CPE Directions,"*IEEE Communications Magazine*, vol. 28, no. 4, April 1990, pp. 39–46.

13. H. Aldermeshian, "ISDN Standards Evolution," *AT&T Technical Journal*, vol. 65, no. 1, 1986, pp. 19–25.

14. S. H. Pandhi, "The Universal Data Connection," *IEEE Spectrum*, July 1987, pp. 31–37.

15. L. L. Stine, "Why Are ISDN Standards Important?" *IEEE Communications Magazine*, vol. 26, no. 8, 1988, pp. 13–15.

16. G. Stix, "Telecommunications," *IEEE Spectrum*, vol. 27, no. 6, 1990, pp. 25–26.

17. K. Martersteck, "ISDN Delivers the 90s Technologies Today," *AT&T Technology*, vol. 5, no. 1, 1990, pp. 2–3.

18. J. Shandle, "ISDN: This Time It's for Real," *Electronics*, vol. 64, no. 5, May 1991, pp. 65–68.

19. R. Roy, "ISDN Applications at Tenneco Gas," *IEEE Communications Magazine*, vol. 28, no. 4, April 1990, pp. 28–30.

20. D. Morgan *et al.,* "ISDN As an Enabler for Enterprise Integration," *IEEE Communications Magazine*, vol. 28, no. 4, 1990, pp. 23–27.

21. J. J. Kauza, "ISDN: A Customer's Service," *AT&T Technology*, vol. 4, no. 3, 1989, pp. 4–11.

22. F. C. Iffland *et al.*, "ISDN Applications: Their Identification and Development," *IEEE Communications Magazine*, September 1989, pp. 6–11.

23. M. M. Roberts, "ISDN in University Networks," *IEEE Communications Magazine*, vol. 25, no. 12, 1987, pp. 36–39.

24. D. Richards and E. Vogt, "The Value of ISDN for Banking Applications," *IEEE Communications Magazine*, vol. 28, no. 4, 1990, pp. 32–33.

25. W. R. Byrne *et al.*, "Evolution of Metropolitan Area Networks to Broadband ISDN," *IEEE Communications Magazine*, vol. 29, no. 1, 1991, pp. 69–82.

26. "Boston Leaning toward Broadband Cable Nets," *Computerworld*, February 27, 1984, pp. SR/56–SR/60.

27. M. Frame, "Broadband Services Needs," *IEEE Communications Magazine*, vol. 28, no. 4, 1990, pp. 59–62.

28. K. Murano *et al.*, "Technologies toward Broadband ISDN," *IEEE Communications Magazine*, vol. 28, no. 4, 1990, pp. 66–70.

29. K. Asatani, "CCITT Standardization of B-ISDN," *NTT Review*, vol. 3, no. 3, 1991, pp. 122–133.

30. M. De Prycher, "Evolution from ISDN to BISDN: A Logical Step towards ATM," *Computer Communications*, vol. 12, no. 3, 1989, pp. 141–146.

31. Y. Inoue and M. Kawarasaki, "Networking toward B-ISDN," *NTT Review*, vol. 3, no. 3, 1991, pp. 34–43.

32. C. J. Dougall, "Broadband Network Evolution in Telecom Australia," *IEEE Communications Magazine*, vol. 28, no. 4, 1990, pp. 52–54.

33. D. Gulick and C. Crowe, "Interface the ISDN to Your PC with a Voice/Data Board," *Electronic Design*, December 10, 1987, pp. 85–88.

ABOUT THE AUTHOR

Matthew N. O. Sadiku received his B.Sc. degree in 1978 from Ahmadu Bello University, Zaria, Nigeria, and his M.Sc. and Ph.D. degrees from Tennessee Technological University, Cookeville, Tennessee, in 1982 and 1984, respectively. From 1984 to 1988, he was an assistant professor at Florida Atlantic University, where he did graduate work in computer science. Since August 1988, he has been with Temple University, Philadelphia, Pennsylvania, where he is presently an associate professor. He is the author of over 40 professional papers and four books, including *Elements of Electromagnetics* (Saunders, 1989) and *Numercial Techniques in Electromagnetics* (CRC, 1992).

His current research interests are in the areas of numerical techniques in electromagnetics and computer communication networks. He is a registered professional engineer and a member of the American Society of Engineering Educators (ASEE) and Institute of Electrical and Electronics Engineers (IEEE). He is presently the IEEE Region 2 Student Activities Committee Chairman.

5

An Overview of the Synchronous Optical Network

Gary C. Kessler
Hill Associates
Thomas A. Maufer
NASA Goddard Space Flight Center

The Synchronous Optical Network (SONET) is emerging as one of the important data transport schemes of the 1990s. Based on optical fiber, it will provide a digital hierarchy that is consistent throughout the world. The motivation for SONET, its interface layers and frame formats, and its impact on metropolitan and wide area networks (MANs and WANs) are described in this chapter.

DIGITAL CARRIERS

Digital carriers were introduced in the telephone network in North America in 1962. These T-carriers used time division multiplexing (TDM) and operated over metallic media such as twisted pair and coaxial cable.

When human voice is carried as a digital signal, a line speed of 64 Kbps is typically used. The voice signal must be sampled 8000 times each second (according to Nyquist's Theorem) and, using pulse-code modulation (PCM), each voice sample is carried as an 8-bit quantity. This 64-Kbps rate is called DS-0 (digital signal level 0).

A T1 carrier multiplexes 24 voice (DS-0) channels on two twisted pairs. The basic unit of transmission is called a *frame*, which carries a single framing bit plus one sample from each of the 24 channels. Thus, a single frame contains 193 bits ($24 \times 8 + 1$); at 8000 frames per second, the T1 rate (also called DS-1) is 1.544 Mbps. In Europe, the first TDM step is to multiplex 32 DS-0 channels, 30 of which carry voice; the E1 carrier operates at 2.048 Mbps.

T1, E1, and higher rates are described in the International Telephone and Telegraph Consultative Committee (CCITT) Recommendation G.703. Table 5.1 lists the digital TDM hierarchy used in North America, Japan, and Europe. Note that all of these TDM schemes are inconsistent from one continent to another, making the development of switches and international network gateways cumbersome. The increment of speeds, number of channels, and frame format is also inconsistent from level to level, which adds to the complexity of multiplexing equipment. Finally, these hierarchies are only defined up to several hundred million bits per second (Mbps), much less than is currently attainable with today's optical fiber-based networks.

Table 5.1   Digital Carrier Multiplexing Levels

Digital Multi-plexing Level	Number of Voice Channels	Bit Rate (Mbps)		
		N. America	Europe	Japan
0	1	0.064	0.064	0.064
1	24	1.544		1.544
	30		2.048	
	48[a]	3.152		3.152
2	96	6.312		6.312
	120		8.448	
3	480			32.064
	480		34.368	
	672	44.736		
	1344[a]	91.053		
	1440[a]			97.728
4	1920		139.264	
	4032	274.176		
	5760			397.200
5	7680		565,148	

[a]Intermediate multiplexing rates.

The international telephone community realized many years ago that higher line speeds, and therefore more telephone conversations per physical circuit, could be economically achieved by using an optical fiber medium. To ensure compatibility at higher speeds, work began in the mid-1980s to define a single digital hierarchy based on fiber and able to incorporate the "low-speed" copper-based digital hierarchies. The digital hierarchy for optical fiber is known in the United States as the Synchronous Optical Network (SONET); internationally this hierarchy is known as the Synchronous Digital Hierarchy (SDH).

SONET OVERVIEW

The SONET standards define a line rate hierarchy and frame format for use with optical fiber transmission systems. Because of the high speeds associated with SONET, 1310- and 1550-nanometer laser optical sources are specified.

SONET originated at Bell Communications Research (Bellcore) in the late 1980s and is now an American National Standards Institute (ANSI) standard for a high-speed digital hierarchy for optical fiber. SONET is not a communications network in the same sense of a local area network (LAN); it is an underlying physical transport network. The Fiber Distributed Data Interface (FDDI), IEEE 802.6 Distributed Queue Dual Bus (DQDB), Switched Multimegabit Data Service (SMDS), and Asynchronous Transfer Mode (ATM) can all operate over SONET. Since these networks will be used for LAN interconnection, SONET's potential importance to the corporate LAN is obvious. SONET is described in ANS T1.105 and T1.106 and Bellcore Technical Reference TR-TSY-000253.

The SONET TDM hierarchy is based upon transmission building blocks of 51.84 Mbps; this rate was chosen because it can accommodate either a T3 or E3 carrier signal. The 51.84-Mbps rate is called the Synchronous Transport Signal Level 1 (STS-1) or Optical Carrier Level 1 (OC-1); an OC-n rate is merely the optical equivalent of an STS-n electrical signal. Standards already define the frame format for rates from 51.84 Mbps (STS-1) to 2488.32 Mbps (STS-48), as shown in Table 5.2. The standard will, presumably, eventually define higher rates such as STS-96 (4976.64 Mbps) and STS-192 (9953.28 Mbps). The standard may be modified to allow for the definition of higher rates.

The Synchronous Digital Hierarchy (SDH) is the CCITT counterpart to SONET. The main difference between the two is that the basic SDH rate,

Table 5.2 SONET/SDH Multiplexing Levels

Line Rate (Mbps)	SONET Level	SDH Level
51.840	OC-1	
155.520	OC-3	STM-1
466.560	OC-9	
622.080	OC-12	STM-4
933.120	OC-18	
1244.160	OC-24	STM-8
1866.240	OC-36	STM-12
2488.320	OC-48	STM-16

designated Synchronous Transport Model Level 1 (STM-1), is 155.52 Mbps (equivalent to SONET's OC-3). SDH is described in CCITT recommendations G.707–G.709. SDH rates are also shown in Table 5.2.

SONET INTERFACE LAYERS

The SONET standards define four optical interface layers. While conceptually similar to layering within the Open Systems Interconnection (OSI) reference model, SONET itself corresponds only to the OSI Physical Layer (Figure 5.1). The SONET interface layers are:

- **Photonic Layer:** Handles bit transport across the physical medium; primarily responsible for converting STS (electrical) signals to OC (optical) signals. Clock recovery and jitter control occur at this layer. Electro-optical devices communicate at this layer.

- **Section Layer:** Transports STS-n frames and Section Overhead (SOH) across the medium; functions include framing, scrambling,[1] and error monitoring. Section Terminating Equipment (STE) communicate as this layer.

- **Line Layer:** Responsible for the reliable transport of the Synchronous Payload Envelope (SPE) (i.e., user data) and Line Overhead (LOH) across the medium; responsibilities include synchronization and multiplexing for the Path Layer and mapping the SPE and LOH into an

---

[1] Scrambling is performed to prevent the occurrence of long runs of 0s or 1s.

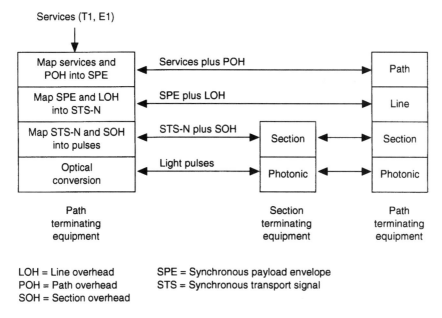

LOH = Line overhead   SPE = Synchronous payload envelope
POH = Path overhead   STS = Synchronous transport signal
SOH = Section overhead

Figure 5.1 SONET protocol architecture.

STS-n frame. An OC-N-to-OC-M multiplexer is an example of Line Terminating Equipment (LTE).

- **Path Layer:** Handles transport of services (e.g., DS-1, DS-3, E1, or video) between Path Terminal Equipment (PTE); the main function is to map the services and Path Overhead (POH) information into an SPE for transport over the medium by the Line Layer. PTE includes SONET-capable switches with an interface to a non-SONET network, such as a T1-to-SONET multiplexer.

SONET FRAME FORMAT

The basic unit of transport defined by SONET is the STS-1 frame. An STS-1 frame (Figure 5.2) is organized as 9 rows of 90 octets, for a total of 810 octets per frame. Octets are transmitted from left to right, one row after another, as drawn. Like other digital hierarchies supporting circuit-switched applications, a SONET frame is generated 8000 times per second, yielding the 51.84-Mbps rate.

SONET rates above STS-1 are created by combining multiple STS-1 frames. An STS-3 frame, for example, is created by octet-interleaving three

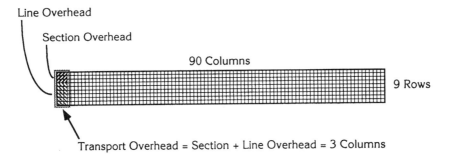

Figure 5.2 Basic SONET frame structure.

STS-1 frames. An STS-n channel will typically be formed by n STS-1 inputs; octet-interleaving allows each individual input to a SONET multiplexer to operate at its normal rate and requires a minimum of buffering at the mux.

The first three columns of an STS-1 frame contain overhead information used for network control and are referred to as Transport Overhead (TOH). The remaining 87 columns comprise the STS-1 Synchronous Payload Envelope (SPE). Although exactly one STS-1 SPE can fit into one STS-1 frame, an SPE will usually begin in one STS-1 frame and end in the next. A payload pointer, described below, indicates the actual beginning of an SPE within the envelope.

Section Overhead comprises 9 octets (3 rows) within an STS-1 frame (Figure 5.3). These octets are:

- **Framing (A1, A2):** Used to synchronize the beginning of the frame; takes on the bit pattern 11110110 and 00101000, respectively.

- **STS-1 Identification (C1):** A number, typically assigned by the LTE, that identifies an STS-1 frame's position within an STS-n frame; this value in the first STS-1 frame within an STS-n frame is 00000001).[2]

- **Section BIP-8 (B1):** Bit interleaved parity 8 (BIP-8) code using even parity for error detection; the i-th bit of this BIP-8 octet contains the even parity value calculated from the i-th bit position of all octets in the previous frame after scrambling.

- **Orderwire (E1):** Optional 64-Kbps voice channel to be used between section terminating equipment, hubs, and remote terminals.

---

[2] Because C1 is a single octet, SONET is currently limited to OC-255 (13.2192 Gbps).

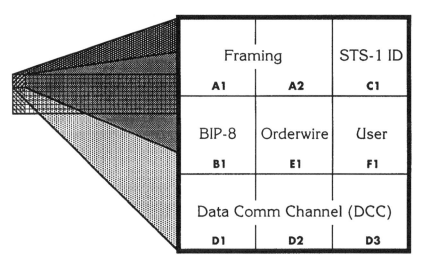

Figure 5.3 Section Overhead.

- **Section User Channel (F1):** Optional 64-Kbps channel for the network provider; passed from one section entity to another.

- **Section Data Communication Channel (D1–D3):** A 192-Kbps message-based data communications channel (DCC) for alarms, maintenance, control, administration, and other communications needs between STEs.

Line Overhead (Figure 5.4) comprises 18 octets (6 rows) in the STS-1 frame. These octets are:

- **Pointer (H1, H2):** A number between 0 and 782 that indicates the octet offset between the pointer and the first octet of the SPE within the STS Envelope Capacity; this pointer is necessary since an SPE is allowed to float within the envelope, allowing SONET to adjust to slightly different frame rates. Pointer adjustments will not occur more than once every four frames under normal operation. Details of the pointer operations are given below.

- **Pointer Action Byte (H3):** Carries data in the event of a negative stuff operation (i.e., decrementing the pointer); otherwise this octet is ignored.

- **Line BIP-8 (B2):** BIP-8 calculated over all bits of the LOH and Envelope Capacity of the previous STS-1 frame.

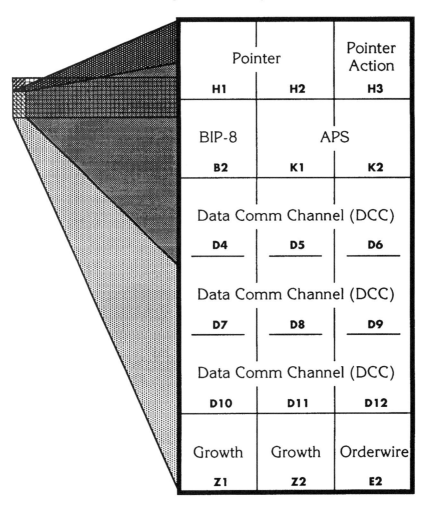

Figure 5.4 Line Overhead.

- **Automatic Protection Switching Channel (K1, K2):** Channel for the exchange of APS signaling between Line level entities; APS uses a bit-oriented protocol that provides for error protection and management of the SONET optical link.

- **Line DCC (D4–D12):** A 576-Kbps message-based channel for communication between LTE.

- **Growth (Z1, Z2):** Reserved for future use.

- **Orderwire (E2):** Orderwire channel between Line entities.

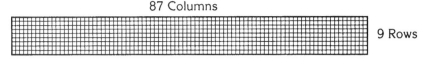

Figure 5.5 STS-1 synchronous payload envelope.

As mentioned earlier, the remaining 783 octets (87 columns × 9 rows) in the frame comprise the STS-1 Synchronous Payload Envelope (Figure 5.5). A single SPE can fit into a single STS-1 frame, although, as mentioned earlier, an SPE is not normally wholly contained in a single STS-1 frame, as depicted in Figure 5.6.

The first column (9 octets) of an SPE forms the Path Overhead, which is attached to (and remains with) a payload until it is demultiplexed. It supports functions necessary for transporting STS SPEs. Per the standard, there are four classes of functions provided by the STS POH:

- **Class A:** Payload-independent overhead functions with standard format and coding. Required by all payloads.

- **Class B:** Mapping-dependent functions with standard format and coding specific to the payload type. More than one type of payload may require these functions, but they are not require by all functions.

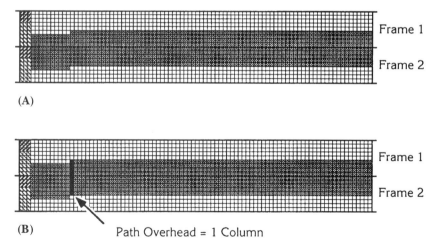

Figure 5.6 (A) SPE mapping into successive STS-1 frames. (B) SPE mapping showing Path Overhead.

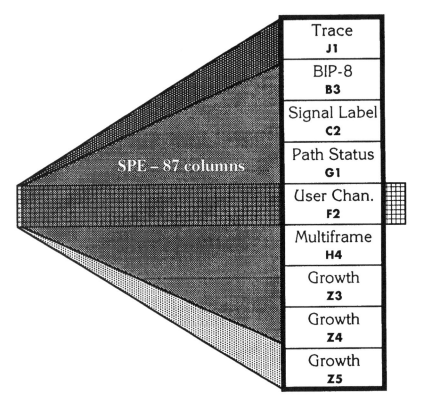

Figure 5.7 Path Overhead.

- **Class C:** Application-specific overhead functions whose format and coding are independently specified in other standard documents.
- **Class D:** Undefined overhead reserved for future use. These may be defined as either Class A, B, or C functions at a later date, with Class A taking priority.

The classification of these overhead functions does not preclude the allocation of other overhead within payload-specific mappings.

The POH is composed as follows (see Figure 5.7):

- **STS Path Trace (J1):** A 64-octet string that is repetitively sent so that the receiver in a path can ensure its continued connection to the intended transmitter (Class A).
- **Path BIP-8 (B3):** BIP-8 calculation over all bits of the previous SPE (Class A).

- **STS Path Signal Label (C2):** Indicates the construction of the SPE; STS SPE unequipped (code 0) means that the Line connection is complete but there is no Path data to send (i.e., the path is not provisioned or it is idle).

- **STS SPE Equipped:** Nonspecific Payload (code 1) is used for payloads that require no further differentiation or for payloads that are differentiated by some other means (i.e., with some sort of protocol identifier). All other values are reserved (Class A).

- **Path Status (G1):** Used to carry path performance and status information. Bits 1–4 are the Far End Block Error (FEBE); the Path BIP-8 octet can indicate the presence of 0–8 bit errors in the previous SPE and this value is placed in the FEBE; bit 5, the STS Path Yellow Indicator, indicates the possible presence of an error on the path; bits 6–8 are unused (Class A).

- **Path User Channel (F2):** Network provider communications channel between Path equipment (Class C).

- **Multiframe Indicator (H4):** The meaning of this octet depends on the payload. For VT-structured payloads (described later in this chapter), it indicates the phase of STS SPE frames in different length superframes; for other payloads, such as ATM, it is a multiframe indicator (Class B).

- **Growth (Z3–Z5):** Reserved for future us (Class D).

The remaining 774 octets (86 columns × 9 rows) of the SPE form the STS-1 Payload Capacity of 49.536 Mbps; this is the bandwidth available in an STS-1 frame for transporting actual data.

VIRTUAL TRIBUTARIES (SUBRATE CHANNELS)

Virtual Tributaries (VTS), or SONET subrate channels, are defined to accommodate today's plesiochronous digital hierarchy (PDH) carriers (i.e., T1, E1, T3, E3, etc.). Their format is more complex than the STS-1 frame/SPE structure; however, there are a few parallels between them. VTs come in four varieties: VT1.5, VT2, VT3, and VT6 (Figure 5.8).

Note that the VT configurations in Figure 5.8 are logical constructs only; for example, a VT3 is equivalent in size to the 6 × 9 grid pictured, but it does not occupy a contiguous 6 × 9 grid within the SPE. Groups of VTs are multiplexed into the frame, as described below.

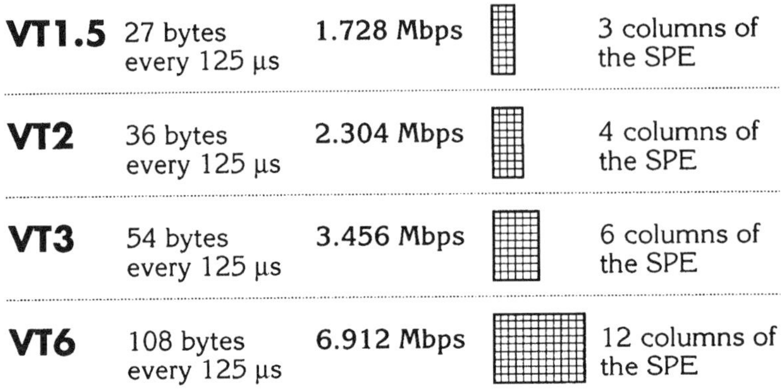

VT1.5
27 bytes every 125 µs
1.728 Mbps
3 columns of the SPE
VT2
36 bytes every 125 µs
2.304 Mbps
4 columns of the SPE
VT3
54 bytes every 125 µs
3.456 Mbps
6 columns of the SPE
VT6
108 bytes every 125 µs
6.912 Mbps
12 columns of the SPE

Figure 5.8 Logical diagrams of VT types.

A VT-structured SPE (i.e., carrying subrate signals) contains 7 VT groups, each containing 12 columns. Between the 7 VT groups (84 columns) and the POH, then, we have only accounted for 85 columns of the 87-column SPE. The two remaining columns are referred to as *Fixed Stuff* columns, and occupy columns #30 and #59. The standard requires SONET hardware to

VT1.5 Group
VT2 Group
VT3 Group
VT6 Group

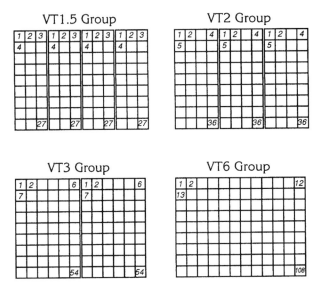

Figure 5.9 VT group types.

ignore these columns when processing VT-structured frames, so they may contain any combination of ones and zeros.

A VT group (which always contains precisely 12 columns) can contain only one kind of VT. This means a VT group can accommodate either 4 VT1.5s, 3 VT2s, 2 VT3s, or 1 VT6 (Figure 5.9).

The SPE can contain any mix of the four VT group types. The VT groups are byte interleaved in the SPE so that one column is taken from each of the seven VT groups in succession, placing each sample column into every seventh column of the SPE beginning with column #2, skipping the "fixed stuff" columns #30 and #59. The octets of each VT are transmitted left to right as is the STS-1 frame (Figure 5.10).

The VT structure above can be operated in either *floating* or *locked* mode. The floating mode is provided to accommodate today's asynchronous network; in the future, the use of floating mode will not be common, as the interconnection of synchronous facilities by locked-mode VTs will be much more efficient. Certain current synchronous payloads (SYNTRAN, for instance) have mappings defined only into SONET's locked mode. In general, current asynchronous payloads have mappings into both modes, so that a service provider can implement the mapping that makes the most sense for its current equipment.

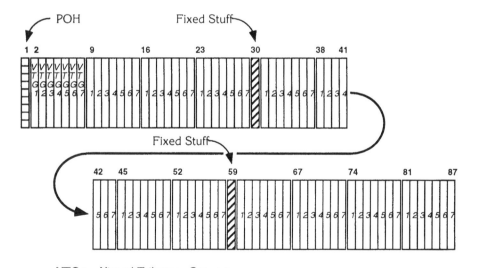

VTGn = Virtual Tributary Group n

Figure 5.10 VT group mapping into the SPE.

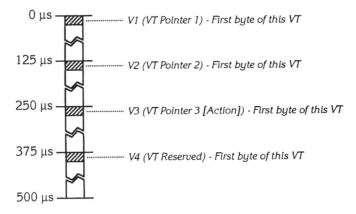

Figure 5.11 VT Superframe.

Floating VT Mode

Four consecutive STS-1 SPEs form a 500-μs Superframe. The VT Superframe contains the VT Payload Pointer and the VT SPE (Figure 5.10). The VT Payload Pointer is analogous to the TOH payload pointer which allows the SPE to float within the STS-1 frame. This pointer allows the VT payload to "float" within the VT SPE (Figure 5.11).

Note that each of the 125-μs time slots must contain the same VT type. Thus, there are four VT Superframe types, one for each VT type, with different bandwidths (Table 5.3).

The equivalent bandwidth is found by multiplying the number of octets in each Superframe by 8 to get the number of bits, and then multiplying by 2000, the number of VT Superframes per second. Note that a VT1.5 Superframe has the same bandwidth as a VT1.5, and so on.

There is a correspondence between the STS-1 frame (Figure 5.2) and the VT Superframe. They are both structures into which data is "poured." Just as

Table 5.3 VT Superframe Capacities

VT type	VT Capacity	VT Superframe Capacity	Equivalent Bandwidth
VT1.5	27 octets	4 × 27 octets = 108 octets	1.728 Mbps
VT2	36 octets	4 × 36 octest = 144 octets	2.304 Mbps
VT3	54 octets	4 × 54 octets = 216 octets	3.456 Mbps
VT6	108 octets	4 × 108 octets = 432 octets	6.912 Mbps

Table 5.4 VT SPE Capacities

VT Type	VT SPE Capacity	Equivalent Bandwidth
VT1.5	108 – 4 = 104 octets	1.664 Mbps
VT2	144 – 4 = 140 octets	2.240 Mbps
VT3	216 – 4 = 212 octets	3.392 Mbps
VT6	432 – 4 = 428 octets	6.848 Mbps

there is a data structure called the SPE, which exists in the STS-1 frame structure that exactly matches its payload capacity in size, there is also a VT SPE that is the same size as the VT Superframe (less the overhead, which, in the case of each VT Superframe type, is always 4 octets). Table 5.4 shows the VT SPE capacities for each type of VT.

The format of the VT SPEs is shown in Figure 5.12. The VT Superframe has elements corresponding to both the Path Overhead (in the first column of the STS-1 SPE) and the Transport Overhead (in the first three columns of the STS-1 frame) (Figure 5.13).

As shown in Figure 5.13, V1, V2, and V3 are VT pointers; V4 is reserved; and V5 is the VT Path Overhead. R stands for *fixed stuff* wherever it appears; R is used throughout the SONET standard to symbolize this function. Depending on the context, R might be a bit, an octet (byte), or a column. In this case, it is a single octet. Figure 5.13 is intentionally drawn with the VT SPE lining up within a single VT Superframe for simplicity. The same consid-

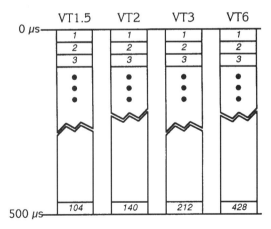

Figure 5.12 VT SPEs.

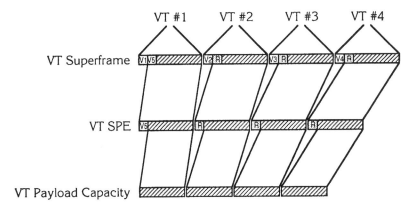

Figure 5.13 VT SPE mapping with VT Path Overhead.

erations apply here regarding pointers, namely that the VT SPE may begin at any octet position within the VT superframe, with the VT Pointer indicating the actual starting point, which can be adjusted to allow for phase differences. Obviously, the floating VT structure is complicated. The net bandwidth available for payload in each VT Superframe type is shown in Table 5.5.

Locked VT Mode

The VT locked mode has the same bandwidth as the floating mode because, although a single VT is one-fourth the size of a VT Superframe, it is transmitted four times faster. The essential difference between the two is that "overhead" in locked mode consists of two "fixed-stuff" octets at the beginning of each VT, contrasting with the floating-mode overhead assignments (over a run of four VTs) of V1, V5, V2, R, V3, R, V4, and R. Thus, locked-mode operation does not require the PTE to do VT payload pointer processing, an obvious reduction in complexity.

Table 5.5 Net VT Payload Capacity

VT Type	VT Payload Capacity	Equivalent Bandwidth
VT1.5	$108 - 4 - 4 = 100$ octets	1.600 Mbps
VT2	$144 - 4 - 4 = 136$ octets	2.176 Mbps
VT3	$216 - 4 - 4 = 208$ octets	3.328 Mbps
VT6	$432 - 4 - 4 = 424$ octets	6.784 Mbps

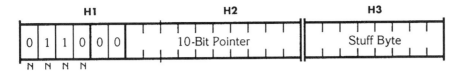

Figure 5.14 Pointer format (normal values).

POINTERS AND SPEs

The STS-1 Payload Pointer (H1 and H2, the first two octets in the Line Overhead) allows dynamic, flexible alignment of the SPE within the Envelope Capacity in a way that is independent of the actual contents of the envelope. Not only can the pointer accommodate phase differences in the Transport Overhead and the SPE independently, it can also handle slight frame frequency differences. The format of the H1, H2, and H3 octets is shown in Figure 5.14.

The first 4 bits of H1 form the New Data Flag (NDF). The NDF allows for an arbitrary change in the payload pointer due to a radical change in the payload. Normally, the pointer can be adjusted by at most ±1 octet every fourth frame; if more adjustment than this is required, the NDF is used. This might happen when equipment is first turned on, or when STEs recover from a severe failure. "New data" is indicated by inverting the NDF; in this case the pointer value will be different than it was in the previous frame (Figure 5.15).

The next 2 bits in the pointer are reserved and are both set to zero. The following 10 bits, which overlap the H1 and H2 octets, contain the pointer. The binary number represented by these 10 bits can have any value in the range from 0 through 782 (00 0000 0000 through 11 0000 1110). A value of 0 indicates that the SPE begins at the position immediately to the right of the H3 octet. A value of 87 indicates a starting point immediately to the right of K2 (i.e., one row down), and so on, with a value of 782 corresponding to the right-most position in the third row from the top.

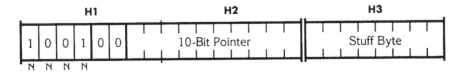

Figure 5.15 Pointer format (new data).

The NDF is one example of how the SONET standard has been written to reduce retransmissions due to isolated bit errors. Certainly ascertaining whether data is new or not only requires 1 bit—a definite yes/no situation. Four bits are sent to provide redundancy. The decoding LTE knows that the last NDF was "0110." It confirms the existence of new data provided that at least 3 of the 4 bits have been inverted. The flag indicating new data is effectively transmitted four times. If the LTE sees 2 bits or less change, it ignores the new pointer and uses the one from the previous frame. In this case, the "new" pointer may or may not have changed. If it did change, it had an error, too.

If there is a frequency offset between the Transport Overhead frame rate and the SPE frame rate, then the SPE must be allowed to drift in the frame, because it must be transmitted as a single entity. During normal operation, pointer adjustments must not occur more often than once every fourth frame; i.e., the pointer value must remain constant for at least three frames following an adjustment. This constraint is needed to preserve the integrity of the four-frame VT Superframe structure; i.e., a pointer adjustment cannot happen more than once per VT Superframe.

Pointer adjustment occurs when the SPE rate is different than the Transport Overhead rate. If the SPE rate is slightly faster, the pointer must be decremented so that the SPE is moved to the left by one position in the STS-1 frame; this is called *negative stuffing* (Figure 5.16).

To alert the receiving equipment that the pointer is being decremented, the 5 bits labeled D are inverted. This is another example of how SONET is designed to incorporate redundancy; at least 3 out of the 5 D-bits must disagree with their previous values. If so, the receiver will expect the next frame to have a pointer value one less than the current value.

Figure 5.17 shows the pointer in action during a negative stuff situation. In the first two frames in the figure, the pointer does not change. The SPE in Frame 3 needs to be adjusted forward in the frame structure, so the D-bits of the pointer are inverted and the octet just to the right of H3 octet is copied into H3, and the remaining octets in the SPE slide to the left (and up, as

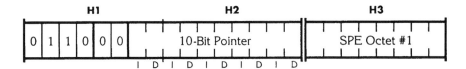

Figure 5.16 Pointer format (negative stuff).

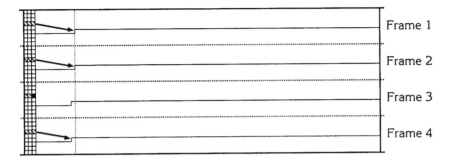

Figure 5.17 Negative stuff operation.

necessary), so that the SPE ends 1-octet position sooner than it did before. The receiver knows that the H3 position contains data rather than a stuff byte because the pointer was decremented. The pointer in Frame 4 reflects the adjustment by having a value one less than it had previously (i.e., in Frame 2).

The other kind of pointer adjustment occurs when the SPE rate is slightly less than the Transport Overhead rate. The pointer value, in this case, must be incremented by one so the SPE is moved to the right by one position. In this *positive stuff* case, the five I-bits are inverted (Figure 5.18) and a majority vote at the receiver (at least 3 of the 5 I-bits must disagree with their previous values) confirms the increment. The next frame is expected to have a pointer value one greater than the value prior to the adjustment.

Figure 5.19 shows how the SPE is manipulated in a positive stuff situation. Frames 1 and 2 contain normal pointers. In Frame 3, a positive adjustment becomes necessary. Thus, the contents of H3 (a stuff octet in this case) are copied into the octet immediately following the H3 octet, and, simultaneously, the rest of the contents of the SPE are displaced to the right (and down, if necessary), until the last octet of the SPE ends up 1-octet position further down in the STS-1 frame. In Frame 4, the pointer indicates the new position by having a value one greater than it had in Frame 2.

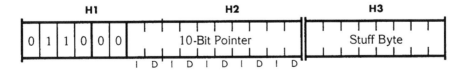

Figure 5.18 Pointer format (positive stuff).

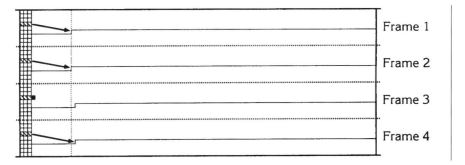

Figure 5.19 Positive stuff operation.

MAKING STS-N FRAMES

Higher-speed SONET signals are formed by byte-interleaving STS-1 signals and transmitting the aggregate signal in the same amount of time that an STS-1 is transmitted: 125 μs. Thus, an STS-n signal is formed from N STS-1 inputs.

In an STS-n frame, the Transport Overhead contains $3 \times n$ columns, and the Synchronous Payload Capacity is $87 \times n$ columns, for a total of $90 \times n$ columns. Note that the STS-n SPE will contain n columns of Path Overhead. Before byte-interleaving the STS-1 frames, the frames must have their Transport Overhead channels frame aligned. The SPEs within the STS-1s do not need to be frame aligned because each SPE's relative position is maintained by an STS-1 pointer.

Figure 5.20 shows an STS-3 frame. Note that some of the TOH octets are replicated three times and others appear only once. This is because some overhead octets have significance only in the first STS-1 frame of an STS-n signal. According to the standard, the objective is that all-zero octets be transmitted in the "unused" overhead slots. Realizing that manufacturers may want to use this extra bandwidth to provide some added functionality, Bellcore requires that all SONET equipment have the ability to be explicitly configured to ignore these values (except that they must be included in BIP-8 calculations). The manufacturers who do make use of this extra bandwidth are required to disclose what features they implement and how they do it; they are also required to give their equipment the ability to disable these nonstandard features.

Byte-interleaving means that, effectively, the STS-n frame is made by taking the first columns from each STS-1 in order, then taking the second

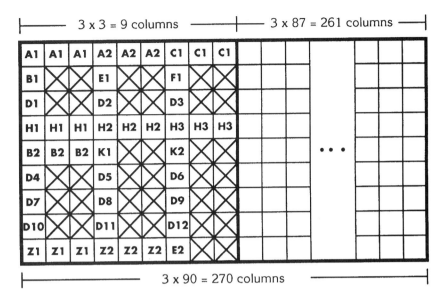

Figure 5.20 STS-3 frame structure.

columns, and so on. This process parallels the way VT groups are folded into the STS-1 SPE. To generate signals with transmission rates higher than STS-3, either STS-3s or STS-1s can be byte-interleaved. The results of both multiplexing processes are required to be byte-for-byte identical.

MAKING SUPER RATE PAYLOADS BY CONCATENATION

In order to provide for the transport of super rate payloads (i.e., those that require greater bandwidth than the STS-1 rate provides), SONET allows for the concatenation of STS-1 signals into STS-nc signals. The main difference between an STS-n signal and an STS-nc signal is that the STS-n signal has n columns of Path Overhead, whereas the STS-nc has only one. The STS-nc signal is treated as a single, large digital channel rather than a group of narrow channels. The SPE in an STS-3 signal, for example, contains 258 columns ($3 \times 87 - 3$), equivalent to an aggregate bit rate of 148.608 Mbps; an STS-3c SPE contains 260 columns ($3 \times 87 - 1$), providing a single channel of 149.76 Mbps.

Concatenation is indicated in the H1 and H2 fields of the TOH. Specifically, the second through Nth payload pointers are set to all ones (an illegal offset because 1023 is bigger than 782) and the NDF is set to "1001."

OPERATIONS DATA NETWORKING IN SONET

The SONET standard provides several message-oriented and bit-oriented channels in the overhead which are to be used for communications between network elements (NEs). Channels that are dedicated to the transmission of operations data are referred to as Embedded Operations Channels (EOCs). Note that the Section and Line Data Communications Channels are not necessarily EOCs. A DCC may be used for any type of communication. The term EOC only refers to a channel that is dedicated to the transport of network operations and management information.

The whole area of communications between NEs (as opposed to data transport) is referred to as Operations Data Networking (ODN). The features of SONET that support ODN are used to support Operations, Administration, Maintenance, and Provisioning (OAM&P) functions for the network providers, and allow the network operations systems (OSs) to directly control and monitor the network remotely. A whole infrastructure of interfaces and communication channels is required to provide this functionality. There are many ways to implement this support network; in addition to using the DCCs and bit-oriented EOCs in the SONET frame, it is possible to use a physically separate network to convey the management and operations data, which could be comprised of private lines, packet radio links, LANs, etc.

The CCITT defines a support network architecture called Telecommunications Management Network (TMN) in Recommendation M.30. SONET will comply with this document, which will provide paths for NE/OS, NE/NE, and NE/Workstation (NE/WS) communications. The SONET standard describes the roles that NEs play in TMN; TMN achitectures are not described. Two functions that TMNs provide are addressed: Local Communications Network (LCN) functions and Mediation Functions (MFs) (mediation implies some sort of protocol and/or message conversion). These pertain to SONET in that NEs and overhead channels are used to implement these functions.

Operations Network Criteria

The specific operations network criteria that apply to a given NE depend on what position in the network the NE occupies. There are several categories: Cateway (GNE), Intermediate (INE), and End (ENE) NEs (Figure 5.21).

As depicted in Figure 5.21, there can either be a direct communications path from an OS to a GNE, or there can be an X.25 link between them. The

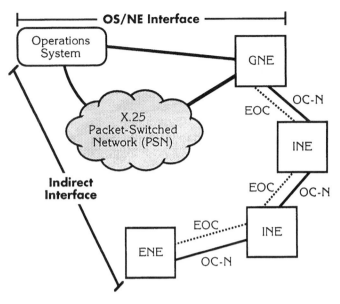

Figure 5.21 Network element types.

indirect interface is a combination of the OS/NE interface and (possibly) multiple NE/NE interfaces using EOCs. The indirect interface does not necessarily terminate in an ENE; in fact, any NE can be engaged in OAM&P communications with an OS. Several different classes of interface are present in the SONET standard, namely OS/NE, NE/NE, and NE/Ws

The OS/NE Interface

The OS/NE specification is fairly complex, as there are many combinations of languages, protocols, and mediation functions (conversions between protocols and messages) which must be implemented to support the full range of possible communications. SONET OS/NE communications are only via message-oriented channels.

The language that must be used for OS/NE messages is Transaction Language 1 (TL1, as Bellcore standard). The standard specifies migration to the use of Common Management Information Service Element (CMISE) and Abstract Syntax Notation One (ASN.1) languages in the future for conveying messages required by transaction-oriented applications and operations information. Operations information that is file-oriented shall use File Transfer, Access, and Management Application Service Element (FTAM ASE) and ASN.1.

There are three protocol stacks defined for OS/NE communications. One is called TPM1 (Transaction Processing using TL1 over CCITT X.25), which is a partial OSI protocol stack (Levels 1, 2, 3, and 7). When Transaction Processing (TP) applications reside over the X.25 protocol, the operations applications messages (which are written in TL1) are encoded using 7-bit ACSII with null parity.

Another possible stack is TPF2 (Transaction Processing Full conformance stack #2). This is a fully OSI-conformant protocol stack for TP applications. Messages are written in CMISE/ASN.1. It is a requirement that every SONET NE having a direct OS interface shall support either TPM1 or TPF2.

The final possible stack is the FT (File Transfer) stack. Operations applications including traffic data access and accounting management require file transfer and also the ability to locate and access portions of a file. Applications such as these shall use the FT stack.

The NE/NE Interface

NEs communicate with each other via either bit-oriented or message-oriented EOCs. The message-oriented EOCs may also be used in OS/NE and NE/WS communications. The bit-oriented channels employed by SONET NEs and their functions are summarized in Table 5.6.

Table 5.6 shows the responsibilities associated with each overhead element listed on the left. Some overhead octets (e.g., K2, G1, and V5) report more than one kind of message. Note that the V1, V2, and V5 octets are only pertinent to floating-mode VT-structured frames. The locked-mode VT-structured frame has no overhead mappings for any operations data.

Table 5.6 Bit-Oriented EOCs for NE/NE Communications

	Line AIS	Line FERF	APS	STS AIS	STS Yellow	STS FEBE	VT AIS	VT Yellow	VT FEBE
H1-H2				■					
K1-K2			■						
K2	■	■							
G1					■	■			
V1-V2							■		
V5								■	■

Layer Name	Service/Protocol
7. Application	ISO 9595, 9596 (CMISE) X.217, X.227 (ACSE) X.219, X.229 (ROSE)
6. Presentation	X.216, X.226 X.209 (ASN.1 Basic Encoding Rules)
5. Session	X.215, X.225
4. Transport	ISO 8073, 8073 DAD2 (TP4)
3. Network	ISO 8473 (CLNP)
2. Data Link	LAPD for SONET DCC applications
1. Physical	Section DCC

Figure 5.22 Protocol stack for transaction-oriented applications.

Transaction-oriented applications shall use CMISE/ASN.1, while file-oriented applications shall use FTAM/ASN.1. Figure 5.22 depicts the full OSI protocol stack used for NE/NE transaction-oriented data communications.

The NE/WS Interface

Local craft access is mandated by the SONET standard for all NEs, and may be provided through a terminal/keyboard or a more advanced microprocessor-based workstation, in combination with direct NE/WS communications path. The standard requires that all of the remote functions available to an OS must be provided by the NE/WS interface.

SONET DEPLOYMENT PHASE

The industry usually refers to the standardization and deployment process of SONET in phases. Phase 1 includes the initial standardization of the SONET hierarchy for early deployment, including the development of T1.105 and T1.106. ANS T1.106 was initially developed between late 1984 and mid-1988, and describes the single-mode optical interface specifications for SONET. ANS T1.105 was written between mid-1985 and mid-1988, and describes basic bit rates, frame formats, payload pointers, and mapping of the G.703 metallic-based TDM hierarchy rates onto SONET.

Phase 2 has been ongoing since early 1988 and involves additions to the T1.105 specification. These supplements will describe such issues as additional timing and synchronization procedures, additional automatic protection switching specifications, use of the DCC, and SONET network management.

Phase 3 will define other issues which are more peripheral to SONET. Some of the "Phase 3" topics are already under discussion, such as mapping FDDI to SONET. Other Phase 3 issues still to be considered include interconnecting the SONET DCC to an LAN, additional operations, administration and maintenance procedures, and protection mechanisms for the DCC.

SONET is currently being widely deployed within North America and Japan, and planning is well underway in Europe for a rich SDH infrastructure, with implementation already occurring in some countries.

SUMMARY

SONET and SDH will have significant impact on the future of data and telecommunications, as they define a standard optical infrastructure for high-speed information transport. Not only will they provide a carrier hierarchy for all foreseeable data rates, but they provide a consistent multiplexing scheme and standard network interfaces, encouraging regional and international interoperability.

SONET and SDH will also play an important role in the availability of public MAN and WAN services. Mappings for FDDI, DQDB, and SMDS to STS-3c signals have been defined so that these services may be offered over a standard, public transport network. The Broadband ISDN specifications define ATM as the underlying transport, and SDH STM-1 (STS-3c) or STM-4 (STS-12c) form the ATM Physical Layer.

SONET and SDH will provide the basis for the optical infrastructure necessary for the broadband services of the next century.

BIBLIOGRAPHY

ANSI, "Digital Hierarchy—Optical Interface Rates and Formats Specifications (SONET)." ANS T1.105.

_____, "Digital Hierarchy—Optical Interface Specifications (Single Mode)." ANS T1.106.

Bellcore, "Synchronous Optical Network (SONET) Transport Systems: Common Generic Criteria." TR-TSY-000253.

CCITT, "Synchronous Digital Hierarchy Bit Rates." Recommendation G.707.

_____, "Network Node Interface for the Synchronous Digital Hierarchy." Recommendation G.708.

_____, "Synchronous Multiplexing Structure." Recommendation G.709.

ABOUT THE AUTHORS

Thomas Albert Maufer was born in Washington, DC. He received his Bachelor of Science degree in Physics and Math from the Virginia Polytechnic Institute and State University in Blacksburg, Virginia, and his Master of Science in Electrical Engineering from the University of Vermont in Burlington, Vermont. He participated in Virginia Tech's cooperative education program at the NASA Goddard Space Flight Center as an undergraduate, and is currently employed there as a senior network engineer working on the Center Network Environment Project. He currently lives in Columbia, Maryland.

Gary C. Kessler is a senior member of the technical staff at Hill Associates in Colchester, Vermont, a technical education and consulting firm specializing in telecommunications technologies and services. He has written several articles for technical journals, is a contributor to _LAN Magazine_, the author of _ISDN: Concepts, Facilities, and Services_, 2nd edition (McGraw-Hill, 1993), and the co-author of _Metropolitan Area Networks: Concepts, Standards, and Services_ (McGraw-Hill, 1992). He is an observer on the ANSI X3T9.5 (FDDI) Task Group; a participant on the IEEE 802.6 (MANs), 802.9 (Integrated Voice/Data LANs), and 802.11 (Wireless LANs) subcommittees; an observer on the SMDS Interest Group Technical Committee; and an observer on the Frame Relay Forum Technical Committee. Electronic mail to Mr. Kessler may be addressed to kumquat@smcvax.smcvt.edu.

6

X.25 and Worldwide Networking

Fred M. Burg
AT&T Bell Laboratories

INTRODUCTION

Since its adoption in 1976, the International Telephone and Telegraph Consultative Committee (CCITT) Recommendation X.25 has often been taken to embody a wide range of networking concepts. Usually this range goes well beyond what was intended by CCITT; Recommendation X.25 (or "X.25" for short) was never meant to provide a full networking solution. Over the years, however, a suite of standards (actually both CCITT Recommendations and ISO/IEC Standards) have been developed that both complement and supplement X.25. In fact, "X.25" has taken us to the point where it, along with its companion set of standards, does indeed provide for a full networking platform.

Recommendation X.25 has been a major factor in the area of data communications for almost 20 years. It has been the basis for "wide area networking" using packet technology on a worldwide basis; most providers of data transport services have implemented it in their networks. Likewise, major computer vendors offer X.25 across their product lines for connecting to these networks. Many value-added environments, such as bulletin boards and news services, depend on it for transport and connectivity. Now, as we move forward to new technologies, such as OSI, ISDN, and broadband ISDN, it might appear that the role of X.25 may start to diminish. However, this is far from the truth. For example, some providers of X.25 services offer speeds in the megabit per second range; likewise, X.25 offers advanced features, such as call forwarding, which are also available to ISDN users.

This chapter starts with a brief review of the origins of packet technology and X.25. This is followed by an overview of what X.25 is and how it works; more detail is given elsewhere [1]. We conclude the chapter by showing how X.25-based capabilities can be extended across a global enterprise network, including a description of other members of the X.25 suite of Recommendations/Standards applicable to these environments.

PACKET TECHNOLOGY AND X.25

In 1972, CCITT had standardized Recommendation X.21 [2] as a method for connecting two data terminal equipments (DTEs) through a Circuit-Switched Public Data Network (CSPDN). This work brought a combination of factors to the standards table:

- Recognition of a *dedicated network* for data communications;
- Use of a *public* network for sharing networking equipment;
- Availability of the user's full communications bandwidth through the network (i.e., *circuit mode* of communication), whether it was actually used or not, for connecting its DTE to another DTE on a permanent (dedicated) or temporary (switched) basis; in the latter case, the bandwidth could be reused for communicating with another DTE only after the connection to the first DTE was released.

Of these factors, the first two were readily acceptable to users in the early 1970s. Rather than continue to share the telephony network for sending data, it was recognized that dedicated data networks could be tailor-made for interactions between computers for exchanging files or between computers and terminals for performing transactions. Likewise, the enormous costs associated with developing, operating, and maintaining such a network could be spread over many customers if it was open to the public.

On the other hand, the third factor still caused concern. Given the relatively high costs of communications facilities at that time, the inefficiences and wastefulness of allocating a fixed amount of resources, even if only for a temporary period, were unacceptable. Many instances of communications were of a bursty nature that did not justify large amounts of bandwidth on a continuous basis while others required fixed resources for a longer duration.

Moreover, some systems needed to communicate with many others simultaneously, for example, a database communicating with several hundred or thousand terminals at the same time. Such communication scenarios made it cumbersome, at best, to have to connect and then reconnect the circuit-switched connection to one destination and then another.

Furthermore, the benefits of packet switching were also starting to be recognized in the early 1970s. Unlike circuit-mode communications, packet switching in its broadest form represents a statistical sharing of resources (access lines, network switches, and trunks, etc.) among many simultaneous instances of communication. With the successes of the ARPANET in the United States and the introduction of IBM's Systems Network Architecture (SNA) at about this time, the need for a companion standard for packet switching was quite apparent in CCITT. Already several networking vendors were offering or planning a packet-switched mode of operation in their public data networks at that time (Telenet and Tymnet in the United States, DATAPAC in Canada, TRANSPAC in France, and DDX-P in Japan, as well as others). Technical work began in CCITT in 1974 on a new packet-switching standard and, 2 short years later, X.25 was adopted [3].

WHAT IS X.25?

Before going further, we need to examine what X.25 is and what it is not. While this has been discussed somewhat above in contrast to X.21 circuit-switching operation, a closer look is in order. The best way forward is to parse the title of Recommendation X.25 to see what it is all about.

The title, then, is: *Interface between Data Terminal Equipment (DTE) and Data Circuit-Terminating Equipment (DCE) for Terminals Operating in the Packet Mode and Connected to Public Data Networks by Dedicated Circuit.*

From the above title, we see that X.25 addresses the following:

- First and foremost, X.25 describes an *interface*; as such, it specifies a set of services available at the interface and the allowed set of interactions by which these services are requested and received.

- The interface is between a DTE (user of service) and a DCE (provider of service).

- Although X.25 describes a single DTE/DCE interface, the goal, although perhaps only implicitly assumed, is to allow communications to take place between two users (i.e., DTEs) of the service without constraining the nature of that communication.

- The mode of operation of the terminal is the *packet mode*, as opposed to circuit mode (which X.21 describes), whereby messages are embedded in *packets* that have a distinct beginning and end; packets for one destination can be interleaved with packets for another, thus providing for the sharing of resources among several instances of communication.

- The terminal is to be connected to a network that is *public* (that is, open to all), as opposed to private.

- The network is dedicated to moving *data*, as opposed to voice or both voice and data; combined with the points above, the network is known as a Packet-Switched Public Data Network (PSPDN).

- The connection between the DTE and DCE is to be by *dedicated circuit*; actually, this aspect was added in 1984 to distinguish connections whereby the network always knew who the customer was by virtue of the dedicated nature of the connection (and, therefore, was able to charge someone for its services), as opposed to cases where the connection was made dynamically (e.g., a *switched connection* via a dial-up line), whereby collection for services might not be possible.

Although it is not explicit in the title, X.25 only describes the behavior of a DCE as viewed at the DTE/DCE interface, but it does not dictate how the DCE should operate internally. Figure 6.1 depicts the elements of "X.25" described above.

From the description above and from Figure 6.1, it should now be clear, at least at a high level, what "X.25" is. In contrast, we have also explicitly identified some aspects of communications that are outside the bounds of X.25 while inferring yet others. These items are equally important in gaining an understanding of what is needed to build a global packet networking environment.

X.25 does *not* address the following areas of communications:

- Operations, administration, and maintenance (OA&M) procedures such as how a customer registers a DTE with the network to obtain service and specifies what services are desired;

- What services are required to be provided by the network and which ones are optional;

- How a DTE obtains service from the network when its interface to the network is via a switched connection instead of a dedicated line;

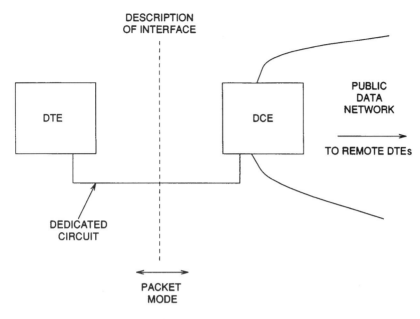

Figure 6.1 Elements of X.25.

- How a DTE identifies the remote DTE with which it wishes to communicate; this aspect involves an *addressing plan*;

- How the network moves information from one DTE to another, once the remote DTE is identified; this involves not only routing strategies but a method for preserving the information conveyed by a user;

- How the network charges for its services;

- How the network interworks with other (public and/or private) data networks;

- What levels of performance need to be provided by the network;

- What management features/functions are available from the network;

- How "X.25" relates to other technologies, such as Open Systems Interconnection (OSI) or Integrated Services Digital Networks (ISDNs).

Although the above list may appear lengthy, it was always understood in CCITT that X.25 by itself would not provide a complete networking solution. Rather, it was recognized that such issues should be addressed elsewhere.

We have set the stage, however, for the discussion to follow later regarding how these "gaps" are filled in a global X.25 networking environment.

GENERAL X.25 OPERATION

As mentioned above, X.25 specifies the allowed set of interactions to be used across the interface to a packet-switched public data network by which services are requested and received by a DTE. This set of interactions, including its method of encoding, is called a *protocol*. While one may speak of *the* X.25 protocol, Recommendation X.25 should actually be viewed as three protocols working together to facilitate communications. However, two of these three protocols actually were "borrowed" from elsewhere; only one of the three members of the X.25 "protocol stack" represented entirely new work in 1976.

Figure 6.2 shows the X.25 protocol stack. A critical element of this stack is the hierarchical relationship or *layering* of the protocols; that is, a higher-layer protocol makes use of the capabilities (*services*) provided by a lower-layer protocol. Furthermore, since this usage only depends on these capabilities being available in an abstract fashion without being tied to the actual protocol, then changes can be made to the lower-layer protocol or an entirely different lower-layer protocol providing the same capabilities can be used without any negative effects (*layer independence*). This is shown at each of Layers 1 and 2, where several protocols can be used interchangeably.

LAYER:

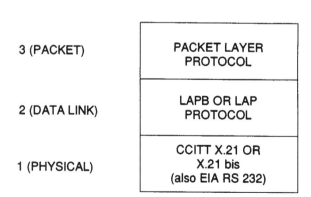

3 (PACKET) — PACKET LAYER PROTOCOL

2 (DATA LINK) — LAPB OR LAP PROTOCOL

1 (PHYSICAL) — CCITT X.21 OR X.21 bis (also EIA RS 232)

Figure 6.2 Protocol stack.

While these concepts were somewhat new in the 1974 time frame, they provided the cornerstone for several key elements (*layer, layer independence, layer service*) to be embedded in work started just a few years later known as the OSI Reference Model (see Chapter 1).

From a functional point of view, the three layers of X.25 provide the following high-level capabilities:

- **Layer 1**, the Physical Layer, provides mechanical, electrical, functional, and procedural means for the transmission and reception of bits over a path between the DTE and DCE.
- **Layer 2**, the Data Link Layer, is responsible for detecting and correcting errors that may occur in the Physical Layer (i.e., across the DTE/DCE interface).
- **Layer 3**, the Packet Layer, defines procedures that allow two DTEs to control the communication and exchange data between them.

Therefore, for a DTE to communicate with another DTE, it must first ensure that the Physical Layer is set up in order to be able to send bits into the network. The protocols used in X.25 Layer 1 are generally associated with some other technology used to access a PSPDN; some were in use even before the advent of X.25. Then Layer 2 must be initialized to ensure error-free communication between the DTE and DCE; likewise, Layer 2 of X.25 was also borrowed from other technology. Finally, the Packet Layer is used to convey information intended for the remote DTE; it is at this layer that global connectivity is established.

Table 6.1 compares the features of Layers 2 and 3 of X.25 in a general way. Although the table shows many features as being available in both layers, many of them operate somewhat differently depending on the layer.

Before discussing the features of X.25 Layers 2 and 3, it is important to recognize the scope of these layers. As indicated in Table 6.1, Layer 2 is concerned with access to/from the network. This layer is viewed as providing the *logical* data link between the DTE and the DCE (i.e., the PSPDN). The data link is viewed as being logical because the connection between the DTE and DCE need not consist of a single physical connection but must maintain analogous properties. For example, the data link between the DTE and DCE may actually be carried over a permanent connection across a CSPDN.[1]

---

[1] In this sense, the DTE and the DCE (i.e., the packet switch of the PSPDN) can both be viewed as DTEs of the CSPDN.

Table 6.1 Features in Layers 2 and 3 of X.25

Feature	Layer 2	Layer 3
Layer Name	Data Link	Packet
Scope of Layer	Access to PSPDN	Communication across PSPDN[a]
Unit of Data	Frame	Packet
Layer Initialization	Yes	Yes
# Concurrent DTE/DCE Connections	1[b]	1 or More
Connection Types	Data Link	Logical Channel
Parameter Negotiation	No	Yes
Layer Termination	Yes	No[c]
Sequenced Delivery of "Normal" Data	Yes	Yes
Data Marking (Qualification)	No	Yes
Segmentation of Large Data Units	No	Yes
Transfer of "Expedited" Data	No	Yes
Request/Receive Acknowledgment	Yes	Yes
Flow Control	Yes	Yes
Error Detection	Yes	Yes
Retransmit Lost Data	Yes	Yes[d]
Reinitialize Data Transfer	Yes	Yes
Error Reporting	Yes	Yes

[a] Although X.25 only describes the DTE/DCE interface, most aspects of the Packet Layer are concerned with communications with a remote DTE.

[b] The X.25 multilink capability, which is an optional feature, allows for more than one DTE/DCE connection at Layer 2. However, these connections appear as one to Layer 3.

[c] Once Layer 3 is initialized, it does not terminate itself. Instead, termination is accomplished by terminating Layer 2 or Layer 1.

[d] The Layer 3 retransmission capability is an optional feature that is rarely implemented.

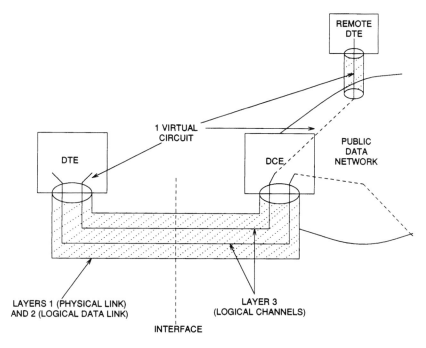

Figure 6.3 Layer 2 versus Layer 3 at the DTE/DCE interface.

Layer 3, on the other hand, provides the means by which a DTE makes known to the DCE the information to be communicated with the remote DTE. The information concerning the communication with each remote DTE is carried on a separate Layer 3 *logical channel.* Each logical channel at a DTE/DCE interface corresponds to one logical channel at a remote DTE/DCE interface once end-to-end communications has been established. This pair of logical channels and the network-internal mechanisms for tying them together form a *virtual circuit.* It is the virtual circuit, whether it spans one network or many networks, that provides for the global connectivity between users. The above concepts are depicted in Figure 6.3.

PHYSICAL LAYER

The Physical Layer of X.25 provides the means by which bits are transmitted between a DTE and a DCE. X.25 specifies several different technologies over which this can be done: dedicated lines, CSPDNs, and ISDNs (frame relay networks can also be used in this fashion, although standardization of this is not yet completed).

Likewise, numerous speeds, up to 2 Mbps, are specified in X.25 for access to a PSPDN. It should be noted that a network may offer even higher access speeds than specified in X.25; this is purely a local matter up to the network provider.

DATA LINK LAYER OPERATION

As mentioned above, the X.25 Data Link Layer is responsible for the movement of information across the communications line that connects the DTE and DCE. As such, it provides an error-free data link by correcting any errors that occur in Layer 1 while providing a transparent data link connection for use by the Packet Layer. The procedures and encodings used at Layer 2 are derived from a subset of those defined by the High-Level Data Link Control procedures (HDLC) [4], which were standardized by the International Organization for Standardization (ISO) starting in the early 1970s. (HDLC is viewed as providing a toolkit from which tools are selected as a foundation for a Data Link Layer protocol. This selection is then fleshed out by the developer to completely specify the operation of the protocol.)

There are two procedures specified in X.25 for use at the Data Link Layer: One is known as *LAP* (for Link Access Procedure) while the other is known as *LAPB* (for LAP-Balanced). From the perspective of the Packet Layer applying the concept of layer independence, it does not matter which one is used. LAP was part of the original specification of X.25 when it was adopted in 1976, but it was found to have problems [5] and was supplemented by LAPB in 1978. Almost all implementations today of X.25 Layer 2 use only LAPB. Although there are numerous similarities between LAP and LAPB, we will restrict our discussion to LAPB. It is conceivable that LAP will be deleted from Recommendation X.25 in the near future.

General Layer 2 Encoding Principles

Figure 6.4 depicts the general format of a *frame*, which is the unit of information transfer at the Data Link Layer. The basic mode of transmission available in all PSPDNs uses *synchronous framing*, where synchronization takes place at the bit level (i.e., no extra bits are added between octets for synchro-

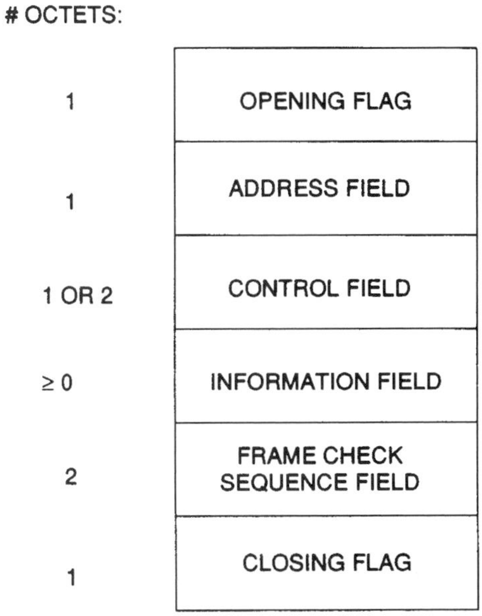

\# OCTETS:

1	OPENING FLAG
1	ADDRESS FIELD
1 OR 2	CONTROL FIELD
≥ 0	INFORMATION FIELD
2	FRAME CHECK SEQUENCE FIELD
1	CLOSING FLAG

Figure 6.4 Frame format at the Data Link Layer.

nization purposes). In addition, a *start–stop framing* option[2] is available in some networks. X.25 Layer 2, as derived from HDLC, uses a unique bit pattern known as a *flag* to mark the beginning and end of a frame;[3] these flags are known as the *opening* and *closing* flags of the frame. Bits, if any, between flags constitute the remaining fields of the frame: the Address, Control, and Frame Check Sequence (FCS) Fields must always be present for a frame to be valid; an Information Field may be present, depending on the frame type. Consecutive flags in the bit stream indicate the absence of a frame. Some Layer 2 implementations purposely send a series of consecutive flags to avoid swamping a slower receiver with too many frames.

To allow the use of any bit pattern by the Packet Layer while still being able to detect a closing flag, the Data Link Layer employs a *transparency*

---

[2] The start–stop option was agreed to in 1991 for inclusion in the 1993 version of X.25. This allows DTEs that transmit in start–stop mode to use the X.25 procedures by surrounding each octet of the frame with start and stop bits to synchronize at the octet level.

[3] Methods used in other environments for delimiting information include time synchronization of the bit stream or violation of the bit-encoding rules of the Physical Layer.

procedure for the information between flags. This procedure inserts bits (for synchronous framing) or octets (for start–stop framing) before transmission while removing them upon reception.

Address Field

The 1-octet Address Field, which is present in every X.25 frame, serves to distinguish between frames that are *commands* and those that are *responses*. This usage is a result of the X.25 Data Link Layer's heritage from HDLC.[4]

Control Field

The Control Field is used to indicate the particular frame type as well as several other items depending on the frame type. Table 6.2 identifies the different frame types used in LAPB and the function(s) each provides. These frames are classified into three groups of formats (not to be confused with the command/response classification mentioned above): Information, Supervisory, and Unnumbered formats.

Information Field

In HDLC and LAPB, there are no explicit indications that an Information Field is present in a frame. Its existence is indicated by the presence of octets after the Control Field but before the FCS Field. In LAPB only two frames contain an Information Field: the I frame and the FRMR frame; any other frame with octets between the Control and FCS Fields is considered to be in error. The Information Field of an I frame contains exactly one Layer 3 packet. In an FRMR frame, the Information Field contains information about the errored frame being reported on and is used for error analysis by Layer 2.

---

[4] In general, HDLC uses the Address Field to identify the destination station to receive a frame, where there can be more than two stations connected by the same Physical Layer. The scope of X.25, where the DTE and DCE are the only two stations, does not require the added functionality of this field. Of more importance is the actual frame type, which is determined by the Control Field augmented by the indication in the Address Field as to whether the frame is a command or a response.

Table 6.2 LAPB Frames

Frame Format	Frame Types	Function	Frame Used As:[a]	Has Sequence Number(s)?[b]	Has Information Field?
Information					
	I (information)	Carry packets for Packet Layer Acknowledge I frames received	C	Send and receive	Yes
Supervisory					
	RR (receive ready)	Ready to receive more I frames Acknowledge I frames received	C or R	Receive	No
	RNR (receive not ready)	Not ready to receive more I frames Acknowledge I frames received	C or R	Receive	No
	REJ (reject)	Request retransmission of I frames Acknowledge I frames received	C or R	Receive	No
Unnumbered					
	SABM (set asynchronous balanced mode)	Request data link initialization with modulo 8 numbering Reset the data link	C	No	No
	SABME (set asynchronous balanced mode extended)	Same as SABM except used with modulo 128 numbering	C	No	No
	DISC (disconnect)	Request data link disconnection	C	No	No
	UA (unnumbered acknowledgment)	Acknowledge SABM/SABME/ DISC frames	R	No	No
	DM (disconnect mode)	Indicate disconnected mode Request initialization	R	No	No
	FRMR (frame reject)	Report certain error types and request data link reinitialization	R	No[c]	Yes

[a] C denotes a frame used as a Command while R denotes a frame used as a Response.

[b] The use of *Send Sequence Numbers* and *Receive Sequence Numbers* is described below under Information Transfer.

[c] The FRMR frame does not carry a sequence number in its Control Field. However, its Information Field may carry sequence number information pertaining to the errored frame it is reporting on.

Frame Check Sequence Field

All frames carry the Frame Check Sequence (FCS) Field, consisting of the 2 octets preceding the closing flag. The FCS Field is used to ensure the integrity of frames transmitted across the DTE/DCE interface. The contents of this field are calculated based on the transmitted bits (not including any extra bits or octets inserted for transparency, start and stop bits, or flags) in the preceding fields of the frame. The receiver of a frame also generates an FCS as bits are received and then compares its FCS to that at the end of the frame. If they are equal, the receiver processes the frame further; otherwise, the frame is ignored.

LAPB Procedures

Rather than describing each frame in Table 6.2 individually, the following discussion focuses on the various functions defined by LAPB. These functions, in turn, involve the exchange of frames across the data link to accomplish their objectives.

Note that a few procedural aspects have already been discussed above under "General Layer 2 Encoding Principles" while describing the frame fields. These included frame delimiting by flags, transparency by bit/octet insertion and removal, and frame integrity by FCS generation and verification. These procedures, which are sometimes referred to collectively as *framing functions*, are considered as very basic functions; they apply to all frames in HDLC, including those not in the LAPB subset, as well as to many other protocols in common use (e.g., the SDLC of IBM's SNA). They are usually implemented in hardware on chips known as *framing chips*, which then can be used as a base for any protocol using the HDLC framing functions (even if not using the rest of HDLC). There are also chips that combine the framing functions with the X.25 LAPB procedures described below.

Data Link Initialization

Initialization of the logical data link at Layer 2 involves the exchange of a SABM or SABME frame and a UA frame. Either the DTE or the DCE can initiate link set-up by sending the SABM/SABME frame. The station receiving this frame indicates its willingness to accept link set-up by returning a UA frame; if the station is not willing to accept link set-up, then it returns a DM frame. In case of collision where both stations send a SABM (or both send a SABME) frame, then both stations also return a UA frame. The DCE may also invite the DTE to initiate link set-up by sending it an unsolicited DM frame.

The choice of which frame, SABM or SABME, to use for link set-up depends on the scheme to be used for numbering I (Information) frames during the information transfer phase. SABM is used for *modulo 8* numbering, whereas SABME is used for *modulo 128*. Modulo 8 numbering is available in all PSPDNs, whereas modulo 128 numbering is an option that is available only in some networks. More detail on how these schemes operate will be given below.

Information Transfer

Once the data link has been initialized, information transfer using I frames may commence. In X.25, the sole purpose of transferring I frames is to carry Layer 3 packets; each I frame carries one packet. Each I frame is numbered using a *Send Sequence Number*, referred to as N(S). The receiver of I frames acknowledges their receipt by returning a *Receive Sequence Number*, referred to as N(R). Each direction of data transfer (DTE-to-DCE and DCE-to-DTE) is independent of the other; a separate N(S) and N(R) is used for each direction.

The counting for N(S) and N(R) starts at zero when link set-up has been completed. It continues up to the value of modulo − 1, as selected during the link set-up process with the SABM or SABME. For example, if a SABM frame was used for link set-up, then the counting for I frames goes from 0 through 7; the next I frame sent after 7 is again numbered 0 and the numbering continues to repeat.

Only a maximum number of I frames can be transmitted by a station before it must stop and wait for acknowledgment of at least the first I frame. This maximum number is referred to as a *window* and is a parameter denoted by *k*. In X.25, the value of k must be the same for both directions of information transfer, although this restriction does not exist in HDLC. For example, if a value of 4 has been agreed for k, then after link set-up the DTE can send I frames with N(S) values of 0, 1, 2, and 3 (as can the DCE in the other direction) before stopping to wait for acknowledgment of at least I frame #0. As mentioned above, the receiver of I frames returns an N(R) to indicate acknowledgment of I frames up through and including N(R) − 1 and that the next I frame expected is the one whose N(S) would equal N(R). However, this does not imply that the receiver must return an N(R) for each I frame it wishes to acknowledge; the receiver may send back an N(R) that acknowledges several I frames at the same time. Upon receipt of an N(R), the transmitter *rotates* its window so that the first N(S) in the window (sometimes referred to as the *Lower Window Edge* or LWE) is equal to N(R). The *Upper Window Edge* or UWE (that is, the N[S] of the last I frame that could be transmitted before being required to stop) is just equal to LWE + k − 1. The concepts of numbering, window size, and window rotation are illustrated Figure 6.5.

Under normal circumstances where I frames are not lost and the receiving station is able to keep pace with the transmitter, the process of transmitting

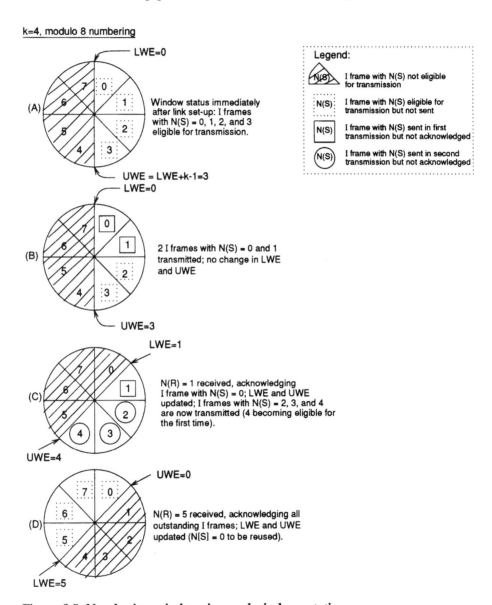

Figure 6.5　Numbering, window size, and window rotation.

I frames, receiving acknowledgments via N(R), rotating the window and updating the LWE, and transmitting new I frames can continue uninterrupted. However, unusual events can occur and the procedures of LAPB must be robust enough to recover in such cases. These procedures are beyond the scope of this overview but are detailed in reference [1].

It is worth examining the issue of selecting modulo 8 or 128 for numbering I frames in a little more detail here. A goal of Layer 2 operation is to *not* become the bottleneck in allowing Layer 3 packets to be transmitted; at the same time, the bandwidth of Layer 1 (i.e., its throughput or the number of bits per second that can be sent) should not be wasted by having the circuit become idle. Since Layer 2 introduces numbering and windows, one must be careful not to choose too small a window lest it be forced to stop transmitting I frames while waiting for acknowledgment. In turn, the window is bounded by the modulo numbering scheme; because of the possibility of errors, the window size cannot be greater than the value of modulo – 1 (because of possible ambiguity as to which I frame an N[R] refers to). The selection of the smallest window size so that Layer 2 does not become the bottleneck depends on several factors. Among the primary factors are the throughput and round-trip delay of the Layer 1 circuit connecting the DTE and DCE. Another important parameter is the maximum I frame size used at Layer 2[5] (LAPB parameter *N1*). In addition, the processing time of a frame by a DTE and a DCE needs to be accounted for, but this is usually small compared to the above factors.

Figure 6.6 [6] shows, as a function of throughput and delay, the dividing line between modulo 8 and modulo 128 usage for efficient Layer 2 operation (i.e., Layer 2 will not be the bottleneck); that is, for a given throughput and round-trip delay at Layer 1, modulo 8 numbering will suffice if N1 is chosen large enough to be a point on or above the dividing line (recalling, however, that N1 is only the maximum frame size, but it is the actual frame-size distribution that matters). In other words, if N1 lies on or above this line, then a window size (k) of 7 or less can be used and modulo 8 suffices. If N1 is chosen to be below the line, then modulo 128 numbering is needed so that a window size larger than 7 can be used. For most X.25 interfaces, the typical values for throughput (usually no more than about 10,000 bits per second), delay (usually no more than about 10 milliseconds), and frame size

---

[5] The actual distribution of sizes of transmitted I frames is more important but there is no way to know this at Layer 2 since it depends on the operation of Layer 3 and higher-layer protocols.

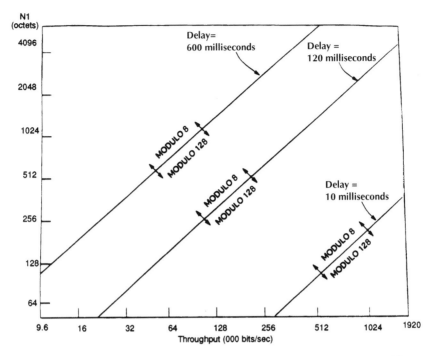

Figure 6.6 Regions for efficient operation using modulo 8 versus 128.

(usually at least 100 octets) are such that modulo 8 numbering suffices. However, if the X.25 interface is operating at a throughput and/or delay measured in the hundreds rather than the tens (bits per second of through-put or milliseconds of delay), than modulo 128 numbering is needed so that a larger window size can be used. For example, the round-trip delay when the Layer 1 circuit uses a satellite link is about 600 milliseconds; this is likely to require modulo 128 numbering for efficient operation, even at low throughput values, if the value of N1 is small. Guidelines based on the above principles have been added to the 1993 version of X.25 to help implemen-tors determine appropriate parameter values.

Receiving I Frames

As the transmitter numbers I frames consecutively, the receiver expects to receive I frames without any gaps in their numbering. The $N(R)$ returned by the receiver indicates acknowledgment for all I frames up through and including $N(R) - 1$ and the fact that the receiver is next expecting the I frame with N(S) equal to N(R). If there are no unusual circumstances, then the N(R) is returned in either an I frame carrying data in the reverse direction[6] or an RR (receive ready) frame (as either a command or a response). The receipt of an N(R) different than the previous N(R) allows the transmitter to release the buffers associated with acknowledged I frames. It also allows the transmitter to update its LWE and to transmit *new* I frames whose N(S) is less than or equal to the revised UWE (however, any I frames in the new LWE-UWE range that were previously transmitted are not sent again). This was depicted in part (C) of Figure 6.5.

One cannot assume that I frames will always be received without errors. For example, a bit error at Layer 1 may have resulted in the receiver's calculated FCS being different than the FCS carried in the I frame. In this case the frame would have been discarded, but a gap in the N(S) values would be detected when the next I frame is correctly received. In this situation, the receiver asks for retransmission of the missing I frame by sending back an N(R) in an REJ (reject) command or response frame. This N(R) still carries the same meaning (vis-à-vis acknowledging I frames and indicating the next I frame to be received), but the use of an REJ frame is taken as a request for retransmission of *all* I frames starting with an N(S) equal to the N(R). This form of error recovery is known as *Go-Back-N* (GBN) since the transmitter goes back "N" frames and resumes transmission from there.

Another problem that may arise at the receiver is a temporary inability to accept more I frames. This may occur, even with a proper choice of window size, because of several reasons; for example, the receiving station's Layer 3 is not accepting packets from Layer 2. In these cases, a station may wish to acknowledge the I frames that it has received but indicate at the same time that the transmitter should stop sending I frames. To do so, the receiver can return an N(R) but in an RNR (receive not ready) command or response frame to indicate a *busy* condition. This allows the transmitter to update its LWE and UWE but requires it to stop sending new I frames. This is known as *flow controlling* the sender[7] When the receiver is ready to accept additional I frames, it sends back either an RR or an REJ frame to clear the busy condition.

---

[6] The ability to acknowledge data for one direction of information transfer at the same time as carrying information in the other direction is known as *piggybacking*.

[7] An alternative method for flow control is to return N(R)s that do *not* advance the sender's LWE, instead of using an RNR frame. However, this leaves previously transmitted I frames as unacknowledged; an undesirable effect as we shall see.

Waiting Acknowlegment

It should be apparent from the preceding discussions that timely acknowlegments are crucial for proper LAPB operation. We have explicitly discussed the acknowlegment of I frames. Other frames may also require acknowlegment; the transmission of an REJ frame is acknowledged by the receipt of the requested I frame. Without acknowlegments, a station may be forced to stop transmitting while waiting for the other station to send a frame. If both the DTE and the DCE find themselves in this situation, then a situation known as *deadlock* has occurred. To ensure timely receipt of acknowlegments, a station starts a timer known as *T1* when it transmits a frame requiring acknowlegment. If this timer should expire before acknowlegment is received, the station invokes the proper recovery procedures as defined by LAPB.

Reinitialization

Certain error conditions are considered severe enough to require the logical data link to be reset. Some of these, such as receipt of a frame with an unrecognized Control Field, may be reported using the FRMR frame prior to reinitializing the link. The DTE or DCE reinitializes the link by sending a SABM/SABME frame. The remainder of the procedure, including setting N(S) and N(R) back to zero, is exactly the same as link initialization. In addition, any busy condition that may have existed as a result of sending an RNR frame prior to the link reinitialization is cleared.

Disconnect

After completing transmission of all I frames (as signaled by some process external to LAPB), the logical data link can be disconnected. The DISC frame is used to initiate the shutdown and needs to be confirmed by a UA frame from the other station. This exchange of frames can be viewed as an orderly disconnect. Of course, an abrupt shutdown (such as turning off the power) will have the same end result if there are no more I frames to transmit and all I frames have been acknowledged.

Multilink Operation

The preceding discussions have focused on the use of LAPB at Layer 2 operating over a single circuit at Layer 1. For a variety of reasons, it may be desirable to have multiple physical circuits at Layer 1; they can be used for reliability purposes or to increase the bandwidth capacity at the DTE/DCE interface. For example, it might be less expensive to lease two low-speed circuits, combining them into one multilink circuit, than to lease a much higher-speed circuit.

X.25 Layer 2 also defines an optional multilink procedure (MLP). The MLP allows for data interchange over one or more *Single Link Procedures* (SLPs) between a DTE and a DCE. Each SLP operates according to the rules of LAPB, as described above, or LAP.

The MLP exists as an added upper sublayer of the Data Link Layer, operating between the Packet Layer and a multiplicity of SLPs in the Data Link Layer. The MLP accepts packets from the Packet Layer and distributes them across the available SLPs for transmission to the remote SLPs. Distribution of packets to SLPs can be done in any desired fashion (e.g., "round robin" for balancing traffic across links or to more than one SLP for redundancy). Depending on how packets are distributed, the receiving MLP may receive packets out of order or multiple copies of the same packet. Since the Packet Layer requires packets to be received in the same order as they were transmitted and without duplication (i.e., it depends on the Data Link Layer as a whole to provide this service), the MLP uses its own sequence number to enable it to resequence packets and to weed out duplicates across all links.

PACKET LAYER OPERATION

Sitting on top of the Data Link Layer is the Packet Layer. This section discusses the operation of the X.25 Packet Layer Protocol (PLP), starting with encoding and then describing the procedures, as was done for the Data Link Layer. Although X.25 strictly defines what goes on at the DTE/DCE interface, most Packet Layer interactions relate to virtual circuit communications between two DTEs. To fully appreciate Packet Layer operation, one must not lose sight of the end-to-end picture. In this section, we focus on communications within the context of a single PSPDN; later we will expand this to a global environment spanning different technologies.

As was shown in Figure 6.3, communication at the Packet Layer is via a virtual circuit which, in turn, is a binding of the logical channel used at each of the two DTE/DCE interfaces involved in an instance of communication. Although logical channels are numbered at each interface, the pair of logical channels associated with a particular virtual circuit need not have the same number; the assignment of logical channel numbers is local to each

DTE/DCE interface. The properties of a virtual circuit are similar to those of the Layer 2 logical data link—perhaps the most fundamental one being the assumption of in-sequence delivery of data on the virtual circuit across the PSPDN(s).[8] X.25 specifies two types of virtual circuit services: a *Virtual Call* (VC) service, where a call set-up and call clearing (i.e., release) phase precede and follow the data transfer phase, and a *Permanent Virtual Circuit* (PVC) service consisting only of the data transfer phase. For PVCs, some of the aspects of call set-up are accomplished in a static, a priori fashion through agreements between the two DTEs and the PSPDN. Although avoiding the call set-up phase would seem to be desirable, this phase offers unique functionality, as illustrated below, which applications may find beneficial. Furthermore, PVCs may not be available on an end-to-end basis when more than one PSPDN is needed to support the virtual circuit between DTEs.

General Layer 3 Encoding Principles

Figure 6.7 illustrates the general format of a *packet*. In contrast to a frame at the Data Link Layer, a packet does not have any explicit delimiters; instead, it is delimited by the boundaries of the Information Field of an I frame. The figure shows that all packets have four fields in common as well as some additional fields depending on the packet type. The common fields are discussed here; the additional fields are described below in the sections dealing with the procedures that use the specific packets.

General Format Identifier

Two bits of the General Format Identifier (GFI) are used to identify the format of the rest of the packet, distinguishing between the use of modulo 8 and modulo 128 numbering in packets that have sequence numbers[9] The use of the other two bits depends on the type of packet.

---

[8] The 1980 version of X.25 defined a *datagram* service, where there was no guarantee of in-sequence delivery, in addition to the virtual circuit services. The datagram option was removed from X.25 in 1984 since no PSPDN operators showed any interest in developing it.

[9] Sequence numbers at the Packet Layer are separate from those at the Data Link Layer. Furthermore, while the selection of modulo 8 or modulo 128 numbering at one layer is independent from the selection at the other layer, there is little if any benefit to using modulo 128 numbering at the Packet Layer with modulo 8 numbering at the Data Link Layer.

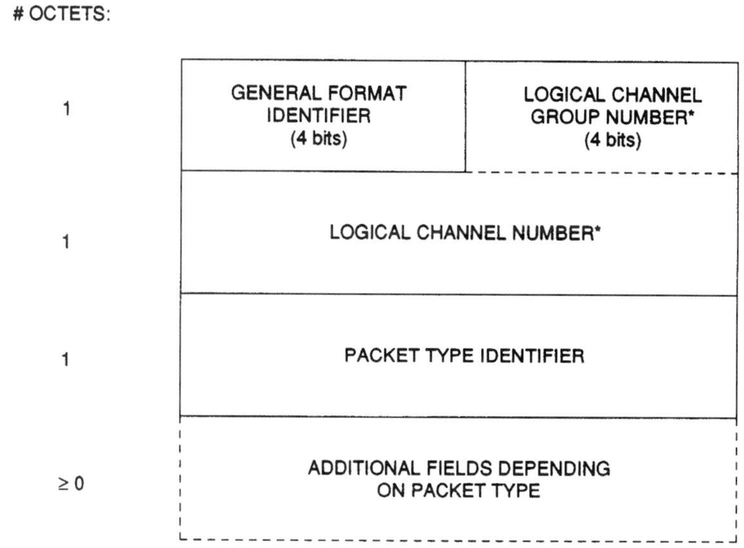

OCTETS:

```
┌─────────────────────────┬─────────────────────────┐
│  GENERAL FORMAT         │  LOGICAL CHANNEL        │
│  IDENTIFIER             │  GROUP NUMBER*          │
│  (4 bits)               │  (4 bits)               │
├─────────────────────────┴─────────────────────────┤
│                                                    │
│         LOGICAL CHANNEL NUMBER*                    │
│                                                    │
├────────────────────────────────────────────────────┤
│                                                    │
│         PACKET TYPE IDENTIFIER                     │
│                                                    │
├ ─ ─ ─ ─ ─ ─ ─ ─ ─ ─ ─ ─ ─ ─ ─ ─ ─ ─ ─ ─ ─ ─ ─ ─ ┤
│         ADDITIONAL FIELDS DEPENDING               │
│         ON PACKET TYPE                             │
└ ─ ─ ─ ─ ─ ─ ─ ─ ─ ─ ─ ─ ─ ─ ─ ─ ─ ─ ─ ─ ─ ─ ─ ─ ┘
```

1

1

1

≥ 0

* These two fields can also be viewed as one 12-bit Logical Channel Idenfitier Field.

Figure 6.7 Packet format.

Logical Channel Fields

As Figure 6.7 showed, there are two fields relating to the logical channel which, for all practical cases, can be regarded as one 12-bit field. When the combined fields contain a value between 1 and 4095, inclusive, this value identifies the virtual circuit to which the packet belongs. Packets with a value of 0 in this field pertain to operation of the DTE/DCE interface as a whole rather than to an individual virtual circuit.

Packet Type Identifier

As its name indicates, this field identifies the type of packet in much the same way as the Control Field of Layer 2 identifies the frame type. Table 6.3 shows the packets used at Layer 3 and their groupings.

Packet Layer Procedures

The procedures of the X.25 Packet Layer can be divided into two sets: those pertaining to a single virtual circuit (associated with the first three groups of

Table 6.3 Packet Groupings, Functions, and Types

Packet Group	Function	Packet Types	Service:[a] VC	PVC
Call set-up and call clearing	Establish and terminate a Virtual Call for DTE/DCE communication; may convey data for higher-layer protocol processing	CALL REQUEST	X	
		INCOMING CALL	X	
		CALL ACCEPTED	X	
		CALL CONNECTED	X	
		CLEAR REQUEST	X	
		CLEAR INDICATION	X	
		CLEAR CONFIRMATION	X	
Data and interrupt	Convey data or interrupt information for higher-layer protocol processing	DATA	X	X
		INTERRUPT	X	X
		INTERRUPT CONFIRMATION	X	X
Flow control and reset	Control the flow of DATA packets across a DTE/DCE interface	RECEIVE READY	X	X
		RECEIVE NOT READY	X	X
		REJECT	X	X
		RESET REQUEST	X	X
		RESET INDICATION	X	X
		RESET CONFIRMATION	X	X
Restart	(Re)Initialize all communication between a DTE and a DCE	RESTART REQUEST	X	X
		RESTART INDICATION	X	X
		RESTART CONFIRMATION	X	X
Diagnostic	Pass error diagnostics to a DTE	DIAGNOSTIC	X	X
Registration	Perform registration procedure	REGISTRATION REQUEST	X	X
		REGISTRATION CONFIRMATION	X	X

[a]VC = Virtual Call; PVC = Permanent Virtual Circuit.

packets in Table 6.3) and those pertaining to the DTE/DCE interface as a whole (associated with the last three groups in Table 6.3). The procedures associated with the first four packet groups are described below; the packets of the last two groups are used only in a few implementations since they are optional.

Call Set-Up and Call Clearing

The call set-up and call clearing procedures, used to establish and terminate a VC, operate in a fashion analogous to a phone call in the voice world. In addition to the common fields shown in Figure 6.7, most of the packets in this group carry addresses (similar to phone numbers) to identify both the calling and called DTEs, *optional user facility* requests and/or indications to change the default mode of operation (see the following section on Optional User Facilities), and some amount of user data for the other DTE.

To establish a VC, a DTE transmits a Call Request packet across its DTE/DCE interface specifying, among other items, the address of the remote DTE. If the PSPDN is able to support the call, it sends an Incoming Call packet to the remote DTE in which it identifies the calling DTE. Various other standards specify the addressing information that can be placed in the Address Fields. If the call can be completed, then the called DTE returns a Call Accepted packet and the calling DTE receives a Call Connected packet. When the DTE sends a Call Request packet and when the DCE sends an Incoming Call packet, they each choose a nonzero logical channel number not in use to represent the virtual circuit at the DTE/DCE interface. These numbers are used to identify subsequent packets associated with the virtual circuit. As part of this process, the network also creates the internal binding that associates the logical channel numbers used with the virtual circuit.

The clearing procedure is used for various reasons to terminate a call. A DTE sends a Clear Request packet across its DTE/DCE interface to indicate normal termination of an already-established VC or to abort a call attempt. Likewise, this packet is used by a DTE to refuse an incoming call. A Clear Indication packet is used by a DCE:

- At the calling DTE/DCE interface if it cannot support a new call (e.g., no available resources in the PSPDN or the remote DTE is not available);

- At a DTE/DCE interface to indicate clearing by the remote DTE; or

- At both DTE/DCE interfaces if the PSPDN must abruptly terminate a call.

Various error cases are also indicated by clearing the call. A station receiving a Clear Request or Clear Indication packet confirms it by transferring a Clear Confirmation packet across the interface to complete the process. Clear Request and Clear Indication packets have Cause and Diagnostic Fields to supply further information as to why the call was cleared. In some cases, further analysis of these fields by a DTE, especially when a new call attempt was cleared, can lead to the DTE retrying the call and possibly succeeding [7].

Figure 6.8 illustrates the call set-up and clearing procedures. Part A of the figure shows that the call set-up procedure is an "end-to-end" procedure; that is, this procedure involves an ordered, four-packet exchange involving

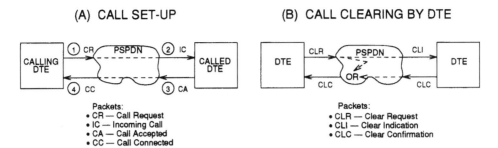

Figure 6.8 Call set-up and call clearing procedure.

both DTEs and the PSPDN in the sequence shown. On the other hand, the VC clearing process can be end-to-end like call set-up or "local" as shown in part B of the figure; this is a design choice of the PSPDN.

Data and Interrupt Transfer

Information transfer takes on several forms at the Packet Layer. For a VC, information transfer can take place only after successful establishment of a call; for a PVC, no call set-up is needed but the remote DTE must be operational. *Normal data* is transferred using Data packets whereas a limited amount of *expedited data* can also be exchanged using Interrupt packets. (Furthermore, a limited amount of data can also be transferred using the call set-up and clearing packets.)

Data packets are numbered with a *Packet Send Sequence Number*, referred to as $P(S)$, which functions in the same fashion as $N(S)$ at the Data Link Layer. These packets have a User Data Field for carrying information for the virtual-circuit user who, in turn, is defined by a standard other than X.25. There are also several other aspects of Data packets that are important.

- The User Data Field of a Data packet has a maximum size that is agreed to by the DTE and DCE. This value, usually referred to as the *packet size*, applies independently for each direction of data transfer at the DTE/DCE interface and to each interface of the virtual circuit. The default packet size is 128 octets; optional user facilities are available to change this value for both VCs and PVCs as well as to negotiate different sizes during VC set-up.

- While PSPDNs limit the packet size that can be used, there is no restriction on the size of the data unit ("message") that the Packet Layer user can request to be transferred to its peer. To preserve the boundaries of the user's data, the Packet Layer provides a *segmentation and reassembly* function, which uses the *More Data* (M)-bit in a Data packet. When the M-bit is set to 1, the User Data Field of the current Data packet is to be logically concatenated with that of the next packet; a Data packet with its M-bit set to 0 marks the end of the sequence of User Data Fields that belong together.

- Another capability is to mark Data packets as carrying *unqualified* or *qualified* data using the *Qualifier* (Q)-bit (part of the GFI). This allows the user of the Packet Layer to transfer two streams of data: one for its own use and one for some other user. The decision to use the Q-bit and the meaning of unqualified (Q-bit = 0) versus qualified (Q-bit = 1) data are controlled by the user of the Packet Layer. Data packets are numbered consecutively regardless of whether their Q-bits are set to 0 or 1.

- The Packet Layer also provides a *Delivery Confirmation* capability using the D-bit (also in the GFI). This capability is related to the flow-control functions of the Packet Layer but will not be discussed here.

Interrupt packets, which are not numbered, are used to carry a small amount of data (up to 32 octets starting in 1984, 1 octet prior to that) from one DTE to the other. Although the routes traveled through the network by Data and Interrupt packets may be different, Interrupt packets are guaranteed to be delivered to the remote DTE prior to Data packets that were transmitted subsequent to the Interrupt packet. An Interrupt packet may, however, get ahead of Data packets that were transmitted before it.

Flow Control and Reset

Flow control and reset operate in much the same fashion at the Packet Layer as they do at the Data Link Layer *with respect to the DTE/DCE interface.* This section will also focus on some of the end-to-end consequences of these procedures as they relate to virtual circuit operation.

Packet Layer flow control makes use of the window,[10] window rotation, and LWE/UWE concepts introduced in the discussion on the Data Link Layer. Numbering of Data packets uses P(S), instead of N(S), and both

---

[10]A different window size can be chosen for each direction of data transfer at the Packet Layer of the DTE/DCE interface, unlike operation at the Data Link Layer. The default window size for each direction is 2.

modulo 8 and modulo 128 numbering are available, as already mentioned. The Packet Layer equivalent of N(R) is known as the *Packet Receive Sequence Number*, or P(R); this value can be carried in RR, RNR, and Reject packets as well as piggybacked in Data packets. RR and RNR packets operate in an analogous fashion as their Layer 2 counterparts. However, the Reject packet, which is an *optional* Packet Layer feature that is rarely implemented, is used only by the DTE to request retransmission of Data packets by the DCE across the DTE/DCE interface (and not by the remote DTE across the virtual circuit). In addition to the above interface-specific aspects, there are also some end-to-end items that pertain to Packet Layer flow control.

- Although the window sizes at each DTE/DCE interface of a virtual circuit can be chosen independently, PSPDNs may force the two window sizes for a given direction of data transfer to be the same. Since PSPDNs cannot absorb an unlimited number of Data packets, they typically operate an internal window for the virtual circuit in conjunction with the interface-specific windows. Coupling of the two DTE/DCE windows simplifies matters.

- Just as one can talk about the throughput of the Layer 1 circuit between the DTE and DCE, the concept of a *throughput class* applies to each direction of data transfer of the Layer 3 virtual circuit. This can be regarded simply as the steady-state rate at which information could be transferred between the two DTEs across the PSPDN(s) under optimal conditions. The actual virtual-circuit throughput is affected by the statistical sharing of transmission and switching resources of the DTEs and the PSPDN. Included in these resources, for example, are the throughput of the Layer 1 DTE-DCE connection and the window sizes at each DTE/DCE interface of the virtual circuit. Because of the multiplexing of many logical channels onto a single physical link (unless MLP is used), it is possible for the sum of the throughput classes of all virtual circuits at the interface to exceed the Layer 1 throughput. The default throughput class for each direction of data transfer for all logical channels is chosen when the interface is established; it is either a value chosen by the DTE or bounded by the data rate of the Layer 1 circuit.

The reset procedure is used to report certain errors in Packet Layer operation, such as a gap in the P(S) numbers of received Data packets (unless the optional Reject packet can be used) or a Data packet size that is too long. Resetting a Layer 3 virtual circuit is similar to many concepts that have already been discussed: P(S) and P(R) are both set back to zero and any busy condition that existed is considered cleared. A DTE initiates the procedure by transmitting a Reset Request packet for the logical channel, whereas a DCE initiates it by sending a Reset Indication packet; in either case, the corresponding logical channel at the remote DTE/DCE interface is also reset. Both of these packets carry Cause and Diagnostic Fields to aid in error analysis and are confirmed by the receiving station sending a Reset Confirmation packet. Just like the VC clearing procedure, DTE-initiated resets can be either confirmed locally or as a result of the confirmation at the remote DTE/DCE interface. When a virtual circuit is reset, any Data and Interrupt packets in transit across the network may be lost.

Restart

The restart procedure is used to (re)initialize the entire Packet Layer operation at a DTE/DCE interface. As such, an exchange of Restart Request/Indication and Restart Confirmation packets must be completed before any VCs can be established or any data transferred on a PVC. While a restart procedure at one interface does not result in the same procedure at other interface(s), it does result in a clearing of any VCs and a resetting of any PVCs at all remote interfaces. The Restart Request and Indication packets also carry Cause and Diagnostic Fields.

Optional User Facilities

Associated with the Packet Layer are numerous *Optional User Facilities* (OUFs) that alter some of the default modes of operation. In all cases, the default set of procedures can be used to achieve simple connectivity. At the Packet Layer, the basic capability to connect DTEs is the Layer 3 virtual circuit (either a PVC or a VC). In many cases, default Packet Layer procedures have also been explicitly mentioned; for example, the use of packet sizes of 128 octets and window sizes of 2. Other aspects have been implicit, such as the DTE originating a VC pays for the call, and the call can only be completed to the originally called DTE (i.e., no "call-forwarding" actions take place). X.25 defines about 40 OUFs, or facilities for short, that can be used to alter the default modes of operation. A DTE is never required to use an OUF but agreement with the network to do so provides a useful alternative to the default approach if needed by an application [8].

The OUFs available in PSPDNs can be categorized in the following groups:

- Addressing-related facilities
- Routing-related facilities
- Charging-related facilities
- Protection-related facilities
- Data transfer–related facilities
- Facilities to convey user data other than during the data transfer phase
- Miscellaneous facilities

Below, the use and application of some of the OUFs available in X.25 are described. Further descriptions can be found in X.25 itself and in newly adopted Recommendation X.7 [9].

Call Redirection/Deflection and Related Facilities

Call Redirection and Call Deflection allow a VC to be completed for a DTE other than the originally called DTE. These OUFs, together with several others, provide complete control and feedback during the call set-up phase of how the call is completed.

Figure 6.9 illustrates the interaction among these OUFs. The figure shows DTE A calling DTE B but Call Redirection is used at DTE B's interface if, for example, it has been taken out of service for preventive maintenance. The PSPDN, using a database associated with DTE B, redirects the call to DTE C. DTE A need have no knowledge of DTE B being out of order. If DTE B had been operable, an Incoming Call packet would have been sent to it by the DCE. However, DTE B might then deflect the call to DTE C based on information in the packet such as the user data; such procedures could be used for security screening based on this data. From this point onward, redirection and deflection operate in the same fashion. A new call is made to DTE C, with the *Call Redirection or Call Deflection Notification* facility indicating that the call is a result of the corresponding action at another interface. Finally, the Call Connected packet sent to DTE A contains the *Called Line Address Modified Notification* facility to indicate that the call was completed to another DTE and the reason. DTE A may also have the ability to explicitly prevent the redirection/deflection action, since such actions could go from one network to another while incurring unexpected charges.

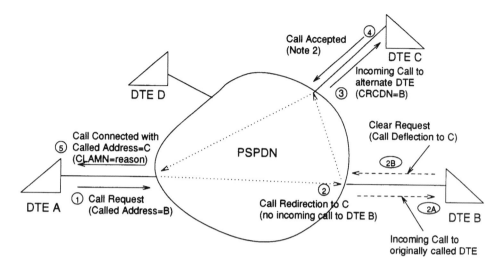

Note 1: Redirections may be logically chained. If DTE C has subscribed to call redirection to DTE D, a call redirection from DTE B to DTE C may be redirected to DTE D.

Note 2: DTE C may also clear the call, in which case (4) is a clear request and (5) is a clear indication.

Legend:
CRCDN = Call Redirection or Call Deflection Notification
CLAMN = Called Line Address Modified Notification

Figure 6.9 Use of call redirection/deflection and related OUFs.

Alternative Addressing

A Call Request packet must identify the remote DTE to which a call is being made. By default, it is assumed that all addresses conform to Recommendation X.121 [10], which specifies the format of addresses used by PSPDNs. The set of *Alternative Addressing* facilities, which has been added to the 1993 version of X.25, allows the called DTE to be identified using an address belonging to some other standard[11] or by a mnemonic address.

---

[11]X.121 also provides for "escapes" to other numbering plans for public networks under the control of CCITT. The standards recognized under the Alternative Addressing capabilities are not CCITT numbering plans. They include, for example, the OSI Network Layer address plan, LAN addresses, and Internet addresses.

The use of these facilities by DTEs requires registration with the PSPDN of a translation of alternative addresses to an X.121 address. Translations can be:

- Of the form *N-to-1* (i.e., N alternative addresses to one X.121 address) or *1-to-N* (i.e., one alternative address to N different X.121 addresses, with translation of the alternative address to a single X.121 address being done by the PSPDN at the time of call set-up);
- Dependent on time of day or call originator, etc. (as in the voice world); or
- Dependent on other parameters in the Call Request packet (e.g., delay).

An example of *1-to-N* mapping is illustrated in Figure 6.10. The example shows a multihomed host. Calls to this host use the alternative address "X" associated with it, which is translated by PSPDN1 into one of the N different X.121 addresses, including into an address on PSPDN2.

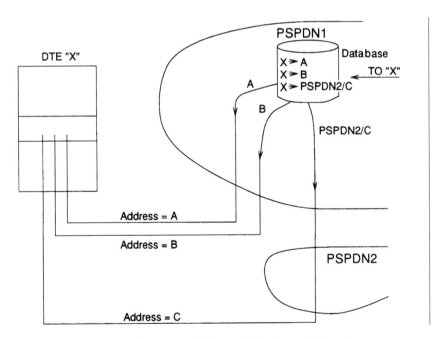

Figure 6.10 Use of alternative address calling in multihoming case.

Closed User Group

The set of *Closed User Group* (CUG) facilities enables a DTE to form one or more groups with different combinations of restrictions for access from or to other DTEs. This provides for an extra level of protection from DTEs that do not belong to the group; the CUG identity can be viewed as an extra "password" needed to access another DTE. The administrative arrangements for operation of the CUG feature, including the assignment of the CUG identity itself, are specified in Recommendation X.180 [11]. If a DTE belongs to more than one CUG, it also specifies a *preferential* CUG. Some PSPDNs allow a DTE to choose not to designate any CUG as being preferred (i.e., specification of a preferential CUG is always allowed).

The following CUG facilities are all optional user facilities that are agreed on for a period of time by the DTE and the PSPDN.

- **Closed user group:** This is the basic facility that enables a DTE to belong to one or more CUGs and to make/receive calls only to/from other DTEs in the same CUG.

- **Closed user group with outgoing access:** This is an extension of the basic CUG facility that also enables the DTE to make outgoing calls to the *open* part of the network (i.e., to DTEs not belonging to any CUG) and to DTEs in different CUGs that accept incoming access (calls from DTEs in other CUGs).

- **Closed user group with incoming access:** This is an extension of the basic CUG facility that also enables the DTE to receive incoming calls from the open part of the network and from DTEs in different CUGs that have outgoing access (they can make calls to DTEs in other CUGs).

- **Incoming calls barred within the closed user group:** This is a supplementary facility to the first three CUG facilities that, when used, applies per CUG and prohibits the DTE from receiving calls from other members of that CUG.

- **Outgoing calls barred within the closed user group:** This is a supplementary facility to the first three CUG facilities that, when used, applies per CUG and prohibits the DTE from making calls to other members of that CUG.

The indication of the relevant CUG pertaining to a call is specified at the time of setting it up. If a preferential CUG has been designated, then ab-

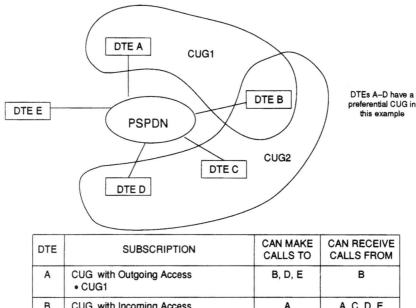

DTE	SUBSCRIPTION	CAN MAKE CALLS TO	CAN RECEIVE CALLS FROM
A	CUG with Outgoing Access • CUG1	B, D, E	B
B	CUG with Incoming Access • CUG1 • CUG2 with Outgoing Calls Barred	A	A, C, D, E
C	CUG • CUG2	B	D
D	CUG with Incoming Access • CUG2 with Incoming Calls Barred	B, C	A, E
E	No CUG Subscription	B, D	A

Figure 6.11 Allowed access capabilities for hypothetical CUG environment.

sence of a CUG when a call is set up is taken to implicitly select the preferred CUG as applying for the call.

Figure 6.11 illustrates some of the allowed combinations of access for a hypothetical set of CUG subscriptions of five DTEs.

Other Optional User Facilities

Below is a sampling of the other optional user facilities available in X.25.

- Modulo 8 is the default method for numbering Data packets at the Packet Layer. The *Extended Packet Sequence Numbering* OUF selects use of modulo 128 numbering of packets. Whichever modulus is chosen applies to all logical channels on the DTE/DCE interface.

- The default use of window size of 2 and Data packet size of 128 can be changed using the *Nonstandard Default Window/Packet Sizes* OUFs. The values chosen using these facilities pertain to all logical channels. For Virtual Calls, values different than the defaults can be negotiated at call set-up using the *Flow Control Parameter Negotiation* OUF. Alternative window sizes that can be chosen range from 1 to modulo – 1; alternative packet sizes range from 16 to 4096 octets in multiples of two.

- When a Virtual Call is established, it is assumed that the calling DTE will be charged for the call. The *Reverse Charging* facility allows the calling DTE to request that the called DTE pay for the call. The network will only send an Incoming Call packet to the called DTE with a request for reverse charging if it subscribes to the *Reverse Charging Acceptance* facility.

X.25-BASED ENTERPRISE NETWORKING

Given the ubiquity of X.25 PSPDNs and products, there are many advantages to basing a global enterprise network on X.25 capabilities. Figure 6.12 illustrates a global X.25-based environment spanning different types of technologies. As noted at the start of this chapter, however, Recommendation X.25 really describes only the interface to a PSPDN; it does not address many of the issues needed to develop such a global network. As also mentioned in the Introduction, there are many CCITT Recommendations and ISO/IEC Standards that have been developed over the years to complement and supplement X.25. This section provides a brief description of these Recommendations and Standards to flesh out the picture presented in Figure 6.12.

Complementary Recommendations and Standards

X.25 was never meant to stand alone, as mentioned at the outset of this chapter. The Recommendations and Standards described below fill in the "gaps" of X.25 in the PSPDN environment.

- **General PSPDN Access Arrangements.** Recommendation X.1 [12] describes the general access arrangements to public data networks. It describes the combinations of speeds and DTE modes of operation that can be used (*user classes of service*) as well as the allowed access scenarios to a public data network through other networks (*categories of access*). Other access speeds and/or modes can also be supported at the discretion of the network provider.

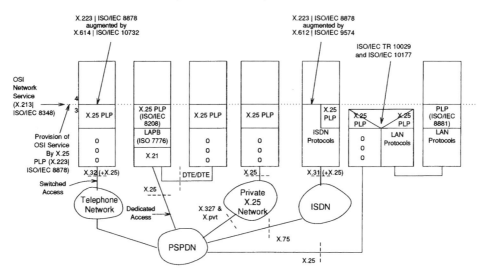

Figure 6.12 Global internet environment using the X.25 PLP.

- **Classification of Services and Facilities.** Recommendation X.2 [13] indicates the level of support required of public data networks for services and optional user facilities. Items that must be supported are designated as *Essential* in X.2, whereas those that a network has the option of supporting are designated as *Additional*. For example, the Flow Control Parameter Negotiation facility is Essential, whereas the Nonstandard Default Packet Sizes facility is Additional.

- **DTE Specifications.** While X.25 describes how a DCE operates, it does not pertain to DTE operation and leaves numerous options for DTEs to select. ISO/IEC International Standards 7776 [14] and 8208 [15] describe, respectively, Layer 2 and Layer 3 DTE operation.

- **Testing.** Many PSPDNs require a DTE to undergo some type of testing before permitting it to connect. In many cases, a DTE may just need to show that it will not harm the network (basically, a Layer 1 test). In other cases, the DTE must also show that it is capable of correctly operating the Layer 2 and 3 protocols. The ISO/IEC 8882 set of International Standards [16] provides Layer 2 and 3 test definitions.

- **Addressing.** As already noted above, Recommendation X.121 defines the numbering plan used in *public* data networks. This plan is a hierarchical scheme consisting of a maximum of 14 digits. Usually, the first four digits define a world zone, a country, and a network within the country. The remaining digits, up to 10, are assigned by the network to identify a particular DTE.

- **Call Progress Signals.** Recommendation X.96 [17] defines the *call progress signals* that may be present in the Cause Field of a Reset, Clear, or Restart Request or Indication packet and classifies them into several categories. For example, the call progress signal of "Reverse Charging Not Subscribed" is classified as a permanent error for which retrying the call with the same Call Request packet will not succeed. However, a DTE may wish to retry a call if it fails for "Number Busy."

- **Arrangements for Providing Capabilities.** As mentioned above, Recommendation X.180 describes the administrative arrangements for provision of the closed user group feature. X.181 [18] provides a parallel description for the X.25 PVC feature. Finally, X.301 [19] provides an abstract description of the flow of information, particularly for call set-up and clearing, within and across networks to support the features defined at the X.25 interface.

- **Performance.** Recommendations X.134 through X.140 [20] define various performance aspects, such as speed of service and availability of PSPDNs. Recommendation X.92 [21] provides a framework for the above recommendations by splitting a virtual circuit in its component parts (e.g., DTE access links, internetwork links).

- **Interworking between PSPDNs.** Recommendation X.75 [22] defines the interface between two PSPDNs for supporting a virtual circuit that spans more than one network. Many of its procedures are similar or identical to those of X.25. Recommendation X.110 [23] describes the routing principles for the establishment of VCs across PSPDNs.

- **Charging.** While PSPDNs are free to specify their own tariffs for use on intranetwork virtual circuits, Recommendations D.10 through D.12 [24] specify the charging principles for virtual circuits that cross international boundaries. For example, D.11 indicates that a network may charge for a call attempt unless it fails due to network congestion or equipment problems.

- **Management.** Two ISO/IEC International Standards define *managed objects* that relate to X.25 resources to allow users to manage their operations. For example, the PVC object allows users to find out information such as the number of Data packets sent for accounting purposes. Likewise, information about the number of FCS errors at the

Data Link Layer can also be obtained for fault-management purposes. ISO/IEC draft 10742 [25] defines objects for the Data Link Layer while ISO/IEC 10733 [26] defines objects for the Packet Layer. The information is conveyed using general-purpose management protocols.

- **Higher-Layer Protocols.** A DTE may have several protocols capable of operating over the X.25 Packet Layer. ISO/IEC Technical Report (TR) 9577 [27] provides a mechanism for identifying these protocols so that the correct procedures can be used over each virtual circuit. This identifier can be carried in the User Data Field of a Call Request packet.

Supplementary Recommendations and Standards

In addition to filling in the gaps, CCITT and ISO/IEC have worked together to extend the use of X.25 (or X.25-like procedures) to environments beyond the packet-mode interface to a PSPDN. It is these Recommendations and Standards, which are described below, that extend X.25 capabilities across other technologies

Switched Access to a PSPDN

As indicated in its title, X.25 assumes a dedicated circuit is used between the DTE and DCE. For backup or other purposes, it may be desirable that a switched connection be used between the DTE and DCE. Recommendation X.32 [28] specifies additional considerations for this mode of operation. For example, X.32 specifies authentication procedures to verify the identity of the DTE when it connects to the network.

Figure 6.13 represents a more general view of the X.25 protocol stack depicted in Figure 6.2, which incorporates the aspects of X.32. In this case, a parallel set of Layer 2 and Layer 3 protocols exist for setting up the path between the DTE and DCE. The protocols on the left are used first to interact with the switched network to establish a path between the DTE and the DCE. Once this path is set up, the X.25 Layer 2 and Layer 3 protocols are used between the DTE and DCE.

DTE-to-DTE Operation

DTEs using ISO/IEC 7776 and 8208 can also operate without an intervening PSPDN, in *DTE-to-DTE mode*. Issues that are prespecified in X.25 for a DTE/DCE environment are resolved for DTE-to-DTE operation in these standards. In the general case, these standards can be viewed as describing a "DTE/DXE interface" since, for the most part, it does not matter if the station at the other side of the interface is a DCE or a DTE (i.e., the other station is a "DXE").

Integrated Services Digital Networks (ISDNs)

ISDNs allow users to combine voice, data, and other information in one network. Recommendation X.31 [29] recognizes X.25 as the initial definition of packet-mode data services for an ISDN terminal. X.31 defines two scenarios for accessing X.25 services: *Case A*, where the X.25 services are provided by a PSPDN, and *Case B*, where they are provided by the ISDN itself (although, in fact, the X.25 packet handler may physically be located in the PSPDN). Depending on the specific details of the scenario, the resulting protocol stack may resemble Figure 6.2, where only Layer 1 is different, or Figure 6.13, with ISDN-specific protocols replacing X.21 on the left side of the protocol stack and at Layer 1. In one of the ISDN Case B scenarios, the Q.921 LAPD protocol [30], which is quite similar to LAPB, is used below the X.25 PLP, again taking advantage of the layer-independence concepts. Recommendation X.75 is also used for interworking between a PSPDN and an ISDN providing packet-mode services (i.e., Case B operation).

Local Area Networks (LANs)

Many of the features of the X.25 Packet Layer, such as the ability to dynamically establish connections using the X.25 VC capability, are useful by sta-

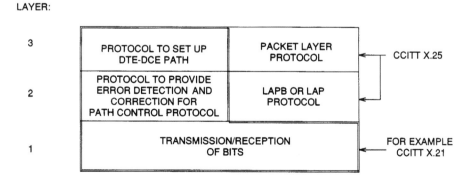

LAYER:

Figure 6.13   Generalized X.25 + X.32 protocol stack.

tions on a LAN. International Standard 8881 [31] provides additional considerations operating ISO/IEC 8208 as the Layer 3 protocol in LANs. In this environment, ISO/IEC 8208 is usually used in the DTE-to-DTE mode and operates over a protocol other than LAPB, again invoking the layer-independence concept.

Public-to-Private X.25 Interworking

Many large organizations have their own private X.25 network to which only their systems can connect. It was decided in the early 1980s that X.25, rather than X.75, would be used as the interface between a PSPDN and a private X.25 network. Several enhancements have been made to X.25 over the years, such as extension of the Closed User Group capabilities, to facilitate this interworking. Recommendation X.327 [32] specifies a general framework for this interworking case. Furthermore, a new Recommendation, X.pvt [33], is being developed to provide more details, such as how addresses are carried between the two X.25 networks.

X.25/PLP-to-X.25/PLP Gateways

In line with X.327 and X.pvt, ISO TR 10029 [34] specifies the detailed procedures for a gateway between two networks for the special case when DTEs on both networks use the X.25 PLP, as specified in ISO/IEC 8208. For example, TR 10029 could be used to connect a LAN where ISO/IEC 8881 is used to a PSPDN.

Open Systems Interconnection (OSI)

The work on OSI started a few years after X.25 was first adopted. Even in its initial drafts, the capabilities defined for the OSI Network Layer service [35] closely resembled the X.25 PLP. A few enhancements have been added over the years to close this gap. Four sets of Recommendations and Standards have been adopted that relate the "real" capabilities of the X.25 PLP to the "abstract" services defined by the OSI Network service.

- The mapping of X.25 PLP protocol elements to the abstract services provided by the OSI Network Layer to the Transport Layer is given in Recommendation X.223 and International Standard 8878 [36]. Note that not all elements of the X.25 PLP are needed in this mapping; some elements, such as the Q-bit, are outside of OSI.

- Special considerations when providing the OSI Network Layer service over specific network types are described in Recommendation X.612 | International Standard 9574 [37] for ISDNs, in Recommendation X.613 | International Standard 10588 [38] for CSPDNs (not shown in Figure 6.12), and in Recommendation X.614 | International Standard 10732 [39] for the telephone network.

- Generic operation of a "gateway" (referred to as an OSI *Intermediate System*) is specified in International Standard 10177 [40]. This standard is an abstraction of the approach of ISO/IEC TR 10029 mentioned above.

- OSI routing in conjunction with Recommendation X.223 or International Standard 8878 is given in International Standard 10030 [41].

SUMMARY

X.25 has come a long way in its nearly 20-year history, from a single CCITT Recommendation for packet switching to one of a family of over 50 related ISO/IEC International Standards and CCITT Recommendations that together provide a complete networking platform. X.25 and packet-switched networks provide the foundation for much of the world's X.400 messaging and electronic-mail services, such as AT&T EasyLink. This application was not even standardized by CCITT until 1984.

Many enhancements have been made to X.25 over the years to keep it current and extend its usefulness to new technologies. Features such as alternative addressing provide current users greater flexibility while start–stop framing, X.31, X.32, and ISO/IEC 8881 extend X.25 capabilities to new users. Today there are several PSPDNs and DTE manufacturers that provide or will soon provide access lines at megabit-per-second speeds, something unheard of just a few short years ago. The primary application for these high speeds is to connect LANs. Further work is planned over the next 4 years to extend X.25 to run at even higher speeds. In the meantime, work continues in the areas of routing, management, security, and multicast operation. Although other technologies are starting to emerge, it is likely that X.25 will continue to play a dominant role in the data communications scene for quite some time.

REFERENCES

1. F. M. Burg, "CCITT Recommendation X.25: Packet Switching and Beyond," *The Handbook of International Connectivity Standards.* New York: Van Nostrand Reinhold, 1992, Chapter 18.

2. CCITT Recommendation X.21, *Interface between Data Terminal Equipment (DTE) and Data Circuit-Terminating Equipment (DCE) for Synchronous Operation on Public Data Networks.*

3. M. A. Sirbu and L. E. Zwimpfer, "Standards Setting for Computer Communication: The Case of X.25," *IEEE Network Magazine*, vol. 23, no. 3, March 1985.

4. ISO/IEC 3309 and Amendments, *Information Technology—Telecommunications and Information Exchange between Systems—High-Level Data Link Control (HDLC) Procedures—Frame Structure.*

   ISO/IEC 4335 and Amendments, *Information Technology—Telecommunications and Information Exchange between Systems—High-Level Data Link Control (HDLC) Procedures—Elements of Procedures.*

   ISO/IEC 7809 and Amendments, *Information Technology—Telecommunications and Information Exchange between Systems—High-Level Data Link Control (HDLC) Procedures—Classes of Procedures.*

5. J. Gostl, "A Problem with the X.25 Link Access Procedure," *ACM Computer Communications Review*, vol. 7, no. 4, October 1977.

6. Paper COM VII-217-E submitted to CCITT Study Group VII meeting of April 1992, *Modulos and Flow Control Parameters in X.2, X.25, and X.75*, Source: Intelsat.

7. F. M. Burg, "Design Considerations for Using the X.25 Packet Layer in Data Terminal Equipment," *Proceedings of IEEE Infocom '83*, April 1983.

8. F. M. Burg and K. T. Tewani, "Signaling for X.25: Meeting User Needs for Advanced Features," *Proceedings of the Eleventh ICCC*, 1992.

9. CCITT Recommendation X.7, *Technical Characteristics of Data Transmission Services.*

10. CCITT Recommendation X.121, *International Numbering Plan for Public Data Networks.*

11. CCITT Recommendation X.180, *Administrative Arrangements for International Closed User Groups (CUGs).*

12. CCITT Recommendation X.1, *International User Classes of Service in and Categories of Access to Public Data Networks and Integrated Services Digital Network (ISDNs).*

13. CCITT Recommendation X.2, *International Data Transmission Services and Optional User Facilities in Public Data Networks and ISDNs.*

14. ISO 7776, *Information Processing Systems—Data Communication—High-Level Data Link Control Procedures—Description of the X.25 LAPB-Compatible DTE Data Link Procedures.*

15. ISO/IEC 8208, *Information Technology—Data Communications—X.25 Packet Layer Protocol for Data Terminal Equipment.*

16. ISO/IEC 8882-1, *Information Processing Systems—X.25 DTE Conformance Testing—Part 1: General Principles.*

    ISO/IEC 8882-2, *Information Technology—Telecommunications and Information Exchange between Systems—X.25 DTE Conformance Testing, Part 2: Data Link Layer Test Suite.*

    ISO/IEC 8882-3, *Information Technology—Telecommunications and Information Exchange between Systems—X.25 DTE Conformance Testing, Part 3: Packet Level Conformance Test Suite.*

17. CCITT Recommendation X.96, *Call Progress Signals in Public Data Networks.*

18. CCITT Recommendation X.181, *Administrative Arrangements for the Provision of International Permanent Virtual Circuits (PVCs).*

19. CCITT Recommendation X.301, *Description of General Arrangements for Call Control within a Subnetwork and between Subnetworks for the Provision of Data Transmission Services.*

20. CCITT Recommendation X.134, *Portion Boundaries and Packet Layer Reference Events: Basis for Defining Packet-Switched Performance Parameters.*

    CCITT Recommendation X.135, *Speed of Service (Delay and Throughput) Performance Values for Public Data Networks When Providing International Packet-Switched Services.*

    CCITT Recommendation X.136, *Accuracy and Dependability Performance Values for Public Data Networks When Providing International Packet-Switched Services.*

    CCITT Recommendation X.137, *Availability Performance Values for Public Data Networks When Providing International Packet-Switched Services.*

CCITT Recommendation X.138, *Measurement of Performance Values for Public Data Networks When Providing International Packet-Switched Services.*

CCITT Recommendation X.139, *Echo, Drop, Generator, and Test DTEs for Measurement Performance Values in Public Data Networks When Providing International Packet-Switched Services.*

CCITT Recommendation X.140, *General Quality of Service Parameters for Communications via Public Data Networks.*

21. CCITT Recommendation X.92, *Hypothetical Reference Connections for Public Synchronous Data Networks.*

22. CCITT Recommendation X.75, *Packet-Switched Signaling System between Public Networks Providing Data Transmission Services.*

23. CCITT Recommendation X.110, *International Routing Principles and Routing Plan for Public Data Networks.*

24. CCITT Recommendation D.10, *General Tariff Principles for International Public Data Communication Services.*

CCITT Recommendation D.11, *Special Tariff Principles for International Packet-Switched Public Data Communication Services by Means of the Virtual Call Facility.*

CCITT Recommendation D.12, *Measurement Unit for Charging by Volume in the International Packet-Switched Data Communication Service.*

25. ISO/IEC 10742, *Information Technology—Telecommunications and Information Exchange between Systems—Elements of Management Information Related to OSI Data Link Layer Standards.*

26. ISO/IEC 10733, *Information Technology—Telecommunications and Information Exchange between Systems—Elements of Management Information Relating to OSI Network Layer Standards.*

27. ISO/IEC TR 9577, *Information Technology—Telecommunications and Information Exchange between Systems—Protocol Identification in the Network Layer.*

28. CCITT Recommendation X.32, *Interface between Data Terminal Equipment (DTE) and Data Circuit-Terminating Equipment (DCE) for Terminals Operating in the Packet Mode and Accessing a Packet-Switched Packet Data Network through a Public-Switched Telephone Network or an Integrated Services Digital Network or a Circuit-Switched Public Data Network.*

29. CCITT Recommendation X.31, *Support of Packet Mode Terminal Equipment by an ISDN.*

30. CCITT Recommendation Q.921, *ISDN User-Network Interface—Data Link Layer Specification.*

31. ISO/IEC 8881, *Information Processing Systems—Data Communications— Use of the X.25 Packet Level Protocol in Local Area Networks.*

32. CCITT Recommendation X.327, *General Arrangements for Interworking between Packet-Switched Public Data Networks (PSPDNs) and Private Data Networks for the Provision of Data Transmission Services.*

33. CCITT Draft Recommendation X.pvt, *Interface between a PSPDN and a Private PSDN, Which Is Based on Modified X.25 Procedures to Define a Gateway Function That is Provided in the PSPDN.*

34. ISO/IEC TR 10029, *Information Technology—Telecommunications and Information Exchange between Systems—Operation of an X.25 Interworking Unit.*

35. CCITT Recommendation X.213 | ISO/IEC 8348, *Information Technology—Open Systems Interconnection: Network Service Definition.*

36. CCITT Recommendation X.223, *Use of X.25 to Provide the OSI Connection-Mode Network Service for CCITT Applications.*

    ISO 8878, *Information Processing Systems—Data Communications— Use of X.25 to Provide the OSI Connection-Mode Network Service.*

37. CCITT Recommendation X.612 | ISO/IEC 9574, *Information Technology—Provision of the OSI Connection-Mode Network Service by Packet-Mode Terminal Equipment Connected to an Integrated Services Digital Network (ISDN).*

38. CCITT Recommendation X.613 | ISO/IEC 10588, *Information Technology—Use of X.25 Packet Layer Protocol in Conjunction with X.21/X.21bis to Provide the OSI Connection-Mode Network Service.*

39. CCITT Recommendation X.614 | ISO/IEC 10732, *Information Technology—Use of X.25 Packet Layer Protocol to Provide the OSI Connection-Mode Network Service over the Telephone Network.*

40. ISO/IEC 10177, *Information Technology—Telecommunications and Information Exchange between Systems—Intermediate-System Support of OSI CONS Using ISO/IEC 8208:1990 in Accordance with ISO/IEC CD 10028.*

41. ISO/IEC 10030, *Information Technology—Telecommunications and Information Exchange between Systems—End System Routing Information Exchange Protocol for Use in Conjunction with ISO 8878.*

ABOUT THE AUTHOR

Fred Burg is supervisor of Networking Standards Planning for AT&T Bell Laboratories. As such, he is responsible for coordination of AT&T's standards strategy, planning, and participation in areas dealing with data networking. He has participated in many of the activities described in this chapter for the past 10 years, serving as author, editor, convenor, and Special Rapporteur in both ISO/IEC and CCITT. Within the United States, he serves as chair of ANSI task group X3S3.7, which is responsible for developing positions on X.25 and related matters for the international arena.

Mr. Burg is also involved in various areas concerning implementation of standards. He serves as chair of the Lower Layer Special Interest Group in the OSI Implementors' Workshop to reach agreements on features of the various OSI Layer 1–4 protocols among product developers. As a member of this group, he also participates in the international efforts at developing functional profiles for these protocols. In addition, he successfully led a demonstration of OSI/ISDN integration at Mather Air Force Base in 1989 as a prelude to inclusion of ISDN as a networking technology in U.S. GOSIP. He also participated in the work on GM's Manufacturing Automation Protocol (MAP) and was technically responsible for AT&T's involvement in this effort.

Beyond X.25 and data networking, Mr. Burg also participates in IEEE committee 802 on Local Area Networks, having served as chair of several subcommittees in the past. He was one of the initial proponents of the frame relay concepts, having participated in the initial phases of its standardization in ECMA and CCITT in the 1983–1985 time frame. He also served in CCITT's Study Group XVII, having been one of the primary developers of the V.42 error-correcting modem protocol.

Mr. Burg received his B.S. degree in Mathematics from the Polytechnic Institute of Brooklyn in 1972 and his M.S. degree in Operations Research from the same school in 1973 on a teaching fellowship. He has since taught classes at both the academic and professional levels. He has written many articles in various journals and served as guest editor for an issue of *IEEE Network* magazine dealing with OSI/ISDN integration. He was elected to Who's Who in America in the East in 1990.

Metropolitan Area Networks

7

Metropolitan Area Networks

Matthew N. O. Sadiku
Department of Electrical Engineering,
Temple University, Philadelphia, Pennsylvania

INTRODUCTION

In the early 1960s, most computers were mainframes, and people communicated with these machines using punched cards. Next, dumb terminals made on-line communication possible. Users could send messages from one mainframe to another using terminals. In addition, users shared storage devices and all the peripherals [1]. With the advent of microcomputers or personal computers (PCs), compatibility of software packages and computer communication became big issues. With the onset of local area networks (LANs) such as Ethernet and Token Ring, communication between PC users became a reality. Over LAN, users can transfer files, send electronic mail, and share peripherals.

However, the performance of LAN usually degrades as the area of coverage becomes large. Also, LANs are typically small, having 20 to 100 users, with limited distance and throughput. Larger companies and college campuses often have more than one LAN and users of one LAN would like to be able to communicate with users of another. Thus, in view of the limitation on the geographical extent, the proliferation of local area computer networks, and the number of devices that a single LAN can handle, the need for interconnection of multiple LANs has become apparent. Interconnection of LANs may be done through private branch exchanges (PBXs), metropolitan area networks (MANs), and wide area networks (WANs). The MAN's packet capability is much better adapted to file transfer or interactive applications than the fixed-bandwidth, circuit-switched connections of the telephone network.

MANs represent LAN technology optimized for longer distances. A primary function of MANs is the ability to provide data interconnection facilities for a myriad of heterogeneous local access network systems. Typically, a MAN spans an entire campus, an entire city, or an office park. The significant advantages of a MAN are high bandwidth, low delay, and high transmission quality. MANs are expected to have more functionality than LANs; whereas LANs are currently used almost exclusively for data applications, MANs are expected to support several traffic types. Typical MAN traffic is expected to include (1) LAN interconnection; (2) connection between PCs, terminals, or workstations to mainframes or hosts; (3) graphics and digital images; (4) bulk data transfer; (5) digitized voice; (6) compressed video; and (6) conventional terminal traffic.

MAN CONCEPTION

A MAN may be viewed as an extension of a LAN to cover a metropolitan-sized area. In a sense, it is a larger LAN with added fixed-bandwidth capability. It performs like a LAN in that users cannot tell the difference in communicating across a room or across a city. Thus, a MAN is basically a network capable of providing high-speed (greater than 10 Mbps) switched connectivity across distances typical of those found within a metropolitan area. The connectivity is of such a nature as to allow different types of traffic (voice, data, video, etc.) to be transmitted simultaneously. The connectivity can be achieved through a number of devices, such as repeaters, bridges, and gateways. A repeater is a physical layer device which merely amplifies and retransmits all signals, including collisions. Thus, the repeater is only used to extend the length of the network. Bridges and gateways are more intelligent. These devices can filter intranetwork traffic and forward only internetwork packets. A bridge operates at the Medium Access Control (MAC) layer, whereas a gateway (also called a router) performs routing at the network layer. For a relatively small number of LANs with similar MAC protocols, such as the standard 802 LANs, a MAC bridge is perhaps the best approach because it is user transparent and requires the least processing time.

The major differences between MANs and LANs can be summarized as follows [2, 3]:

Distance: City and suburbs versus a few kilometers. IEEE Project 802 set a distance optimization of 50 km diameter in order to match the dimensions of typical large metropolitan areas.

Backbone: Use interconnecting LANs and large computers. The switching function is free; no large up-front expenditure for a switch is necessary in a shared-medium network.

Service: Most of the traffic is digitized voice, not computer data. MAN must be optimized for carrying voice and video as well as computer data, thus having a more demanding access requirement. Voice has stringent requirements: a guaranteed bandwidth (64 Kbps per voice channel) and bounded delay (2 μ at worst for round trip). These requirements for so-called isochronous channels cannot be met by conventional LANs.

Central operation: Provides maintenance and billing.

Public operation: MAN is shared between many user organizations, which raises privacy and security issues, in addition to requiring centralized operation and a source of rights of way.

In a MAN, the speed of the backbone network is anticipated to be 10 to 100 times greater than that of the LAN. This speed disparity between the high-speed backbone and the lower-speed LANs that are connected to it creates a bottleneck situation at the gateways [4]. If, for example, we run our Ethernets at 10 Mbps, then interconnecting them at 10 Kbps (a factor of 1000 less) surely results in bottlenecks. A control policy is necessary to regulate the flow of traffic, primarily that of traveling across the gateways from the backbone to the LANs.

MAN TECHNOLOGY

Physically, a MAN consists of a transmission medium and nodes that provide customer access to the medium. Thus, a MAN consists of a medium and a MAC. In terms of protocol architecture, these fit into the Open Systems Interconnection (OSI) reference model, as shown in Figure 7.1.

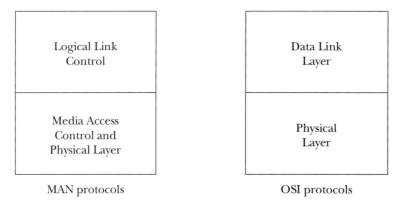

MAN protocols   OSI protocols

Figure 7.1 MAN protocols and the OSI reference model.

Although standards for MAN are yet to be fully established, several schemes have been proposed for MANs. One may classify the different proposed MANs into three categories [5]: (1) tree-based MANs, (2) Toroidal-based MANs, and (3) LAN-based MANs.

Tree-Based MANs

These MANs have the same tree topology as in community antenna television (CATV). Two types of tree-based MANs have been proposed: those that use the CSMA/CD protocol and those that use a controlled access method called group polling.

An advantage they have is that they can be implemented in existing CATV networks. Also, since the CATV network is essentially a broadband network, it provides several logical networks, each of which can be used in a manner that optimizes the performance of a particular application. A major drawback of the tree-based MAN is its reliability. The failure of the head end brings the network down. Also, the failure of a hub or subhub disconnects a set of subgroups from the network. Other inherent problems in implementing tree-based MANs are discussed in references [6 and 7]. In view of these disadvantages, the possibility of seeing a tree-based MAN in the near future seems dim.

Toroidal-Based MANs

In a toroidal-based MAN, each node represents a switching device to which are connected computing devices such as PCs, workstations, file servers, and hosts. A typical example of such a MAN is the Manhattan Street Network. One major advantage of the toroidal-based MANs is their fault tolerance. A fault-tolerant network has at least one redundant path between any pair of nodes. The redundant path is used to bypass a failed network component (link or node) on the primary path. This is in contrast to the tree network, where one link or node failure can disconnect a pair of users.

LAN-Based MANs

For LAN-based MANs, interconnection of the existing LANs is achieved either directly or through a backbone network [5].

A direct interconnection is made using a bridge or a gateway. Two homogeneous LANs (i.e., having the same access control [MAC] protocol) are connected with a bridge, which performs routing and flow control functions. A gateway is used to connect two heterogeneous LANs. In addition to routing and flow control (as the bridge), the gateway implements protocol conversion, particularly reformatting the packets that go from one LAN to another. A typical example of direct interconnection of two bus and two ring LANs is shown in Figure 7.2.

Interconnection via a backbone network is achieved by means of either a broadcast network or a switched network. A broadcast network is one in which the stations in the network share a common transmission medium; data transmitted by one station is received by some or all the stations. The

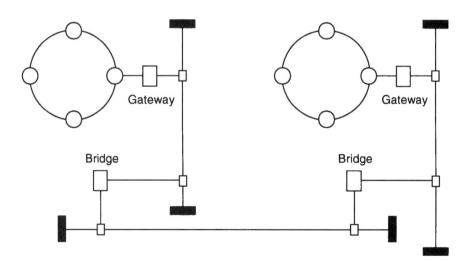

Figure 7.2 Direct interconnection of LANs.

connection of a LAN to a broadcast network is made via a bridge or a gateway, depending on whether or not the backbone uses the same MAC protocol as the LAN. Figures 7.3 and 7.4 illustrate LAN-based MANs with backbone Token-Ring network and backbone CSMA/CD bus network, respectively. A typical example of a LAN-based MAN with a broadcast backbone network is the fiber distributed data interface (FDDI) network, which consists of an optical fiber Token-Ring network as the backbone and a set of LANs accessing the backbone via bridges. The main disadvantage of this class of MAN concerns reliability; if the backbone fails, then inter-LAN communication is disrupted.

A switched network consists of an interconnected system of nodes in which data are transferred from source to destination by being routed from one node to another. Because a switched network uses a different protocol from that of a LAN, all connections to a switched backbone network are made via a gateway. The switched backbone generally enhances the system reliability by providing alternate paths between every pair of stations in the network. It can span a wider area than a broadcast network since the latter has distance limitation. Also, the switched backbone network can interconnect more LANs than a broadcast network since there is a limit to the number of LANs that can be connected to the latter. A major drawback of the switched backbone network is that it is more expensive than the broadcast backbone network.

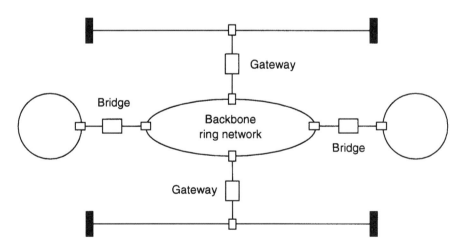

Figure 7.3 LAN-based MAN with a backbone ring network.

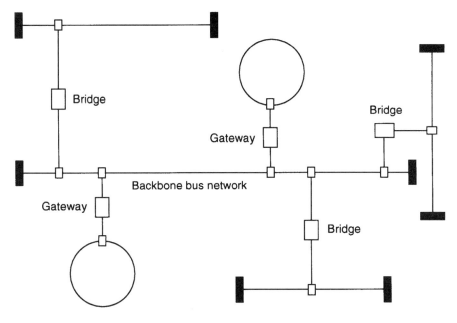

Figure 7.4 LAN-based MAN with a backbone bus network.

The interconnection via a backbone, as typically shown in Figures 7.3 and 7.4, offers superior performance to that of direct interconnection, as in Figure 7.2, for the following cases [5, 8]:

- **Administration:** For ease of administration, it is better to use a backbone network scheme. It is easier to expand the network, since existing LANs need not add new bridges each time another LAN is added to the network. Also, independent communication channels exist which prevent lockout by uncooperative networks or by network failures.

- **Traffic Regulation:** In an independent network, such as MAN, it is easier to obtain global information to regulate traffic efficiently, to handle errors, and to control malicious traffic disruption or illegal use of the network.

- **Cost:** The cost is comparable to other networks where the internetwork distance is larger than the intranetwork distance. Having a standard translation at a MAN node eliminates the need to rewrite the protocol software for each additional interconnection. Protocol conversion can be carried out in the backbone network, thus eliminating the need for each LAN to know the protocol used in the other LANs. In other words, a LAN does not have to know the protocols of others except the MAN it is connected to.

- **Security Reasons:** A LAN owner may not be willing to accept en route traffic as well as go through other people's domain. The access to the MAN can be closely monitored at each of the nodes (or gateways).

KEY ISSUES

MANs need to address problems that local area networks do not face. The key issues to be addressed in implementing MANs include [1, 8] (1) cost, (2) security, (3) reliability, (4) compatibility with current and future networks, (5) human factors, and (6) network management. Although some of these issues are interrelated, they are the major factors influencing the choice of scheme.

The cost of a network is measured by such parameters as the total number of links (in a backbone network), bridges, gateways, and transceivers in the system [5]. The cost of connecting a network to a MAN, relative to the cost of the network itself, is an important issue from a user viewpoint. Connection costs include both the cost of the electronic interface and the cost of the cable and its installation [9]. Because the cost per direct connection is very high, only the most powerful devices are costly enough to justify direct connection to a MAN. Low-speed, low-cost devices neither need, nor can they afford, a direct connection to a high-speed medium. Hence, there is the need for at least a two-level hierarchy of networks. A low-speed device (e.g., 5 Mbps) is connected along with other similar devices to a low-cost network, which is then connected to a high-speed (e.g., 100 Mbps) backbone network via a bridge. Since many organizations already have more than one LAN, the most common approach to building a MAN is the interconnection of LANs; it is more economical to interconnect them than to build a network that will serve the same purpose.

Security is an issue because MANs will likely be owned and operated by common carriers, rather than being privately owned. No customer will be satisfied with his or her confidential data passing through a competitor's stations and no operator will be pleased with a network in which one customer could disrupt the service of others, either accidentally or maliciously. Thus, privacy, protection against nonauthorized access, and correcting billing must be ensured. These problems are not faced with LANs, which are typically owned and operated by the same organization that uses them.

However, MANs as public networks can probably provide better security for the cost than anything else.

The reliability issue concerns two basic functions: namely, the transmission and the routing functions. The transmission function relies on both the integration of the transmission media and the correct operation of the access protocols, while the reliability of the routing function depends on the reliability of bridges and gateways. A failure in a bridge may isolate a LAN. However, each of the resulting networks is not affected in its internal communications. With the aid of optical directional couplers, a fiber optic MAN can be constructed whose reliability equals, if not exceeds, that obtained in hierarchical structures.

Compatibility with the existing and future networks is an important issue. Much care has gone into providing good compatibility between the 802.6 standard and new standards for wide area networking. For example, telephone companies have established certain quality goals for their digital transmission systems in support of the integrated services digital networks (ISDN). Any MAN being used for a telephone should act as an extension of the ISDN and so should meet these quality goals as well [9]. Thus, the proposed MANs are compatible with ISDN. In particular, the new broadband ISDN (BISDN) is ideal for interconnecting MANs. BISDN is a rethinking of the present ISDN, running at fiber optic speeds and largely packet oriented. The motivation for the packet orientation is the new asynchronous transfer mode (ATM) switching technology. ATM switches can operate at several hundred megabits per line at a very low cost by routing data through a switch a packet at a time [10].

Human factors such as user friendliness and user adaptability are crucial. Educating the service provider and potential customers is an important strategy. In order to provide a MAN, a company would have to be attuned to what a customer's needs are and how to meet them. New services would have to be developed to aid customers and show them how to benefit from these new services.

Network management is a broad issue. A MAN requires a central organization to install it, operate it, and bill users for services. For ease of administration, it may be expedient to use the scheme with a backbone network.

STANDARDS

Since a MAN interconnects computer systems belonging to a large number of organizations, the problem of harmonizing standards with different industrial sectors involved (electronics, telecommunications, and building construction industry) must be addressed. Unless there is a standard, network operation is impossible. Also, MAN must be capable of interfacing LANs on one side and WANs on the other. Development of MAN standards requires consideration of standards in these areas [2, 11].

Standardization activity for MANs started within IEEE Project 802 out of a concern for how high-speed LANs could be interconnected across distances greater than a few kilometers without introducing a low-speed bottleneck. Consequently, LAN interconnection has always been a main objective. However, communication needs include voice and video, which are not currently accommodated by the family of IEEE 802 LAN protocols [12].

Initially, the 802.6 committee focused on standards applicable to systems based on CATV, due to the availability of bandwidth and space cables in the CATV franchises. By 1984, however, the medium was changed from CATV-type coax to optical fiber. The committee approved lifting the 20 Mbps maximum speed for Project 802 LANs, allowing MAN to go as fast as the fiber or other media permit. The IEEE 802.6 MAN standard was expected to be approved in 1990; trials and products based on this standard were supposed to appear in 1990/1991.

The IEEE P802.6 Working Group is working towards the definition of a MAN called DQDB (Distributed Queue Dual Buses), which is based on a system proposed by Telecom Australia. The DQDB MAN is a communication switch allowing integration of voice and data over circuit and packet switching. Its architecture comprises two unidirectional looped buses, as shown in Figure 7.5. Every node of the network is attached to both buses allowing full duplex communication between each pair of nodes. Nodes act as gateways to interconnect LANs with DQDB.

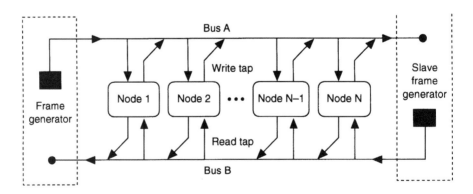

Figure 7.5 DQDB dual bus network.

The DQDB protocol combines the advantages of a bidirectional medium and the Token Ring [10]. At low load it offers the ability to transmit almost immediately, like Ethernet. At high load it is well behaved and efficient, like a token-based system. In addition, it has a fail-safe feature; it can be looped into a near-ring, with one station serving as the head of both buses, as shown in Figure 7.6. The fact that the loop always has an opening provides an important fault tolerance. Scheduling is another area where the dual bus shines. The existence of two full-time buses makes it possible to implement a unique distributed queue, which has been shown to be equivalent in operation to a single queue except for the effects of network propagation delay.

For a given DQDB network the frame, and therefore the transmission bandwidth, is segmented in slots, where each slot is allocated either to isochronous traffic or nonisochronous traffic. The slot structure is shown in

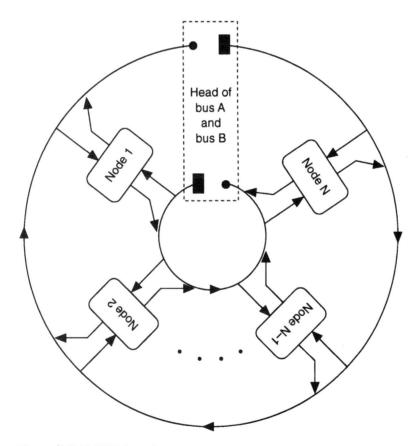

Figure 7.6 DQDB loop bus structure.

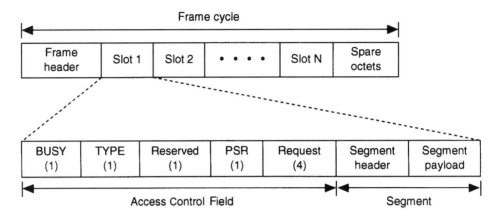

Figure 7.7 Frame format for a DQDB MAN.

Figure 7.7 and is approved by IEEE 802.6 as well as by T1S1.1 to switch packets from the MAN to BISDN and vice versa. Each slot contains a 5-byte header and a 64-byte payload. The so-called Access Control Field (ACF) is a part of the header of any slot and is used to control access to the slots. The Busy bit indicates whether a slot is occupied or not. The Type bit indicates the slot type. The Reserved bit is for future use and is presently set to 0. The PSR bit indicates whether or not the Previous Slot has been Received [13, 14].

APPLICATIONS

Corporate MANs may come into existence in many areas before public MANs. A single corporation can fund the installation of a network from the beginning, while public networks must handle installation of facilities before revenue comes in.

Since MAN is intended to serve more users than the LAN, it is important to design access protocols that are not as sensitive to network size as those used in LANs. Also, the basic speed of the transmission medium must be greater based on the extended number of users. MANs are ultimately expected to transmit data at rates above 1 Mbps within the areas of 50 km or so in diameter and serve large industries, university campuses, and research laboratories where there is a need for high-capacity backbones to interconnect the LANs in the individual buildings. A good business example is the network built by Teleport Communications for the Port Authority of New York and New Jersey to link up bridges, tunnels, and other transit facilities in and around New York City. The Bellcore METROCORE network [15] is a 150-Mbps fiber optic MAN which uses a slotted attempt-and-defer protocol. The network is based in two separate unidirectional buses with signals propagating in opposite directions. The most upstream station and the most downstream station act as master stations, performing round generation, which enables METROCORE to support traffic with three different priority levels. ExpressMAN is a metropolitan area network architecture which is based on Expressnet access mechanism [16]. The overall network structure is halfway between a linear bus and a two-level hierarchical structure in which several subnetworks are connected by a backbone network. However, it does not need complex routing facilities like bridges.

There are several potential services a metropolitan area network can provide. The potential users might have PCs, terminals, mainframes, LANs, and peripherals at remote locations. This is typical of large businesses including educational institutions, hospitals, banks, accounting firms, computer companies, insurance companies, state and local governments, manufacturing companies, and credit companies. Services MANs can provide to these diverse users include the following [6]:

- **Timesharing:** A public access timesharing computer system could be accessed by subscribers with terminals or personal computers connected to the network.

- **Connection:** Connection between subscribers would allow two users to connect their terminals or personal computers via the network. Connections might also be to other computer networks outside of the local MAN and to national systems such as ARPANET.

- **Voice/Image Service:** Calls might be placed to other network subscribers or to phones elsewhere via bridges to the normal phone system.

- **Mail Service:** This could be the current electronic mail provided by many computer networks or it could be a complete mail service. It might include mail order services such as grocery, shopping, reservation, and banking transactions. Professors of colleges with several campus locations in a metropolitan area could send mail to each other comparing tests, classes, memos, and a number of other possible communications.

The potential uses of a MAN by the general public, government, and industry are endless. Initial services offered by MANs will focus on high-speed connectionless data applications, followed by connection-oriented isochronous and statistical services [17].

CONCLUSION

A brief introduction to MAN has been presented. As a backbone network, a MAN can be used to interconnect a large number of heterogeneous LANs. The need for MAN and the various issues confronting MAN's implementation are discussed.

Because MAN is optimized for metropolitan and not continental dimensions, it is not likely to be available for WANs without some major changes. However, MAN seems to be the most likely solution to the need for high-speed backbone networks that will be able to provide broadband services. The implementation of ISDN will provide wide area facilities that can be interfaced to the MAN invisibly to the user and can provide much greater speed than present facilities such as X.25 [10]. Internetworking between MANs and other components of the public telecommunications network will evolve over time as the capabilities of both MANs and other network components evolve.

As we move towards the next generation of MANs, we have greater architectural choice than ever before through the bandwidth of optical communications and the processing power of customized VLSI. The use of fiber optics is predicted to increase substantially for several reasons, including the emergence of high-performance processors, the movement toward low-cost laser sources, the development of the proposed fiber distributed data interface (FDDI) standard (ANSI X3T9.5), and higher functionality and easier design-in through integrated packaging.

Imagine two users in different buildings, sitting in front of their terminals, and interacting and conversing in full view of each other via the screens of the terminals. One can expect such an activity to occur in the office of the near future. Such an activity will require the real-time video, data, and voice integration of MAN described in this chapter. As MANs become accepted and used to widen the choices of intercommunication for users, demand for even wider coverage grows.

REFERENCES

1. C. J. Cranfill, "Issues in Implementing a Public Metropolitan Area Network," *Proceedings of the IEEE International Conference on Communications (ICC '90)*, 1990, pp. 1572–1575.

2. J. F. Mollenauer, "Standards for Metropolitan Area Networks," *IEEE Communications Magazine*, vol. 26, no. 1, 1988, pp. 15–19.

3. J. F. Mollenauer, "Metropolitan Area Networks and ATM Technology," *International Journal of Digital and Analog Cabled Systems*, vol. 1, no. 4, 1988, pp. 225–228.

4. L. N. Wong and M. Schwartz, "Flow Control in Metropolitan Area Networks," *Proceedings of IEEE INFOCOM*, 1989, pp. 826–833.

5. O. C. Ibe and R. C. Howe, "Architectures for Metropolitan Area Networks," *Computer Communications*, vol. 12, no. 6, December 1989, pp. 315–323.

6. A. I. Karshmer and J. N. Thomas, "Inherent Problems in Implementing Cable TV–Based Metropolitan Area Networks," *Proceedings of the 22nd Annual Hawaii International Conference on System Sciences*, vol. IV, 1989, pp. 338–347.

7. A. I. Karshmer and J. N. Thomas, "TVNet II: A Cable TV–Based Metropolitan Area Network Using KEDS Protocol," *Microprocessing and Microprogramming*, vol. 30, no. 1–5, 1990, pp. 627–635.

8. O. W. W. Yang and J. W. Mark, "Design Issues in Metropolitan Area Networks," *Proceedins of the IEEE International Conference on Communications (ICC '86)*, pp. 899–902.

9. Daniel T. W. Sze, "A Metropolitan Area Network," *IEEE Journal on Selected Areas in Communications*, vol. SAC-3, no. 6, 1985, pp. 815–824.

10. J. F. Mollenauer, "Metropolitan Area Networks: A New Application for Fiber," *Photonics Spectra*, vol. 24, no. 3, 1990, pp. 159–161.

11. J. F. Mollenauer, "Metropolitan Area Networks: Where Many Standards Meet," *Proceedings of the IEEE Computer Standards Conference*, 1988, pp. 2–6.

12. R. W. Klessig, "Overview of Metropolitan Area Networks," *IEEE Communications Magazine* vol. 24, no. 1, January 1986, pp. 9–15.

13. K. Sauer and W. Schodl, "Performance Aspects of the DQDB Protocol," *Computer Networks and ISDN Systems*, vol. 20, 1990, pp. 253–260.

14. M. Zukerman and P. G. Potter, "The DQDB Protocol and Its Performance under Overload Traffic Conditions," *Computer Networks and ISDN Systems*, vol. 20, 1990, pp. 261–270.

15. A. Albanese *et al.*, "Overview of Bellcore METROCORE Network," *Proceedings of the IFIP WG 6.4 Workshop HSLAN '88*, April 1988.

16. F. Borgonovo, "ExpressMAN: Exploiting Traffic Locality in Expressnet," *IEEE Journal on Selected Areas in Communications*, vol. SAC-5, no. 9, 1987, pp. 1436–1443.

17. W. R. Byrne *et al.,* "Evolution of Metropolitan Area Networks to Broadband ISDN," *IEEE Communications Magazine,* January 1991, pp. 69–82.

ABOUT THE AUTHOR

Matthew N. O. Sadiku received his B.Sc. degree in 1978 from Ahmadu Bello University, Zaria, Nigeria, and his M.Sc. and Ph.D. degrees from Tennessee Technological University, Cookeville, Tennessee, in 1982 and 1984, respectively. From 1984 to 1988, he was an assistant professor at Florida Atlantic University, where he did graduate work in computer science. Since August, 1988 he has been with Temple University, Philadelphia, Pennsylvania, where he is presently an associate professor. He is the author of over 40 professional papers and four books, including *Elements of Electromagnetics* (Saunders, 1989) and *Numerical Techniques in Electromagnetics* (CRC, 1992).

His current research interests are in the areas of numerical techniques in electromagnetics and computer communication networks. He is a registered professional engineer and a member of the American Society of Engineering Educators (ASEE) and Institute of Electrical and Electronics Engineers (IEEE). He is presently the IEEE Region 2 Student Activities Committee Chairman.

8

An Overview of the Switched Multimegabit Data Service

Gary C. Kessler
Hill Associates

The Switched Multimegabit Data Service (SMDS) is a metropolitan area network (MAN) service currently offered by local and long distance telephone companies in the United States. The service is also growing in popularity in Europe and the Pacific Rim.

This chapter will describe the forces driving the development of SMDS, features and characteristics of the service, and some applications for it. A brief examination of SMDS-related protocols will also be provided, as well as the relationship of SMDS to other technologies.

HISTORICAL DEVELOPMENT

The development of SMDS is the result of several independent yet related factors, including changing technologies, the evolution of MAN standards, and politics.

During the 1970s and early 1980s, the number of personal computers in business and industry saw near-explosive growth. During the 1980s, one of the important networking issues became PC interconnection using local area networks (LANs). LAN technology, while relatively new in the late-1970s, matured rapidly in the 1980s.

As the number of LANs increased, interconnecting them became a major issue. LAN interconnection was, in fact, one of the original forces driving the development of MAN standards. In the mid- to late-1980s, however, remote LAN interconnections were mostly limited to packet-switched or T1 networks; both solutions are limited in speed, particularly when compared to the speed of the LAN itself.

Every market study that has come out in the last several years shows an increase in the number of installed LANs. This leads to the conclusion that LAN interconnection devices and services will take on an ever-increasing significance into the 1990s. Indeed, most studies also show large growth in the bridge, router, and gateway markets. These same studies also suggest real growth in LAN interconnection networks, including MANs and MAN services.

In 1980, the Institute of Electrical and Electronics Engineers (IEEE) formed their Project 802 committee to develop LAN and MAN standards. The original LAN committees, namely 802.3 (carrier sense multiple access with collision detection, or CSMA/CD), 802.4 (token-passing bus), and 802.5 (Token Ring), each had a product or specification upon which to base their work; in particular, their early work started with the Digital/Intel/Xerox Ethernet specification, General Motor's Manufacturing Automation Protocol (MAP), and IBM's Token Ring, respectively.

The 802.6 MAN committee, however, was charged with developing a MAN standard. This was hardly an easy task since the definition of just what a MAN is evolved considerably during the 1980s. Originally, MANs were viewed only as data networks for the interconnection of LANs; later, they were viewed as initial implementations of Broadband Integrated Services Digital Networks (BISDN). In December 1990, the IEEE 802.6 MAN committee adopted the Distributed Queue Dual Bus (DQDB) standard, based upon the Queued Packet and Synchronous Exchange (QPSX) proposal from Telecom Australia. The DQDB standard defines a physical layer and medium access control (MAC) sublayer to support packet and isochronous (time-sensitive) data transport over a metropolitan area. The adoption of DQDB was a very important step in our discussion of SMDS since the two are closely related; it is important to note, however, that DQDB describes only a transport subnetwork and not a network service, per se.

LANs are typically geographically small networks, limited in size to just a few kilometers. Due to their small size, they are usually located on the user's premises and are, therefore, usually thought of as private networks. MANs, on the other hand, will have a larger geographic scope and will usually be service offerings of public network providers, such as the telephone company or public data network service.

After the break-up of the Bell System in 1984, the Regional Bell operating companies (RBOCs) were no longer able to utilize the basic research capabilities of Bell Laboratories. Since the Bell system telephone companies relied so heavily on Bell Labs, and because all of the RBOCs have common operational systems and service offerings, part of Bell Labs was spun off to form Bell Communications Research (Bellcore); the RBOCs, in turn, fund Bellcore as their research and development arm. In order to evolve the RBOC's networks and services in a consistent fashion, Bellcore publishes a variety of documents that define requirements for RBOC services. Vendors manufacturing to Bellcore's specifications ensure equipment and service interoperability across the regions.

In response to the requirements of the RBOCs, Bellcore described SMDS as a MAN service offering for the telephone companies. As currently specified, SMDS will provide the MAN service using DQDB as the underlying transport network between the user and the network, and between networks.

DESCRIPTION AND APPLICATIONS

SMDS is a service specification for a metropolitan area, high-speed data service. It is a response to several important network objectives, shared by the RBOCs and other public data network providers. Its goals are to:

- Provide a high-speed data service within a metropolitan area
- Provide features similar to those found in LANs; in particular, high throughput and low delay
- Allow easy integration of the service within existing systems and provide the capability to evolve gracefully with the network
- Define and implement security features
- Provide a connectionless high-speed packet service

The applications for MAN services, in general, and SMDS in particular, are quite varied. Any application requiring high-speed data transfer, such as imaging, computer-aided design/engineering, publishing, telemedicine, disaster recovery, or financial applications, can benefit from SMDS.

SMDS is particularly well suited for users that:

- Have multiple locations, each with its own LAN and/or host computer system
- Have locations that are geographically dispersed

- Have a requirement to exchange information among the different locations and/or with other organizations
- Expect a growth in data traffic
- Require a high-speed backbone network with greater capacity than is currently available and/or affordable
- Want to use a public network service rather than a private line solution

SMDS OVERVIEW

LANs provide a high-speed transmission service with high throughput and low delay. LAN technology, however, is not applicable to the large geographic scope of a MAN. The relatively small inefficiencies of LAN MAC schemes (i.e., token rotation delay or contention network collisions) are greatly exaggerated when the size of the network increases from a few kilometers to over 100 km.

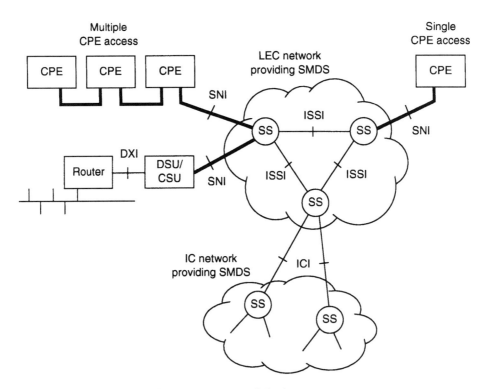

Figure 8.1 SMDS network components and devices.

Customer access to SMDS utilizes an underlying DQDB subnetwork. IEEE 802.6 DQDB is a cell relay network, switching and transmitting 53-octet cells; these cells have the same general format as those defined in BISDN standards. In addition, SMDS data frames use a format that is similar to DQDB data frames. Thus, DQDB provides a compatible format to carry SMDS data and to interoperate with emerging BISDN switching technologies, including Asynchronous Transfer Mode (ATM).

Figure 8.1 shows the general components of the networks and devices providing SMDS. The SMDS is provided to a customer from an SMDS switching system (SS). Customer-premises equipment (CPE) accesses the service using SMDS protocols across a subscriber–network interface (SNI); both the *single CPE* and *multiple CPE* access arrangements are shown in Figure 8.1. LANs can access the service via a router; the router will attach to the digital access facility using a channel service unit/data service unit (CSU/DSU). The router and CSU/DSU communicate with each other using a specification called the Data Exchange Interface (DXI).

Switching systems are interconnected via an Inter-Switching System Interface (ISSI); the collection of SSs provides a local exchange carrier's (LEC) SMDS service. For service across local access and transport area (LATA) boundaries,[1] an interexchange carrier's (IC) network must be used. Connection between a LEC's SS and an IC's SS is over an Interexchange Carrier Interface (ICI).

Figure 8.2 shows an example of customer access to a network providing SMDS from the perspective of the CPE. User Site A is a LAN, attached to the SMDS network via a bridge or router. The SNI describes the access point to the SMDS service and is the point where the public network ends and the customer premises' network begins. The SMDS Interface Protocol (SIP) comprises a protocol suite that describes the network services and how those services are accessed by the user. The SIP defines the frame structure, addressing, error control, and transport of data at the SNI.

User Site B contains a host system that is connected to the SMDS network. The host, like the LAN's bridge/router, connects to the SMDS network via the SIP. The customer is responsible for interworking and end-to-end protocols.

---

[1] A LATA is the area in which a LEC may provide service; except in a few special cases, LECs may not carry traffic across LATA boundaries even when both LATAs are within the same LEC serving area.

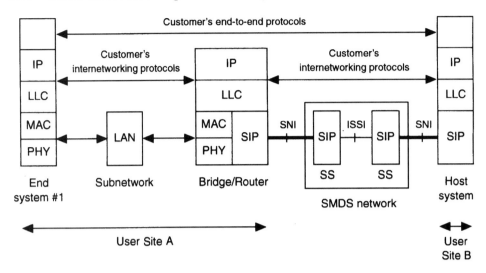

Figure 8.2 Example SMDS configuration from the perspective of user equipment.

Access to the network providing SMDS will be over DS1 (1.544 Mbps) or DS3 (44.736 Mbps) digital transmission facilities. DS1 access provides a user data rate of 1.17 Mbps. For DS3 access, *service classes* have been defined to support a sustained transfer rate of 4, 10, 16, 25, or 34 Mbps. DS3 or Synchronous Optical Network (SONET) OC-3 interfaces (155.52 Mbps) may be used in the network backbone. Other access rates are also under consideration, including DS0 (64 Kbps), E1 (2.048 Mbps), E3 (34.368 Mbps), and higher SONET rates.

SMDS provides a number of features that make it an attractive public network service offering. SMDS uses 60-bit network addresses, corresponding to international ISDN numbers defined in CCITT (International Telephone and Telegraph Consultative Committee) Recommendation E.164. These addresses are similar to today's telephone numbers, are limited to 15 digits in length, and provide "anywhere-to-anywhere" connectivity between SMDS users. Use of E.164 also signifies the future compatibility with BISDN. Up to 16 individual E.164 addresses may be assigned to a single user interface.

Users can create virtual private networks within the public network by defining *group addresses*, much like X.25 closed user groups (CUGs). A security feature called *address screening* allows the user to specify a set of addresses identifying the allowable destinations for frames they send and allowable sources for frames they may receive. The combination of group addresses and address screening is a potentially useful feature for many organizations in order to limit access to their resources; a single point of entry to and from a corporate network can be provided by opening a single system to addresses beyond the network. This single gateway for external systems allows the organization to control the information flow in and out of a corporation and is a valuable security tool in case the organization decides that, for some reason, it needs to quickly remove itself from outside access. A group address can comprise up to 128 different customer interfaces and a given customer interface can be a member of up to 48 group addresses.

It is theoretically possible that a user outside of a virtual private network could "break in" to the group by supplying its own frames with a source address that legitimately belongs to the group but not to this station; this is known as *spoofing*. To eliminate the spoofing threat, all SMDS switching systems perform *source address validation*, which ensures that every frame from a customer contains a source address that belongs to that interface.

As shown in Figure 8.1, the network is a collection of SMDS switching systems. In some of the early SMDS literature, a switching system was referred to as a MAN Switching System (MSS); the term was changed to reflect the fact that the SS may be any system capable of supporting SMDS using any technology, including MAN technology. This again points to the evolutionary path that is being mapped out for SMDS as a platform for BISDN and other services.

SMDS deployment is often described by Bellcore in terms of *phases*. Phase 1 efforts, or early availability of SMDS, are aimed at single SS, intra-LATA (i.e., local) service, and limited customer network management (CNM) capabilities. Phase 2 issues include inter-LATA (i.e., long distance) and inter-carrier service and extended CNM capabilities. Phase 3 adds higher speeds and other features, such as directory services and evolution to BISDN.

SMDS SPECIFICATIONS AND SOURCES

While originally defined by Bellcore, different aspects of SMDS are described by a variety of sources. Before examining some of the different SMDS specifications, it is important to know who the different players are.

The most important organization in terms of SMDS specifications is, of course, Bellcore itself. Bellcore is responsible for defining implementation standards and service requirements for the RBOCs. Their specifications include:

- **Technical Advisories (TA):** Preliminary technical specifications which are circulated for industry review and comment

- **Technical References (TR):** Finalized versions of TAs; technical specifications for implementation

- **Framework Technical Advisories (FA):** General information and guidance on technology; provides a framework for further TAs and TRs

- **Special Reports (SR):** Provide general, nontechnical information

The first SMDS TAs were released by Bellcore in October 1989 and TRs started to appear in May 1991. These specifications include descriptions of the user–network interface, long distance (inter-LATA) SMDS network components, billing elements, and network management. The European Telecommunications Standards Institute (ETSI) has adopted a series of SMDS specifications for use in the European Community, based largely upon the Bellcore specifications.

In early 1991, an industry consortium of SMDS vendors, manufacturers, service providers, and users formed the SMDS Interest Group (SIG). The SIG focuses on some of the issues that are beyond the direct purview of Bellcore, such as CPE interfaces to SMDS, customer education, and intercarrier issues. A European SIG (ESIG) was formed in late 1991 and a Pacific Rim SIG (PRSIG) in 1992.

The Internet Engineering Task Force (IETF) is responsible for many of the technical aspects of the operation of the worldwide Internet, including the definition and maintenance of the Transmission Control Protocol (TCP)/Internet Protocol (IP) suite. IETF specifications and other major documents are published in a series of Requests for Comments (RFCs). Compatibility between SMDS and TCP/IP (including TCP/IP-based network management) is important because of TCP/IP's pervasiveness in the LAN environment.

SMDS INTERFACE PROTOCOL

As shown in Figures 8.1 and 8.2, the SIP is the protocol suite that defines customer access to the network. The SIP comprises three protocol layers corresponding to the physical and MAC layers described by the IEEE 802 standards. The three SIP levels are described below and in Figure 8.3.

SIP Level 1 (L1) describes the SMDS access path and corresponds to the IEEE 802.6 Physical Layer. The SIP L1 Transmission System sublayer, the lower sublayer of SIP L1, defines the digital carrier systems that can be used for the SNI. Current Bellcore specifications support DS1 and DS3 digital carrier access, and it is anticipated that DS0, E1, and SONET transmission

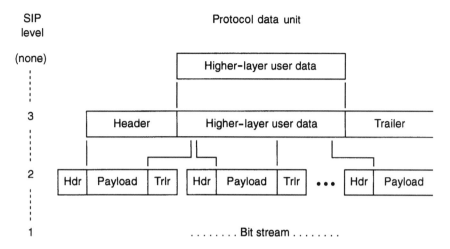

Figure 8.3 SIP protocol layers.

rates will be incorporated in the future. The upper sublayer of SIP L1, the Physical Layer Convergence Protocol (PLCP), defines how the 53-octet cells are mapped onto the specific Transmission System. The SIP L1 PLCP is taken directly from the IEEE 802.6 DQDB standard.

The SIP Level 2 (L2) protocol describes the medium access control mechanism for the MAN. SIP L2 uses the same MAC scheme as the DQDB standard for *queued arbitrated* access in support of connectionless data service. IEEE 802.6 describes two types of access to the network, namely queued arbitrated and prearbitrated. Prearbitrated access is designed for isochronous services, such as voice and video, where time is reserved on the network for a specific number of cells. Prearbitrated access is not supported by SMDS.

Queued arbitrated access refers to the fact that all data users must contend for the network's bandwidth. The actual operation of the DQDB standard is beyond the scope of this chapter; however, a brief description is in order. Stations on a DQDB subnetwork are connected with two unidirectional buses; thus, a station must know which bus to use to send information to another station. The DQDB scheme provides a mechanism so that stations request access to the network in such a way that all stations gain access *in the same order that they requested access.* Furthermore, every station maintains counters so that they always know the length of the queue and their place in it; thus, a *distributed queue.* When a station gets to the front of the queue, it is allowed to send data at the next opportunity. The queued arbitration procedures of DQDB are supported by SMDS.

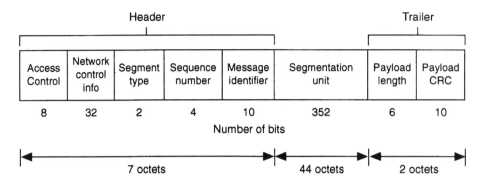

Figure 8.4 SIP Level 2 cell (L2_PDU) format.

The SIP L2 protocol data unit (PDU) is a 53-octet cell that uses the same general format as a BISDN *cell*; DQDB refers to this 53-octet entity as a *slot* (Figure 8.4).

The fields of the SIP L2_PDU are:

- **Access Control:** Indicates whether this cell is empty or if it contains user data; may also carry reservation priority information (8 bits).

- **Network Control Information:** Used to indicate whether the L2_PDU contains data or is empty (32 bits).

- **Segment Type:** Indicates what portion of the SMDS frame is contained in this cell; if the entire frame is contained in this cell, it is a single-segment message (SSM); if this is the first, intermediate, or last cell transporting fragments of a frame, the cell is denoted as a beginning-of-message (BOM), continuation-of-message (COM), or end-of-message (EOM), respectively (2 bits).

- **Sequence Number:** Used to reassemble the SMDS frame in the correct order from the individual cells (4 bits).

- **Message Identifier:** A unique identifier that is placed in every cell associated with a frame; used to ensure that the proper cells are used to reassemble a frame (10 bits).

- **Segmentation Unit:** Contains a 44-octet portion of an SMDS frame (352 bits).

- **Payload Length:** Indicates how many of the octets in the Segmentation Unit field actually contain user data; this value will always be 44 in BOM- and COM-type cells (6 bits).

- **Payload CRC:** Contains a cyclic redundancy check (CRC) remainder to detect bit errors in the cell, except for the Access Control and Network Control Information fields;[2] used to detect bit errors or, possibly, correct single-bit errors (10 bits).

SIP Level 3 (L3) transports data from higher-layer protocols. The L3_PDU is a variable-size frame that can contain up to 9188 octets of user data and is identical to the DQDB frame in support of the connectionless data service. Larger frames will require an additional protocol describing fragmentation and reassembly.

A Level 3 frame can, obviously, be significantly larger than a single cell; in fact, up to 210 cells (L2_PDUs) may be required to transport a single frame (L3_PDU). It is the responsibility of the SIP L2 to fragment and reassemble L3 frames. SIP L2 and L3, together, correspond to the IEEE 802.6 DQDB Layer.

The SIP Level 3 PDU format (Figure 8.5) is similar to a DQDB MAC frame.[3] Several of the fields are present only to provide alignment for transport in SIP Level 2 cells and compatibility with the IEEE 802.6 standard; these fields are marked "X+" in the figure and are not processed by the network.

The fields of the L3_PDU are:

- **Reserved (r):** Reserved and set to all zeros (1 octet).

- **Beginning-End Tag (BEtag):** A sequence number from 0 to 255 that is carried in both the header and the trailer; used to associate the header and trailer of the L3_PDU with each other at the receiving interface (1 octet).

- **Buffer Allocation Size (BAsize):** The number of octets between the Destination Address and CRC fields; tells the receiver how many Level 2 cells to expect (and, therefore, how many memory buffers to reserve) to complete the frame (2 octets).

- **Destination Address (DA):** Contains the address of the intended receiver. The first 4 bits indicate whether this is a 60-bit individual (1100) or group (1110) address. The next 4 bits are set to 0001; this "1" prefix

---

[2] The 48 octets protected by the Payload CRC field are equivalent to a Derived MAC PDU (DMPDU) in the IEEE 802.6 standard.

[3] The L3_PDU, or SMDS frame, is equivalent to an Initial MAC PDU (IMPDU) in the IEEE 802.6 standard.

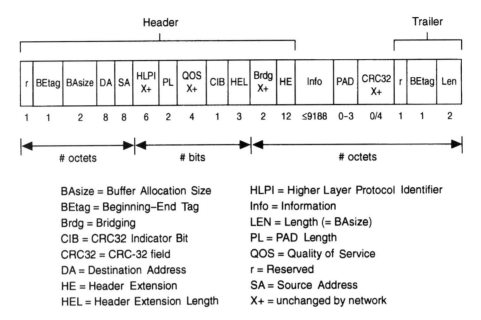

Figure 8.5 SIP Level 3 frame (L3_PDU) format.

for SMDS addresses indicates world zone #1 for international telephony applications. The SMDS address itself is a 10-digit number that has the same structure as North American telephone numbers; the next 40 bits in the DA field contain these 10 binary coded decimal (BCD) digits.[4] The remaining 16 bits are set to 1 (8 octets).

- **Source Address (SA):** Contains the address of the sender; the format is the same as that for an individual DA (8 octets).

- **Higher-Layer Protocol Identifier (HLPI):** Provides alignment of the SIP Level 3 PDU with the cells of the SIP Level 2 protocol. While this field is not processed by the network providing SMDS, it is coded 000001 to indicate support of the IEEE 802.2 Logical Link Control (LLC) protocol (6 bits).

- **PAD Length (PL):** Indicates the number of octets in the PAD field, which is used to ensure that the L3_PDU is aligned on 32-bit boundaries (2 bits).

---

[4] The address format will vary from country to country, but will comply with CCITT Recommendation E.164, i.e., a country code followed by a national (significant) number, coded in BCD. The field will be padded with ones.

- **Quality of Service (QOS):** Used to provide octet alignment (4 bits).

- **CRC32 Indication Bit (CIB):** Indicates the presence or absence of the CRC32 field (1 bit).

- **Header Extension Length (HEL):** Indicates the number of 32-bit (4-octet) words in the Header Extension field; currently, this field is set to 3 to indicate a 12-octet header extension (3 bits).

- **Bridging (Brdg):** Provides 32-bit alignment of the L3_PDU (2 octets).

- **Header Extension (HE):** Used to provide additional information regarding the connection. Currently, there are two elements defined: Version, an indication of the SMDS version in use; and Carrier Selection, which allows the subscriber to select up to three interexchange carriers for use with inter-LATA SMDS. This field will be padded, if necessary, so that it is exactly 12 octets in length.

- **Information:** Data from higher layers; this is a variable-length field and can be up to 9188 octets in length. This field is large enough to encapsulate frames from other LAN standards, including IEEE 802.3, Ethernet, IEEE 802.5 token ring (4 Mbps), and Fiber Distributed Data Interface (FDDI); a notable exception is 16-Mbps Token-Ring frames, which may be up to 17,800 octets in length.

- **PAD:** Used to ensure that the Information and PAD fields are aligned on 32-bit boundaries; varies from 0 to 3 octets in length depending upon the length of the Information field.

- **CRC32:** If present, provides CRC bit-error detection protection between the DA and CRC32 fields, inclusive (0 or 4 octets).

- **Length (Len):** Contains the BAsize value as an additional check to ensure the correct reassembly of the SIP L3_PDU (2 octets).

All of these fields contain information that the SIP uses to ensure correct delivery. Frames will be discarded if certain errors occur, such as if:

- The two BEtag field values do not match,
- The BAsize and Length field values do not match,
- There are bit errors, or
- The address formats are incorrect.

If a frame is discarded, it is the responsibility of the higher layers to request retransmission the data; this is beyond the scope of the SMDS specifications.

CUSTOMER NETWORK MANAGEMENT

An objective for customers using public network service offerings is the ability to access accurate, timely information about the performance and utilization of the service. In today's data networking environment, users cannot wait for their monthly bills to determine whether or not there is a problem. In addition, access to on-going information provides the customer with a charge-back capability.

SMDS Customer Network Management, described in a Bellcore TA, defines the basic mechanisms so that a customer's network management system can access appropriate information from the public network providing SMDS to aid the network manager in tracking the performance of their own sites. The CNM procedures have been chosen so that they are similar to the management procedures used in LANs and LAN interconnect equipment, such as routers and bridges.

One of the guiding design principles for SMDS CNM is that it provide a framework to accommodate the needs of a broad range of capabilities within the user community, including customers with sophisticated internal network management procedures and staff, customers who have minimal network management experience, and customers who want the SMDS provider or a third party to perform management functions.

The first management application protocol endorsed by Bellcore is based upon the IETF's Simple Network Management Protocol. The major reason for choosing SNMP is due to the overwhelming industry support for this protocol, particularly within the LAN industry. A major objective of SMDS is that all aspects of the service maintain compatibility and synergy with existing LAN-based products, including network management.

As Figure 8.6 shows, the customer's SNMP Manager is an application that resides in the Network Management System of the customer's LAN. The network providing SMDS, the SNMP Manager's local SMDS router, and this customer's other routers contain an SNMP Agent, allowing the customer to access necessary management information. The agents and management station exchange information across the SMDS network; the Bellcore CNM specifications describe only the actions of the network's SNMP agent.

SNMP provides management functions by accessing relevant network management databases called Management Information Bases (MIBs). MIBs for DS1, DS3, and the SIP have already been defined by the IETF, and an SMDS subscription MIB (for service-specific issues such as customer contact and address screening options) is currently under development.

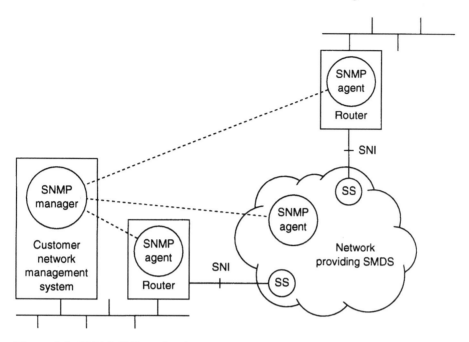

Figure 8.6 SMDS CNM using SNMP.

The protocol to access and exchange information in the MIBs is relatively straightforward. SNMP defines five types of messages:

- **GetRequest and GetNextRequest:** Requests to obtain MIB parameter value information

- **SetRequest:** Request to set a particular MIB parameter to a specified value

- **GetResponse:** Response to any of the request messages; contains the requested parameter value(s)

- **Trap:** Automatically generated as a response to alert conditions, including coldStart, warmStart, linkDown, linkUp, and enterprise-Specific

SMDS DATA EXCHANGE INTERFACE

The most common initial application for SMDS will be the interconnection of LANs. From the LAN's perspective, access to the SMDS service will be via a bridge, router, gateway, host, or some other internetworking device.

Physical access to the SMDS service will typically be over DS0, DS1, DS3, or other digital transmission facilities. Attachment to a digital carrier requires use of a CSU/DSU.

In 1991, the SIG recognized that there were no SMDS interworking devices with CSU/DSU capabilities. CSU/DSUs and bridge/routers have been optimized to perform their specific tasks. CSU/DSUs for T1 and T3 carriers, for example, are already mature products and most do not possess the CPU power to perform the protocol management that SMDS demands. Routers and bridges, on the other hand, are well designed for protocol handling, conversion, framing, and formatting, but do not typically have CSU/DSU capabilities. The general trend in the industry, so far, has been to keep these functions separate.

What emerged initially, then, were alliances between some bridge/router and CSU/DSU vendors, so that a given bridge/router transferred SIP packets to the CSU/DSU via an agreed-upon proprietary interface protocol. The problem was, if one vendor's bridge/router only worked with one other vendor's CSU/DSU, it significantly limited the equipment choices for the customer.

The SIG's Technical Working Group has led the development of two interrelated specifications to solve this problem; namely the SMDS Data Exchange Interface Protocol and the DXI Local Management Interface (LMI). The DXI provides an open standard interface between SMDS data terminal equipment, or DTE (such as hosts, bridges, and routers), and data communications equipment, or DCE (namely, the DSU). As shown in Figure 8.7, the SIP functions are split between the two devices; the DTE handles SIP Level 3, while the DCE handles SIP Levels 1 and 2.

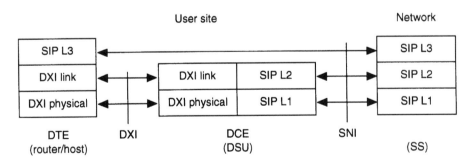

Figure 8.7 The SMDS Interface Protocol (SIP) and Data Exchange Interface (DXI) protocol architecture at the DTE (bridge, router), DCE (DSU), and SS.

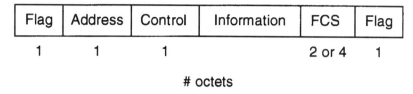

Flag	Address	Control	Information	FCS	Flag
1	1	1		2 or 4	1

octets

Figure 8.8 SMDS DXI frame format.

The DXI Physical Layer describes connectivity between the DTE and DCE. It specifies use of an EIA-530, EIA-449, CCITT Recommendation V.35, or Recommendation X.21 interface for DS1/E1 access to SMDS, and the High-Speed Serial Interface (HSSI) for DS3/E3 access.

The DXI Link Layer protocol is loosely based upon the High-Level Data Link Control (HDLC) protocol. The fields of the DXI frame (Figure 8.8) are:

- **Flag:** As in all bit-oriented protocols, the Flag is the 8-bit pattern 01111110 and is used to delimit the beginning and end of the frame. Bit stuffing (0-bit insertion) is used to prevent data from being misinterpreted as a Flag; the transmitter automatically inserts a 0 into the bit stream between Flags after any transmission of 5 contiguous 1 bits.

- **Address:** Contains a bit indicating whether this frame is a command or response, a bit indicating whether this frame is coming from or going to the DSU, and 5 bits indicating the DXI logical link (1 octet).

- **Control:** Indicates the type of frame; the DXI currently uses HDLC Unnumbered Information (UI) and TEST frames (1 octet).

- **Information:** Contains data and/or messages specific to each DXI logical link (see below).

- **Frame Check Sequence (FCS):** 16- or 32-bit CRC remainder to detect bit errors in the frame; support for a 16-bit FCS is mandatory and support for a 32-bit FCS is optional (2 or 4 octets).

The DXI identifies the logical link in the Address field. Identifying the type of information flow by logical link number allows devices to prioritize frames for transmission. In addition, the different protocols for the applications associated with each logical link can be developed and modified in parallel as long as there is adherence to the same basic formatting rules.

The DXI currently defines two logical links, numbered 0 and 1 (2–15 are reserved for future standardization and 16–31 are reserved for user definition):

- **Data Logical Link (0):** Uses UI frames to transport SIP L3_PDUs containing user data. On this logical link, the first 2 octets of the Information field comprise a 2-octet Header subfield (containing a single Congestion notification bit and 15 reserved bits) and up to 9232 octets in the Data subfield.

- **Management Logical Link (1):** Used to carry status, control, and diagnostic information between the DXI DTE and DCE for network management and reporting; LMI PDUs are carried in UI frames. TEST frames are employed in the Heart Beat Poll procedure, used by either the DTE or DCE to periodically determine the status of the DXI link.

The LMI is designed to work with a network management station running SNMP and utilizing SMDS-related management information bases, as mentioned above. It is a simple, adaptable, and generic protocol designed to provide end users with appropriate network management information.

The LMI is an asymmetric protocol; that is, DTEs and DCEs send different types of messages. The LMI defines five types of PDUs (à la SNMP):

- **GetRequest and GetNextRequest:** Requests sent by the DTE to obtain parameter value information from the DCE

- **SetRequest:** Request sent by the DTE to set a particular parameter value at the DCE

- **GetResponse:** Response sent by the DCE to provide the DTE with the requested parameter value(s)

- **Trap:** Automatically generated by the DCE as a response to an alert condition

The SNMP proxy agent resides in the DTE and is responsible for determining when to query the DCE in response to a request from the network manager. The DTE sends appropriate requests to the DCE, which then responds with the GetResponse PDU.

Some in the SMDS community have observed that the DXI provides an adequate data link protocol for the direct transfer of SMDS frames (L3_PDUs) between CPE and the network, and the fragmentation of a frame into cells merely adds unnecessary overhead and complexity. To address this concern, the SIG has proposed an HDLC-like frame-based interface for SMDS. This frame-based DXI eliminates L2_PDUs across the SNI, instead encapsulating the SMDS L3_PDU into a DXI frame, as described above. This DXI also expedites support of lower-speed Nx56 Kbps and Nx64 Kbps access to the network. One significant departure between the frame-based interface and the DXI is that the LMI is not supported; logical link #1 is used only for the exchange of TEST frames for the Heart Beat Poll process.

BRIDGING AND FDDI

Interoperability with other networking schemes is of particular interest to the SMDS community since this aspect is critical to the successful deployment and utilization of the service. LAN and FDDI bridging over IEEE 802.6 DQDB subnets and SMDS is one part of that picture.

SMDS can be used to bridge any type of IEEE 802–compatible LAN traffic, including FDDI. Since the IEEE 802.6 standard forms the technology platform for today's SMDS, the remote bridging work being done in the 802.6 committee will provide a standard that will also apply to networks providing SMDS. The IEEE 802.6i specification describes the interconnection of IEEE 802 LANs by encapsulating a LAN frame in the Information field of an SMDS packet (L3_PDU). Other related bridging standards are the IEEE 802.1d (MAC bridging) and 802.1g (remote bridging) standards.

The University of California at Berkeley's Bay Bridge Project has designed an encapsulation bridge to transport FDDI packets transparently across an SMDS network. This capability has generated interest in both the SIG and the American National Standards Institute (ANSI) X3T9.5 (FDDI) Task Group.

SMDS AND FRAME RELAY

Frame relay is a connection-oriented, fast-packet data service, conceptually similar to X.25. Whereas X.25 has three protocol layers and provides a guaranteed, virtual circuit packet delivery service, frame relay has only two layers of protocol and relies on higher-layer protocols for end-to-end message assurance. X.25 identifies virtual circuits by use of a Logical Channel Identifier carried in Packet Layer Protocol (Layer 3) packets; frame relay uses a Data Link Connection Identifier (DLCI) carried in Data Link Layer (Layer 2) frames.

Several vendors and service providers are interested in providing some form of interworking between SMDS and frame relay. One reason is that this

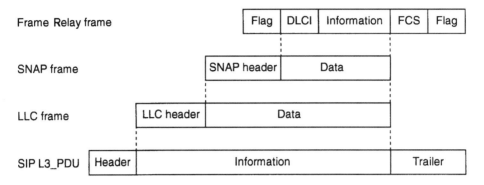

Figure 8.9 Frame relay encapsulation in SMDS.

allows a provider to offer both services over one type of user–network interface. This also allows internetworking between a frame relay service provider and an SMDS provider.

A Frame Relay frame comprises five fields, namely, two Flags to delimit the beginning and end of the frame; the Address field, containing congestion control bits and the DLCI to identify the virtual circuit; an Information field containing higher-layer data; and a Frame Check Sequence (FCS) field with the remainder from the CRC error-detection calculation. The SIG is examining two different schemes for SMDS/frame relay interworking, namely, *encapsulation* and *protocol conversion*.

Frame relay encapsulation into SMDS uses a standard IEEE 802 technique (Figure 8.9). The DLCI and User Data are carried in an IEEE 802.1 Subnetwork Access Protocol (SNAP) frame; information in the SNAP header identifies the protocol as frame relay. The SNAP frame, in turn, is carried in an IEEE 802.2 Logical Link Control frame; LLC header information indicates use of the SNAP protocol. The LLC frame is carried in a SIP L3_PDU.

Encapsulation of frame relay into SMDS implies that the network providing SMDS is acting as a bridge between two frame relay networks; that is, a Frame Relay frame is encapsulated in an SMDS frame at the entry side of the SMDS network and a new Frame Relay frame is created at the exit side. It is the responsibility of the SMDS/frame relay gateway at the entry side to translate the source DLCI to the destination DLCI *and* to determine the SMDS network address of the appropriate exit-side gateway.

Frame relay protocol conversion to SMDS removes most of the protocol overhead of encapsulation and obviates the requirement for there to be a Frame Relay network at both the source and destination side (Figure 8.10). An SMDS converter accepts a Frame Relay frame and creates an SMDS

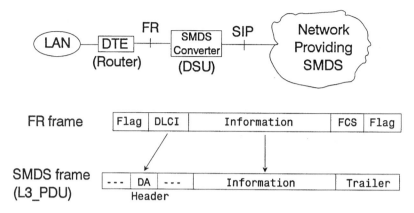

Figure 8.10 Frame relay/SMDS protocol conversion.

frame; only the Frame Relay user data is transported in the SMDS frame. It is the responsibility of the SMDS converter to map the Frame Relay DLCI to an appropriate SMDS Destination Address.

SMDS AND ATM

ATM is a cell relay transport scheme that is similar to SMDS in many ways. Telephone network planners widely view ATM as the underlying basis for next-generation networks transporting voice, data, video, and other types of traffic. In particular, BISDN services will be offered over an ATM network. Although a detailed description of ATM is beyond the scope of this chapter, a brief examination of its relationship to SMDS is in order.

CCITT ATM specifications define four ATM service classes, categorized by the bit rate, timing relationship between the source and destination, and connection mode requirements of the service (Figure 8.11). In particular, ATM class D provides a connectionless data service, an example of which is SMDS.

The ATM protocol suite is divided into three layers (Figure 8.12). The Physical Layer (PHY) will be SONET (or the Synchronous Digital Hierarchy [SDH], its CCITT counterpart). The ATM Layer provides a connection-oriented service and is responsible for managing the cells. Since ATM can support several types of service classes, an additional layer is needed to provide the interface between the ATM Layer and the additional requirements of the specific service class; this layer is the ATM Adaptation Layer (AAL).

SERVICE CHAR.	CLASS			
	A	B	C	D
Bit rate	Constant	Variable		
Timing	Time sensitive		Time insensitive	
Mode	Connection-oriented			Connectionless
Example	Voice, CBR	VBR	X.25, FR	SMDS

Figure 8.11 ATM service classes.

Like SMDS, ATM uses 53-octet cells. All cells have a 5-octet header, which is created and managed by the ATM Layer. The format of the remaining 48 octets, the Payload field, is the responsibility of the AAL. To date, several AAL types have been defined. AAL types 1 and 2 are defined for ATM classes A and B, respectively. AAL types 3 and 4 were intended for both classes C and D; the cell format and procedures were so similar, however, that their specifications were merged and they are usually referred to as AAL3/4. The AAL3/4 cell format is very similar to the SMDS (and IEEE 802.6) cell format, as shown in Figure 8.13.

A new AAL type 5 was defined in 1992 to provide greater efficiency. As Figures 8.3 and 8.13 show, ATM-like cell relay has at least 17 percent protocol overhead. In an attempt to reduce the overhead and increase throughput, AAL5 cells use the entire 48-octet Payload field for user data, making them incompatible with SMDS/DQDB cells. The current trend seems to be moving towards the AAL5 format and away from AAL3/4; as a result, the IEEE 802.6 committee is examining ways to use AAL5-type cells in DQDB

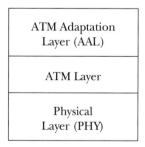

Figure 8.12 ATM protocol architecture.

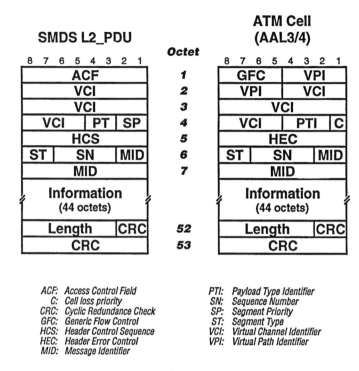

Figure 8.13 SMDS/DQDB cell and AAL5 cell formats.

and any solution that they derive will most likely be adopted for use with SMDS.

IP OVER SMDS

One of the design objectives of SMDS is compatibility with existing networks, products, and protocols. Since SMDS will act as a LAN interconnection network, its compatibility with existing LAN interworking protocols is particularly important. As TCP/IP is widely used on LANs, then, a relationship between SMDS and the TCP/IP protocol suite is quite important.

RFC 1209 describes how IP and Address Resolution Protocol (ARP) packets can be encapsulated for transmission over a DQDB network providing SMDS service. The purpose of this RFC is clear; users running TCP or User Datagram Protocol (UDP) applications over IP can use the SMDS public network for the transport of their data.

User Application
TCP or UDP
IP/ARP
SNAP
LLC
SIP L3
SIP L2
SIP L1

Figure 8.14   Protocol architecture described by RFC 1209.

Figure 8.14 shows the protocol layers described in RFC 1209. The encapsulation scheme described here is similar to that for frame relay encapsulation and is common throughout the Internet community. Although the actual encodings are beyond the scope of this chapter, the various layers include:

- End-user application data, which is carried as a TCP or UDP message, is transported in an IP datagram.

- The top layer, from the perspective of this RFC, is IP or ARP.

- The IP/ARP datagram is transported in a SNAP frame.

- SNAP frames are carried in LLC frames.

- LLC frames are carried in SIP L3_PDUs.

- SIP L3_PDUs (frames) are then segmented and carried as SIP L2_PDUs (cells).

ARP was originally designed to provide address translation between Ethernet 48-bit addresses and Internet 32-bit addresses. ARP procedures can also be used to map 60-bit SMDS addresses to Internet addresses.

RFC 1209 demonstrates that IP protocol information can be easily carried over SMDS. Since the TCP/IP suite has emerged as one of the most important interworking *and* open systems protocol suites, this ability is significant.

SMDS, then, has the potential to have a positive impact on internetworking in a number of ways:

- Use of a connectionless wide area service should improve gateway performance and decrease delays compared to today's connection-oriented WANs. SMDS also offers a larger packet size, decreasing the amount of segmentation and reassembly processing at LAN gateways.

- The availability of a multicast addressing capability may simplify wide area routing processing.

- As SMDS becomes a ubiquitous connectionless data service, administration of internets may be facilitated through the use of a single service. (SMDS has already been deployed in the U.S. Internet backbone.)

- Interconnected public local and interexchange SMDS networks will provide a more uniform quality of service than a collection of autonomously operated private networks.

- The high speeds offered by SMDS provide an opportunity to play an important part in evolving high-bandwidth applications such as medical imaging, image processing, high-speed data transport, and desktop publishing.

SMDS SERVICES AND PRODUCTS

The first trial of a MAN service in the United States was conducted by Bell Atlantic Corporation and Temple University in Philadelphia. This trial was held between the summer of 1990 and spring of 1991, using QPSX Communications switches supplied by Siemens Stromberg-Carlson. The main focus of the trial was high-speed LAN interconnection and medical imaging (for the customer), field testing the equipment (for the switch vendor), and experience providing the service (for the network provider). One result of this early trial was that Bell Atlantic, in 1991, became the first network provider in the United States to offer a public SMDS service.

By late 1990, several other service providers had begun trials of SMDS, including Pacific Bell, NYNEX, BellSouth, and US WEST. In a significant announcement in May 1992, all seven RBOCs and GTE (the largest independent telephone company in the United States) jointly announced their initial SMDS (and frame relay) rollout plans. AT&T and MCI have subsequently announced their plans to offer inter-LATA SMDS. SMDS was

Table 8.1 Sample List of SMDS Product Vendors[a]

BRIDGE/ROUTER/HUB/CONCENTRATOR	CSU/DSU
Ascom Timeplex	ADC-Kentrox Industries
Cisco Systems	Advanced Computer Comm.
Digital Equipment Corp.	Digital Link
NetVantage	NEC America
Network Systems Corp.	Verilink
Primary Rate Inc.	
Proteon, Inc.	
3Com	
Ungermann-Bass	
Vitalink Communication	
Wellfleet Communications	

SWITCHING SYSTEMS	INTERFACE CARDS
Alcatel	Hewlett-Packard Co.
AT&T Network Systems	Multiaccess Computing Corp.
Digital Switch Corp.	Pacific Access Computers
Fujitsu	Sun Microsystems
NEC America	
QPSX Communications	
Siemens Stromberg-Carlson	

PROTOCOL ANALYZERS	CHIP SETS
ANDO Corp.	AT&T
GN Navtel	Base$_2$ Systems
Hewlett-Packard Co.	Pacific Microelectronic
Wandel & Goltermann	Transwitch Corp.

[a]This list is not exhaustive nor intended as an endorsement of any product or vendor.

available in at least 20 metropolitan areas in the United States by the end of 1992 and as many as 75 cities may be served by the end of 1993.

SMDS is not isolated to the United States The world's first MAN trial was started in 1990 in Australia using QPSX Communications' equipment, resulting in Telecom Australia's FASTPAC MAN service. MAN trials and/or services have been held or planned in Germany, France, Italy, Sweden, Switzerland, Taiwan, the United Kingdom, and other countries. International SMDS implementations will probably comply with, or be very similar to, the Bellcore specifications.

As with any communications technology, the success of SMDS will lie with its adoption not only by service providers, but also by product manufacturers and vendors. To date, a large number of SMDS products have been brought out to market (Table 8.1), including:

- Switching systems
- Bridges, routers, hubs, and concentrators
- SMDS CSU/DSU
- Interface boards for PCs, Macintoshes, and other host systems
- Chip sets
- Protocol analyzers

CONCLUSIONS

This chapter has provided an overview of the SMDS service and has surveyed several important SMDS technical contributions from various segments of the industry. The creation of SMDS-related standards will minimize the expense and effort required by CPE vendors to support SMDS in their equipment and will, therefore, accelerate the number and variety of CPE and switching equipment that can support SMDS. In addition, interoperability in the multivendor environment is greatly enhanced.

The complementary work of Bellcore, the SIGs, the IETF, and others will also increase the attractiveness of SMDS to both service providers and potential customers. These industry-accepted specifications will provide a pathway for early implementations as well as future evolution.

GLOSSARY OF ACRONYMS AND ABBREVIATIONS

AAL	ATM Adaptation Layer
ANSI	American National Standards Institute
ARP	Address Resolution Protocol (IETF)
ATM	Asynchronous transfer mode
Bellcore	Bell Communications Research
BISDN	Broadband integrated services digital network
CCITT	International Telephone and Telegraph Consultative Committee

CNM	Customer Network Management (SMDS)
CPE	Customer premises equipment
CRC	Cyclic redundancy check
CSMA/CD	Carrier sense multiple access with collision detection
CSU	Channel service unit
DCE	Data circuit-terminating equipment
DLCI	Data link connection identifier (frame relay)
DQDB	Distributed Queue Dual Bus (IEEE 802.6)
DSU	Data service unit
DTE	Data terminal equipment
DXI	Data Exchange Interface (SIG)
ETSI	European Telecommunications Standards Institute
FDDI	Fiber Distributed Data Interface (ANSI)
HDLC	High-Level Data Link Control Protocol (ISO)
IC	Interexchange carrier
ICI	Interexchange Carrier Interface (SMDS)
IEEE	Institute of Electrical and Electronics Engineers
IETF	Internet Engineering Task Force
IP	Internet Protocol (IETF)
ISO	International Organization for Standardization
ISSI	Inter-Switching System Interface (SMDS)
LAN	Local area network
LATA	Local access and transport area
LEC	Local exchange carrier
LLC	Logical Link Control (IEEE 802.2)
LMI	Local Management Interface (SIG)
MAC	Medium access control
MAN	Metropolitan area network
MIB	Management information base (SNMP)
PDU	Protocol data unit
QPSX	Queued Packet and Synchronous Exchange
RBOC	Regional Bell operating company
RFC	Request for Comment (IETF)
SIG	SMDS Interest Group
SIP	SMDS Interface Protocol (SMDS)
SMDS	Switched Multimegabit Data Service
SNAP	Subnetwork Access Protocol (IEEE 802)
SNI	Subscriber-network interface (SMDS)
SNMP	Simple Network Management Protocol (IETF)

SONET	Synchronous Optical Network
SS	Switching system (SMDS)
TCP	Transmission Control Protocol (IETF)
UDP	User Datagram Protocol (IETF)
UI	Unnumbered Information frames (DXI)

BIBLIOGRAPHY, STANDARDS, AND FURTHER READING

Bellcore, *A Framework of High-Level Generic Requirements for SMDS Exchange Access Operations Management (XA-OM) Service*. FA-TSV-001237, Issue 1, October 1992.

_____, *Generic Requirements for SMDS Customer Network Management Service*. TA-TSV-001062, Issue 2, February 1992.

_____, *Generic Requirements for SMDS Networking*. TA-TSV-001059, Issue 2, August 1992.

_____, *Generic System Requirements in Support of Switched Multi-Megabit Data Service*, TR-TSV-000772, Issue 1, May 1991.

_____, *Local Access System Generic Requirements, Objectives, and Interfaces in Support of Switched Multi-Megabit Data Service*. TR-TSV-000773, Issue 1, June 1991.

_____, *Operations Technology Generic Criteria in Support of Exchange Access SMDS and Intercompany Serving Arrangements*. TR-TSV-001063, Issue 1, December 1992.

_____, *Operations Technology Network Element Generic Requirements in Support of Inter-Switch and Exchange Access SMDS*. TA-TSV-001061, Issue 1, May 1991.

_____, *SMDS Generic Criteria on Operations Interfaces—SMDS Information Model and Usage*. TR-TSV-001064, Issue 1, December 1992.

_____, *SMDS Operations Technology Network Element Generic Requirements*. TR-TSV-000774, Issue 1, March 1992.

_____, *Switched Multi-Megabit Data Service First Phase for Exchange Access and Intercompany Serving Arrangements*. SR-TSV-002395, Issue 1, July 1992.

_____, *Switched Multi-Megabit Data Service Generic Requirements for Exchange Access and Intercompany Serving Arrangements*. TR-TSV-001060, Issue 1, December 1991.

_____, *Usage Measurement Generic Requirements in Support of Switched Multi-Megabit Data Service*. TR-TSV-000775, Issue 1, June 1991.

Cox, T. A., and K. Tesink (eds.), *Definitions of Managed Objects for the SIP Interface Type*. RFC 1304, February 1992.

European Telecommunications Standards Institute, *Metropolitan Area Network (MAN) Principles and Architecture*. ETR 300 211. (This is the first in a family of MAN-related specifications.)

Feit, S., *TCP/IP: Architecture, Protocols, and Implementation*. New York: McGraw-Hill, 1992.

Institute of Electrical and Electronics Engineers, *Distributed Queue Dual Bus (DQDB) Subnetwork of a Metropolitan Area Network (MAN)*. ANSI/IEEE 802.6.

_____, *Logical Link Control.*, ANSI/IEEE 802.2.

_____, *Overview and Architecture.*, ANSI/IEEE 802.

Kessler, G. C., "IEEE 802.6 MAN," *LAN Magazine*, April 1990.

Kessler, G. C. and D. A. Train, *Metropolitan Area Networks: Concepts, Standards, and Services*. New York: McGraw-Hill, 1992.

Piscitello, D., and J. Lawrence, *The Transmission of IP Datagrams over the SMDS Service*. RFC 1209, March 1991.

Rose, M. T., *The Simple Book: An Introduction to Management of TCP/IP-Based Internets*. Englewood Cliffs, New Jersey: Prentice Hall, 1991.

SMDS Interest Group, *Frame-Based Interface Protocol for SMDS Networks—DXI*. Version 3, January 5, 1993.

_____, *SMDS Data Exchange Interface Protocol*. SIG-TS-001/1991, Revision 3.2, October 22, 1991.

_____, *SMDS DXI Local Management Interface*. SIG-TS-002/1992, Revision 2.0, May 19, 1992.

Tesink, K. (ed.), *Definitions of Managed Objects for SMDS Subscription*. Bellcore draft, March 1991.

SOURCES OF SMDS INFORMATION AND STANDARDS

Bell Communications Research (Bellcore)
Documentation Coordinator
60 New England Avenue
Piscataway, NJ 08854
908-699-5800 / 1-800-521-CORE (2673)

European SMDS Interest Group (ESIG)
InterConnect Communications Ltd. (ICC)
Merlin House
Station Road
Chepstow
Gwent, United Kingdom NP6 5PB
+44-0-291-620425 (voice) / +44-0-291-627119 (fax)

European Telecommunications Standards Institute (ETSI)
B.P. 152-F-06561 Valbonne Cedex
France
+33-92944200 (voice) / +33-93654716 (fax)

Institute of Electrical and Electronics Engineers (IEEE)
445 Hoes Lane, P.O. Box 1331
Piscataway, NJ 08855-1331
908-981-0060 (voice) / 908-981-9667 (fax)

Internet Engineering Task Force (IETF) Secretariat
Corporation for National Research Initiatives
1895 Preston White Drive, Suite 100
Reston, VA 22091
703-620-8990 (voice) / 703-620-0913 (fax)
Electronic mail: ietf-info@nri.reston.va.us

SMDS Interest Group
480 San Antonio Road, Suite 100
Mountain View, CA 94040-1219
415-962-2590 (voice) / 415-941-0849 (fax)
Electronic mail: smdstc@nsco.network.com (SIG Technical Committee)

ABOUT THE AUTHOR

Gary C. Kessler is a senior member of the technical staff at Hill Associates in Colchester, Vermont, a technical education and consulting firm specializing in telecommunications technologies and services. He has written several articles for technical journals, is a contributor to *LAN Magazine*, the author of *ISDN: Concepts, Facilities, and Services*, 2nd edition (McGraw-Hill, 1993), and the co-author of *Metropolitan Area Networks: Concepts, Standards, and Services* (McGraw-Hill, 1992). He is an observer on the ANSI X3T9.5 (FDDI) Task Group; a participant on the IEEE 802.6 (MANs), 802.9 (Integrated Voice/Data LANs), and 802.11 (Wireless LANs) subcommittees; an observer on the SMDS Interest Group Technical Committee; and an observer on the Frame Relay Forum Technical Committee. Electronic mail to Mr. Kessler may be addressed to kumquat@smcvax.smcvt.edu.

PART 4

Local Area Networks

9

Ethernet/802.3 and Token Ring/802.5

John Enck
Forest Computer Incorporated

INTRODUCTION

Overview

Many people believe the two major local area network (LAN) standards are Ethernet and Token Ring. The fact that what looks like an Ethernet network may, in reality, be an IEEE 802.3 is often dismissed as technical nitpicking. Similarly, pointing out that the Token-Ring LANs may be implemented according to IBM specifications or to the IEEE 802.5 specifications generates a similar lack of concern.

In reality, Ethernet, IEEE 802.3, IBM Token Ring, and IEEE 802.5 all describe different LAN environments. Although the IBM Token-Ring specifications and the IEEE 802.5 specifications are very similar, differences do exist. In contrast, the specifications for Ethernet and IEEE 802.3 are dramatically different—different to the point where the two can coexist but not interoperate.

Behind the technical differences is a significant philosophical difference. The IEEE 802.3 and 802.5 specifications are driven by the Institute of Electrical and Electronics Engineers (IEEE). The IEEE is a noncommercial standards-producing organization. The IEEE reports its recommendations to ANSI (American National Standards Institute) which, in turn, contributes them to ISO (International Standards Organization).

On the other side of the fence, the commercial implementations of Ethernet and Token Ring are driven, for the most part, by Digital Equipment Corporation and IBM. This is not intrinsically bad; however, it is worth considering that their motivation may not be as altruistic as the IEEE. For example, during the years that IBM chose not to support Ethernet and Digital chose not to support Token Ring, those choices were not purely made on a basis of technology (although both companies had reams of documents to prove the superiority of their LAN of choice).

Fortunately, the LAN wars are rapidly coming to an end and most major manufacturers now support some mixture of Ethernet, IEEE 802.3, IBM Token Ring, and IEEE 802.5 specifications. To see how we got to this point in time—where commercial specifications and noncommercial standards have become so intertwined—we need to take a brief stroll down the memory lanes of Ethernet and Token-Ring LANs.

History of Ethernet/802.3

Ethernet and 802.3 are similar (but not identical) implementations of a Carrier Sense, Multiple Access with Collision Detection (CSMA/CD) LAN. Ethernet was developed in the commercial market, while 802.3 was developed by an independent standards organization. Specifically:

- Ethernet was created by Xerox Corporation in 1972; however, the first commercial implementation of Ethernet, Version 1, was developed in a joint effort by Xerox, Digital Equipment Corporation, and Intel Corporation and introduced in 1980. The Version 1 specification was subsequently refined and introduced in 1982 as Ethernet Version 2.

- The 802.3 implementation was designed by the IEEE as part of its 802 series of LAN specifications. These specifications were approved by the IEEE in 1983.

The 802.3 design was, in fact, based on the Version 1 Ethernet implementation. The IEEE enhanced the design to the extent that the two implementations were incompatible with one another. In response, Xerox, Intel, and Digital created the Version 2 implementation of Ethernet so 802.3 and Ethernet could coexist on the same physical LAN.

Because of the similarities, and the fact that both Ethernet and 802.3 can coexist on the same physical LAN (or in the same system), the two terms are often used together, or interchangeably. In point of fact, they are not interchangeable and network software using the Ethernet specifications cannot communicate with a network software using the 802.3 specifications. Additional technical information on the differences between Ethernet and 802.3 are presented in the Ethernet versus 802.3 section of this chapter.

History of Token Ring/802.5

The design for Token-Ring networking dates back to 1969; however, Token-Ring technology did not become a major factor in LANs until the mid-1980s. Specifically, in 1982, IBM presented a series of papers on Token-Ring technology to the IEEE, who were beginning the development of the 802 series of LAN standards. IBM's presentation became a driving force that resulted in the development of the IEEE 802.5 standard for token-passing ring networks, released in 1985.

IBM's first foray into Token-Ring networking also took place in 1985 with the announcement of a Token-Ring LAN for PCs. This offering was then broadened in 1986 to include other platforms in the IBM computer family. Since that time, Token Ring has been the backbone of IBM's LAN strategy.

IBM's implementation of Token-Ring and the IEEE specifications for the 802.5 are extremely similar, but not exactly identical. The specific differences between IBM Token Ring and 802.5 are described in the IBM Token Ring versus 802.5 section of this chapter. To be sure, an IBM Token-Ring network can be installed and operated according to the 802.5 specifications; IBM has simply chosen to "tweak" the specification in certain areas. In general, the differences between IBM's implementation and the IEEE specifications are not worth losing any sleep over.

IEEE 802.2

The commercial implementations of Ethernet and Token Ring have very little in common. The IEEE implementations of 802.3 and 802.5, however, have a great deal in common.

Specifically, when the IEEE embarked on defining a set of standards to apply to LANs, it wanted to create a common framework for those standards. To accomplish this, the IEEE broke LAN functions into two general areas:

- **Logical Link Control (LLC):** This interface defines how the LAN interacts with higher-level network protocols (e.g., SNA, IPX).

- **Media Access Control (MAC):** This interface relates to the LAN access methodology (token-passing or collision-sensing) and the physical aspects of the LAN.

The LLC definition is defined by the IEEE 802.2 standard. The 802.3 and 802.5 standards, in turn, address the MAC definitions. Also note that the LLC definition is incorporated into both MAC structures, as shown in Figure 9.1.

The LLC structure contains two fields of particular importance: the Destination Service Access Point (DSAP) and Source Service Access Point (SSAP). The purpose of these Service Access Points (SAPs) is to identify the logical network that originated the message (SSAP) and the logical network where the message is to be delivered (DSAP). For example, the SAP has been assigned values that relate to following network protocols:

SAP	Assignment
00	Null
04	IBM SNA (station operations)
05	IBM SNA (group operations)
06	Internet Protocol (IP of TCP/IP)
80	Xerox Networking Services (XNS)
E0	Novell NetWare
F0	IBM NetBIOS
F4	LAN management (station)
F5	LAN management (group)
F8	IBM Remote Program Load (RPL)
FE	Open System Interconnect (OSI) network layer
FF	Global

The ultimate significance of the DSAP and SSAP, then, is that they enable multiple protocols to share the physical LAN and coexist with one another.

Specifically, when a system receives a broadcast frame or a frame specifically addressed to it, it then looks at the DSAP field to determine what to do next. If the SAP value is unknown to the system, the message is rejected or ignored (depending on the context). If, however, the SAP is known to the system, the system then locates the program/service handling that SAP. This mechanism works fine for a system that only handles one network protocol (one SAP), or for a system that can potentially handle a number of network protocols (several SAPs) over one physical LAN connection.

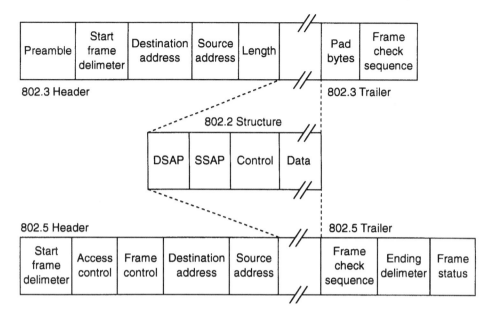

Figure 9.1 802.2.

The IEEE 802.3, IEEE 802.5, and IBM Token-Ring specifications employ the SSAP and DSAP fields. Ethernet, which has a different frame format, uses a single "Type" field to identify the network protocol present in the frame.

ETHERNET/802.3

Theory of Operation

Ethernet and 802.3 specify a LAN operation at speeds of 10 Mbps using frames that can carry up to 1500 bytes of user data. The keys to Ethernet and 802.3 operation are the carrier-detection and collision-sensing mechanisms. These two mechanisms allow multiple systems to contend for access to the LAN and to detect (and recover) from data collisions that can occur on the LAN. These mechanisms are part of the CSMA/CD access discipline.

Under CSMA/CD, a system that wants to make a transmission "listens" to the LAN to see if any data is currently being transmitted. If the LAN is quiescent (no carrier is detected on the receive circuit), the system transmits a frame of information. If, however, the LAN is busy, the system waits for a brief period of time and then retests the condition of the LAN. A system may repeat this process many times before it is able to transmit its information.

In the event that two systems detect an idle LAN at the same time and start transmitting at the same time, a data collision occurs and the information is garbled beyond recognition. The transmitting systems of the LAN will recognize that a collision has occurred because of the electrical disturbance generated by both systems transmitting at the same time—the signal level will be twice what it should be.

After experiencing a data collision, each system waits for a small random interval of time before attempting to transmit again. If another collision occurs on the next attempt, the system will wait for a longer period of time. This process is repeated until the information is successfully transmitted or the operation is aborted.

Data collisions can only occur when two or more systems begin transmitting at the same time, because if one system accesses the LAN first, others will detect a carrier and will not attempt to transmit. Once a data frame is successfully transmitted (no collisions are reported), Ethernet regards the network transaction as complete. No acknowledgments are generated at the CSMA/CD protocol level to indicate if the frame was successfully received or not.

The strength of CSMA/CD lies in how it allows a minority of devices to dominate the LAN if the majority of systems have little or no information to transmit. For example, if only two systems in a 100-system LAN have information to exchange, they can dominate the LAN for the duration of the exchange.

Conversely, in a heavily loaded LAN the same aspect of CSMA/CD becomes a weakness. When LAN activity is high, systems must wait for LAN access and they also experience a high number of data collisions. Both of these factors affect LAN performance and can produce periods of unusually slow response times.

Topology and Construction

As shown in Figure 9.2, Ethernet and 802.3 networks can be configured using a bus topology, tree topology, hub topology, or any combination of the three topologies. Large Ethernet and 802.3 networks normally begin with a main bus cable that establishes the main "backbone" of the LAN, and then employ tree and/or hub segments originating from the main backbone to reach groups of systems.

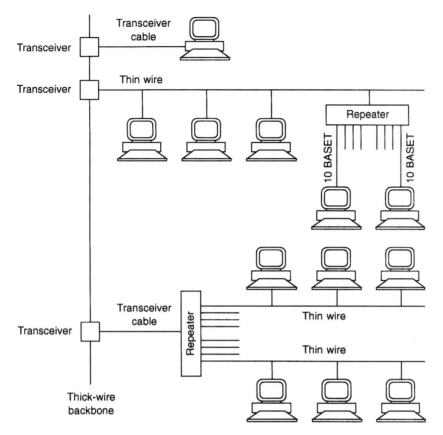

Figure 9.2　802.3/Ethernet topology.

Connecting a device to an Ethernet LAN requires the use of an attachment device called a transceiver. A transceiver may be a physical external device or the transceiver functions may be integrated into the network adapter. As a general rule, this is a function of the type of media; connection to the thick coaxial backbone is typically handled by an external transceiver, while connections to thin coaxial segments use internal transceivers. Twisted-pair connections can go either way.

The term "transceiver" (TRANSmitter/reCEIVER) is for the most part an Ethernet term. In the formal specifications for the IEEE 802.3 network, the attachment functions are handled by a Medium Attachment Unit (MAU). The popularity of the term transceiver, however, resulted in a spill-over of its use in the 802.3 environment.

The primary function of the transceiver/MAU is to translate the digital information generated by the system into the electrical format appropriate for the connection media. Beyond the managing send and receive operations, a transceiver (or the transceiver logic on an interface adapter) performs several functions of particular interest and value to Ethernet and 802.3 LANs:

- **Collision detection.** The transceiver contains the circuitry that detects when a collision occurs on the media. When a collision is detected, the transceiver performs two actions. First, the transceiver generates a signal to notify the transmitting system that a collision has occurred. Second, after notifying the transmitter about the collision, the transceiver then broadcasts a "jamming" signal on the LAN. The jamming signal alerts other systems that a collision has occurred and also allows the LAN to "settle" before transmission resumes.

- **Heartbeat.** A heartbeat is a brief signal generated by the transceiver after every transmission to ensure the main adapter that the transmission was free of collisions. A heartbeat uses the same electrical interface used to report collisions; however, it occurs *after* transmission and is much shorter in duration. Although the heartbeat function is defined in both Ethernet (as the Collision Presence Test) and 802.3 specifications (as Signal Quality Error [SQE] Test), it is rarely used because many adapters confuse a heartbeat with a collision signal.

- **Jabber.** The jabber function allows the transceiver to discontinue transmission if the frame being transmitted exceeds the specified limit (1518 bytes). This prevents a malfunctioning system or adapter from flooding the LAN with inappropriate data.

- **Monitor.** The final function allows the transceiver to prohibit transmit functions while enabling receive and collision detection functions. As a result, the attached system can monitor LAN traffic, but it cannot originate any traffic.

Smaller LANs are often constructed solely with cable, connectors, and transceivers. Large networks, however, usually employ some or all of the following devices:

- **Repeaters.** Repeaters are used to connect two segments together to form a single logical segment. Repeaters do not filter the traffic between segments. Multiple repeaters may be used to interconnect consecutive segments.

- **Multiport repeaters.** A multiport repeater is a hub that allows the connection of systems or additional LAN segments to a central point. A single multiport repeater may be used to create a small stand-alone network using a hub topology.

- **Local bridges.** Given that all systems compete for LAN access under the CSMA/CD access discipline, Ethernet and 803.2 networks are often broken down into smaller network segments that are linked together using intelligent local bridges. When bridges are employed, local traffic on a LAN segment is isolated from the other LAN segments; only traffic destined for the other LAN segment moves across the bridge. This dramatically reduces network-wide competition for access to the main LAN, because systems compete for access to their local segment, and the bridge contends for access to another LAN if needed.

- **Wide area bridges.** Wide area bridges perform the same function as local bridges; however, they connect the two LANs (or LAN segments) over wide area links such as X.25 packet-switching networks, leased analog or digital phone lines, frame relay networks, and so on.

- **Routers.** Routers are similar to wide area bridges because they too interconnect multiple Ethernet networks over wide area links. The level at which bridges and routers operate is, however, quite different. Specifically, a bridge is oblivious to the network protocol in use (i.e., TCP/IP, IPX, DECnet, etc.) and makes its decisions on when to bridge and when not to bridge based on the Ethernet/802.3 frame information alone. In contrast, a router interacts at the network protocol level and forwards frames based on the network protocol type or on information contained in the network protocol information, such as logical addresses.

Additional devices are available to convert media types, to extend the length of Ethernet links using fiber optic cable, and to perform other specialized functions.

Cabling

Physical construction of an Ethernet or 802.3 LAN is as much dependent on the type of media as it is on the overall topology. The types of media commonly used are:

- **Thick cable (10BASE5).** As the name implies, this is a thick (10 millimeters in diameter) coaxial cable that can be up to 500 meters in length per segment. Thick cables are usually employed as a main LAN backbone. External transceivers are then used to make the connection between the main LAN cable and the attached systems or devices. Each transceiver is permanently attached to the thick cable and presents a 15-pin D-shell connector for attachment to a system, repeater, or other device.

- **Thin cable (10BASE2).** Thin cable is common coaxial cable (e.g., RG-58 A/U) that can be up to 185 meters in length per segment. Thin cable uses twist-on BNC connectors to attach to a series of systems or devices. Each system or device attachment uses a T-shaped connector to daisy-chain the connection to the next system or device. The final "T" in the chain must be fitted with a twist-on termination plug. In most 10BASE2 implementations, transceiver functions are integrated into the LAN adapter card.

- **Unshielded Twisted Pair (UTP) (10BASET).** UTP cable is very similar to twisted-pair phone cable. A UTP segment can be up to 100 meters long and attaches to a single system or device. Because of this single attachment design, UTP connections are typically used in conjunction with a multiport repeater (sometimes called a "hub" in this context), which provides a number of UTP connections. The physical connection is normally an eight-wire RJ-45 push-in connector. UTP implementations can use either internal or external transceivers, depending on the systems and devices being interconnected.

The different styles of media can be interconnected using repeaters. For example, one or more thin-wire segments can be connected to a thick-wire segment. A UTP multiport repeater can be attached to a thick or thin segment. A UTP segment can even be converted into a thin-wire segment. This flexibility makes installing, expanding, or reconfiguring an Ethernet or 802.3 a relatively easy and painless task.

Ethernet and 802.3 both use the Manchester encoding scheme to transmit and receive data on the LAN. In thick and thin cable these signals are carried over the coaxial media. When transceiver cables or UTP cables are employed, these signals are carried over copper wire pairs.

A transceiver cable uses a 15-pin connection. The assignment of these pins varies slightly between Ethernet and 802.3, as will be shown in the next section. UTP cable, on the other hand, must be composed of two sets of twisted-pair wires. The assignment for these wires using a standard RJ-45 connector is as follows:

Typical 10BASET Cable

Wire	*Assignment*
1	Transmit +
2	Transmit –
3	Receive +
4	
5	
6	Receive –
7	
8	

Using this arrangement, wires 1 and 2 should be twisted together, and wires 3 and 6 should be twisted together. This is the subset of the four-pair 10BASET implementation where 1 and 2, 3 and 6, 4 and 5, as well as 7 and 8 are twisted as pairs.

Ethernet versus 802.3

Both Ethernet and 802.3 specifications can coexist in a common LAN environment; however, they are not completely compatible. The two specifications differ in two key areas: (1) frame format and (2) transceiver cable circuit assignments.

As shown in Figure 9.3, the Ethernet and 802.3 are similar but not identical. Although they are similar enough to coexist in the same LAN, network

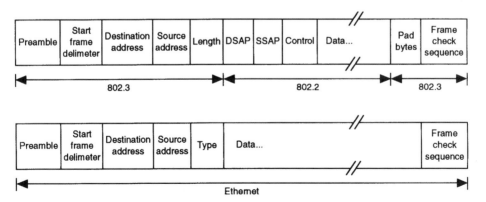

Figure 9.3 802.3 and Ethernet frame formats.

software must explicitly be written to interpret the Ethernet frame, the 802.3 frame, or must have sufficient digital intelligence to handle both formats. One of the key differentials between the two formats is that Ethernet relies on a single "Type" field to identify the type or network, or the network protocol it is carrying (well over 100 Ethernet Types are currently registered). Some examples of Ethernet Type assignments are:

Type	Assignment
0800	Department of Defense Internet Protocol (IP)
0807	Xerox XNS network protocol
0BAD	Banyan Systems network protocol
6000–6009	Digital Equipment Corporation protocols
6010–6014	3Com network protocols
8137–8138	Novell network protocols

In contrast, the 802.3 frame uses the 802.2-level SSAP and DSAP to determine what network the frame came from and what network it is going to. Please refer to the 802.2 section at the beginning of this chapter for more information on SAPs.

In terms of transceiver cable circuits, 802.3 and Ethernet use the following pin assignments:

Transceiver Cable

Pin	802.3	Ethernet
1	Control In Ground	Ground
2	Control In A	Collision Presence +
3	Data Out A	Transmit +
4	Data In Ground	
5	Data In A	Receive +
6	Voltage Common	
7	Control Out A	
8	Control Out Ground	
9	Control In B	Collision Presence –
10	Data Out B	Transmit –
11	Data Out Ground	
12	Data In B	Receive –

Pin	802.3	Ethernet
13	Power	
14	Power Ground	
15	Control Out B	

The 802.3 specification defines four circuits with each circuit composed of three wires (A, B, and ground). Of these circuits, one is used to transmit (Data Out), one to receive (Data In), and one for collision detection (Control In). The fourth circuit (Control Out) is not currently used. In contrast, Ethernet defines three circuits (transmit, receive, and collision), which share a common ground.

The common circuits between Ethernet and 802.3 share the same pin assignments. Although this means that the same cable can function in both environments, using one type of cable with the other environment is not recommended due to the differences in the grounding methods.

Specifications

General

Speed:	10 Mbps[1]
Maximum frame size:	1518 bytes
Maximum data unit:	1460 bytes (802.3), 1500 bytes (Ethernet)

Thick Coax Media

Specification:	10BASE5
Impedance:	50 Ohms
Connector:	DB-15
Maximum segment length:	500 meters
Maximum attachments per segment:	100
Minimum distance between nodes:	2.5 meters
Combined length of repeated segments:	2500 meters

---

[1] IEEE 802.3 was designed to accommodate operation at 20 Mbps, but no commercial implementation of that rate is available.

Thin Coax Media

Specification:	10BASE2
Impedance:	50 Ohms
Connector:	BNC
Maximum segment length:	185 meters
Maximum attachments per segment:	30
Minimum distance between nodes:	.5 meters
Combined length of repeated segments:	925 meters

UTP Media

Specification:	10BASET
Impedance:	85–110 Ohms
Connector:	RJ-45
Maximum segment length:	100 meters
Maximum nodes per segment:	1
Minimum distance between nodes:	Not applicable
Combined length of repeated segments:	2500 meters

Frame Formats

Figure 9.3 shows the field definitions for 802.3 and Ethernet frames. The purpose of each field is as follows:

802.3/802.2 Fields

- **Preamble:** A 7-byte pattern of binary ones and zeros to establish synchonization.

- **Start Frame Delimiter:** A 1-byte pattern indicating the start of the frame.

- **Destination Address:** The address of a specific station or group of stations to receive the frame. May be 2 or 6 bytes in length.

- **Source Address:** The address of the sending station. May be 2 or 6 bytes in length.

- **Length:** A 2-byte field containing the length of the 802.2 structure (header and data).

- **DSAP:** The 1-byte 802.2 DSAP. See the discussion under the IEEE 802.2 section of this chapter for more information.

- **SSAP:** The 1-byte 802.2 SSAP. See the discussion under the IEEE 802.2 section of this chapter for more information.

- **Control:** An 802.2 field used for various commands, including exchange identifier, test, connect, disconnect, and frame reject. May be 1 or 2 bytes long, with the length defined by the first 2 bits.

- **Data:** The actual information being transmitted.

- **Pad Bytes:** Optional nondata bytes added to ensure that the frame meets minimum length requirements.

- **Frame Check Sequence:** A 4-byte field containing a checksum of the frame information beginning with the destination address and ending with the data.

Ethernet Fields

- **Preamble:** Same as corresponding 802.3 field.

- **Start Frame Delimiter:** Same as corresponding 802.3 field.

- **Destination Address:** The 6-byte address of a specific station or group of stations to receive the frame.

- **Source Address:** The 6-byte address of the sending station.

- **Type:** A 2-byte field that identifies the network protocol or protocol service carried in the frame.

- **Data:** The actual information being transmitted.

- **Frame Check Sequence:** Same as corresponding 802.3 field.

TOKEN RING/802.5

Theory of Operation

Token-Ring networks can operate at 4 or 16 Mbps. IBM's original implementation of a 4-Mbps ring used a frame size of approximately 2 KB. This speed and frame size, however, put Token Rings at a disadvantage when compared to the performance of Ethernet networks. To compensate for the difference, the frame size was subsequently increased to 4 KB for 4-Mbps rings, and operation at 16 Mbps was introduced supporting frame sizes up to 16 KB. The increased frame size for 4-Mbps operations allowed Token-Ring networks to come close to the performance of Ethernet/802.3 networks, and operation at 16 Mbps allowed it to exceed the performance of Ethernet/802.3 networks.

In a Token-Ring network, a special message, a token, is passed from one system to another. The flow of the token is a logical ring (regardless of how the network is physically cabled); therefore, the token will always end up back at the originating system.

A system possessing information to transmit on the network must wait to receive a token. Once it has possession of the token, it transmits a frame of data to another system. When the receiver obtains the data, it sets a flag in the frame acknowledging receipt and releases the frame back into the ring. The originator sees that the frame has made it (or not) and it generates a new token to allow another system to have access to the ring.

The strength of the Token-Ring methodology is that it guarantees that every system on the LAN will have the opportunity to transmit. Furthermore, Token-Ring behavior is extremely predictable; tokens and data frames travel from one system to another in a logical fashion and time frame.

In larger networks, however, the strength of the Token-Ring LAN can become a weakness. Specifically, each system must wait to receive a token before it can transmit; therefore, when more systems are added to a LAN, this increases the opportunities for transmissions from multiple systems, which can, therefore, decrease the opportunity any one system has to receive a token. One compromise on this issue is to divide a large ring into several small rings. However, dividing systems into smaller rings is really only practical if traffic on the smaller rings can be self-contained. In other words, breaking a large ring into smaller rings which constantly access one another is not a dramatic improvement.

Ring Monitoring

The overall flow of frames through the ring is regulated by an active ring monitor. Any system can potentially be an active ring monitor, although only one active monitor may be in effect at any one time. The responsibilities of an active monitor include:

- **Looking for data frames that travel around the ring more than once.** The active monitor will remove any offenders from the ring and discard them.

- **Detecting the loss of a token.** In this case the active monitor initiates a purge of the ring and then originates a new token.

- **Clocking and timing.** The active monitor is responsible for providing the master synchronization of the ring. This is the clock source used by all other systems to ensure that they are using the same timing to send and receive data.

The loss of a token or the perpetual circling of a data frame are "soft" errors. They can be incited by accidental disruptions in the LAN, such as those caused by vacuum cleaners running over LAN cable, or by powering down systems when they are in possession of a token or involved in a message exchange. In all of these situations, the active ring monitor can normally resolve the problem automatically.

An active monitor is elected. When a system detects the absence of a ring monitor or a failure of a ring monitor, it initiates an election procedure known as "token claiming." When one system detects the absence of the active monitor (based on the absence of a ring monitor present message), it initiates a "claim token" message which, in effect, is a request to become the active monitor. When another system receives the claim token message, it takes one of the following actions:

1. If the system does not want to participate in the election process, it simply passes on the message.

2. If the system wants to participate, but the address of the system that generated the claim is higher than its own, it passes the message on.

3. If the system wants to participate and has a higher address than the system that generated the claim, it initiates a new claim token message.

In the end, the system with the highest address participating in the claim procedure will end up being elected as the new active monitor.

Ring Access

Individual systems are responsible for testing and participating in ring integrity checking. The bulk of this testing is performed when a system accesses a ring for the first time, and it involves five specific phases:

- **Phase 0 (Lobe Test).** In this phase the system sends a series of test messages to itself in order to test the connection between itself and the MAU. If this phase fails, the system will not proceed any further.

- **Phase 1 (Monitor Check).** During this phase the attaching system "listens" to the ring to see if an active monitor is present. An active monitor is a system that assumes responsibility for resolving correctable problems on the ring. An active monitor indicates its presence by periodically transmitting "active monitor present" messages on the ring. If the attaching system does not receive a broadcast from an active monitor, it initiates the procedure used to elect an active monitor (or it assumes the role of the active monitor if it is the only system on the ring). Once the operation of an active monitor is resolved, the system proceeds to the next phase. More information about the role of the active monitor is presented in the next section.

- **Phase 2 (Duplicate Address Check).** In this phase the system initiates a test message that checks for duplication of its own address in another system. If a duplicate address is detected, the system stops communicating with the ring.

- **Phase 3 (Neighbor Notification).** During this phase the attaching system sends test messages to learn the address of its Nearest Active Upstream Neighbor (NAUN) and to notify its downstream neighbor of its address. The concept of NAUN is important in deciphering Token-Ring problems. Specifically, when a serious problem occurs in the ring, the system that detects the problem starts complaining and identifies its upstream neighbor as the probable cause. This mechanism is called "beaconing" and will be discussed later.

- **Phase 4 (Request Initialization).** The final phase is used to receive any special parameters implemented through a ring parameter server. For example, this could include software-level IDs or ring number assignment. The use of initialization parameters is optional (although all systems should make the request in this phase).

These access-time tests and the activities of the ring monitor are the two key areas that facilitate the automatic monitoring and resolution of many Token-Ring network problems.

Problem Notification

When a problem arises that cannot be corrected by the active ring monitor or by the individual system that detected the error, the problem is escalated to a higher level through "beaconing." The intent of beaconing is to isolate the malfunctioning system and to inform the human operator (or any network management products that may be running) that a serious and uncorrectable problem is occurring.

A beacon is a special type of network message originated by the system that first detects the problem. The beacon message identifies the system reporting the problem and also identifies the address of its Nearest Active Upstream Neighbor (NAUN). This information is included in the beacon message to help isolate the problem; in theory, if a system is causing problems on a LAN, these problems will first be detected by its downstream neighbor.

If the beaconing system's NAUN is capable of recognizing the beacon message, it will watch for eight beacon messages to pass by and then it will take itself off the ring and perform self-tests. These self-tests correspond to the Phase 0 (Lobe Access Test) and Phase 2 (Duplicate Address Test) checks performed during the normal attachment process. If the NAUN successfully completes these tests, it assumes the problem has been corrected and rejoins the LAN. If, however, these tests do not complete successfully, the NAUN remains off the ring.

The beaconing system itself will wait for a period of time (based on ring size and speed) for the problem to be resolved. If the problem remains after the timer expires, the beaconing system will assume the NAUN has taken appropriate action. At that point the beaconing system will take itself off the LAN and perform the Lobe Access Test and Duplicate Access Test. If the tests are successful, the system rejoins the LAN. If they are unsuccessful, the system remains detached from the ring.

If a system is experiencing an internal hardware problem that can be detected but not corrected, the net result of the beaconing process will be that it will be identified as the NAUN, it will perform self-tests, and it will detach from the ring and remain detached until human intervention corrects the problem.

If, however, a system is exhibiting radically deviant behavior on the LAN, but the hardware itself cannot detect that it has a problem, the beaconing process will be repeated over and over until human intervention occurs—the defective system will be identified by the beacon and perform a successful self-test, as will the beacon, but the problem will continue. Needless to say, this has a negative impact on normal LAN activities.

Unfortunately, the latter case is more prevalent than the former; most hard errors are detected and resolved by humans, not by software.

Optional Behavior

In the token-passing methodology previously described, each system has equal access to the token; no one system has priority over others. An option in most Token-Ring implementations is the use of multiple access priorities for systems on the LAN. These priorities may be applied to LAN traffic to allow higher-priority systems to "override" the transmissions of lower-priority systems. In effect, one system can interrupt the current traffic on the LAN to handle a higher-priority traffic.

When a system has a message to transmit but senses a data frame instead of a token, it compares its own priority to the priority of the current data frame. If the system wishing to transmit has a greater priority, it sets a flag in the data frame indicating that it wants to interrupt the current flow of data. When the data frame returns to its point of origin, the system notes that a higher-priority request has been received. Instead of generating a standard token, the lower-priority system generates a higher-priority token, which corresponds to the priority level of the system requesting the interrupt.

This high-priority token then makes its way to the interrupting system following the normal flow of data. Systems that see the token will not seize it unless they have an equal or higher priority than the system that requested the interrupt. Once the high-priority token is received by the interrupting system, it transmits data at that priority level. When the system is done with its priority transmissions, it generates a new token with a priority level that corresponds to the original interrupted token. At that point the original flow of information is restored.

Another option in Token-Ring LANs is early token release. When this method is employed, a system originating a data frame releases a token immediately after the transmitting data frame, instead of after receiving the data frame on its return trip. This approach allows multiple data frames to be present on the ring at the same time; therefore, it facilitates greater possible throughput.

Topology and Construction

The original Token-Ring networks were, in fact, wired in a physical ring. Cables were daisy-chained from one system to another until they formed a closed loop. This was not a great architecture, however, because any break in the ring disabled the entire LAN; if you disconnected a PC, you disconnected the LAN. Given this limitation, very few physical-ring networks have survived into the 1990s.

Today's Token-Ring LANs are cabled in a hub configuration. In this configuration systems are attached via a cable (termed a "lobe") to a central device called a Multistation Access Unit (MAU), which supports a number of lobe connections. For example, the IBM 8228 MAU can support up to eight lobe connections. Every Token-Ring network must have one MAU. If the number of required lobes cannot be accommodated by one MAU, multiple (up to 33) MAUs can be connected together using dedicated "Ring In" (RI) and "Ring Out" (RO) connections on each MAU.

When multiple MAUs are used, the distance between MAUs is dependent on the type of media. If conventional Type 1 cable is used, a MAU can be placed within 100 meters of the adjacent MAU. Longer distances may be achieved through the use of copper repeaters, which extend that distance to 740 meters, or fiber repeaters, which can extend the distance up to 4 kilometers.

A lobe connection from a MAU often normally attaches directly to a system. If multiple systems are at that location, a "Lobe Access Unit" (LAU)—sometimes referred to as a hub—may be used to split the single lobe into two or more lobes. Using this scheme, a LAU can be placed on a single cable drop to accommodate the connection of two or more systems. Many LAUs also support a dedicated attachment to accommodate another LAU, so LAUs can be chained together to provide additional attachments.

In theory, the difference between a LAU (or hub) and a MAU is that a LAU cannot be used alone to create a stand-alone ring. Unfortunately, different manufacturers use the terms "LAU" and "hub" loosely; therefore, some LAUs are, in reality, MAUs. If you are purchasing a LAU or a hub, you should find out whether or not it can be used as a stand-alone device.

The Token-Ring approach to cabling accommodates all sizes of networks:

- As shown in Figure 9.4, a two-system ring can be constructed with a single 2-port MAU.

- As shown in Figure 9.5, complex networks can be constructed by chaining 8-port MAUs to one another and optionally attaching additional 2-port hubs to lobes leading from the 8-port hub. Notice that the 8-port MAUs are connected together using RI and RO cables to extend the physical ring over multiple MAUs.

MAUs and LAUs maintain the integrity of the ring. When a lobe connection is made to a MAU or a LAU, it "opens" the ring to facilitate the new attachment. Similarly, when a lobe is disconnected from a MAU or a LAU, the connection point is automatically "closed" to keep the ring intact. This

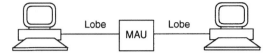

Figure 9.5 Simple Token-Ring topology.

flexibility allows the construction of the network to be changed without bringing it down.

Token-Ring networks are often implemented as a set of interconnected rings. When this approach is used, a bridge is used to tie the two networks together. The way that a bridge works in this environment, however, is dependent on which standard is being followed: IBM Token Ring or 802.5. Please see the IBM Token Ring versus 802.5 section of this chapter for more information.

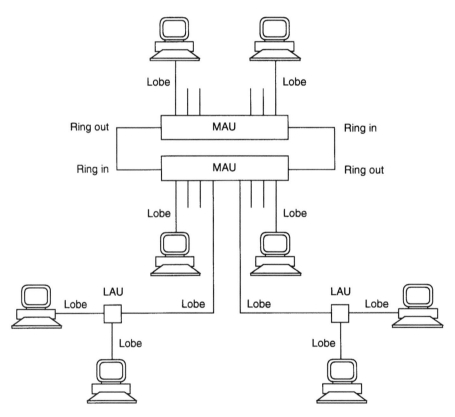

Figure 9.4 Complex Token-Ring topology.

Cabling

The physical construction of a Token-Ring LAN is dependent on the type of media as well as the placement of MAUs and hubs. Token-Ring networks are generally constructed out of two types of cable media:

- **Shielded Twisted-Pair (STP) cable (a.k.a. IBM Type 1).** STP cable is composed of shielded twisted-pair strands and is suitable for lobe connections up to 100 meters in length. STP cable is terminated in either a 9-pin D-shell connector or a "patch" connector. As a general rule, patch connectors are for MAU attachments, male 9-pin connectors are for system and LAU attachments, and female 9-pin connectors are used to originate a daisy-chain attachment from one LAU to another. STP cable is available for indoor and outdoor environments, with indoor variations for plenum and nonplenum jackets.

- **Unshielded Twisted-Pair (UTP) cable (a.k.a. IBM Type 3).** UTP cable is composed of unshielded twisted-pair strands similar to telephone cable. The connectors used with Type 3 cable are RJ-45 quick connect/disconnect plugs. UTP cable may be used for lobe connections in the neighborhood of 45 meters in length (the actual length depends on the speed of the LAN and the characteristics of the environment).

IBM also supports the use of Type 2, Type 5, Type 6, Type 8, and Type 9 cable in Token-Ring networks. However, these cable types are specialized for certain environments or applications:

- Type 2 is a combination of Type 1 and four twisted pairs of telephone-grade cable.

- Type 5 is a nonstandard fiber optic cable used to interconnect repeaters.

- Type 6 is a low-cost, low-distance (maximum of 45 meters) cable often used for MAU-to-MAU connections.

- Type 8 is for subcarpet installation and can run up to 50 meters.

- Type 9 cable is plenum-jacketed data-grade cable that can run up to 65 meters. It is a lower-cost alternative to Type 1 plenum cable.

Token Ring uses the differential Manchester encoding scheme to transmit and receive data on the LAN. In both STP and UTP cables, signals are carried over two balanced circuits, one circuit for transmit and one for receive. Each circuit is then made up of two wires, one used to carry the positive signals and the other used for the negative signals. This means that Token-Ring cable requires two twisted pairs of cable.

When STP cable is used, the pin assignments for the two twisted pairs are as follows:

STP Pin Assignments

Signal	9-pin	Patch
Transmit –	5	Black
Receive +	1	Red
Receive –	6	Green
Transmit +	9	Orange

When UTP cable is used, the wires are normally assigned to a standard RJ-45 connector as follows:

Typical 10BASET/UTP Cable

Wire	Assignment	Type 3 Wire Color
1		
2		
3	Transmit –	Blue with white strip
4	Receive +	White with orange strip
5	Receive –	Orange with white strip
6	Transmit +	White with blue strip
7		
8		

Using this arrangement, wires 3 and 6 should be twisted together, and wires 4 and 5 should be twisted together. This is the subset of the four-pair 10BASET implementation where 1 and 2, 3 and 6, 4 and 5, as well as 7 and 8 are twisted as pairs. (Also note that this wiring is different from Ethernet over 10BASET, which uses the 1/2 and 3/6 pairs.)

IBM Token Ring versus 802.5

Although the differences between the IBM Token-Ring specifications and the 802.5 standard are not nearly as dramatic as the differences between Ethernet and 802.3, two differences are particularly important:

1. IBM specifications state a ring can support up to 260 attachments, while the IEEE 802.5 specifications limit support to 250.

2. IBM specifications use a feature known as "Source Routing" when bridges are employed. The IEEE 802.5 specifications do not include this feature.

The number of attachments is a straightforward issue. Source Routing, however, needs additional clarification:

*   With Source Routing, a system inquires about the location of its destination and then includes the returned address in the message so the bridge knows how to route it to the appropriate ring. Both the bridge and the system participate in route discover and route delivery.

*   The 802.5 standard does not use the Source Routing feature. In this case, the bridge must perform routing functions independently (and transparently) from the systems in the ring. A range of bridge intelligence is available. On the low-end bridges send all messages to the adjoining ring. On the high end, bridges "learn" which systems are in which ring, and only send to the adjoining ring when necessary.

In cases where both types of protocols following both standards (e.g., SNA and NetWare) operate on the same LAN, a bridge must be capable of performing both Source Routing and transparent bridging.

Specifications

General

Speed:	4 or 16 Mbps
Maximum frame size:	4511^2 bytes (4 Mbps), 17,839 (16 Mbps)
Maximum data unit:	4414^2 bytes (4 Mbps), 17,742 (16 Mbps)

---

[2] Note: The original implementation of 4-Mbps Token Ring on the AS/400 was limited to a maximum frame size of 2091 bytes with a 1994-byte data unit size.

Type 1 (STP) Media

Connector: DB-9 or Patch
Maximum lobe length: 100 meters
Maximum attachments: 260 (IBM), 250 (802.5)

Type 3 (UTP) Media

Connector: RJ-45
Maximum lobe length: 45 meters
Maximum attachments: 72

Frame Formats

Figure 9.6 shows the field definitions for 802.5 and IBM Token-Ring frames. The purpose of each field is as follows:

802.5/802.2 Fields

Start Frame Delimiter: A 1-byte pattern indicating the start of the frame.

Access Control: A 1-byte field used for control and maintenance functions. The fourth bit of this field is the "token" bit. If set to 1, the frame is a token and is composed of just the Start Frame Delimiter, Access Control, and End Delimiter fields (total of 3 bytes in length).

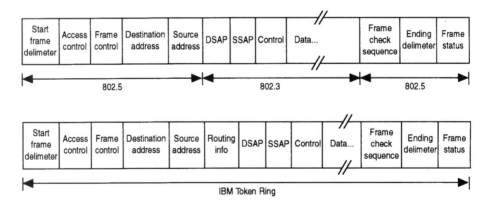

Figure 9.6 802.5 and IBM Token-Ring frame formats.

Frame Control: A 1-byte field used to identify specific information, control, and maintenance functions.

Destination Address: The address of a specific station or group of stations to receive the frame. May be 2 or 6 bytes in length.

Source Address: The address of the sending station. May be 2 or 6 bytes in length.

DSAP: The 1-byte 802.2 Destination Service Access Point. See the discussion under the IEEE 802.2 section of this chapter for more information.

SSAP: The 1-byte 802.2 Source Service Access Point. See the discussion under the IEEE 802.2 section of this chapter for more information.

Control: An 802.2 field used for various commands, including exchange identifier, test, connect, disconnect, and frame reject. May be 1 or 2 bytes long, with the length defined by the first two bits.

Data: The actual information being transmitted.

Frame Check Sequence: A 4-byte field containing a checksum of the frame information beginning with the Frame Control field and ending with the data.

End Delimiter: A 1-byte pattern signaling the end of the frame.

Frame Status: A 1-byte field used for status information. Specifically, this field is set by a receiving station to indicate that it has recognized and copied a frame addressed to it.

IBM Token-Ring Fields

Start Frame Delimiter: Same as corresponding 802.5 field.

Access Control: Same as corresponding 802.5 field.

Frame Control: Same as corresponding 802.5 field.

Destination Address: The 6-byte address of a specific station or group of stations to receive the frame.

Source Address: The 6-byte address of the sending station.

Routing Information: The presence of this field is indicated by the first bit of the Source Address field. If that bit is set, the Routing Information field contains addressing information used to reach the destination station over one or more bridges. Note that if the Source Address field is not set, this field is not present.

DSAP: Same as corresponding 802.5/802.2 field.

SSAP: Same as corresponding 802.5/802.2 field.

Control: Same as corresponding 802.5/802.2 field.

Data: The actual information being transmitted.

Frame Check Sequence: Same as corresponding 802.5 field.

End Delimiter: Same as corresponding 802.5 field.

Frame Status: Same as corresponding 802.5 field.

ETHERNET VERSUS TOKEN RING: BATTLE OF THE NETWORK STARS

The lay of the LAN has long been the demarcation between Digital Equipment Corporation and IBM systems. Digital has traditionally used Ethernet for its LAN activities while IBM has focused on Token-Ring LANs. In the old black-and-white world of noncooperative processing, this made life extremely simple. IBM equipment and PCs or PC/2s that needed to communicate with IBM equipment went on the Token-Ring LAN; Digital equipment and Digital-oriented PCs or PC/2s went on the Ethernet LAN—end of discussion.

However, with the increasing need for systems of all sizes and shapes to share common LANs, these artificial boundaries have begun to erode and crumble. The unmanageability of running separate LANs for IBM equipment and Digital equipment has taken its toll on the minds and budgets of intermediate system (IS) managers across the globe. Furthermore, the rising needs for cooperative processing between dissimilar systems and the maturity of de facto integration products like Novell NetWare, TCP/IP, and OSF DCE have also produced pressure for LAN consolidation.

IBM saw these changes coming and responded by releasing direct support for Systems Network Architecture (SNA) over Ethernet and 802.3 LANs in Version 1 Release 3 of the OS/400 operating system for the AS/400. With support for Token-Ring *and* Ethernet *and* 802.3 networks, IBM had positioned the AS/400 as a potential player in almost any LAN environment. Digital responded in kind by releasing support for DECnet over Token Ring.

And although IBM has not reached complete parity between Ethernet and Token Ring (mainframe SNA services are still restricted to Token Ring), the full implementation of SNA over Ethernet/802.3 is inevitable.

These trends lead into a brave new world where system vendors and networking protocols no longer impose teeth-gnashing constraints on physical network selection. Although this may not be new territory to some—TCP/IP and Novell NetWare have been able to run over a variety of LAN types for many years—this is certainly a remarkable change for massive and lumbering proprietary architectures like DECnet and SNA.

Unfortunately, this flexibility and freedom of choice create a new problem: Which LAN to choose?

Of course there is no single, simple answer to that question. Every environment has its own special constraints and considerations. A better way to look at the issue is to explore the questions commonly asked during the LAN selection process. In particular, the following questions serve to highlight the strengths and weakness of Ethernet/802.3 and Token Ring.

Which Is Easier to Troubleshoot?

Token Ring. The Token-Ring access protocol includes test procedures that are invoked every time a system first accesses the ring. When one of the procedures fails, messages are blurted out on one or more of the systems, indicating probable causes of failure, including suspicious addresses. Ethernet has no such provisions, and is, for the most part, diagnosed through a combination of isolation procedures and will-power.

Which Is Easier to Install?

Ethernet. The flexibility to mix and match star, bus, or tree topologies makes it extremely easy to plan and install an Ethernet network of any size. This is especially true with thin-cable Ethernet, where systems can be daisy-chained together with T-connectors. In contrast, Token Ring forces you to use a hub topology, where you must plan connections back to the main MAU for every system or every hub.

Which Is Best for IBM Connections?

Token Ring at 16 Mbps. A 16-Mbps Token-Ring network using 16-KB frames will kick the bits out of Ethernet, which uses 1518-byte frames running at 10

Mbps. Of course, you need to be doing operations that will actually fill the frame to realize any benefits. If, for example, you are doing character-oriented terminal access (e.g., using a VT100 emulation package), you will not notice much of a difference between Ethernet and Token Ring. But if you are doing file transfer using SNA services, you should see a dramatic difference.

Which Is Best for a Multivendor Environment?

Ethernet. Most non-IBM systems support Ethernet as the primary (and in many cases only) LAN of choice. For example, Digital Equipment, Hewlett-Packard, and Sun Microsystems networks are normally implemented using Ethernet. Although Token-Ring technology has begun to garner some popularity and support from these and other players, Ethernet remains the mainstream preference.

Which Supports More Stations?

Debatable. Anyone who implements a self-contained network with more than 200 systems is pushing the limits of reality. A better strategy is to implement small segments/rings and interconnect them as needed. In this regard, both Ethernet and Token Ring can be easily carved up into small LANs and then interconnected.

Which Offers Better Performance?

Go fish. Ethernet is better suited for LAN environments where LAN activities are random and bursty in nature. Token Ring favors environments where access is methodical and predictable. In theory, a 10-Mbps Ethernet network will outperform a 4-Mbps Token-Ring network, and a 16-Mbps Token-Ring network will outperform a 10-Mbps Ethernet network. But in reality, the actual performance is mitigated by the average amount of data being transmitted, the number and locations of devices transmitting, and the frequency at which each device transmits. In other words, the raw throughput of a LAN is only one factor in determining overall LAN performance.

Which Has a Better Future?

Tie. The sheer number of installed Ethernet and Token-Ring networks guarantee that both types of LANs will be significant factors in the on-going evolution of LAN technology. For example, Token-Ring has been a driving force in the evolution of 100-Mbps FDDI/CDDI, and Ethernet has been the motivation behind development of 100-Mbps 100BASE-VG. (Of course, both of these 100-Mbps solutions will require new adapters, hubs, repeaters, and cable, but the spirit of Token Ring and Ethernet will live on within them.) Just remember, nothing lasts forever.

SUMMARY

Finally, you might want to consider an entirely different approach to the problem. Instead of choosing between the two, why not implement both? By doing so you might be able to offset the disadvantages of one type of LAN with the advantages of the other. The risk in this approach is insignificant, because with today's technology it is as easy to bridge a Token Ring and Ethernet network together as it is to bridge Ethernet to Ethernet or to bridge Token Ring to Token Ring.

If this approach sounds intriguing, all you have to do is shift the question from "Which is the best overall LAN?" to "Which is the best LAN for a particular set of systems?" (or for a specific application). The technological considerations remain the same.

ABOUT THE AUTHOR

John Enck is a data communications and networking specialist with over 12 years of hands-on experience. Presently a network analyst with Forest Computer Incorporated, Enck has also worked for Burroughs Corporation, Electronic Data System Corporation, the Illinois Law Enforcement Commission, and the U.S. Department of Defense. He is the author of *A Manager's Guide to Multivendor Networks*, published by Cardinal Business Media, of "Signals," a monthly column appearing in *NEWS 3X/400*, and of articles featured in *DEC Professional, HP Professional, NEWS 3X/400, MIDRANGE Systems, UniReview,* and *Network World*.

Portions of this chapter have been adapted from:

"Dressing for Battle," *NEWS 3X/400*, December 1992. Copyright 1992 by Duke Communications International. Used with permission.

"True LAN Confessions: The TR in Trouble," *NEWS 3X/400*, December 1992. Copyright 1992 by Duke Communications International. Used with permission.

10

Local Area Network Cabling Considerations

William Carltock
Equinox Systems Inc.

INTRODUCTION

The importance of the wiring system in corporate networks is often underestimated. A great deal of thought and planning go into the evaluation and selection of equipment and software for the network, but that same diligence is often lacking when specifying and installing a wiring system. Studies have shown that nearly half of the problems with installed local area networks (LANs) relate to the cabling system. These problems can be difficult to diagnose, often consuming a great deal of a network technician's time. Combined with the resulting downtime a corporation experiences, these problems become more than an annoyance, affecting productivity and profitability.

In the constantly changing world of data communications, it is important to consider future requirements as part of the evaluation process. Corporations have spent fortunes over the last decade recabling with each new computer system that was installed. With technology changing at a very rapid pace, and increasing demands for bandwidth, planning for the future is more important now then it has ever been. Fortunately, equipment vendors and cable manufacturers have recognized this problem and have taken steps to reduce these incompatibility problems. Wiring systems are available from a variety of vendors and equipment vendors have taken steps to allow their equipment to operate over a variety of media. Standards have been specified by independent agencies such as the Electronics Industry Association and Underwriters Laboratories to assure the end user that cables will be capable of supporting their existing and future environments.

It is important to understand the issues and options for selecting a wiring system, to ensure compatibility with the corporate networking scheme. Selection of the cabling system should be determined by the networking applications that are planned, and other factors such as cost and facility requirements.

This chapter explores the various aspects of wiring systems, from the definition of a structured wiring system, through planning and installation. The information presented provides a basic understanding of the issues surrounding the installation of a wiring system from the prospective of a systems designer. Much of the material presented is of practical value, avoiding intricate details of electrical characteristics and building codes which concern the installer or contractor. Building and fire codes vary by region, and a comprehensive guide to these issues can be obtained from the local chamber of commerce. The vendors of the networking equipment that will be used with the system can verify if the cabling system being considered is supported by their equipment.

The purpose of this chapter is provide basic information about wiring systems as they relate to data communications systems, and to help network designers avoid some of the potholes and problems common to building wiring systems.

Cabling Topologies

Cabling systems for data communications use a variety of methods for connecting the devices together to form a network. The method used for connecting devices is known as the *topology* of the network. Common topologies and their applications are described below:

Bus

Networks cabled with a Bus topology use a common "bus" to which all devices connect. Typical applications for bus wiring include coaxial-based Ethernet systems and broadband applications. The figure that follows illustrates a typical bus-wired network:

Bus Wiring

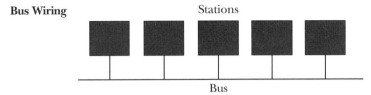

Star

Networks cabled using a Star topology are wired such that all cables originate from a single point. Typical applications for star wiring include twisted-pair–based Ethernet systems and RS-232 applications. The figure below illustrates a typical star-wired network:

Star Wiring

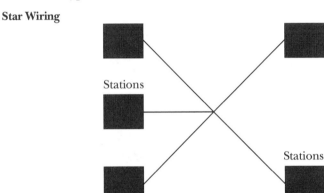

Ring

Networks configured for Ring wiring require a closed loop to complete the data path. Typical examples of ring-wired systems include Token-Ring networks and fiber optic applications. The figure below illustrates a typical ring-wired system:

Ring Wiring

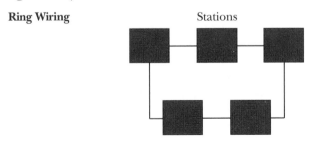

Some systems use a combination of these methods. One example is a typical Token-Ring network. These systems are commonly wired using what is known as a *Star-Wired Ring* method. An illustration of a Star-Wired Ring is shown below:

Star-Wired Ring

Stations

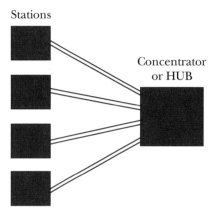

Concentrator
or HUB

In this example, the integrity of the ring is preserved, but the topology is changed to allow the system to be star wired. The topologies listed can all be intermixed to form compatible configurations. For example, Ethernet systems that use unshielded twisted pair (UTP) are typically wired in a star-wired bus configuration. Star wiring provides the most flexibility, allowing stations to be easily added or relocated. As indicated above, most systems can be converted to star wiring, and, as a result, this has become the de facto standard for computer system wiring.

Structured Wiring and Premises Wiring

Structured wiring is a term used to describe the wiring method selected for use in a building or campus environment. A structured wiring system is usually specified before the wiring is installed in a facility, and details the method and type of wiring that will be used, as well as how the wiring will be terminated. Most structured wiring systems use a star topology for distribution of the cables to the stations.

In the past, wiring systems were installed as they were required, such as when a new computer or telephone system was being implemented. This eventually leads to a wiring mess throughout the facility, with old, obsolete cabling from an old system clogging the ceilings and wiring ducts. In a structured wiring facility, cabling requirements for all devices are examined before system installation. Other factors are also considered, including the layout of the building or facility and the future requirements for the phone and computer system.

Structured wiring systems, sometimes called Premises Wiring systems, are relatively new terms, but are similar to systems that the telephone companies have used for many years. Almost all telephone systems use a structured wiring system to provide a method for the telephones in a building to connect to a central telephone system.

In the past, cabling requirements varied greatly for all the various systems used in a facility. Telephone systems used UTP and computer systems used various forms of shielded cable such as coaxial (Coax), twinaxial (Twinax), and multiconductor cable. Using these various types of cabling created a multitude of maintenance problems. Often, a new system required a different type of cable, resulting in costly recabling and obsoleting the previous system. Many older buildings are strewn with the remains of old computer system cables, making the installation of a new system even more difficult.

Recognizing the problems that arise from utilizing these disparate systems, many vendors began to develop solutions to the problem. A wiring system that could accommodate any computer system would solve most of these problems. In the early 1980s, a few vendors began introducing solutions to these problems. IBM introduced the IBM Cabling System, and, to stress its significance, dubbed it "The Fourth Utility." Other vendors also introduced systems, which are covered in more detail later in the chapter.

A very significant step towards integration of wiring systems into structured wiring systems was the use of UTP cable for transmitting data. As a result of deregulation in the telephone industry and other rulings in the early 1980s, the wiring in a facility became the property of the owner of the building. This change offered corporations the ability to use the existing telephone wiring in a building for other purposes. One immediate problem was that many computer systems were designed to operate on specific types of cables. These systems could not be directly connected to the telephone wiring without causing problems with the operation of the computer system.

Many vendors began producing adapters that would allow these systems to operate over ordinary telephone wiring. Today, adapters are available to allow almost any computer system to operate over UTP, and many manufacturers of communications equipment have designed their equipment specifically for use with UTP.

Adapters that allow almost any system to run over UTP are commonly available. These include

Baluns: For using 3270 and other coax-based equipment
Media Filters: For using Token Ring
Transceivers: For using Ethernet
Modular Adapters: For using RS-232 asynchronous equipment

Several vendors of networking equipment today offer what are commonly referred to as HUBs. These HUBs concentrate the networking equipment into a single chassis, which allows the wiring from each station or device to be concentrated in a single location. Many of these were specifically designed to be implemented into structured wiring systems. Most vendors offer UTP options for these HUBs, allowing station cabling to use UTPs for connection to the HUB. The HUBs often include as part of their design an outlet that allows the HUB to be connected to a backbone, a common component of structured wiring systems.

As a result of the equipment that is now available for running data over UTP, it has become the most popular medium for use in structured wiring systems. Many of the structured wiring systems available today use UTP as the primary medium for both voice and data. Other types of cabling are used when the bandwidth requirements or environmental concerns (such as interference) are unsuitable for UTP.

Recognizing that many corporations have already designated and implemented UTP wiring systems, most of the newer technologies for networking include support for UTP. Some of these newer technologies include 16-MB Token Ring, CDDI, and Fast Ethernet, all of which operate at faster speeds than common networks of today.

TYPICAL LAYOUT OF A STRUCTURED WIRING FACILITY

Structured wiring systems vary greatly based on the application and facility, but most follow the same fundamental scheme. Most of these schemes are based on common practices used by the telephone companies for many years. These schemes include a central location, where all the wiring will eventually connect to, and intermediate locations. In telephone terms, these are commonly referred to as the Main Distribution Frame (MDF) and Intermediate Distribution Frame (IDF). For a computer system, these might be the Main Computer Equipment Room and Satellite Equipment Rooms.

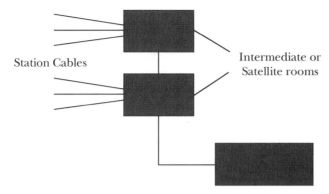

Figure 10.1 Layout with main equipment room.

These satellite equipment rooms are typically the telephone rooms designed into most buildings. Many of today's computer systems use a distributed computing environment and only use satellite equipment rooms, as it is often the case that there is not a main computer equipment room. Figure 10.1 illustrates a typical layout using a main equipment room. Figure 10.2 illustrates a distributed computing environment without a main equipment room.

In many instances, there are separate rooms for the computer systems and telephone systems. In these instances there is a separate MDF for the telephone system and a main computer room. The satellite rooms remain shared by both systems.

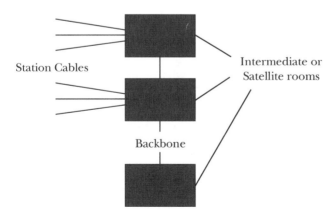

Figure 10.2 Layout without main equipment room.

Common to both these types of systems are cables that connect the satellite rooms together. These cables can be multiconductor, bundled cables, fiber links, composite cables, or any combination of the cables. These cables are commonly referred to as the *backbone*, and separate backbones may be required for voice and data systems. For telephone systems, these are sometimes referred to as *Riser* cables. As Figures 10.1 and 10.2 illustrate, there are separate horizontal and vertical components, each with its own requirements. The exact requirements for the horizontal components are determined by the networking equipment selected and the application.

PLANNING FOR A STRUCTURED WIRING SYSTEM

Facility Planning

Most newer buildings are constructed with consideration for a structured wiring system. This is normally due to the requirements of the telephone system. Often, when designing a building, the special requirements of the computer system are not considered. The requirements for the telephone system and computer system can be quite different. This section covers some of the facility requirements that should be explored to avoid possible problems in the implementation of the computer system.

Determine the Location of the Main Computer Room and the Telephone Rooms

Conduits, raceways, and other paths are normally provided to allow the telephone wiring to access the main telephone room or MDF. The main computer room could be located in a different area of the building and consideration should be given to how the wiring will access this room. This may require additional conduits or paths from the satellite rooms to the main computer room. Special thought should be given to the size of the conduits and raceways being used to be sure they can accommodate the required amount of wiring and to allow for future expansion of the system or additional cabling. Since the telephone system and the computer may share the cabling, it is often necessary to connect the telephone and main computer room to allow easy access to the cabling from a central distribution point. Most computer systems need some type of access to the phone system, so it always a good idea to verify that there is a path between the two systems, even if it is not an immediate requirement.

A review of the blueprints of a facility will reveal the paths that have been designed for routing cables. These pathways are usually designed into the building with considerations for telephone, electrical, and other utilities and may provide clues as to the best method for implementing a structured wiring system. Consulting with the architect can provide details and avenues not immediately obvious from the blueprints.

The contractor responsible for these systems could be the electricians, telephone systems installers, or the general contractor. It is important to communicate the requirements to these contractors to ensure a smooth installation. Electrical requirements can be easily overlooked, and special care should be taken to ensure that there are plenty of electrical outlets for the existing and future needs in both the telephone and computer rooms. A standard recommendation for electrical outlets that will be used for data equipment is to request special dedicated, isolated circuits for the data equipment. These types of electrical circuits will help to isolate the equipment from interference from other electrical sources. Always request that a high-quality earth ground be provided in the equipment rooms. Following these guidelines will avoid costly additions later, improve system performance, and will reduce downtime on the systems. It is always recommended that the consultant who specializes in wiring systems be used to assist in some of these considerations.

Satellite Room Considerations

The satellite rooms, or telephone closets, located throughout the building require a great deal of consideration. These rooms are typically small and primarily designed for the telephone company's use. Since these rooms will also need to handle data, there are many special requirements to consider. The first consideration should be the layout of the room itself. Specific areas for exclusive use by the telephone and data should be designated. Sometimes these rooms also contain electrical equipment, and steps should be taken to locate the data area as far from the electrical area as possible. There are also laws that regulate the location of equipment in relation to electrical equipment, and the electrical contractor or general contractor should be consulted when planning the layout of these rooms.

Modern design of these satellite rooms often includes provisions for networking equipment. This equipment typically consists of wiring HUBs and telecommunications equipment. Because these rooms are usually designed with only the telephone concerns in mind, many factors can be overlooked that can create serious problems. These include substantial electrical and cooling requirements, normally not required with telephone systems. Electrical requirements should also be specified for these rooms. Request dedicated, isolated circuits for all data equipment, and request a high-quality earth ground for the room. All equipment should be grounded to this earth ground, and any racks that house the equipment should also be grounded.

Station Wiring Considerations

There are few considerations here, as the responsibility of getting cables to the individual stations is normally assumed by the contractors. Some of the considerations include verifying that there will be enough space to get all the required cables to the stations. Keep in mind that additional cabling may be required in the future to support other systems. This can be easily accomplished by ensuring that the contractor is fully informed of the cabling requirements. Another consideration is to wire extra locations that may not be needed now, but will save time and inconvenience later. It is always a good idea to install separate cables for the telephone and data system(s). This will help prevent possible problems such as cross-talk or interference between the systems. For example, some telephone systems apply high voltages to the station lines in order to get the phone to ring, and these high voltages can interfere with data transmissions.

One of the biggest problems with the station wiring occurs during system installation. Cables are frequently labeled incorrectly, or not labeled at all. Ensuring that all cables are properly identified at both ends, and labeled with permanent marking, will save hours of time during installation.

SELECTING A WIRING SYSTEM

The selection criterion for a wiring system is determined by the equipment that will be used with the wiring system. Current and future needs should be determined, as well as the costs involved with the selection. Some wiring systems may cost more initially, but will save the cost of recabling later when a new computer system is installed. Other systems may be cost prohibitive. For example, installing a system that is completely fiber optic based would ensure that the system could be used for many years and would satisfy the requirements of any future networking scheme, but would be very expensive to install.

UTP Systems

Most computer systems today can use UTP cable for transmitting data. This allows the same type of wiring and accessories to be used with the data system as are used with the phone system. This type of system has become the most popular and common method for installing wiring systems because of its simplicity and low cost. Manufacturers of networking equipment have reacted quickly to this trend, and most offer solutions and equipment designed for use with UTP cabling. Cable manufacturers have also reacted to this trend, producing cable that meets the special requirements for high-speed data transmission. As a result, structured wiring systems that use UTP exclusively are commonplace. Formal structured wiring systems that specify and use this method as the primary component are available from telephone vendors including AT&T and Northern Telecom, as well as from manufacturers of cable and connectors such as AMP, MOD-TAP, and Panduit. A listing of providers of structured wiring systems is included at the end of this chapter.

Using UTP wiring is not without its drawbacks. UTP is unshielded, and, as a result, is susceptible to interference from outside sources. An additional problem is support for high-speed data rates. The electrical characteristics of UTP make it difficult to transmit high-speed data reliably, reducing the maximum cable distance and limiting the maximum speed. Some of the newer networking schemes that operate in excess of 150 Mbps will not be able to operate over UTP. Recent advances in production of the cable and the technology used with it have eliminated many of these problems, if the proper combination of cable and equipment is used. Some vendors of wiring systems, such as DEC and IBM, offer shielded twisted pair as part of their solution to overcome these restrictions, allowing longer distances and more reliable data transport. Demand from users that already have a UTP wiring system installed has pressured the industry to find solutions to running very high-speed data over UTP. Equipment that can operate at 100,000,000 bits per second (100 Mbps) over UTP is becoming available, with even higher speeds possible in the future.

The ability to support high data rates and most networking systems makes using UTP as the primary component of a structured wiring system a practical and inexpensive solution which should meet the requirements of most networking equipment through the end of the century.

As a result of the domination of UTP, the Electronics Industry Association (EIA), in conjunction with the Telecommunications Industry Association

(TIA), has recently established industry standards. These standards, known as EIA/TIA-568, specify the electrical and performance characteristics of various types of cables and connectors. A summary of the specifications detailed by EIA/TIA-568 are provided later in this chapter. Underwriter Laboratories Inc. also has established standards for various types of cables. UL's complete LAN cable program covers safety, performance, and quality assurance for a variety of cabling products. This verification program assures a consumer that an approved cable meets industry standards for safety, performance, and quality.

UTP cable is the cable of choice for most of today's structured wiring systems. Using this type of cable as the basis for the horizontal wiring scheme has many advantages:

Cost. UTP cable is the least expensive cable to install. The cable itself is inexpensive, as are the associated connectors and other accessory components.

Ease of Installation. UTP is a very small diameter cable, reducing the difficulty of installing large numbers of cables in a small area.

Industry Acceptance. Almost all of the networking systems today can be operated using UTP. Some of the newer technologies, such as 16-Mbps Token Ring and Fast Ethernet also support UTP connections to the desktop. The amount of installed systems that use UTP will force vendors to provide solutions that can utilize their existing cabling scheme.

Shielded Cabling Systems

Shielded twisted-pair systems allow for greater isolation against interference and typically support higher data rates than UTP. This high-grade cable typically uses a lower gauge of copper and, as a result, can offer greater distances. The electrical characteristics of shielded cable are much different from UTP, and attempting to mix the two different types of cable can cause problems for many systems. Shielded systems are more expensive than UTP, but due to their ability to support higher data rates, may be compatible with systems that UTP is not capable of supporting. Shielded twisted-pair systems are available from many cable suppliers, and are a part of many of the systems from suppliers such as Digital Equipment Corporation and IBM. The IBM Cabling System uses shielded twisted-pair (STP) as the primary component of the system. Adapters are available to allow any IBM system to operate using the IBM Cabling System, and the characteristics allow the cabling system to support speeds up to 600 Mbps.

Composite Systems

Composite systems are also available to system designers. These composite systems typically incorporate different types of cables in a single jacket. Composite systems are the most expensive, and are usually manufactured to a specific customer's specification. The benefit of using a composite cabling system is that a system can be constructed that supports your current and future requirements. A composite cable might include UTP, coaxial, and fiber all in the same jacket. Composite cabling systems are available from most of the major manufacturers and suppliers of cabling systems, such as Beldon Wire and Cable and Vertex Corporation.

Fiber Optic Systems

Fiber Optics is an expensive solution for an overall wiring system plan, but it is commonly used as a component of the other wiring systems. Fiber is typically used as part of the "backbone" or "riser" component of the system. The benefit of using fiber is its immunity to interference and its ability to support almost unlimited bandwidth. It is expected that it will be well into the twenty-first century before fiber becomes the dominant media in structured wiring systems.

AVOIDING PROBLEMS

Many corporations are downsizing, or rightsizing, to distribute the processing throughout the organization. Although downsizing theoretically saves a company money, studies have shown that the cost of supporting these distributed systems is higher than the support costs associated with mainframe installations. Other studies have shown that a large portion of the problems with supporting these systems, and a large portion of the problems that occur with systems, are cabling related. The majority of the problems with the cabling system are in the following categories:

- Improper or inadequate termination of the cables
- Improper design of the cabling system
- Improper labeling/documentation of the cables

These problems can be reduced or avoided by following some of the simple suggestions and guidelines offered in this chapter.

Improper Termination of Cable

This is the leading cause of problems with network cabling. These types of problems can be disastrous to a network, causing the network to crash, and are often difficult to track down. Fortunately, many modern network systems have the capability built-in to eliminate segments of the network that could cause problems for the entire network, but this only cures half the problem. Even with the best equipment, tracking down these problems can sometimes take hours, and often utilizes time that could be spent much more productively by network technicians and systems administrators. Some suggestions for avoiding these problems are listed below:

- **Always use experienced Data Communications Cabling installers.** Using the phone installer to install your data communications cabling is often a convenient solution, but not always the best. If your system uses only UTP, using the phone installer is not a bad idea, but if your system uses other types of cabling such as shielded or coaxial cable, using a specialist will save much trouble down the road. Phone systems are not as sensitive to the cabling, and if you do decide to use the phone installer, make sure he understands the special requirements for your data.

- **Always ensure that the cable terminations are firmly mounted.** Standard wallplates and inserts for cubicles should always be used. Leaving cables loose in a cubicle or office is just asking for trouble.

- **Keep terminations to a minimum.** The more places a cable is terminated, the more possible places there are for problems. Terminations should always be in easily accessible places, such as equipment rooms, and never in the ceiling or floor trenches.

Improper Design of the Cabling System

Improper design of the cabling system can be a relative term. Sometimes the cabling was designed for use with a different type of system, and is not well suited to the present requirements. Companies sometimes try to use older existing cabling instead of installing new cable with a new system. This is especially true for installations using UTP cable. Some common problems related to cabling system design are listed below:

- **Cables are too long.** Phone cables can be run very long distances with little degradation in the quality and functionality of the phone set. Computer network systems are always limited. The distance that can be run using a given data communications system is normally a function of the data rate; the higher the speed, the shorter the distances.

- **Too many terminations.** Every termination causes a loss of signal strength. The distance to a station may not be too long, but it is possible that there are too many terminations along the way. This is particularly true if the system is using "66"-type punch-down blocks for cable terminations. These connection blocks use very poor quality metal that introduces resistance to the flow of data.

- **Multiconductor cables.** Many installations use multiconductor cables to connect locations within a facility. These multiconductor cables often carry phone and data in a densely packed jacket. Some of the problems encountered when using these cables are interference from outside sources and "cross-talk" between cables in the same jacket. If multiconductor cables are part of the system design, try to keep data separate from voice whenever possible.

- **Environmental problems.** Data running through cables is often high speed and low voltage. This makes the cables susceptible to outside interference, especially from sources of electrical interference. Phone cables have a great deal of immunity to these sources of interference, due to the relatively low signal rates and high voltages. As a result, phone installers are not concerned about most possible sources of electrical interference. When cabling for data, every effort should be put forth to keep the cables away from possible sources of electrical interference. Two of the most common sources of detrimental interference are fluorescent lights and electrical transformers commonly found in equipment rooms.

Improper Labeling/Documentation of Cable

Improperly labeled or unlabeled cables are every network installer's nightmare. It should always be a requirement that every cable be clearly labeled at both ends, and documented. Trying to find an unlabeled cable in the telephone room can turn a 5-minute installation into a 2-hour installation. Wallplates and termination blocks should always be labeled using a permanent method such as an indelible marker, so the labeling is still readable and identifiable after a long period of time. A labeling method should be determined before any installation begins, saving time and grief later. A floor plan that identifies the location of the cables is also a good idea. Cable distances should also be documented, as this will be valuable information in determining the network layout either immediately or in the future, when higher data might be used on the network. A good rule of thumb that also adheres to most industry specifications is to restrict station cable distances to less than 90 meters (about 290 feet). An installer who specializes in data cabling installation often will use a device known as a Time Domain Reflectometer (TDR). This device measures the distance of a cable, and often provides other information such as the impedance and DC resistance.

SUMMARY OF EIA/TIA-568 SPECIFICATIONS

The table below illustrates some of the characteristics for various cables:

Cable Type	Description	Maximum Data Rate
Category 3 UTP	Common UTP	10 Mbps
Category 4 UTP	Data Grade UTP	16 Mbps
Category 5 UTP	High-performance UTP	100 Mbps
Shielded STP	Shielded Twisted Pair	<155 Mbps

The shielded twisted-pair specifications primarily relate to the IBM Cabling System, since shielded twisted pair is the primary component.

VENDORS OF STRUCTURED WIRING SYSTEMS

Many of the formal cabling systems available from the vendors listed below may not be cost effective for installations with fewer than 100 stations. All of the following vendors offer products that are compliant with EIA/TIA-568 specifications:

		Wiring Types Supported				
Vendor	*Product*	*UTP*	*STP*	*Fiber*	*COAX*	*Other*
AT&T	Systemax Premises Distribution System	✔	✔	✔		
AMP Incorporated	NetConnect Open Wiring System	✔	✔	✔	✔	✔
DEC	OPEN DECconnect	✔	✔	✔	✔	
IBM	IBM Cabling System	✔	✔	✔		
Northern Telecom Ltd.	Integrated Building Distributed Network	✔	✔	✔		
Panduit Incorporated	PAN-NET Network Wiring System	✔	✔	✔	✔	✔

AT&T, DEC, IBM, and Northern Telecom are considered the "Big Four" in structured wiring systems. All offer comprehensive solutions for larger businesses that have a wide variety of connectivity requirements.

Most vendors offer documents that can help determine the cabling requirements for your application. The documents listed below are available free of charge in most cases, and can provide valuable insights into selecting and specifying a wiring system.

Vendor	*Document*	*Description*
AMP Inc. 800-522-6752	NetConnect Open Wiring System	A complete listing of all the cabling products available from AMP
Berk-Tek 800-BerkTek	The Seven Secrets to Specifying Cable	Details specifications for cables
DATAPRO	LANs and Internetworking Cabling	Details specifications and features of various cabling systems

Vendor	*Document*	*Description*
Du Pont Co. 800-441-9494	The Du Pont Blue Book	How to specify and install low-voltage cable
Panduit Inc. 708-532-1800	PAN-NET Wiring System	Catalog of products for cabling systems
Underwriters Laboratories, Inc. 800-676-WIRE	Directory for UL's Verified LAN Cable Products	Lists manufacturers of cables that have been approved by UL

A nonprofit organization called Building Industries Consulting Services International (BiCSi) is chartered with helping organizations with building wiring. BiCSi specializes in premises wiring systems, providing consulting and referral services. Several helpful documents are available from BiCSi (telephone 813-979-1991).

Other sources for information on wiring systems are available from the vendors of structured wiring systems listed earlier in this chapter.

GLOSSARY OF COMMON TERMS

Backbone	Normally the vertical component of a LAN system. The backbone is typically used to connect LANs in various locations within a facility.
Balun	A transformer-like converter device. Baluns are used to match the impedance required for different types of systems. Typical applications for baluns are for converting cables and equipment to operate over UTP.
Data Connector	A type of hermaphrodite (nongender) connector used with the IBM Cabling System.
Ethernet	A LAN system. Ethernet operates at 10 Mbps over a variety of media.
Fast Ethernet	A LAN System. Fast Ethernet operates at 100 Mbps over a variety of media.
Fiber	Optical fiber cable used with communications systems. Typical designations for fiber are single or multimode, with diameters from 50 to 125 microns.
LAN	Local area network.

Mbps	Megabits per second. One Mbps equals 1,000,000 bits per second.
Media	The type of cable.
Media Filter	A device that filters interference and allows only a specific range of frequencies to be passed. Typical applications for media filters are for operating Token-Ring systems over UTP.
Plenum	A type of cable specifically designed for use in ceilings and other open areas. Many building codes specify that this type of cable be used due to fire code regulations. Plenum cable does not produce toxic smoke or carry flames.
PVC	Polyvinyl choride. A manmade material that is commonly used for the outside jacket of cables.
Riser	A vertical chamber. The riser is an area specifically designed into buildings to provide a path for cables and other utilities.
RJ	A specification for the connectors used with UTP systems. Typical designations are RJ-11, RJ-12, RJ-21, and RJ-45.
Shielding	A metal barrier. Shielding on cables is commonly a group of braided wires that completely surround the internal wires. Another type of shielding is metal foil surrounding the wires.
Token Ring	A LAN system. Token Ring operates at 4 or 16 Mbps over a variety of media.
Topology	The physical layout of the cabling system. Topologies include bus, star, and ring.
Transceiver	A device that communicates in two directions. Transceivers are used to connect devices to cabling systems. Typical applications for transceivers are in Ethernet systems.
TYPE	A designation for specific cables used in the IBM Cabling System. TYPEs range from 1 to 9, and specify characteristics of the cable.
UTP	Unshielded twisted-pair cable. Typically 22- or 24-gauge copper wires twisted into pairs.

ABOUT THE AUTHOR

William Carltock has been in the data communications industry since 1977, and is currently the product line manager for Equinox Systems Inc., located in Fort Lauderdale, Florida. Mr. Carltock has received specialized training in Structured Wiring Systems from AT&T, Digital Equipment Corporation, ROLM Incorporated, and IBM, and has held a low-voltage contractor's license since 1985.

11

Disaster Recovery Planning for Local Area Networks

Marc Farley
Palindrome Corporation

INTRODUCTION

People have been recovering from disasters for centuries. And as long as they have been recovering from them, they have also been trying to prepare for the next disaster in order to minimize their losses. One of the oldest disaster recovery plans on record is the biblical Noah story. In this story, Noah is visited by God and instructed to build a large ark to carry one pair of each animal species; God tells Noah that he plans to destroy the world with cataclysmic flood and the animals in Noah's ark will be needed to repopulate the earth.

The ark plan is a simple one in concept but would be very difficult to accomplish. All the animal types would have to be identified, located, captured, and loaded onto the ark, without injury. Domesticated animals would be simple, but wild and dangerous animals like large cats would require careful planning and rehearsal. The preparation and use of tranquilizers, nets, or traps is obviously not trivial. And the roundup operation is only the beginning; the challenges of keeping all of them alive would also necessitate complicated plans. Food for all of them would have to last approximately 2 months. Medical and veterinary skills would be needed; it would probably be necessary to keep a variety of medical minerals and plants. Finally, after the

317

storm subsided, they would have to safely unload the boat and transport many of the animals to a habitat where they could survive.

Trying to generate a list of tasks for the capture, transport, and release of any wild animal stimulates a complex and detailed thought process. This sort of mental exercise can be useful for newcomers to the disaster recovery world in order to help them grasp the scope of their assignment. Due to the technical content of the local area network (LAN) administrator's job it is natural to think of disaster recovery within a narrow context of technologies and the equipment operations. However, if the logistics required to assemble a complete system are not dealt with adequately, the recovery will certainly fail. Thinking about Noah's disaster recovery operation is analogous to considering all the critical components of your own disaster recovery plan.

Noah was fortunate to know in advance what kind of disaster was going to occur. If he had been surprised by an ice age instead of a flood, his plans would not have done him much good. The year 1992 was a year of many disasters—some predictable and some not. Hurricanes struck Florida and Hawaii, destroying buildings and scattering possessions at random. Businesses with disaster plans that included the possibility of hurricanes faired far better than those that had no plans. The riots in Los Angeles in the summer and the underground tunnel flooding in Chicago in the spring are excellent examples of unanticipated disasters. Although both of these events were unexpected, there were businesses in both cases that were able to recover quickly because they were prepared for the loss of their facilities. This kind of heroic response does not happen without a lot of careful thinking in advance.

In disaster recovery planning we ask the question: "What will it take to make my *business* operational?" We do *not* necessarily ask: "What will it take to make my *systems* operational?" In fact, at many large corporations the disaster recovery planning staff have titles or positions in "business continuity planning" or "business contingency planning."

In spite of the overwhelming difficulty of Noah's job, he did have one critical thing going for him: He had a boss who supported his efforts. Management must be committed to the process or it will be very difficult to create a plan and maintain it. The final result of a disaster recovery plan is a document that details the steps required to recover, which, unfortunately, is likely to become obsolete in 18 months due to changes on the network. For that reason, management should fund the disaster recovery planning process as an ongoing business expense to cover the costs of maintaining the plan.

There are disaster-planning packages available in the marketplace that utilize relational database technology for easier maintenance. While these packages can save time when developing the original plan, their most significant benefit is that they are easy to maintain; a change of information in one part of the plan is immediately reflected in other components. Even with an automated software package, one should still expect to spend a fair amount of time collecting all the data needed to assemble a plan. Disaster recovery software is not well known in the LAN market, probably because most of them have been developed and marketed to needs of the mainframe market. They may be hard to find, but some of these products are now being delivered to the LAN marketplace.

Disaster recovery planning does not require the talents of a genius. Instead, it is an exercise in thoroughness. Disaster recovery services started as an industry for mainframe data centers in the 1970s. The industry grew quickly and has matured a great deal since then. Since its inception, a few simple fundamental ideas have evolved that are part of virtually every disaster plan. If you do nothing else, adhering to these recommendations will improve your ability to recover your systems should you experience a disaster.

1. Run backup operations at least once a day and verify their successful completion. Backups normally run at night when there is little contention for files and the impact on performance is minimal. Data is usually copied to magnetic tape. At the time this was written, LAN tape backup systems had single-tape capacities ranging from 150 MB to 5 GB. It is a good idea to have a drive capacity larger than the amount of data you are backing up for ease of operations. For large networks or locations without skilled administrators, there are robotic autoloader systems that will automatically change tapes.

2. Take tapes off-site on a regular schedule. If your primary computer center is destroyed, you will need to recreate your systems from tapes that are stored elsewhere. You will also want to keep your disaster recovery plan and possibly some equipment off-site. There are data courier services that specialize in the transfer of tapes from customer sites to storage vaults. Some LAN administrators manage the off-site transfer themselves, but be aware that tapes are somewhat fragile insofar as they can be made unreadable by temperature extremes and high humidity.

3. Practice restoring data to simulate a variety of situations. Do not count on being able to read the manuals coherently when you are under

pressure and when people are waiting for you to show your stuff. By far the best way to prepare is to practice and stay in practice. The more familiar you are with your backup system, the easier it will be to operate in a real disaster situation.

Beyond these basic principles, the disaster recovery industry has developed a general methodology for developing more detailed disaster recovery plans. Depending on the source, this methodology takes on a different look. The basic steps of this methodology are listed below:

1. Analyze the risks
2. Assess the risks
3. Prioritize applications systems
4. Define recovery requirements
5. Create a detailed plan
6. Implement and test the plan
7. Maintain the plan and continue testing

The following section describes each of these steps.

ANALYZE THE RISKS

In the risk analysis phase of building a disaster recovery plan, three simple questions are asked: What is at risk? What events could cause me to lose data? and What is the likelihood that they will occur? One way to look at this for the LAN environment is to draw a distinction between major disasters and minor disasters. Major disasters are things such as fires, floods, tornadoes, hurricanes, and power failures. Minor disasters are things such as hardware failures, software bugs, viruses, and human errors.

The ability to use the LAN or access data stored there is at risk. This includes current production data and also includes historical records that you might be saving. A disaster that completely wipes out your computing facility will probably also wipe out all the data that is stored there on disks and tapes. This is the primary reason for storing data regularly off-site. Personnel are also at risk. It is not pleasant to think about, but the disaster recovery plan should include contingency plans if people are injured or unavailable for some other reason.

After living in an area for a few years a person becomes familiar with the sorts of major natural disasters that could occur there. For instance, people in the Gulf states, Atlantic Seaboard, and Hawaii anticipate hurricanes every year; the West Coast is more likely to see earthquakes and volcanoes; and the

Central States experience a yearly tornado season. Less spectacular, but capable of causing serious difficulties, are electrical storms, heavy rains, ice storms, hail storms, high winds, and blizzards. The potential for bad or unusual weather exists everywhere and the disaster plan should reflect the severity of the storms that can occur in the region.

Almost all locations are subject to flooding and fire. Every geographical region in the United States experienced flooding in 1992. Every spring and fall the news services carry stories about flooding in some part of the country. The tidal wave that struck Nicaragua is a testimony to the destruction that these incredibly powerful events can cause; the flash flooding in Texas happened with very little warning; heavy storms flooded part of New York City. But floods are not always in the news or caused by bad weather. There are numerous cases of broken water pipes causing localized flooding inside buildings, causing extensive damage.

Fires are particularly disruptive. The direct damage caused by the extreme heat and smoke of a fire will ruin a building and everything inside. One safeguard against this is a fireproof safe. What many people do not realize is how long a building can be inaccessible following a fire; the records in a safe may have survived, but you may not be able to access the safe. The high temperatures of fires can release toxins which are extremely dangerous. Fires involving old electrical equipment such as transformers are among the worst. The Environmental Protection Agency and local health authorities test for the existence of toxins and have the authority to close access to a building indefinitely. Retrieving data and records from such a building is possible at a significant cost by hiring companies that specialize in hostile environment operations.

The disaster plan should also take manmade or industrial disasters into account. Chemical accidents can force evacuations and prohibit access to equipment. Disruption of phone service can completely isolate a business from its customers. The most infamous phone service interruption in history occurred in May 1988 when a fire completely destroyed the AT&T switching center in Hinsdale, Illinois. Some businesses were without phone service for nearly 2 months and had no way to get it unless they moved their offices.

Total loss of electrical service can be caused by many things. In the mainframe world this is countered by large UPS systems (uninterruptible power supplies) and diesel generators. It is not likely for LAN servers to need a gas generator, but a good UPS system is highly recommended. If remote access and continuous availability for a database server is required, a small generator may be appropriate. Remember, it will not work unless there is sufficient power to run all the necessary telephone equipment too. Before installing a generator make sure to check with your facilities management, as there are building codes that govern its installation and use.

Unfortunately, rioting, acts of terrorism, political protests, and other forms of civil unrest can also result in damaged or inaccessible facilities. The World Trade Center bomb in New York City in March 1993 is a prime example. Personal vendettas by individuals attract less news, but still occur. The intentional destruction of equipment and data by employees or insiders occurs sporadically. Usually, this takes the form of somebody trying to destroy or steal data, but more extreme cases involve fires set by firefighters and the discharging of firearms into computing equipment.

The most common source of lost data on LANs are end users. While most end users do not have the knowledge or power to make major mistakes on mainframe or midrange systems, they know how to delete valuable files on their own personal computers (PCs), and, by extension, their networks. Depending on the nature of the error, the LAN administrative staff must be prepared to respond quickly.

LANs are constructed of many components made by many manufacturers. The quality of LAN equipment is constantly improving, but still components fail. A disaster recovery plan for LANs should take into account the replacement of disk drives, controllers, NICs, system RAM, motherboards, system software, and peripherals.

ASSESS THE RISKS

This is where you get to pretend you are an insurance actuary. The questions to ask in this phase are, What is the cost to protect against the disaster? and What is the cost to recover if it occurs? Estimating these costs can be frustrating due to lack of detailed information, but you ought to have some cost criteria for deciding which disasters to spend the most time preparing for. Remember to include common small-scale events such as disk failures and user errors which occur many times in a year.

Sometimes the worth of a system is easy to calculate. For example, if you are in the distribution business and you lose the server for a day when your order entry system is running, it is fair to calculate the lost revenue as the average daily sales. In the legal industry, if you cannot access a file, the cost is equal to the hourly billable rate of the lawyer who needs it. Both of these minor disasters could wind up costing a lot of money but both could be recovered from easily. For that reason they should be covered in detail in the disaster recovery plan.

There are four kinds of costs to be aware of: (1) lost productivity; (2) lost sales opportunities; (3) loss of hardware, software, and data; and (4) loss of image or customer confidence. The first three are simple algebraic exercises, but the loss of customer confidence is difficult to measure. Unfortunately, you will not know this number unless it is already too late.

While it would be nice to fully prepare for every kind of disaster, the cost to prepare a detailed plan for all disasters may be prohibitive. So, instead of creating separate plans for hurricanes, tornadoes, and fires, you can create one general plan for the complete loss of your facilities. If you take this approach, try to include as much information about vendors and service providers in the plan. The feasibility plan may point to the necessity of including outside service organizations to provide assistance following a disaster.

PRIORITIZE APPLICATION SYSTEMS

This is perhaps the most important aspect of the plan. Do not focus your attention on server hardware. Instead, concentrate on application systems. Hardware is relatively unimportant to the operation of a business; the applications that employees use are the key to productivity. For instance, in the distribution industry, the order entry system is considered one of the most important application systems. It would be one of the first systems to restore following a disaster.

The application system is composed of all the software, data, hardware, and network equipment required for an employee to use the application. A distributor's order entry system may use 300 MB of disk space for application code and data, a server with at least 300 MB of space available, five workstations with monitors for end users, network cards, a 24-pin printer for multipart forms, a printer cable, a wiring hub, and cabling. The disaster plan should account for the restoration of each of these items for a fully functioning order entry system. The entire network of a business may be much larger than this, with three servers, 50 workstations, and four printers. One approach to disaster recovery for this business would be to restore all the servers first, then all the workstations, then cabling, and, finally, the printers. This could take several days to complete. A better sequence of operations for getting order entry on-line as fast as possible would be to restore a single server and five workstations, then install cabling to connect them on a small network and attach the printer to one of the workstations. After this small network has order entry operational, the other systems can be recovered.

The point here is to determine the most important applications for the well-being of the business and develop an efficient plan to restore them first. The line of questioning should be, Which application system ought to be restored first? And after that, Which one comes next? and so on. Departmental managers often disagree over which application is most important. It may be necessary to ask the help of senior management to make this determination. With management's prior agreement, should a disaster occur, there will be less pressure to change your operations midstream to satisfy a nervous executive.

Consider a manufacturing business that has three server LANs: servers A, B, and C. Server A has the cost accounting system on it and office automation applications. Server B has the order entry and payroll. Server C has the inventory control, billing, and accounts receivable. It has been determined that inventory control and cost accounting are the two most important application systems because production operations cannot run without them. Now let us assume that a fire has destroyed the offices where the servers are located. Temporary office space is established in the parts warehouse, a spare replacement server is set up, and cables are run. First, the cost accounting system will be restored and then inventory control. But instead of restoring all of Server A and then all of Server C, a smarter plan would be to rebuild a single server first and restore the cost accounting and inventory control systems on it. After these systems are operational, the rest of the applications can be restored on the same or other servers.

As shown in Figure 11.1, there are three ways to restore the cost accounting and inventory control systems on a single server: rebuild Server A and restore to it, rebuild Server C and restore to it, or build a completely new server and restore to it. Using any of these methods will involve something called a redirected restore. This is where information is restored to a volume or directory that is different than the one it had been backed up from. If Server A was rebuilt, then inventory control would be redirected from Server C; if Server C was rebuilt, then cost accounting would be redirected from Server A: if a new server name is used, both costs accounting and inventory control would be redirected. Redirected restore operations can be more difficult than normal restore operations, so it is important to know how this is done with the backup system. The server requirements of the cost accounting and inventory control systems may dictate that a different server be built that can accommodate both. This may mean larger disks or different volume definitions.

Once the server is running and the data is restored, all that is left to do is make sure that users can access it and that sufficient security is in place. In

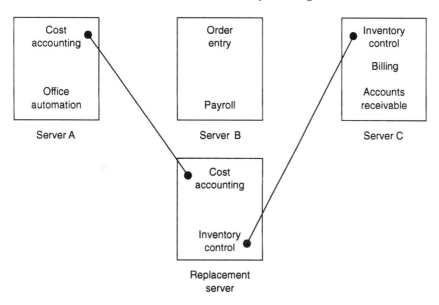

Figure 11.1 Restoring high-priority applications to a single replacement server.

Novell environments prior to Release 4.0 of NetWare there is a NetWare internal database called the binderies. Binderies use something called object identifications (IDs) to internally reference users, groups, print queues, and other logical entities. Externally a user's name may be Chris, but internally it is some number. The problem in multiserver environments is that the name Chris may exist on all servers, but the internal object ID for Chris may be different on all servers. Binderies cannot be merged or combined and, depending on the backup system, they may or may not be able to be redirected to another server from tape. Files and directories are restored with their security assigned based on the object IDs that are attached to them. Therefore, files restored to a server with a different bindery will probably be restored with the wrong security.

In Figure 11.2, MYFILE.DOC is restored with correct ownership to Chris on Server A. On Server B, Pat is assigned ownership. The same situation applies to entire application systems redirected onto different NetWare servers. In the previous example, only one of the critical systems—inventory control or cost accounting—will be restored with the correct security. The LAN administrator will then have the responsibility to grant and limit access to the system, which has the incorrect security. This is not usually a difficult task and, considering the circumstances, does not have to be done completely as long as the system is usable. There are several products on the

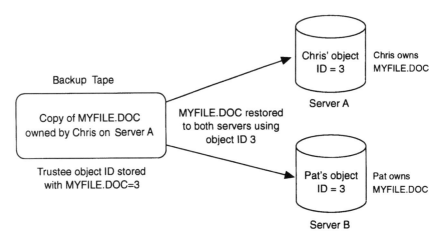

Figure 11.2 When MYFILE.DOC is restored to Server A, Chris is given ownership, but when it is restored to Server B, Pat is given ownership.

market that can be used to record bindery information and create reports; such products are generally referred to as *LAN Inventory* products. The reports they create could be extremely helpful in trying to rebuild network security following a disaster.

Other network operating systems implement security differently. LAN Server and LAN Manager use a single server among multiple servers in a domain to control user access. Therefore, following a disaster on one of these networks, time can be saved if the domain controller can be restored first. If this cannot be done, the user access will have to be recreated by the administrator. Also, the restoration of data and its accompanying security information will be most complete if the same type of file system is installed on the server: either FAT or HPFS. On FAT systems, the security information for the whole file system is contained in a file. On HPFS systems, security information for each file is physically located near the file on disk in a separate storage area, similar to extended attributes.

Banyan Vines uses a directory services facility called StreetTalk, which shares security information across the network. The StreetTalk system is a database that runs on each server in the network and is updated on all machines whenever changes occur. This means that all servers have information about every other server's users. A Vines server that is restored back into a functioning network with other Vines servers will have its security information rebuilt automatically by StreetTalk. If the server will not be able to communicate with other Vines servers, the StreetTalk database information must either be restored or reconstructed manually. Banyan customers may want to verify that their backup system supports backup and restore of the StreetTalk information.

NetWare 4.0 replaces the bindery system with implementation of directory services. Similar to Banyan Vines, a single server restored to a network with other servers will have its directory services automatically rebuilt. If the NetWare 4.0 server is restored and is unable to communicate with other servers, its directory services information will either need to be restored by the backup system or manually rebuilt. At the time this chapter was written, it was unknown if there were utility packages available to record directory services information to help with the manual recreation of directory services information.

DEFINE RECOVERY REQUIREMENTS

The question asked in this phase is, How much time until we are operational again? It is essential to have a realistic objective for the length of time it should take to recover critical systems. In the words of the disaster recovery industry, this is known as the RTO, or recovery time objective. Start with the top of the prioritized list of application systems and work down the list, assigning a length of time to each one. Consult management to find out how long they can be without their system if they have to be. Do not promise things that cannot be done. It is a good idea for them to be prepared for the worst and ready to rely on manual contingency systems.

Business management should work together with LAN administration to determine the RTO for every critical application system. Nobody benefits from being overly optimistic about the RTO. Many variables can affect it; some of them are hot spare availability, time required to acquire necessary equipment, access time to data tapes, number of backup systems that can be used simultaneously, time to generate system software, transfer rates, and amount of data to restore. It may become necessary to update the backup system to meet the RTO. Restoring data is normally a serial process, so be careful not to assume that too many things can be accomplished simultaneously. It may be useful to have a Gantt chart showing the relative timings of the entire recovery operation.

CREATE A DETAILED PLAN

This is the real nuts and bolts of disaster recovery planning. The goal of the entire process is to have a plan that can be used. Expect this plan to need updating from time to time, so do not spend too much time making it beautiful. As mentioned before, there are disaster recovery planning software packages that can greatly reduce the time it takes to generate a plan.

A disaster plan for LANs should contain at least the following sections: (1) notification lists including phone numbers and addresses, (2) detailed task assignments and procedures, (3) hardware and software acquisition information, (4) wiring diagrams, and (5) user environment and workstation information.

Everyone who needs to be notified of a disaster must be named in a list. This list should be prioritized so the people who need to respond quickly are notified first. It is important that this list be updated periodically for obvious reasons. It should include the names and telephone numbers of every employee or vendor who might be needed.

The detailed task assignments describe the steps and operating procedures required to recover. An example of this would be a list of the commands entered to run a redirected restore of an application system to a spare server. It would also include the names of those responsible for completing this task and any backup personnel. It is probably not possible to complete this section of the plan without experience in operating the backup system (covered in more detail in the next section). There should be a contingency plan for all points of failure. For instance, if it becomes necessary to drive to the off-site storage facility to get tapes, a map should be included and any security information you need to retrieve them should be included. If you plan to be able to recover at a remote site, make sure that you have the required hardware, software, and manuals for the backup system at an off-site facility.

Acquiring replacement hardware and software may be much more difficult than you think. The PC industry lives on the principles of just-in-time manufacturing and fast inventory turns. It is a prudent exercise to determine where equipment is warehoused and how quickly it can be accessed by which vendors. It may be a good idea to have some spare server equipment in reserve. Find out what the replacement policy is of your major software products. Covers of manuals and license agreements that burn will not work. If you have a software inventory listing including serial numbers, it should be stored off-site too.

If you need to purchase equipment, you will probably need a purchase order. Generating a purchase order in the midst of a major disaster is not easy. If the equipment is to be delivered to a remote site, make sure to have the address for the remote site available and be sure that the equipment is delivered the that site instead of your normal place of business.

Wiring diagrams come in handy for troubleshooting network problems and locating failed components during minor disasters. Network analyzers can save a great deal of valuable time. You may find it useful to have a general wiring plan available if you need to set up at a remote site; that way, a wiring contractor will be able to finish the job much more quickly and you will be able to set up user workstations much faster.

Anything you can do to preserve the user's normal way of working will be a major benefit. This includes such things as log-in processes that set up system variables, invoke system processes, and assign drives and printers. There are LAN inventory products available that allow you to save information about the user's environment including their config.sys and auto-exec.bat files. Backup systems can be used to protect user workstation data, but the restore process is slow and therefore should not be used to restore a lot of workstation data. Of course, reinstalling software is not fun, but it is an easy task to contract out.

The goal of the plan is to become operational as fast as possible. Inadequate PC equipment will make it harder to do this. Therefore, do not make the mistake of getting PCs that are too small or slow for the job.

IMPLEMENT AND TEST THE PLAN

After the plan is finished, you will want to test it for accuracy. This purpose of testing is not to pass, but to find out what does not work. Testing a disaster plan is an iterative process; things that are found to be incorrect should be corrected and updated in the plan.

There are many ways to test components of the plan without testing an entire recovery operation. For instance, phone numbers can be called to make sure they are still current, vendors can be called to see if they have systems in stock, and restore operations can be checked to see if old commands still work with new versions of the backup/restore software. It may be wise to see whether or not server equipment can be attained, on loan, to try restoring critical high-priority applications. Verify that your tapes, spare server, and backup system can be located and brought to a remote site. Every day, verify that backup is running correctly. Make sure you get plenty of practice with your backup system. Become familiar with it requirements. Try to perform every operation indicated in your plan. Practice restore operations regularly to keep your skills sharp; there is nothing worse than trying to read the manual or remembering how to restore something while people are breathing down your neck. It can be difficult finding the time to practice, but it is time well spent.

Do not create a disaster by testing your plan! Experimenting on production systems in the middle of the day is a good way to get fired.

MAINTAIN THE PLAN AND CONTINUE TESTING

As mentioned, a plan that is not periodically updated will probably not have the correct information about the LAN. Changes to phone numbers, equipment, applications, vendors, personnel, and new systems need to be reflected in the disaster plan. Some people do this monthly, some do it yearly, and others never do it. Because LANs change so rapidly it is a good idea to update the plan at least once a year.

Testing the plan is one of the best ways to practice disaster recovery skills. One of the other benefits of testing the plan is that you may uncover weaknesses or necessary changes that need to be made. An example is discovering that an important member of the recovery team has a different home phone number.

THE BACKUP AND RECOVERY SYSTEM

The choice of hardware and software used for backing up and restoring will have a major impact on the time it takes to respond following a disaster. Unfortunately, backup/recovery systems are often one of the last things considered when putting together a network system. This means that the capital budget for the network is mostly spent and the backup system gets underfunded. The result is too little hardware or inadequate software, or both.

Capacity planning should be carefully done to ensure the backup system is not overburdened. An undersized system puts extra wear and tear on the tapes and tape drives. Expect to have problems with equipment that is regularly being used beyond its capacity. There are a wide variety of tape drives available, but for network applications, there are basically four technologies to choose from: quarter-inch cartridges (QIC), digital audio tape (DAT), 8-mm tape, and digital linear tape (DLT). Table 11.1 summarizes their capacities.

There will be additions to this list as new products are introduced. In general, the newest technology is desirable for the best reliability and performance.

Table 11.1 Tape Drives Available for Network Application

Drive Type	Capacity Range	Maximum Data Transfer Rates
Quarter-inch cartridge	60 MB–2 GB, up to 4 GB with data compressions[a]	8 MB/minute
Digital audio tape	1.3 GB, 2.0 GB, up to 4 GB with data compression[a]	17 MB/minute
8-mm tape	2.2 GB, 5.0 GB, up to 10 GB with data compression[a]	29 MB/minute
Digital linear tape	6 GB	48 MB/minute

[a]Compression drives are listed as doubling the capacity of the drive. The actual compression ratio depends on the data being compressed. For instance, image files do not compress well. Transfer rates of compression drives will also depend on the compression ratio of the data.

The criteria for software selection depends on your environment and your disaster recovery requirements. The following is a list of questions you may want to explore:

- How easy is it to restore entire volumes?
- How easy is it to restore individual files?
- How easy is it to install, run backups, and verify their completion?
- What effort is required to adapt it to network changes?
- How is tape scheduling done?
- Does it monitor tape condition?
- Does it back up and restore all the different file systems on my network?
- What facilities does it have for permanently archiving data?
- Does it provide any additional functions for data management?
- Which adapter cards, tape drives, optical drives, and media changers are supported?

OTHER TECHNIQUES

There are a number of ways to protect data. Tape is the most common way to protect data, but there are other techniques that can be used too. In NetWare 3.x, there is a salvage facility that allows deleted files to be recovered from their original location on disk. Salvage is far from ironclad, as it depends on excess volume capacity and file system activity. If NetWare needs the disk space for another file, the old one is overwritten and salvage will not be able to retrieve it.

Disk duplexing should be used to protect data against disk subsystem failures. There are a variety of RAID (redundant array of inexpensive disks) subsystems on the market which offer varying levels of fault tolerance. Novell has announced and is expected to soon deliver its SFT Level III level of NetWare. In a nutshell, SFT Level III provides immediate and constant duplication of the primary server to a hot spare, which is always ready to go on-line should the first machine fail. Some sites make a nightly copy from one server to another to keep a "warm" spare available for use the next day. Similarly, some sites copy their most critical data to another disk on the network to have it immediately available should a minor disaster crash their primary server. The advantage of using hot and warm spares is that it saves time compared to restoring it from tape.

Another technique that is sometimes used is televaulting. Televaulting is backing up data over a wide area network to a remote site. If there is a disaster at the primary site, the business restores all the data they can at the remote site and resumes operations there. This typically requires a high bandwidth line service and intelligent software to allow the operation to complete overnight.

Tape-on-tape copy facilities are valuable for keeping all the data on-site and off-site. The idea is to complete normal backup operations and then make copies of those tapes to take to the off-site storage facility.

There is almost always room to improve an existing disaster plan. The key to a useful plan is knowing your business and the application systems that are the most important. Then develop the capability to return them to operation as soon as possible using whatever techniques are at your disposal. Plan for both major and minor disasters and test your equipment and operations regularly.

ABOUT THE AUTHOR

Marc Farley is a consulting engineer at Palindrome Corporation.

Palindrome Corporation

Palindrome is one of the leading technology providers of backup and data management software to the PC network marketplace.

12

Selecting a Tape Backup System

Nick Blozan
Product Marketing Manager
Mountain Network Solutions, Inc.

Selecting a business computer today is no simple task. Potential buyers are confronted with a complex series of hardware and software choices. Which bus is best: ISA, EISA, or MCA? What operating system is correct for their environment: DOS, OS/2, or UNIX? Which is the correct processor to choose: 386, 486, or Pentium? What will be the GUI of choice: Windows, NT, Workplace Shell, MS-DOS 6.2 shell, or DR DOS 6.0.

Once a user has decided on a basic hardware and software platform, the same type of decisions must be made in choosing peripherals, especially in the secondary storage arena. While the importance of data backup is well documented, a surplus of backup products in various sizes and formats has confused the market and is partially responsible for more people bypassing backup systems altogether. However, things are not really as bad as they appear.

The simple answer to the question, "Which backup system is best?" is, of course, "The one that best meets your individual requirements." This chapter will look at application requirements and the technology available to meet specific system backup needs. While various high-capacity storage technologies (i.e., Bernoulli, optical disk storage, floptical disks, etc.) have emerged, tape remains, by far, the most well-accepted and most cost-effective means of backing up networked data. For this reason, the focus will be limited to choosing the proper tape backup systems.

Typically, the tape-drive market is segmented into categories based on the physical tape medium: quarter-inch minicartridge, quarter-inch data cartridges, and 4- and 8-mm data cartridges. (A new addition to half-inch tape, Digital Linear Tape, may make significant inroads into the high-end networking marketplace, but will not be covered in this chapter.) In addition, these tapes may be formatted differently depending upon the drive being used. For example, quarter-inch data cartridge drives may utilize either a QIC-40 or QIC-80 format. It is also important to note that tapes formatted in one drive may not be read- and write-compatible with drives using an alternative format.

The physical size of a tape is one way to categorize a system, but evaluating your tape-drive requirements on this factor alone addresses only one part of the equation.

To adequately analyze and define the best tape-drive solution, a user must first define the application requirements and computing environment independently of tape formats. In the process of the analysis, if a requirement for backward compatibility exists, only then does a particular tape format become an integral part of the evaluation process. Beyond that, these systems should be analyzed on other parameters, including capacity, data throughput (not always the same as the data transfer rate, which is usually quoted as a best case maximum speed), operating system and network compatibility, and cost.

It is important to note that when doing a cost analysis, it is common for products to be compared on a cost-per-megabyte basis. While this appears to be a logical basis for product comparison, the cost per solution offers a better comparison. Higher-capacity products typically offer better cost-per-megabyte (now cost-per-gigabyte) specifications, but it is easy to pay for substantially more capacity than you require. Even when considering future system growth, a $200 drive with a 120-MB capacity may address your backup needs better than a $2000 drive with a 4.0-GB capacity.

In a broad sense, the personal computer (PC) storage market can be segmented into five general categories based on systems and computing environments:

- Entry-level systems and portables
- Advanced PC workstations
- Advanced PC workstations with need for backwards compatibility
- Department networks
- Corporate-wide network servers

While the cost and performance level of these system environments varies dramatically, the application's usage of tape systems is remarkably similar across all environments. Certain functions are limited to more advanced tape systems, but applications usage generally falls into the following areas:

- Fixed disk backup and restoration
- Disaster recovery
- Long-term archival data storage
- Software distribution
- Data logging and acquisition
- Image storage and retrieval
- File inquiry
- Data interchange

In general, there is a direct correlation between the cost and capacity of tape backup systems and the price and performance level of the system that it is attached to.

BACKUP FOR ENTRY-LEVEL AND PORTABLE SYSTEMS

Entry-level systems in today's market are PCs using the 80486SX and DX microprocessors. These systems are available complete with hard disk and VGA monitor for about $1000, making price a key consideration for tape systems in this segment. The trade-off, of course, is performance. But again, the performance of the tape, while slower than other high-cost products, is effectively matched to the performance and capacity of the system it is backing up. For example, a quarter-inch minicartridge drive utilizing QIC-80 formatting can offer one of the best values on the market today. It is possible to purchase a unit for around $200 which supports file-by-file back-ups of up to 250 MB on a single minicartridge and is a good match for most 80486SX- and DX-based systems.

Another key feature of QIC-80 drives is their ability to operate off a floppy disk controller, alleviating the cost of a dedicated tape controller which would also take up an expansion slot. The other major attraction to these drives is size. Most QIC-80 drives are now available in a 3.5-inch form factor; some are even available in a 1-inch high profile. Historically, these smaller form factor tape drives have been associated with lower-performance products, but that situation is rapidly changing. Following a general industry trend towards more power, speed, and capacity in 3.5-inch products, some of these systems now offer speeds and capacities comparable to some full-size data cartridge tape systems with a SCSI interface. These advanced minicartridge tape drives are ideally suited as internal backup devices for systems demanding 3.5-inch form factor drives.

This new class of high-performance minicartridge drives is a cost-effective solution for midrange systems requiring 3.5-inch peripherals. Their capacity is also attractive for peer-to-peer local area networks (LANs) and some larger entry-level network environments that use a standard PC as a host instead of a multidisk dedicated server.

An important feature to look for in minicartridge products is the ability to read multiple tape formats. Typically, high-capacity QIC-80–type drives are backward read-compatible with the QIC-80 format. There are, however, even more flexible designs available that incorporate high performance along with QIC standard compatibility.

QIC-80 standard drives use a floppy disk interface, which provides a large base of compatible PCs. However, the relatively slow throughput of the floppy controller limits the speed and general performance of these devices. This is a drawback for those needing a high-performance solution for large-capacity hard disk backups.

There are options available to overcome these limitations. With the addition of a dedicated controller, the functionality of QIC minicartridge drives can be greatly expanded—in some cases, offering more than 300 MB of capacity and a data transfer rate of up to 10 MB/minute with software compression.

Parallel port minicartridge drives also provide an alternative to serial port devices. Since these systems easily connect to a system's parallel port, they are ideal for portable computers such as notebooks and laptop systems that often do not have expansion ports for SCSI devices. The small form factor of these units also make them useful for backing up individual workstations on a small network.

Further advancements in minicartridge technology have overcome one of the main drawbacks to most tape formats—the need to format the media before use. This can be a time-consuming process, taking more than 2 hours in some cases.

New systems available on the market do not require a lengthy formatting cycle and costly preformatted tapes are unnecessary. With the breadth of the product offerings, from low-cost entry-level systems to high-performance devices, minicartridge tape systems are often the best solution for applications requiring 300 MB of capacity or less. In the near future, we will also see minicartridge technology capture more of the high-end market as well. SCSI-based minicartridge products, currently in the evaluation stage, will offer capacities as high as 400 MB (uncompressed to 800 MB compressed).

BACKUP FOR ADVANCED PC WORKSTATIONS

High-powered PC Workstations, such as those using high-speed 486 and Pentium microprocessors, comprise the middle range of PC hardware platforms. These systems cover a comprehensive range of price and performance capabilities, encompassing everything from a base 486 system selling for around $1200 to cache-based 66-MHz systems designed as a host to support multiple UNIX terminals. Backup systems for these applications typically utilize higher-capacity DC600 data cartridge units. DC600 drives have been widely available for over 10 years with an unmatched record of reliable performance. Tape drives based on this full-sized quarter-inch cartridge cover a wide spectrum of capacities—from 60-MB to over 2-GB native capacity. The popularity of this format and its ability to read data on tapes created by previous generations of lower-capacity drives make this the format of choice for installations that already have an installed base of DC600 devices. The current generation of 525-MB and 2-GB quarter-inch cartridge systems offers users the best of everything—the ability to perform a 1:1 backup of a high-capacity disk, while maintaining compatibility with the installed base of data tapes.

High-performance QIC drives with over 2.0 GB of capacity using the SCSI interface will soon be appearing on the market. These drives take advantage of new developments in magnetic media and recording technology. The growth path for this class of drives calls for 10+ GB drives by 1995.

A major factor in the success of QIC systems is its compatibility with previous QIC formats. Backward compatibility, for instance, is a critical issue for 386, 486, and RISC installations used in UNIX environments. Much of the applications software written for UNIX and XENIX, and even the operating system itself, is distributed on data cartridges. Because of the ability of the new drives to read multiple QIC formats, software developers are not forced to port their software to a new format, and users are not required to make any conversions.

BACKUP FOR DEPARTMENT NETWORKS AND LARGE NETWORK SERVERS

Users who do not have a strong requirement for compatibility with current data can look to the helical scan tape format to provide very high-capacity storage solutions. They are available in two main formats: 4-mm systems, based on Digital Audio Tape (DAT) technology, and 8 mm, derived from mechanisms used in compact video recorders.

The 8-mm helical scan systems are based on a format developed by Sony Corporation and provide capacities from 2.5 to 5 GB per cartridge. Using data compression techniques, 8-mm helical scan drives provide up to 10 GB of data storage. Either way, these systems provide sufficient capacity for complete backups of large network file servers.

Whether we are talking about 8-mm drives or 4-mm DAT drives, helical scan tape devices are a radical departure from traditional cartridge tape designs.

The two major differences of helical scan technology are the use of a rotating recording head, rather than a stationary head, and the methods in which the data are recorded on the tape. In DAT drives, the read/write heads are mounted on a repeatedly rotating drum. The tape is pulled past the head at less than 1 inch per second (ips), but the resulting relative speed of the tape moving past the rapidly rotating head at a $6°$ angle is 123 ips, slightly faster than most of the quarter-inch cartridge tape systems.

In contrast to conventional quarter-inch tape systems, which record data in a series of longitudinal tracks running along the entire length of the tape, helical scan systems record tracks diagonally on the tape with a length of less than an inch. DAT drives record these tracks using a method called alternate azimuth recording.

With alternate azimuth recording, two sets of read and write heads are positioned $90°$ apart around the rotating drum with the alternating head tilted at different angles relative to the tape. Each track is written overlapping the previous track by 25 percent. Because alternating tracks are recorded at an azimuth opposite to the adjacent tracks (minimizing cross-talk), the tracks are recorded physically on top of each other, but do not interfere with the track currently being read. This technique provides extremely high track densities, as it eliminates the need for guardbands between tracks, which are required in longitudinal recording. As a result, DAT drives can maximize the available recording area on the tape, producing extremely high data densities and the accompanying gigabyte-plus capacity offered by this technology.

Information is also organized differently on the 4-mm DAT tapes than on quarter-inch cartridges. The tracks on DAT tapes are associated into frames, two tracks per frame, with the 22 frames comprising a group. Within the group, certain frames are used for indexing and storing the C3 Error Correction Code (ECC) recovery data. The indexing of the groups contributes to the rapid file retrieval of the DAT technology.

One of the prevailing myths about DAT is that it will open new application areas for tape by allowing the systems to function as random access devices. However, all tape drives, regardless of format, are still sequential access devices. Even though new methods of storing and retrieving data dramatically reduce DAT file search times, compared to traditional tape technologies, tape is still primarily a secondary storage medium.

The Digital Data Storage (DDS) format, the dominant format for 4-mm DAT drives, stores data on the tape in a sequential fashion, much like the quarter-inch data cartridge drives. Files or the disk "images" are committed to the tape as the application software or operating system delivers them. No update in place feature is available. Random retrieval for data is permitted. The DDS format is better suited for the rapid backup and retrieval of files, and fills the traditional role of magnetic tape as the backup and archiving media for hard disk and optical drives.

The applications for DAT are, to a large extent, the same ones that QIC tape has traditionally dominated: fixed disk backup, long-term archival storage, and disk image storage and retrieval.

There is, however, a new application area for which DAT, when coupled with the appropriate software, is ideally suited: distributed backup and data management.

The traditional model of fixed disk backup defines a system where the backup medium offers a 1:1 capacity match for the system's hard disk drive. Unfortunately, this model no longer applies, as today's computing environments have changed significantly. Most modern computing work groups are equipped with the central network server(s), along with local disk storage, throughout the organization. The old model dictates that the backup tape systems be equal in capacity to the server disk capacity, which is likely to include multiple disk drives. There is also a requirement to back up and protect corporate data stored locally on individual workstations. The advent of DAT autoloaders will accommodate the capacity of the network, but the problem remains in having enough time available to back up the multigigabytes of data that are on LANs today.

Network data security and data management represent a prime application opportunity for DAT. Until the 4-mm system, and, more recently, 1- and

2-GB QIC drives appeared, users were faced with a significant capacity gap between quarter-inch data cartridge systems with 525 MB of capacity and expensive 2.5- or 5-GB 8-mm systems. DAT offers an economical, high-capacity solution to fill this midrange gap with both 2- and 4-GB versions available today. Not only is the capacity substantial enough to back up LAN servers and local workstations in a single session, but since most restore operations on a network are for a single file, the fast access mode allows users quick access to data they might inadvertently erase from their disk.

In addition to desirable performance attributes, the ability to add capacity without sacrificing the existing hardware investment is another attractive feature of suitably configured DAT systems. Earlier tape systems would not allow users to increase capacity by adding drives in a daisy-chain fashion, which limited the growth path for this technology. However, certain integrators of SCSI-based DAT systems give users the ability to daisy-chain multiple drives, providing logical capacity upgrades as needed without discarding current hardware.

DAT STANDARDS

Unlike the very early efforts of quarter-inch cartridge drive vendors to sell various format products to the OEM market, the DAT industry designed recording format standards before drives were available. Although other options are available, the industry is clearly backing the DDS format created by Hewlett-Packard and Sony as the preferred DAT format. Leading drive suppliers such as Hewlett-Packard, Sony, WangDAT (recently acquired by Wangtek), Archive (ARDAT, recently acquired by Conner Peripherals), and Wangtek, as well as computer system OEMS, including Digital Equipment Corp. (DEC), have endorsed DDS, assuring users of long-term support and upgrades of DDS-compatible products.

This strong support of the DDS format is producing a market in which highly standardized hardware will be differentiated in end-user products by the level of optimization of the hardware and software technologies included in the package. While the basic underlying tape drive technology may be very similar, significant differences are beginning to emerge in how the products are supported by the manufacturers and the growth path that exists for their products.

Perhaps the most substantial variations in DAT performance and ease of use will be directly related to the design of the software that is included with the system. In the rush to get these advanced storage systems into the hands of anxious users, some products are being sold without being fully optimized for backup and restore performance.

To take advantage of the Quick File Access (QFA) features of the DAT drive, one of the methods employed requires two partitions to be set up on the tape. One of the partitions holds the directory information and the other holds the data. The directory partition holds the information on where to rapidly locate the file in the data portion of the tape. Once the files have been selected for restoration, the QFA properties of the DAT drive are used to seek to the address given by the directory partition in coordination with the application software. Setting up the two partitions is a type of formatting, but it is complete within a few minutes. Some DAT drive suppliers require that this process be completed before the backup operation begins.

DAT buyers should also be wary of excessively low-priced media. Media pricing has been touted as a major advantage of DAT technology, but while pricing can be below that of traditional quarter-inch data cartridge media, it is not at the cost of video and audio cassette tapes.

Tape drive manufacturers recommend certain media they have certified for use with their drives. The quality of media available varies greatly and lower grades may actually shorten the life of the DAT drive. To ensure the highest data integrity, it is recommended that only drive manufacturer–certified, data-grade media be used in these systems. Standard off-the-shelf DAT media designed for audio recording should not be used. While users may be tempted to use this low-cost media and might even be able to successfully record data with it, it does not ensure the long-term storage stability that is provided with higher-quality tape developed expressly for data storage applications.

There are other requirements that DAT buyers should be aware of as well. Not all currently available products offer the comprehensive features users need to take full advantage of DAT technology and maximize their return on investment. The ability to match the performance of the DAT drive with the hard disk or transfer rates across a network will determine if DAT will be the best backup choice for their needs.

Because the technology is relatively new compared to other tape technologies, buyers should make a point of considering the reputation for quality and service of the manufacturer as well as the manufacturer's experience in the tape industry. Be sure that the company has a track record in providing network backup solutions and is recognized for meeting those needs.

SELECTING A LAN BACKUP SOLUTION

The following is a list of other important questions to ask when considering a LAN backup system:

- Does the tape drive software produce a report of files that were skipped during a backup session? The files may be open, locked, or in use on a network server during the backup session. The user or supervisor needs to be notified that these files should be backed up at a later time. This is a mandatory requirement for managing the vast amounts of data that will be stored on high-capacity backup systems.

- Does the tape system support the latest versions of Novell NetWare 286, NetWare 386, and NetWare 4.0? Support for the most popular network operating systems is critical. Any backup system lacking Novell support is incomplete. But network support does not end with Novell. The software should also be flexible enough to work with other operating systems such as IBM OS/2 and IBM's LAN server, IBM PC LAN, and Artisoft LANtastic.

- Does the system provide password protection for backup volumes? The system administrator has to rely on a secure system for sensitive data on a corporate LAN.

- Does the backup system include an extensive batch processing capability to automate the process of publishing and backing up local hard disks? Local hard disks are also a corporate asset and may contain important information for the operation of the company. Disk failures on network workstations can cripple the smooth flow of information in the workplace.

- Can the drive and software support local hard drive backup and peer-to-peer communications on Novell, NetBIOS, and peer-to-peer networks? If so, is the software robust enough to support an adequate number of local drives for your installation or is it limited to a specified number of workstations per backup session? Not all networks are running Novell's NetWare and its IPX transport. Small networks rely on NetBIOS as their transport. Flexibility to name drives by their assigned volume names enhances the administration of the entire network backup.

- Does the system provide adequate information during the backup process? Ideally, the DAT system will supply a comprehensive progress report during the backup session, including the size of the backup, number of files to be backed up, percentage complete, and number of files remaining to be backed up.

- Can the DAT system back up local drives without file server intervention? If the workstation must be logged into the server to perform a backup, network security is at risk.

- Does the software support verification of the data that has been written to the tape? Without this feature, users have no way of ensuring the data were actually recorded properly. Some systems check to see only if the directory of the tape can be read. The only true verification would be to do a byte-for-byte comparison of the data on the tape with data on the hard disk.

- Does the system software take full advantage of the speed and access features of the DAT drive, especially QFA, or is it simply modified from another medium and patched to work on a DAT drive? The old adage that backups are done at leisure and restores are done in a panic still holds true. If it takes minutes or hours to find a file on a tape, useful productivity time is lost.

- Is the software sophisticated enough to properly handle backup in Novell environments, including the backup of extended attributes in the current releases of NetWare and all files and namespace information of non-DOS data located on the file server? The increased use of Macintosh and computers with other operating systems on LANs requires additional attention to addressing the backup needs of these clients. Cooperation with the network operating system suppliers will enhance the support for backup systems in these environments.

- Can a full restore be made to a different disk than was originally backed up? A backup tape has little value if it cannot be easily restored when a hard disk fails. Servers grow in size and data must be migrated from the original disk to the larger-capacity drives.

- Does the software provide for adequate disaster recovery?

DATA MANAGEMENT

When selecting a tape backup system, one must evaluate more than just the hardware. In fact, as prices of tape drives continue to decline, industry leaders in the backup arena are placing an increasing amount of focus on the software solutions that accompany their systems. This has led to the emergence of systems that offer a variety of data management functions as well as simple backup procedures.

Data management, as defined by leading industry analysts, is "the administration of data in a system such that it can be stored, backed-up, cataloged, and protected in the most cost-effective way." Today, a comprehensive backup system should provide both the hardware and software solutions to meet all aspects of data management. Data is the lifeblood of all computing needs, and it is imperative that its integrity is maintained. Personal finance records, business forecasts, manufacturing records, and database information are typical types of data that need to be managed.

Proper data management assures data integrity—the preservation of data for its original intended use—and provides the means for data manipulation and detailed reports on how data is being used. Data management also provides complete recovery of data after a catastrophic failure. Several tools available guarantee data integrity on computer systems and networks and ease the complexity of data management tasks. Elements of data management include:

Virus protection. A computer virus is aptly named. As with humans, a virus is invisible, can be caught unknowingly, and can be devastating to the infected system. Viruses are passed through networks and removable storage media (i.e., floppy disks). Viruses can jeopardize data integrity and the operation of the entire system or network. The fear of lost or corrupted data has fueled a new market for virus protection software that systematically detects and eliminates viruses. Virus detection provides a mechanism for determining if data has been infected and notifying the system administrator to correct the problem. Data management tools make every attempt to warn users if data integrity has been compromised.

Tape/media cataloging and maintenance. One of the problems with traditional network backup methods is in the handling of the tape logistics—which tapes to use and in what order. This becomes more unmanageable as more sites are included in the management process and the amount of maintained data increases. While tape/media cataloging and maintenance is a popular topic of industry forums and analyst papers, few companies have been able to implement the complete solution.

File grooming and data migration. Primary on-line hard drive space is at a premium in most networking environments. It seems users will always fill whatever space is available. Creating more hard drive space usually means an investment in additional hard disks, but if LAN administrators could groom hard drive files to archive old files onto secondary off-line storage media, valuable on-line resources could be freed to the networking environment and its users.

Extended reporting services. Reporting allows the LAN administrator to gather valuable information regarding the usage of data on the network, including information on accessed data, time of use, and storage space allocation. For example, if a LAN administrator needs to know how often the file server is used for data management functions, a report can be generated showing which users requested backup procedures. This information could be accumulated and used to forecast file service load across the network.

When a company experiences a system crash, it is imperative that there be a simple and effective means of bringing the system back up and running as quickly and completely as possible. Unfortunately, disaster recovery programs are often ignored until it is too late.

In January 1990, AT&T's long distance network failed. The problem was caused not by heavy phone traffic, but by a failure of its new network software. It took more than 24 hours to correct the problem, and AT&T is still suffering from consumers' lack of confidence in the system.

The 1993 bombing of the World Trade Center in New York City downed thousands of computer networks disrupted by the blast. It is estimated that over 50 percent of the companies affected by the disaster have lost valuable data permanently. A number of these companies may never recover from that loss.

In 1990, the Internal Revenue Service (IRS) touted its new computerized tax filing system that promised early returns to users. However, because of a problem with its network software, users who used this method to file their taxes did not see fast returns. Additional staff hours were required to fix the problem, at a time of the year when resources were least available. This situation not only cost time and money to resolve, but further damaged the IRS' already tenuous reputation with the taxpaying public.

These highly publicized system failures are only two examples of the thousands of system crashes that businesses experience each year. In 1989, an Infonetics Inc. (San Jose, California) survey of Fortune 1000 companies found that networked corporations lost nearly $3.5 million in employee productivity annually due to LAN downtime, some of which was directly related to failed storage devices. These same companies reported revenue losses in lost data and lower employee productivity averaging more than $600,000, or more than 3.5 percent of their total revenue (information provided by *LAN Times*, "Considering the Critical Issue of Network Data Storage," December 10, 1990).

Even more harrowing are the statistics from a recent study by the University of Texas, at Arlington, which found that 43 percent of the companies that lose their data via a major disaster will never reopen; 90 percent will be out of business in 2 years. This is due, in part, to the fact that a downed system can cost a company hundreds of thousands of dollars for each hour that it remains inoperable.

The fact remains that one small breach in data integrity can result in significant financial losses, extra hours to correct problems, and a loss of credibility to corporations. Even more significant than the loss of data integrity would be the consequences if data could not be completely recovered after a catastrophe.

In order to provide the data protection that today's networks require, various companies in the backup industry are refocusing a greater amount of their attention on disaster recovery. Now, instead of offering simple 1:1 backup, these firms are developing complete software solutions designed to protect and recover data from downed networks. The strategy for disaster recovery may differ greatly from one product to another but the goal is the same: to provide a fast and simple means of restoring a network to a chosen state, prior to a disaster.

While planning for a system crash seems straightforward enough, getting a system back up during a real emergency is usually an example of Murphy s Law: "Whatever can go wrong, will." For this reason, each component of the disaster recovery plan should be designed to be implemented under the worse possible scenario. Its simplicity should assume that someone less qualified than the network manager will be the one with the responsibility of bringing the system back on-line. It should presuppose that those system components that can fail, will.

REQUIREMENTS FOR EFFECTIVE DATA MANAGEMENT

A typical networked data processing environment consists of several PCs running DOS and Windows on a Novell NetWare LAN. These may be connected to another LAN with several Macintosh systems using AppleTalk. The LANs may also include mixed network topologies.

As more manufacturers of networking software enter the market, the more complex data management becomes. Single-source support for all of these environments is not available.

Storage Requirements

A growing number of companies are downsizing their mainframe applications, thus putting more demands on the size and sophistication of their LAN. Many networks now face increased requirements for both primary on-line and secondary off-line storage. It is not unusual to find networks with 10 to 50 GB of primary storage and, in order to provide sufficient backup capacity, 50 GB of secondary storage in an autoloader library.

Ease of Use

Data management must also be made easy. Graphical user interfaces have made applications development and user interface much easier by providing an intuitive environment for users. Tape rotational schemes have made it easy to quickly locate the tapes necessary to bring a system back up and running in as short a time period as possible.

Shared Resources

Following the client/server model of networking, data management software should offer shared resources. The data management server "engine" must be able to handle requests from multiple clients at the same time. In addition, access to off-line storage devices must be provided in a distributed, multiuser fashion, whether the device is attached to a file server or another workstation on the network.

Interoperability

Interoperability is the key to the network industry growth and will allow both client and server environments from multiple vendors to work together. Successful interoperability can be achieved through focused efforts of the following vendors and systems:

- Novell, Artisoft, and their associated product families
- Microsoft and its operating systems, MS-DOS and Windows
- IBM with its PC-DOS and OS/2 and LAN Server systems
- Apple and its Macintosh family of products
- The entire UNIX family of computers and file systems including A/UX

By supporting interoperability through effective data management, this group of computers and operating systems can be configured to offer an effective and viable interenterprise networking solution.

ABOUT THE AUTHOR

Prior to his appointment as product marketing manager at Mountain Network Solutions Inc, Mr. Blozan worked for 3 1/2 years on Mountain software development projects. he aslo has nine years of experience in software development with such companies as Emerald Systems Inc., Computer Associates, and Data GraphiX. Mr. Blozan holds B.S. degrees in Business Administration and Computer Science from San Diego State University.

Mountain Network Solutions, Inc.

Founded in 1977, Mountain is a leading producer of computer and network tape backup systems. Mountain Network Solutions Inc. is headquartered at 360 El Pueblo Road, Scotts Valley, California, 95066; Voice (408) 438-6650, FAX (408) 439-3249.

PART 5

Data Communications

13

Electronic Messaging

Mikael Edholm
Ericsson Hewlett-Packard Telecommunications, A.B.

The objective of computer networks is to provide a mechanism for access and manipulation of information. This information is typically dispersed across multiple locations, in differing formats, and in a variety of computer systems. While some types of information might require virtually instantaneous communication, most information flows can be handled on a store-and-forward basis. The network services and associated applications providing this functionality are typically referred to as electronic messaging services.

Electronic messaging can take many forms. Today, the most commonly implemented messaging services are used for enterprise electronic mail, linking individuals within corporate entities at multiple geographical locations, through wire-line networks. Messaging is, however, rapidly expanding beyond the confines of the corporate office. Mobile messaging has become more and more frequent as the use of nomadic computing devices has spread across the world. Wireless computing is not yet as common as the ubiquitous cellular phone, but it is rapidly gaining in popularity.

Electronic messaging is simultaneously moving beyond mere electronic mail. Mail-enabled services are rapidly being added to the core communications services. Word processing software packages now come with integrated mail capabilities. Compound document transfer services allow for combined text, graphics, and images within an e-mail message. Structured business communications such as Electronic Data Interchange (EDI) and Electronic

Funds Transfer (EFT) through messaging services are now also commonly available.

Finally, messaging is adding intelligence to its basic functionality. So-called rules-based messaging, or "smart" messaging, makes use of programmable agents that perform complex sequences of operations without direct user involvment. Event-based information retrieval, event-triggered query operations, and individually designed message filters are taking messaging far beyond its humble e-mail origins. The addition of workflow capabilities to standard eletronic mail systems is proving to be an efficient means of increasing knowledge of worker productivity.

ENTERPRISE MESSAGING

The basic service provided by most messaging systems is electronic mail. A great many organizations today are using this indispensable business tool to facilitate enterprise communications. In most cases, the electronic mail system was originally implemented on the corporate headquarters mainframe, while access was provided to any employee capable of locally or remotely logging on to the central system. Messages could be composed, sent, stored, retrieved, replied to, or forwarded from any authorized user terminal. These mainframe-based e-mail systems gradually became more and more sophisticated, as additional applications such as group calendars and schedulers were added to the basic service. Although primarily used for intraenterprise communications, a few successful mail systems even started to incorporate users outside of the core enterprise domain. Manufacturing suppliers were given limited access to plant e-mail addresses. Certain customers became able to enter orders or receive technical information through their vendor's e-mail system. For a few years, mainframe e-mail was the dominating enterprise communications service in most major corporations.

The mergers and acquisitions frenzy of the late 1980s, combined with the rapid spread of personal computers, changed this once stable situation. Multiple incompatible mainframe and midrange computers appeared within the restructured organizations. Previously rigid Management Information System (MIS) guidelines and recommendations were no longer applicable to the entire enterprise. The corporate computer networks gradually fell apart into entity domains, offering similar but incompatible applications and services. Electronic messaging users, in particular, suffered from this evolution, as one e-mail system could not easily be linked to another, due to differences in the underlying network technologies and application formats.

A major cause was the rapid deployment of personal computers (PCs) and local area networks (LANs). At first, PCs were stand-alone systems, complementing the mainframe terminals. PC applications, such as spreadsheets and word processors, were originally developed for individual usage and dependent on locally available information. Soon, however, the need for shared access to data and peripherals led to a rapid growth of LANs. The formerly stand-alone PCs and peripherals became part of what is now referred to as a client/server architecture. PCs became desktop clients to a range of back-end servers. These network servers managed shared data (file servers), shared peripherals (print servers), and shared communications services (communications servers). With the network servers came network applications, one of which was LAN e-mail. Within a few years, most file servers offered their clients a user-friendly mail system, complete with a mail engine, message storage facilities, and graphical user interfaces. But only occasionally did the LAN mail system include an external communications facility.

Thus, in a very short period of time, most major organizations had developed isolated islands of information. Focused, mutually exclusive solutions proliferated throughout large and small organizations alike. Computer systems vendors and software providers benefited handsomely from this situ-

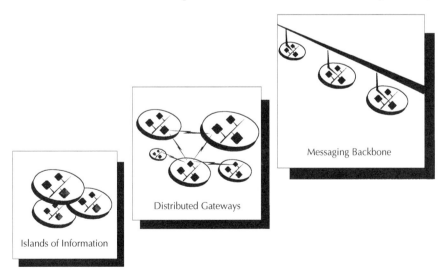

Figure 13.1 Technology trends.

ation since products could be designed to lock users into specific architectures or applications. Although clearly serving a need and being highly appreciated by their users, the PC networks were not always a part of the corporate information mainstream. Sending a message from one desktop to another, within an entity, was an easy task. The entity file server could easily handle the message transfer on the LAN. Sending or receiving messages between entities was usually not as easy, if at all possible. The LANs became isolated islands of information. With the addition of other networked applications, these islands soon drifted further and further apart. Much to the dismay of the frustrated corporate MIS manager, user expectations increased while the MIS span of control rapidly diminished. Worst of all, from a corporate standpoint, was the daunting task of providing a ubiquitous electronic mail service. (See Figure 13.1.)

ENTER THE GATEWAY

From a corporate point of view, the situation had deteriorated because of a lack of connectivity. During the mainframe era, e-mail was provided from a single point, through a single network, to multiple users. After the introduction of LANs, multiple servers provided similar functionality, but from multiple locations and through multiple networks. If these disparate networks could communicate, any given user might view the complete system as one network. As long as a message could be passed on from one desktop to another, what possible reason could an end user have to worry about how this feat was actually accomplished?

With this in mind, LAN mail gateways were developed and deployed. More and more LANs added a mail gateway to their mainframe counterpart. This gateway enabled desktop users to address users of the corporate network as if they were also on the LAN, and vice versa. As long as there was only communication between one LAN and one mainframe mail system, the network usually operated as expected. Soon, however, there were several gateways in the network. The local LAN mail users did not only need to communicate with mainframe mail users, but with other LANs, and other mail applications. Two different systems needed only one gateway. Three different systems needed three gateways. Four systems needed nine gateways.

Sales of e-mail gateways mushroomed. In 1990, the North American market for e-mail gateways was valued at $165 million. In 1991, that number had risen to $255 million. By 1992, $360 million worth of gateways were sold in the United States and Canada alone. Projections through 1995 expect e-mail gateways to become close to a $1 billion market. Worldwide, that number would be achieved much sooner.

Unfortunately for the corporate mail system administrator, as well as for the LAN e-mail administrators, the communication problem had not really been solved, only temporarily fixed. With each new revision of mail software and with each new revision of communications software, it became necessary to review the operation of the gateways. While theoretically it should be an easy task to update the various parts of the system, in practice some part was always unable to fully utilize the network. The reason was mainly software upgrade incompatibilities, due to new and improved features and associated bugs. Although eventually fixed, the delays often led to profound user dissatisfaction with the corporate mail system.

To make things worse, the e-mail gateways could not always provide the corporate e-mail administrator with the necessary tools to maintain the overall system. Directory structures were different on the different sides of the gateways. Statistics from the LAN mail servers could not be gathered from the mainframe side of the fence, and administrative responsibilities were more often than not shared between corporate entities and highly independent local entities. In short, proliferation of e-mail gateways had resulted in an administrative nightmare.

THE BACKBONE CONCEPT

The advent of client/server computing, coupled with some recent developments of standard protocols for electronic mail transmission, created a new opportunity: the e-mail backbone. Instead of relying on multiple gateways, a single transmission protocol could be implemented at a back end, while desktop mail users maintained the front-end user interfaces and services they had become accustomed to. Multiple back-end servers would make up a backbone network. The backbone eliminated the need for multiple gateways since each LAN mail system would depend on only one conversion to take place; that between its own protocol and the backbone protocol. The backbone protocol could then be managed, maintained, and controlled from a single source, through any back-end server in the system. In other words, the backbone put the corporate mail system administrator back in charge.

Originally, there existed several viable choices for the backbone protocol. Both proprietary protocol suites, such as IBM's System Network Architecture (SNA) and the de facto standard TCP/IP (Transmission Control Protocol/Internet Protocol) include services that can perform this critical function. Both of these have the technical functionality required, and are in widespread use. If intraenterprise messaging is all that is required of a corporate mail system, there would usually be no reason to look further. Either choice would suffice, although none would be ideal.

Over the last few years, however, interenterprise messaging has become more and more frequent. If one intraenterprise backbone had chosen SNA as its communications architecture, another might have chosen TCP/IP. Interenterprise messaging would then once more require the use of additional gateways. Fortunately, there is another solution: X.400. As the only set of protocols that has been developed specifically with backbone message handling in mind, X.400 is in may ways unique. It is also universally accepted, being the result of an international standards effort conducted under the auspices of the International Telephone and Telegraph Consultative Committee (CCITT).

The marketplace acceptance of X.400 was initially slow, but as its more recent revisions added much needed functionality, X.400 usage rapidly increased. In 1990, X.400-based gateways made up less than half of the overall mail gateway sales volume. But by 1991, X.400 gateway sales had surpassed sales of all other mail gateways by a wide margin. North American sales volume of X.400 gateways were $80 million in 1990. In 1991, sales doubled to $160 million. By 1992, sales had reached over $250 million, nearly two and a half times as much as sales of all other mail gateways combined. By this time, X.400 was also offered by all major service providers. AT&T, Sprint, and MCI in the United States, and a very impressive range of other carriers and PTTs worldwide. In the United Kingdom and abroad, British Telecom offered X.400 access through its BT GOLD service, France Telecom had its Atlas 400, and Deutsche Bundespost had its TeleBox 400. In Japan, Australia, and Taiwan similar offerings were also underway.

In terms of market penetration, the numbers were even more impressive. Fortune 1000 users of X.400 in the United States grew from 6 percent in 1990, to 18 percent in 1991, to 30 percent in 1992. Market projections made in mid-1992 assumed that by the mid-1990s, X.400 would be used by over two-thirds of U.S. Fortune 1000 companies. In Europe, X.400 penetration was already close to this level in 1993.

STORE AND FORWARD

The keys to X.400's success are in its architectural merits and in the functionality it provides. CCITT developed the X.400 specifications as guidelines for a message handling system, not only an electronic mail system. E-mail is just one application within a broad spectrum of messaging applications. The CCITT X.400 series of Recommendations for Message Handling Systems provide both an architecture and a set of communications protocols for interconnecting disparate mail systems. In other words, CCITT anticipated the evolution towards a multiprotocol world and took advantage of the emerging client/server architectures to provide a new and unique solution to a common business problem.

The X.400 Message Handling System (MHS) is made up of three main parts: UA, MTA, and MS (see Figure 13.2). The client submitting or receiving messages on behalf of a user is called the User Agent (UA). UAs submit or retrieve messages via Message Store (MS) servers. Message stores use Message Transfer Agents (MTA) to forward messages along the backbone.

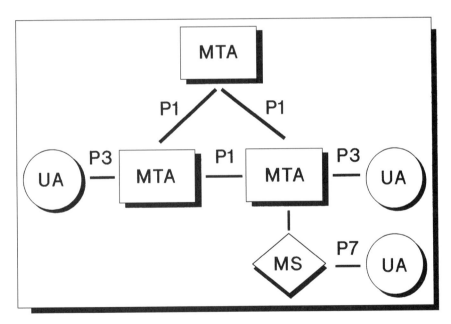

Figure 13.2 Message handling system.

In addition, external entities may address the MHS through a fourth part: a gateway called an Access Unit (AU).

The three parts of the MHS communicate through the use of one or more of four interconnecting protocols, P1 through P7.

P1 specifies how the MTA servers should relay messages along the backbone.

P2 specifies how the contents of these messages should be structured.

P3 specifies how the clients (UAs) and servers (MTAs) should communicate.

P7 specifies how the interaction between UA and the MS is conducted.

The benefits of this architecture are immediate. The clear separation of the message envelope and its contents enable X.400 to be used as a transport mechanism for a multitude of messaging applications, beyond the core e-mail application widely in use today. Different body parts within the X.400 envelope can accommodate different representations of data. Examples include memos, forms, office documents, telex, fax, graphics, and schematics, as well as voice messages. X.400 is also rapidly being deployed as a transport mechanism for structured business transactions, such as Electronic Data Interchange (EDI) or Electronic Funds Transfer (EFT).

In order to accomodate such applications, the basic X.400 specification has been extended by the introduction of X.435 for electronic data interchange. X.435 is similar to the basic X.400, but it has additional features for structured business exchanges. Key features include acknowledgments, tracking of transactions, responsibility forwarding, and a separate message store, the X.435 message store. During 1993, X.435 was implemented by several large corporations throughout North America. In addition, public EDI services, based on X.435, were being considered by several carriers.

A second benefit is the address format. Contrary to the TCP/IP environment, for example, X.400 is in no danger of running out of addresses. The open-ended format allows for originator/recipient (O/R) addresses to include any type of end user, whether it is a person, an electronic device, or a service.

A third benefit is its independence of the user applications. X.400 was designed to accommodate disparate mail systems, not to replace them. Desktop mail users, familiar with a certain set of user interfaces, need not learn new ones when confronted with an X.400 system. When using X.400, the front-end systems remain intact, while the back end becomes transparent.

Still, X.400 is not a user-friendly system. Designed as a global back end, the addressing is highly complex and cumbersome. A complete X.400 address includes information about the Administrative Management Domain (ADMD), the Private Management Domain (PRMD), the country, the organization, and the individual. An O/R address is invariably a long string of data. Bringing X.400 to the front end requires major improvments in usability. Such improvements have been made by several software providers. The most commonly used scheme involves "beautification" of X.400 addresses. This refers to the process by which an MTA can "strip" a complete O/R address down to only the essentials needed by an end user. This process can be implemented for outgoing messages as well as for incoming messages. In both cases, full O/R addresses are stored at the MTA, but a separate database is generated to maintain the "beautified" names that the end user sees. In most cases, the front-end mail user would see only his usual address syntax, not the underlying X.400 O/R address.

DIRECTORY SERVICES

Messaging backbones cannot be designed with only the transport mechanism in mind. It is also necessary to make sure that the location of data and resources are known to users, and to the backbone itself. Mainframe-based mail systems use their own proprietary ways of dealing with this issue. Public carrier services have their own subscriber databases. LAN mail systems have yet other ways of knowing where to find addressees.

A backbone transport mechanism such as X.400 requires a fully functional directory service. The CCITT once again recognized this fact at an early stage. As a companion standard to X.400, the CCITT developed its Recommendations and International Standards for an Open Systems Interconnection Directory Service, called X.500. These recommendations provide a model for a fully scalable information retrieval service applicable not only to X.400 O/R addresses, but to any network object. These objects can be people, network information such as routing tables, or client/server configurations and locations.

X.500 is structured in a way similar, but not identical, to X.400. The X.500 logical database is known as the Directory Information Base (DIB) with an internal structure known as the Directory Information Tree. This logical

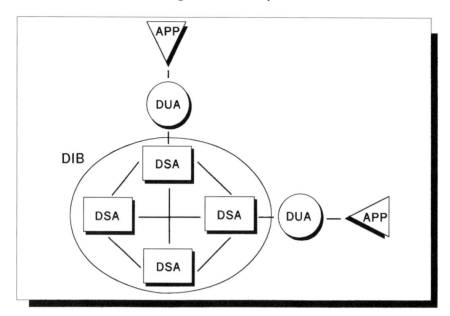

Figure 13.3 Directory services.

directory is physically located in a scalable number of Directory Service Agents (DSAs). A user of the directory would access information contained in a DSA through the use of a Directory User Agent (DUA). (See Figure 13.3.)

When a user wishes to view, modify, or create an entry in the directory, the DUA ensures that the request is correctly formatted. The DUA then accesses one or more DSA servers. Because the directory can be far larger than is possible to contain within a single DSA, each DSA contains sufficient knowledge to pass a request on to any other DSA that might contain the desired information. The DIB is thus distributed across the network. Information in the DIB is classified as objects which are divided into classes. X.500 defines certain default classes, but it also allows for creation of new classes. Objects within these classes are stored as entries with a set of attributes, each of which can have one or more values. X.500 associates each attribute with an attribute syntax that makes sure each entry is unique by providing a way of defining the entry's relative position in the DIT hierarchy. This is achieved by defining so-called Relative Distinguished Names (RDN) and Distinguished Names (DN). An RDN is made up of an attribute–value pair. The DN is made up of all RDNs in the path from the top of the Directory Information Tree to the actual entry in question.

It is important to note that, although this structure in many ways mirrors the structure of the X.400 transport mechanism and was developed as a complement to X.400, there is one major difference. X.500 operates in real time. Any deployment needs to be carefully planned in order to meet user expectations regarding performance and availability. It is important to choose X.500 implementations based on the expected needs of the user organizations. For example, should the directory be optimized for size and ease of object additions? Or should it be optimized for speed, allowing for fast scans and searches? Depending on the vendor implementation, vastly different results may be obtained when benchmarking an X.500 system.

The original X.500 recommendation was published by the CCITT in 1988. This specification was in many ways incomplete, lacking certain features for access control and replication of data throughout a complex system. Implementations of the specification during the early 1990s suffered from this lack of functionality. Although sufficient functionality was specified in the original recommendations, it would not have been advisable to begin large-scale deployment based on X.500 (88). Also, several vendors who might have been tempted to provide products based on this technology chose instead to wait for the first revised specification, the X.500 (92). Market acceptance of X.500 thus remained low for the first few years.

By 1992, however, several products had appeared on the market. Some implemented only the originally specified functionalities, some were enhanced by proprietary additions. Most notable among these additions were the replication features. By allowing information requests to be serviced through replicated portions of the DIB, response-time performance could be significantly improved.

In spite of such improvements, general acceptance of X.500 directory services has been slow. This is not only due to the real or perceived lack of funtionality of the original specification, but also because of the lack of clear migration paths from existing messaging directories to X.500, and, to some extent, due to lack of commitment from public carriers. While X.400 acceptance, to a high degree, has been driven by the European PTTs and their U.S. and Asian counterparts, X.500 is not currently a part of any carrier's general data communications services.

The emphasis on X.400 as a backbone technology has, however, increased market awareness of X.500 as a companion standard. Large corporations have operational pilots and are beginning to convert these into production services. The carriers can be expected to follow soon, by introducing pilot services to limited audiences. Although still a long way from being a global data information directory, X.500 has become accepted as an enterprise backbone directory service, in conjunction with existing directories. X.500 (92) functionality has enabled the development and deployment focus to shift from plain directory protocol implementations to directory synchronization and integration issues.

BACKBONE MANAGEMENT

Even when using a combination of messaging transport (X.400) and global directory (X.500), a messaging backbone would not be complete without the addition of a management service structure. For an enterprise to maintain a messaging backbone and allow mission-critical data to be transported, the backbone must be fully manageable. It is necessary to obtain a consistent view of network and systems operations in order to guarantee users the services they expect. Backbone management can be divided into two broad categories: network management and systems management.

Network management involves the monitoring and control of traffic on the network. How many messages are being processed at a certain segment of the network? How long does a message have to queue before passing from one MTA to another? What is the average message size? Message type? The answers to these questions might prove indispensable when deciding on the design of routing tables, which take into account variables such as the cost of using certain message types. A backbone may, for example, implement least-cost routing as an alternative to standard routing. A backbone may alternatively provide for priority routing of certain messages, depending on type, originator, or recipient. With the proper management tools, the critical decisions can be greatly simplified. (See Figure 13.4.)

Systems management is equally important. If a certain MTA is underperforming, it might be due to lack of processing power. If a message store is unable to adequately perform, it may be due to lack of storage space. By implementing systems management, MTAs can be remotely reconfigured, messages rerouted, or prioritized.

In addition, a large number of applications can be developed for the backbone using the network and systems management technologies as a basis. Billing and auditing applications can take advantage of historical data logged. Emergency routing applications can be triggered by historical trend analysis and network status combinations. Routine maintenance and configuration applications can be launched from centralized management stations on the backbone.

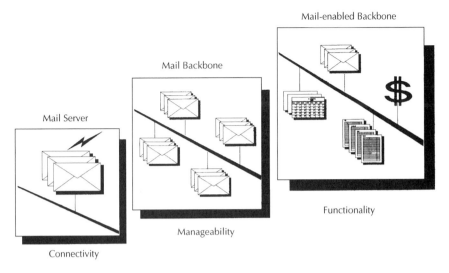

Figure 13.4 Messaging deployment strategies.

Messaging backbone management requires that all resources become manageable objects with defined properties. Each resource must be capable of communication through the use of agents. The key capabilities of these agents are discovery, diagnosis, control, and configuration. Extensible agents are located at the respective MTA, providing information to network and systems managers, and capable of acting upon decisions made at this level.

While Open Systems Interconnection (OSI) provides for network management through its Common Management Information Specification and Common Management Information Protocol (CMIS/CMIP), this is not a widely used protocol. And as CCITT has yet to provide a complete set of recommendations for network and systems management of messaging backbones, most backbones rely on the de facto standard, Simple Network Management Protocol (SNMP). This implies the use of dual protocol stacks at the MTA level. SNMP was designed for use with TCP/IP-based networks, while X.400 and X.500 were designed for use with underlying OSI protocol stacks. Given time, it is expected that this situation will change and a single protocol stack will be used. Most likely, this will mean greater use of the OSI protocol stack, although combinations based on TCP/IPs RFC 1006 transport conversion could be a possible solution in the short term. Until CMIS/CMIP becomes more widespread, most vendors of network management products use SNMP and extensible SNMP agents as the ways to monitor and control backbone networks.

The use of SNMP as a management protocol has one important benefit: It makes it possible to use generic network and systems management platforms. Such platforms are available from several computer systems vendors, under brand names like OpenView (Hewlett-Packard) and NetView (IBM), among others. Based on these management platforms, a large number of management applications can be obtained off the shelf from multiple independent software developers. The built-in toolkits that these management platforms provide also allow for additional application development, customized for the backbone in question. Because most providers of X.400 and X.500 software will have hooks into their protocol offerings, the extraction of data from the backbone can be a comparatively easy task.

Currently available applications for backbone management, based on the above-mentioned platforms, include network node managment, protocol stack configuration, network diagnostics, and message queue analysis, among others.

APPLICATION PROGRAMMING INTERFACES

As previously mentioned, electronic mail is only one of many applications supported by a messaging backbone. Other applications using the transport mechanism and directory services of the backbone are commonly referred to as mail-enabled applications. In older computing environments, application dialogs were conducted through the use of detailed, system-specific calls. Each computer system required a different type of dialog. Applications were custom made, efficient but hard to modify, and difficult to adapt to changing surroundings.

In a standardized backbone architecture, applications can have generic dialogs with the underlying services. Applications request services through application programming interfaces (API). APIs provide sets of macro commands that translate generic application service requests into system-specific commands. Applications developed for use with standard APIs become highly portable, from one system to another, from one user interface to another, from one database to another, etc.

In a messaging backbone, APIs surround the infrastructure, the transport mechanisms, and the management services, providing a common mechanism for accessing and utilizing the underlying transport, directory, and management capabilities. Although proprietary APIs exist and provide certain valuable functionalities, adherence to standards will greatly enhance the usability of the messaging backbone. The X/Open Company Ltd. publishes a set of portability guides for open systems. In these guides, recommendations for mail gateway APIs, as well as APIs to underlying services, are specified. X/Open specifies an API for each and every level of the backbone network protocol stack.

Most mail-enabled applications developers need to concern themselves with only a few of these APIs. For X.400, the X/API provides a generic set of commands for the design of gateways between X.400 and non-X.400 mail applications. For X.500, the X/DS API provides a similar functionality for designers of directory applications. As these APIs are part of generic standards specifications, they include a large number of calls and options in order to cover a wide range of possible usages. Many of these calls may not be applicable to every application developer's efforts. For this reason several vendors of backbone messaging protocols and services have implemented so-called high-level APIs which simplify and reduce the need for extensive X/Open API usage. A typical high-level API includes some 5 to 10 calls, rather than the approximatley 50 calls available in the generic specifications. High-level APIs complement the richer X/Open APIs and are normally positioned as an addition to the generic API, hiding the complexity of the underlying protocols.

Developers of structured business messaging applications frequently make use of these high-level APIs in their development of EDI applications or EFT applications, to name just a few examples. An EDI translator based on the U.N. specification Electronic Data Interchange for Administration, Commerce and Trade (EDIFACT) requires, for example, only some basic API calls in order to make use of an X.400 messaging backbone. The full X.400 X/APIA would not be necessary in this case. EFT applications are often more complex, specifically in terms of security aspects, and may need certain additional options, but seldom the complete mail gateway functionality.

In addition to these APIs, there are also some APIs that promise to take the messaging backbone concept a step beyond pure e-mail: the front-end vendor or vendor organization APIs. Messaging capabilities, such as those provided by X.400 and X.500, are currently being added to operating systems provided by desktop software or LAN software vendors. This approach completely frees the desktop client from the mail network, and a true client/server messaging architecture becomes possible. Key functions are performed at the front-end desktop client; the back-end server provides the messaging infrastructure services. Key APIs that fall into this category are the Microsoft API (MAPI), the Vendor Independent Messaging API (VIM), and Apple's Open Collaborative Environment API (OCE). Currently, a vast multitude of applications based on these APIs are under development. In several cases, existing desktop applications are being rewritten to take advantage of integrated messaging.

SECURE MESSAGING

In a large distributed system, such as an enterprise messaging backbone, security concerns abound. Overall OSI specifications, as well as the individual X.400 and X.500 recommendations, address this issue to some extent, although not in the detail required by many users of messaging systems.

The overall OSI security framework is divided into two areas: upper- and lower-layer security. A typical messaging backbone administrator need only be concerned with the former, since the application layer functionality is generally responsible for mechanisms involving the identity of senders and receivers of messages. The OSI security model defines a number of Generic Security Functions (GSF) that can be invoked by applications using the messaging service. GSFs support the confidentiality of message exchanges. Although this would most often be the key concern of the backbone administrator as well as of the users of the messaging backbone, there are also certain internal security functions available. These functions support the integrity of the messages through so-called security check-value routines.

As mentioned above, the functions are typically invoked through the network application layer. A major exception occurs when encryption is used. Encryption can be applied to the message transfer syntax, in which case the security function needs to be performed at the layer immediately below the application layer, the OSI presentation layer. Otherwise, senders and receivers would be required to use the same syntax, which would obviously limit the value of the presentation layer to any multivendor system.

Messaging systems usually implement security both in the transport mechanism (X.400) and the directory service (X.500). Basic X.400 security involves the exchange of passwords between the servers (the X.400 MTAs). Each sending MTA will exchange passwords with the receiving MTA each time a message transfer is to take place. This guarantees that only MTAs belonging to a certain backbone can send and receive messages along the backbone. No outside party can claim to be part of the backbone or make use of its facilities without using the proper passwords. Although it is possible to encrypt these passwords, they are normally sent as clear text.

The X.500 directory was designed for two aspects of security: authentication and authorization. Authentication routines are intended to determine whether or not a user actually is who he or she claims to be. Authorization routines determine the user's rights to information access.

Authentication of users and the distributed components of the directory system can be performed at two levels: simple and strong. Simple authentication makes use of passwords and is easily implemented and used. Strong authentication requires that public key encryption techniques are used. X.500 recommendations include a discussion on the use of encrypted, digitized signatures. This is not a widely used security scheme, however, since it significantly lessens the usability of the system in addition to requiring independent certifying authorities.

Authorization is less well covered in the X.500 recommendations, as it is mainly seen as a local matter for the enterprise directory manager or managers. When used on an intracompany basis, authorization may be a fairly simple matter since most employees would require similar access privileges to the backbone. Interenterprise messaging, however, implies the use of the messaging backbone by outside parties. Many organizations may not be willing to let their X.500 directory disclose, in detail, the corporate structure or the locations of their entities. If this is the case, the X.500 directory can be made partially available to outside parties through the use of access control lists. These lists specify which individuals or groups can access what information. Access can be restricted to certain object classes, certain attribute types, or certain subtrees within the DIT. In this way, a corporate messaging directory can be linked to a carrier's global directory, or to other organizations' directories without disclosing sensitive information to nonauthorized users.

NOMADIC MESSAGING

Access to a messaging backbone is made possible through traditional wireline hook-ups or through wireless communications media. Desktop PCs on LAN have access to messaging servers, which in turn form the enterprise messaging backbone. Laptop PCs, notebook PCs, and personal communicators are now moving computing power out of the office. Still, the need for access to messaging services remains.

Airports and hotels have already started upgrading their phone switches with new ones that provide better access to mobile data communication devices through simple wire-line hook-ups. While this enables out-of-office computing, it does not easily lend itself to fully nomadic computer communication. To achieve the full potential that mobile devices promise, wireless communications must be implemented. The combination of analog cellular telephone technology with data communications is the beginning of this next phase of messaging, nomadic messaging. Such mixed voice and data systems have been around for some time. For example, computer terminals in police cars transmit messages regarding services or license checks. Fire stations and vehicles have deployed wireless messaging in several North American and European cities. Global parcel tracking systems utilized by independent mail carriers or field service messaging used by computer companies are other familiar examples.

These systems are usually tailor-made for their respective organizations. Few standardized components have been used. The client/server architecture has not been fully realized. In order to improve productivity through messaging, it is necessary to integrate the messaging backbone concept with the emerging nomadic messaging technologies. Such integration is now taking place in several parts of the world, based on recent standardization efforts in the wireless messaging communications arena.

Currently, the most developed wireless front-end messaging system, which is also capable of linking into an enterprise backbone, is the Mobitex system. Mobitex is widely implemented in North America and Scandinavia, covering all major cities and metropolitan areas in those countries. It is rapidly expanding in continental Europe and Australia, with more countries likely to follow. The system makes use of a trunking technology based on multiple radio base stations with multiple channels. Channels are automatically switched as services are requested. Each data packet channel supports around 500 simultaneous users. Some 30 channels per geographic service area are currently in use, allowing thousands of messaging requests to be serviced concurrently.

At the front end, any mobile computing device with a serial port can be used, whether it is a laptop, a notebook, or a personal communicator. What is needed is the wireless e-mail software and the attachment of a Mobitex modem. The nomadic device may then send and receive messages at a standard rate of 9600 baud. As the Mobitex system is based on published standards, which are readily available to developers of integrated messaging systems, compatibility with a large number of devices is assured.

At the back end, there is an information repository and reformatting facility. This facility converts any incoming message to the backbone protocol standard and forwards it to its recipient. Messages from the enterprise backbone (or any other source) that arrive at the information repository are converted into radio format. They are then downloaded to the mobile recipients whenever their nomadic devices are activated within a service area.

Using this system, any LAN e-mail user who also has a mobile computing device can, for example, autoforward wire-line messages to the repository. In this way he or she will have continuous access to the same information that he or she would have had at the home office. This information can then be processed and acted upon in an instant, dramatically increasing the productivity of the traveling knowledge worker.

MAIL-ENABLED APPLICATIONS

As mentioned above, a messaging system is now capable of much more than electronic mail. EDI is today the primary mail-enabled application, already being in widespread use. The introduction of a toolkit for the Open Document Architecture (ODA) in early 1993 promises to make compound document transfer a second widespread mail-enabled application. The ODA toolkit provides specific tools, documents, and libraries, developed by a mix of European- and U.S.-based computer vendors. Since ODA is a message type within the X.400 (88) specification, documents including a mixture of text, graphics, and images can now be sent across the backbone to a mix of multivendor applications platforms. Work is under way to further expand these capabilities. In 1994, support for desktop publishing will be added. ODA extensions for large images, color, and security, as well as publishing layouts, alternate representation, and stylistic relationships between parts of documents are expected in the near future.

Both EDI and ODA are primarily related to the back-end messaging server functionalities, although front ends are expected to make extensive use of the ODA capabilities once the toolkit is in widespread use. Meanwhile, front-end application developers are rapidly moving forward in adding mail-enabled applications for workgroups to the desktop. Workgroup applications that make use of messaging systems are now available from various software companies, database providers, and major systems vendors.

Through the use of ODA, the server database can store and transmit compound documents in a generic form acceptable to a wide range of vendor systems. With the addition of a replication function, the database allows users or other applications to synchronize document contents through detection and resolution of differences between document versions. Replication can also be used to periodically update nomadic users of mobile computing devices.

Generic mail-enabled groupware in the form of mail-enabled spreadsheets, newsclip services, financial information, software distribution, and document management applications all entered the market during the early 1990s. In addition, several vertical market applications appeared, primarily in the health care and service sectors.

INTELLIGENT MESSAGING

Most existing messaging applications require more or less interaction from an end user. The amount of interaction depends on the user interface and the complexity of the application. As applications tend to become more and more complex, there is a growing need to minimize routine user interaction and to filter the vast amounts of information becoming available. Several organizations have developed, or are in the process of developing, various types of rules-based messaging. Rules-based or "Smart messaging" involves the addition of an amount of intelligence to the network itself. The ability of customizing and hiding various routine tasks behind programmable agents is a typical example. Messaging agents can be instructed to automatically route or reroute messages. They may provide standard replies to expected messages or identify and prioritize incoming messages based on originator, topic, or content type. Messaging agents can also automatically query information sources. Even more important, they can integrate messages with key applications for automated information processing.

Four major categories of mail-enabled information sources exist today on an interenterprise basis: news services, travel services, on-line information services, and specialized business data services. Custom-tailored news is provided filtered and selected to suit organizational or individual preferences. Travel and navigation services include travel guides and maps. On-line information services can be queried for legal, financial, or other types of data. And, of course, there is a wide range of specialized business data about products and services.

With the addition of a workflow engine, the messaging server can also manage multiple-users' calendars, schedule resources, and automate tasks such as flows of requests and approvals. Workflow monitoring systems can track documents, trigger automatic creation of documents, and automatically route documents to predefined locations and users. This type of messaging is currently the fastest growing segment of the messaging market.

In a similar manner, messaging systems can be designed to distribute software upgrades and administer site license agreements. They can also be used as an electronic publishing vehicle for newsletters and other publications seeking wide distribution.

It is becoming increasingly clear to many individuals and organizations that messaging systems may finally provide that elusive improvement in white collar productivity that the computer revolution promised years ago.

USING THE MESSAGING INFRASTRUCTURE

Many organizations and industries have implemented messaging infrastructures. Many have replaced older systems with updated messaging technology; some have implemented messaging backbones and some have moved mission-critical applications onto the messaging environment. A few examples may show the reasons behind this shift and the benefits reaped from efficient messaging.

In the first example, a global manufacturer of consumer goods, based in North America, maintains operations in approximately 50 countries. On average, there are two locations per country. By 1992, about half of the total number of employees used electronic mail, but the number was growing by 10 to 12 percent per year. The company maintained three different main-frame-based e-mail systems, a legacy from earlier acquisitions. There were also five different PC LAN mail systems implemented by independent entities around the world. Some of these were off-the-shelf mail systems; some were in-house designed. The host mail systems also had some mail-enabled applications, mainly for the finance, logistics, sales, and human resources departments.

The overall messaging architecture depended on a multitude of gateways, linking all remote systems with a central host in North America. Every message transmitted to the system was routed to North America, even if the recipient was located next door from the sender. Software revisions frequently caused segments of the overall system to be out of commission for shorter or longer periods of time.

In the early 1990s, the company conducted a survey of the messaging usage within the company. Among other findings, it was discovered that approximately 80 percent of all messages sent from within a local entity were received by addressees within the same entity. Only 20 percent of the messages needed to move further. Of the messages that did need to move beyond the entity, 80 percent remained within the country of origin. Clearly, there was no need to maintain a central North American focal point for all intracompany messaging purposes.

The follow-up to the survey resulted in a blueprint for a messaging back-bone to replace the gateway-oriented approach previously deployed. Some 250 X.400 MTAs were to be installed around the globe. While the local entities were free to maintain their existing mail systems, nonlocal traffic was to be routed through the messaging backbone. The backbone was logically split into four levels: local, country, regional, and global. MTAs were config-ured to handle expected flows of up to 10,000 messages per hour at the local level and corresponding amounts at other levels.

While designing the backbone network, a financial evaluation plan was also defined. Based on the redesign of the messaging architecture, the com-pany could safely project an overall dollar savings rate of over 20 percent per year. Individual items showed even higher savings rates. Telecommunica-tions costs, in particular, went down nearly 50 percent, mainly by eliminating the majority of the traffic between local entities and the North American headquarters. The company is currently in the process of redesigning its mail-enabled applications to take full advantage of the backbone concept deployed, and is actively investigating the possibility of extending the back-bone infrastructure through wireless access.

In another example, similar results occurred at a European financial institution responsible for a country-wide interbank clearinghouse opera-tion. In the late 1980s, there were approximately 2000 banks in the country. Merchant banks, savings institutes, and rural banks all depended on this central clearinghouse operation to balance interbank accounts on a daily basis. The clearinghouse was responsible for credit and debit depositions, cash dispenser transactions, and corporate payments. It also handled cus-tomer credit information and support services to affiliated organizations. Until the late 1980s, all these functions were based on the use of batch-proc-essing computers located in one remote computer center. Each bank and financial institution that was part of the clearing system maintained a link to the processing center. These links used a wide variety of communications protocols, all of which were converted through gateways at the processing center or at the banks themselves.

As transaction volumes grew through the decade, the system was gradually becoming obsolete. The amounts of information began to overwhelm the existing networks, and frequent software revisions at both the computer platform level and the gateway level caused a number of local network outages. It became increasingly clear to the clearinghouse operators, and the affiliated banks, that a major overhaul was necessary.

After conducting a technology survey, a decision was made to replace the gateway approach with a consistent, standardized messaging backbone capable of handling massive electronic funds transfer applications. The choice was made to utilize the CCITT X.400-specified network protocols, with certain adaptations for customized usage. The enhanced security that the clearinghouse required was the most important of these adaptations. The clearinghouse wished to retain the openess of the X.400 approach, as the multivendor benefits were too important to be sacrificed; but since the X.400 specification did not provide for specific EFT security measures, it was decided to implement encryption techniques at a lower level in the protocol stack.

The solution was message rerouting. As a message was passed down from X.400 to the underlying OSI session layer, the message was extracted from the protocol stack using calls from the CCITT session layer access library. The message was then handed over to a separate device and encryption algorithms invoked. The encrypted message was handed back to the OSI protocol stack at the OSI transport level. This exchange made use of the X/Open transport level API, X/TI. Finally, the message continued down through the protocol stack and out to the messaging backbone. At the receiving end, the process was carried out in reverse. In this manner, the OSI multivendor aspect was preserved, but the enhanced security was achieved without violating the standards approach.

The successful implementation of the messaging backbone helped the clearinghouse meet transaction volume demands and enhance the services offered to affiliated financial institutions. Results could also be quantified easily, as the following example will demonstrate. An individual in the country has a checking account with an affiliated bank. He or she writes a check and presents it to a teller at a bank other than his or her own. This check will then be processed through the clearinghouse, using the messaging backbone. At the time of writing, every single check that is presented to a bank other than where it was issued in the country in question, is handled by the interbank messaging backbone, and it is cleared, safely and securely, within a determinable and predictable time frame.

SUMMARY

Messaging systems have evolved considerably over the years, from simple host-based electronic mail to nomadic information transfer, from isolated islands of information to soon-to-be ubiquitous personal communication enablers, from basic e-mail to structured business communications, from user-intensive memo transfers to rules-based intelligent information filters, and from individuals to workgroups.

By providing a global information highway, messaging systems finally can deliver on the elusive promise of white collar productivity gains through information processing. Knowledge workers need no longer be limited to local information sources. Messaging-based workflow applications are now changing the way organizations operate, and the way they are structured.

ABOUT THE AUTHOR

Mikael Edholm is a frequent speaker on open systems networking at major seminars and symposia around the world. He has published several articles on networking and related topics, including chapters in the *Handbook of Manufacturing and Automation Integration* (Auersbach Publishers, 1990), the *Open Systems Interconnect Handbook* (McGraw-Hill, 1991), and the *Handbook of International Connectivity Standards* (Van Nostrand Reinhold, 1992).

He is a former member of the European MAP Users Group, has served on the Corporation for Open Systems marketing committee, and has been a member of the advisory board of the *Euro-American Communications Newsletter*, published in Palo Alto, California, and London, United Kingdom.

Mr. Edholm is currently business development manager of Ericsson Hewlett-Packard Telecommunications, A.B. in Stockholm Sweden. He has held marketing positions with Hewlett-Packard in Cupertino, California, and Grenoble, France. Prior to Hewlett-Packard, he held marketing positions with Allen-Bradley Company, based in Amsterdam, the Netherlands; 3M, based in Stockholm, Sweden; and ABB Electronic, based in Västerås, Sweden.

Mr. Edholm is a graduate of Uppsala University, Sweden, and Ashridge Management College, United Kingdom. He specializes in industrial and international marketing.

14

Workgroup Applications

Conall Ryan
Chairman of the Board
ON Technology Corporation

Historically, there have been three problems with groupware applications: Vendors do not know how to sell them; distributors do not know how to distribute them; and customers are not sure they want to use them.

Two of these three conditions still exist. But customers have decided to move forward. Under intense pressure to downsize operations and streamline processes across the board, forward-thinking businesses have adopted new collaborative software applications, in some cases to do the same work they have been doing more efficiently; in others, to enable new ways of working together that give their businesses a competitive advantage.

The best evidence that customers are embracing groupware is the spectacular growth of local area network (LAN)–based electronic mail over the last 3 years. Estimates put the number of e-mail users at nearly 7 million today, growing to more than 30 million by 1996.

This chapter focuses on the major issues involved in evaluating, buying, and maintaining workgroup software applications on your network. There is ample focus elsewhere in these pages on setting up the infrastructure of the network, itself. If you are in a mixed environment of personal computers (PCs) and Macs, or Macs and UNIX workstations, you have already wrestled protocol routers to the ground, struggled with e-mail gateways, and recoiled at the expense of delivering Ethernet to the desktop. Now that you have incurred the enormous cost of constructing your network, it is time to start seeing some of the return on investment in measurable, and *sustainable,* increases in end-user productivity.

Regardless of which workgroup applications you invest in, you must review several technical issues:

- Does the application run cross-platform?
- Does it work with the directory services you already have?
- Does it scale from two users to two thousand? To twenty thousand?
- How sophisticated are its security features?
- Will it coexist with the other applications on the network?
- Is it easy to install the program? Train users? Support users?
- How much time will it take to back up and otherwise administer the servers?
- Is the application transportable? Can mobile users dial in while on the road?

As you begin to add more and more applications onto your network, it helps to develop checklists like this to better gauge the investment you are about to make.

ELECTRONIC MAIL

Electronic mail is a good starting point because *groupware* is a place-holder word, waiting for specific products like electronic mail to define it more precisely. Some of the distinct categories that have emerged under the groupware umbrella include group scheduling, document sharing, screen sharing/conferencing, and forms routing/management. Organizationally, many of these applications tend to fall somewhere in between the enterprise-wide implementations of electronic mail and the traditional desktop (or pen and paper) individual productivity tools (Figures 14.1 and 14.2).

We understand mail because we can break it down into a linear process with a pen-and-paper analog: write letter, address envelope, insert letter into envelope, close envelope, lick stamp, drop in mailbox, hope it gets there. The computer is great at automating this task, removing some of the irksome steps along the way, and adding capabilities you do not get with pen and paper, such as a mail log that notifies you when someone has read your message, and, more recently, rule-based "agents" that can automatically file messages by topic, priority, and even send standard replies for you.

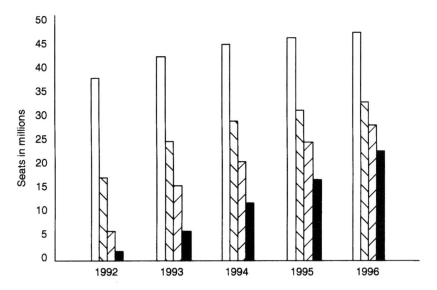

Figure 14.1 U.S. e-mail and group scheduling penetration. The explosive growth of e-mail and scheduling on LANs suggests that the stand-alone, "disconnected" CPU is rapidly becoming the exception rather than the rule. (*Sources:* IDC, Gartner, Info Corp.)

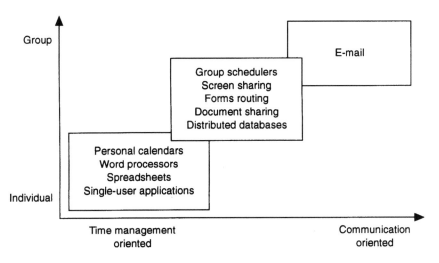

Figure 14.2 Workgroup applications fall between the individual and the enterprise.

Figure 14.3 Like a phone conversation.   **Figure 14.4 Like a radio broadcast.**

Figure 14.5 As interactions increase, e-mail becomes less effective.

E-mail is great for one-to-one or one-to-many communications. It is essentially a broadcast medium, concerned with getting messages from Point A to Points B and C. As the number and complexity of interactions in your workgroup increase, the effectiveness of basic electronic mail begins to diminish. (See Figures 14.3–14.5.)

File-based, store-and-forward e-mail can send, receive, route, and file. But it cannot arbitrate, reconcile, consolidate, and present evolving data in the way that is possible to do with a distributed client/server application such as Lotus Notes. If you use e-mail to manage XYZ project, your in-box quickly fills up with out-of-sequence, out-of-context messages. Instead of gaining clarity and momentum, the information contained in all of those Re:XYZ messages becomes mixed up and, in some cases, unintelligible.

Electronic mail will get simpler (the basic message handling service that will be subsumed into the NOS) and fancier (the front-end applications that add forms, rules, etc.). However, e-mail as we know it today is to workgroup applications what the 10-MB hard disk was to mass storage: A great start, but destined to become obsolete. Remember when you wondered how you would ever fill up 10 megabytes? These days, you can barely squeeze some major applications, with all of their help and tutorial files, into 10 megabytes. So, if the people on the network you support are asking the question, "What could I possibly want to do with the other people in my company that I can't already do with e-mail?"—the answer is: "Plenty."

Let us explore some of those applications.

THE WORKGROUP APPLICATIONS UMBRELLA: MAPPING THE CAPABILITIES OF WORKGROUP TOOLS TO YOUR ORGANIZATIONAL NEEDS

Workgroup software facilitates communications in one or more of the following areas:

Same Time, Same Place: Real-time meeting facilitation, shared screen software

Same Time, Different Places: Teleconferencing, audio conferencing, electronic meeting software, telephone

Different Times, Same Place: Electronic mail, scheduling/calendaring, group editing/authoring, computer conferencing, workflow, document management, voice mail

Different Times, Different Places: Electronic mail, scheduling/calendaring, group editing/authoring, workflow, document management, voice mail

Start your planning process by following these steps:

1. Clearly define the workgroup problem you are trying to solve.

2. Describe the linear events that accomplish this process now.

3. List the elements of the process that the software automates.

4. List the elements that still must be accomplished on pen and paper, or through face-to-face interactions.

5. Which of the above time/place requirements must be met?

6. Does the software you're considering meet these requirements?

7. Estimate ballpark time and cost savings if you adopt the software.

8. Call vendors and ask them to refer you to happy customers. Then call the happy customers and ask if they can refer you to unhappy customers!

9. Start a scrapbook of clippings on the product, concentrating on detailed comparative reviews.

The next step is to make sure you have identified all of the participants in the decision-making process. Whether your company treats this group as a loose confederation or a formal voting committee, getting everyone to agree on the purchasing objectives is critical. If a third of your team wants to buy a real-time meeting facilitator, another third wants to buy a group scheduling package, and the final third wants to buy a "meeting minimizer," someone is bound to be disappointed. Although they may sound similar, these three product areas are actually quite different. Meeting facilitation software manages and enhances the meeting process, using networked machines around a "same place, same time" table or conference area to capture and synthesize the *content* of the meeting as it occurs. A group scheduler has nothing to do with the meeting beyond setting up an actionable agenda. Group schedulers are friction removers, designed to attack the wasted time an organization spends every day trying to *set meetings up*. Meeting minimizers, whether they distribute information through live documents, shared databases, or other means, are time-shifters whose main purpose is to cut down on the number of meetings by preprocessing topics for discussion and reaching decisions through asynchronous communication. Agreeing in advance on which solution you want will save you a lot of time and headaches later.

PARTICIPATIVENESS, OR OVERCOMING THE "WHAT'S IN IT FOR ME?" SYNDROME

No workgroup package can truly benefit your organization unless employees are willing to use it.

All of the popular business literature to the contrary, the fact is that most organizations still make software decisions in the traditional way: methodically and hierarchically. The software used in these organizations is mandated, not chosen. A new employee arrives at his or her desk and finds a 486 Windows machine equipped with the company-standard memory, disk, and display configuration. Powering on the machine, the employee can get to work right away on a hard disk that has been preloaded with the company's approved word processing, spreadsheet, database, and e-mail packages. An incoming message may arrive, inviting the employee to sign up for training. Otherwise, no one is about to ask this person—who is being paid to apply noncomputer-related expertise—to stay current on all the latest developments in *PC Magazine.* And he or she is quite happy to be allowed to focus on other issues. However, if you want this employee to electronically publish his or her competitive research on a new FDA-approved drug, grant access rights to his or her pharmaceuticals database, or simply attend a meeting, the immediate (if often unspoken) response will be the same response we would all have: "*What's in it for me?*"

A statement like "*This is what everyone else is going to use,*" will not gain this person's cooperation, because it doesn't really answer the question.

On the other hand, if using a new forms package will save the company $100,000 in 6 months, and $25,000 of that has already been earmarked by management for R&D, a statement like "*the new lab equipment you've been asking for*" could make our researcher a forms fanatic almost overnight.

As paradoxical as it may sound, every workgroup application must overcome the what's-in-it-for-me barrier. People prefer familiar, inefficient systems to learning something new. You must arm yourself with compelling data that supports the workgroup tool you plan to deploy. Sharing your needs analysis and purchasing objectives will boost participation dramatically.

Some simple guidelines for minimizing the anxiety of installing workgroup software are listed below:

1. Be prepared to explain how it delivers individual, as well as group, benefits.

2. Do not tell users that the software you are planning to implement will make them better. Instead, focus on how the software is going to make things *easier.*

3. Stay away from software that makes people uncomfortable or uncharacteristically belligerent. If people complain about having to use a new workgroup tool, the probability that something is wrong with the software and the people who designed it is much higher than the probability that something is wrong with your users. People should never be subordinated to software.

4. Reassure people that using the software will not force them to surrender control over their personal schedules, data files, etc. If the software *does* undermine individual control, return to step 3. Repeat as necessary until users buy into your decision.

5. Think through training and support issues in advance.

6. Find product champions within the departments and get them to help you.

THE DISTRIBUTED DATABASE MODEL

Many of the newer client/server applications have taken a different approach than e-mail toward workgroup computing, viewing the asynchronous flow of data within an organization not as a series of discontiguous messages but as a structured exchange of tasks, events, and results. For these applications, moving information around is less important than how fast (and how well) users can synthesize that information with the rest of their work at the desktop (or laptop) level.

Distributed databases typically use a two-way message store in which master copies of documents, schedules, and the like reside on a server. The server in turn replicates copies of these files, as well as updates as they occur, to the local client machines. Distributed object-oriented databases arbitrate and reconcile complex, evolving information better than traditional file-based, store-and-forward messaging architectures.

If User A changes a file, the server updates the master copy, then notifies Users B and C of the change (Figure 14.6). User B may be a mobile user, who resyncs with the central data store from a hotel room 3000 miles away. Any user can make subsequent changes within the constraints of his or her access privileges. Since they can view each other's input in context, some users may be responsible for adding information, while others edit, refine, and delete information that is no longer relevant. Though constant database pruning is required to keep such systems performing optimally, the number of data "harvesting" events is relatively few in number. Unlike single-user

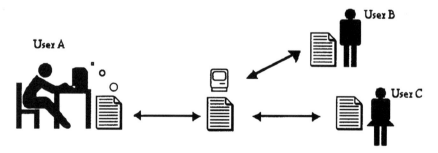

Figure 14.6 Two-way message store.

individual productivity applications geared toward producing static hard-copy reports, workgroup tools are friction removers, designed to increase the velocity and throughput of information within the organization.

The products that fit this general description are listed in Table 14.1.

The best thing to do if you are considering a distributed database product versus a more traditional file-based messaging package is to refer back to the problem you are trying to solve, and the linear (and potentially recurring) sequence of steps the software must perform. If arbitration and reconciliation rate high in this analysis, and overall security and mass storage concerns rate low by comparison, a distributed database is probably for you.

THE DIRTY SECRETS OF COLLABORATIVE COMPUTING

The true cost of a workgroup application has very little to do with the price per seat you pay at retail. As a quick exercise, assume you are buying 1000 seats of a new forms management product. The sales representative offers a volume purchase price of $99 per seat, providing you buy all 1000 seats within a year. To understand what you are really paying for the application, you need to do some math based on your answers to the following questions:

Question 1. How hard is the software to install? Can it be installed remotely, or will someone from MIS have to visit every machine? Can users install it themselves? Having someone from MIS load the software onto each user's machine is a time-consuming and costly task.

Question 2. Do our end users' desktop machines satisfy the system requirements of the software? Is more memory needed or more disk? Are dedicated server(s) required? Capital equipment can burden the cost by several thousand additional dollars.

Question 3. Will people need to be trained before they can use it? This is a tricky calculation, because asking end users to sacrifice an hour of their time to be trained with 50 other people in a large conference room may be far more cost-effective than relying upon end users to train themselves (which could lead to 50 users calling you with the same problems, one at a time). Modest goals lead to great workgroup tools. To get everyone's participation, ease of use is probably the most important feature to look for in a workgroup tool. Studies of individual desktop products like spreadsheets and word processors have shown that the average person uses less than 20 percent of the functionality of those packages. Work-

Table 14.1 Strengths and Weaknesses of the Distributed Database Approach

Strengths	*Weaknesses*
Replication: The server stores everyone's information. Client gets a local copy of the information that is relevant to him or her.	Requires significantly more mass storage volume, due to replicated data; don't forget the backups, either!
Arbitration: Server is typically capable of comparing records between users and facilitating agreement on who/what/when types of information.	Many distributed database products require separate directory services, which can be hard to maintain when you already have NetWare and e-mail installed.
Portability: Client can take work *on the road*. Any incremental changes he or she makes on a plane or in a hotel room are captured in his or her local copy of the database.	In a multiple-server environment, user and resource progagation can be a problem. Make sure you understand how users on Server A find out about new users on Server B. Once a connection is established between servers, what happens if the servers get out of sync? Look for some sort of rollback feature that addresses the data recovery issue.
Reconciliation: When the traveling client dials in from the road, the application downloads any changes made to the central database during the time the client has been off-line. The client's changes upload to the server, which notifies other clients if what has been changed affects them.	Data is less secure. It stands to reason that when there are more entry points, constructing an enterprise-wide defense system to prevent unauthorized entry gets harder.
Off-loads server of connect-intensive work, which boosts server performance and can result in reduced network traffic.	
Multiple copies of data make recovery easier; there is no single place where all of your data can be wiped out.	

group software needs to be leaner, because the usage patterns are much higher (e-mail users probably exercise 50 to 75 percent of their products every day). When you are buying workgroup software, do not look for the most features. Look for the *right* features. And imagine the least experienced person in your organization trying to train him- or herself in how to use the product.

Question 4. Who will internally support the product? The way people in MIS departments get assigned new tasks when they are already working at 100 percent capacity is not very different from the movie *The Producers*. In the movie, Zero Mostel sells several hundred percent of the ownership in a play that he is certain will be a bomb. When the play turns into an instant hit, he and Gene Wilder have to figure out how they're going to pay. And pay. And pay. If you already have five full-time people trying to support 10,000 seats of electronic mail, and no help desk hiring requisitions to fill, the departments that use the forms management package will have to support themselves. Can they do it? Will they? If the answers are yes, are you willing to let departments install 1000 seats of an unsupported product on *your* network?

Question 5. Does the vendor provide free, unlimited customer support? Is the support team responsive? To contain costs and protect the already dwindling margins in software, vendors have begun charging for product support on an annual basis, or even by the call. Be sure to ask if vendors provide unlimted support as part of their annual maintenance agreements.

All of these factors can constitute hidden costs which you must recognize and measure to determine if the product investment is cost-effective. If you have to visit 1000 machines because the group forms management product requires a special IPX driver, and you also have to upgrade a large percentage of the CPUs to provide the necessary disk and memory to run the application, the *true* cost per person might look more like this:

Initial price per seat	$ 99
Installation	$ 30
System upgrades	$ 30
Training	$ 75
Support/Maintenance	$ 75
Vendor support	$ 0?
Upgrade @ 15%	$ 15
True cost per seat	**$324**

Before you buy any workgroup applications, you should do a highly detailed cost analysis that accounts for all of the factors mentioned above. If you are sure you can justify the cost now, ask yourself if you will still be able to justify the purchase decision 1 or 2 years from now. And before you move on to constructing a feature matrix for evaluating the software, never stop asking yourself if the features you want added to the software are also adding unwanted cost.

THE EVALUATION CYCLE: CONSTRUCTING THE FEATURE MATRIX

Evaluating workgroup products requires the same careful planning you would use to select an individual productivity tool. The process of choosing which workgroup application your organization should use is actually quite different, however. If getting a product that requires no training is more important than having a harder-to-use competitor with all the bells and whistles, a workgroup product with fewer features actually may be a better purchase decision.

Remember, the average spreadsheet customer uses less than 20 percent of the product's features. This, in and of itself, is a powerful argument for workgroup software. Why would anyone buy a whole cow to make a couple of hamburgers?

The average group scheduling customer uses between 70 and 75 percent of the product's features *every single day*! With workgroup products, modest goals lead to great products. Again, what the vendor leaves *out* is almost as important as what the vendor puts in, so structure your evaluation accordingly.

As a way of helping you prepare for your next workgroup software evaluation cycle, the charts below take you through a hypothetical case of buying a group scheduling package. The purpose of the charts is to help guide you in defining your requirements. The check marks (✔) have been arbitrarily arranged, and do not reflect actual commercial products.

Boilerplate Product Evaluation Matrix
Internal Use Only
Group Scheduling Applications

✔ = Feature
blank = Not a feature

Cross-Platform Operations	Product A	Product B	Product C	Product D	Product E
Supports Windows and Macintosh from the same server	✔				
Windows or Mac server option	✔			✔	

Cross-Platform Operations	Product A	Product B	Product C	Product D	Product E
Both Windows and Macintosh client and server in the same box	✔		✔		
Same user interface on both platforms	✔				✔
UNIX client		✔			✔
UNIX server		✔			✔

Scheduling Meetings	Product A	Product B	Product C	Product D	Product E
Autopick: Automatically find available meeting times	✔	✔		✔	
Shows conflicts as you change the meeting time	✔	✔		✔	✔
Reschedule a meeting after sending proposal	✔	✔			✔
One step to cancel a meeting	✔		✔		✔
Change guest list, agenda, or location of a meeting; automatically inform guests	✔		✔		✔
Automatic confirmation (guests can attend)	✔				✔
Visual indication that a meeting is confirmed	✔				✔
Automatic notice to guests when meeting is confirmed	✔				
Schedule recurring meetings	✔	✔	✔	✔	✔
Required and optional meeting participants	✔			✔	
cc: and bcc: meeting participants	✔			✔	
View multiple calendars at once	✔			✔	✔
Composite schedule of guest availability	✔	✔		✔	✔
Send agendas with meeting invitations	✔	✔	✔	✔	✔
Agenda attached to meetings in daily calendar	✔	✔	✔	✔	✔
File attachment to meeting invitations		✔			
First-come, first-served meeting rooms, etc.	✔	✔			

(continued)

Scheduling Meetings	Product A	Product B	Product C	Product D	Product E
Track and log guest responses to meeting proposal	✔	✔			✔
Public and private groups	✔	✔	✔	✔	✔
Address books		✔		✔	✔
Message Window for easy status information		✔		✔	
Print your meeting information in a convenient summary	✔	✔	✔	✔	✔
Send invitations via e-mail to users not on calendar		✔		✔	✔
Tile Daily option for open proxies	✔		✔		
Auto-pick for conference rooms			✔		
Schedule over midnight	✔				

Responding to Meeting Invitations	Product A	Product B	Product C	Product D	Product E
Ability to change your mind about attending a meeting	✔	✔			✔
Send comments back to proposer about the meeting	✔	✔		✔	
Have confidential comments from guests (in daily calendar)	✔				
User options to Accept, Decline, or Defer accepting the meeting	✔	✔		✔	
Automatically place accepted meetings into your calendar	✔	✔	✔	✔	✔
All meeting changes highlighted for quick understanding	✔				

Organizing and Viewing Schedule	Product A	Product B	Product C	Product D	Product E
Day at-a-glance	✔	✔	✔	✔	✔
Multiple days at-a-glance	✔				✔
Week at-a-glance	✔	✔	✔	✔	✔
Month at-a-glance	✔		✔	✔	✔
Customize your calendar for your work hours—daily basis	✔				
Customize your calendar for your work hours—all days only		✔			

Organizing and Viewing Schedule	Product A	Product B	Product C	Product D	Product E
Display schedule in 15-minute increments	✔		✔	✔	✔
Indicator for activities not in daily view	✔			✔	
Monthly busy time view with rapid navigation for details	✔	✔	✔	✔	✔
Prioritized To-Do list with automatic sorting	✔	✔	✔	✔	✔
Flexible time (time you are still available for meetings)	✔				
Graphically reschedule and resize activities	✔	✔			✔
Allow overlapping activities and meetings (double-booking)	✔	✔			✔
Add detailed notes to activities or To-Do list items	✔		✔	✔	
Export schedule to tab-delimited file		✔	✔	✔	✔
Search all text in calendar/notes	✔	✔	✔		✔
Repeat events automatically	✔	✔	✔	✔	
Repeat events with any frequency	✔	✔	✔		✔
Change one repeat activity or meeting without affecting others	✔	✔	✔		✔
Allows for work hours crossing midnight	✔		✔		

Proxy Access to Calendars	Product A	Product B	Product C	Product D	Product E
No passwords need to be shared between users to access others' calendars	✔	✔	✔		✔
Change people with proxy access any time	✔		✔	✔	✔
Allow meeting invitations to go to your proxy	✔				
Keep private activity and To-Do list items from your proxy	✔	✔			
Read-Write and Read-Only proxies	✔	✔	✔		✔

(continued)

Proxy Access to Calendars	Product A	Product B	Product C	Product D	Product E
"Public" events everyone is invited to					
Multiple Proxies on screen at the same time	✔		✔		
"Tile" option for proxies	✔				

Printing and Display	Product A	Product B	Product C	Product D	Product E
Print from all views	✔	✔	✔	✔	✔
Pocket size (3.75" × 6.75")	✔		✔		
Organizer size (5.5" × 8.5")	✔		✔	✔	✔
Folio size (8.5" × 11")	✔	✔	✔	✔	✔
Wall charts (up to 34" × 44")					
Folded and facing pages			✔		
Guidelines for cutting					
On-screen preview	✔				✔
Import and export (text)	✔	✔		✔	✔
Import and export (appointments)		✔		✔	✔
Custom fonts and styles	✔	✔	✔		✔
Color	✔	✔	✔		✔
Banners					
Post-It notes					
Icons and graphics					

Reminders and Alarms	Product A	Product B	Product C	Product D	Product E
Remind at the time of an event	✔	✔	✔	✔	✔
Warn of upcoming events	✔	✔	✔	✔	✔
Alert while in other program	✔	✔			✔
Snooze alarm and warnings		✔		✔	✔
Adjustable warning and snooze	✔	✔		✔	
Travel time reminder					

To-Do List Features	Product A	Product B	Product C	Product D	Product E
Propose Group To-Do items to others	✔			✔	
Track acceptance of Group To-Dos	✔			✔	

To-Do List Features	Product A	Product B	Product C	Product D	Product E
Allow users to accept, decline, or decide later before accepting a Group To-Do	✔			✔	
Reminders on To-Dos	✔	✔	✔	✔	✔
Priorities	✔	✔	✔	✔	✔
User-definable priorities	✔				✔
Keep confidential from proxy	✔	✔			✔
Associate To-Dos with a date	✔	✔	✔	✔	✔
Recurring tasks			✔		
Sort tasks	✔	✔	✔	✔	✔

General User Features	Product A	Product B	Product C	Product D	Product E
Application	✔	✔	✔	✔	✔
Automatic log-in at start-up	✔	✔	✔	✔	
Password security for each user	✔	✔	✔	✔	✔
Check calendar from any PC with software installed	✔			✔	
Easy dial-in from the road method	✔				
Time Zone support				✔	
Voice attachments					
User-level archiving		✔	✔		✔
Installer	✔	✔	✔	✔	✔

Administration	Product A	Product B	Product C	Product D	Product E
Define resources as first-come, first-served	✔	✔			
Simple set-up and management of server and user accounts	✔	✔	✔	✔	✔
Remote administration of all servers	✔	✔			✔
Define work hours	✔				
Easy import of user lists from e-mail products	✔	✔		✔	✔
Designate and display company-wide holidays			✔	✔	✔
Server controls for backup and restore operations	✔	✔			

(continued)

Administration	Product A	Product B	Product C	Product D	Product E
Purge old calendar data to optimize performance		✔			
Server-to-server		✔		✔	
Servers can run in background on any Windows machine	✔		N/A		✔
Run without e-mail	✔			✔	✔
Scales enterprise-wide		✔		✔	✔
Cross-platform	✔				
Administrative statistics		✔			
Automatic backup		✔			

Modes of Operation	Product A	Product B	Product C	Product D	Product E
Single user			✔		✔
Networked group	✔	✔	✔	✔	✔
Remote	✔			✔	✔
Portable	✔				✔
Off-line	✔	✔			✔

Pricing	Product A	Product B	Product C	Product D	Product E
Suggested retail price (per seat)	$129.95	$82.50	$79.50	$119	$50
Volume purchase pricing	✔		✔	✔	
Site licenses offered?	Y	Y	N	N	N
Maintenance agreements offered?	Y	N	Y	N	Y

Once you have compiled and analyzed all of the above factors, you should apply a weighted ranking to each category prior to adding up each product's "score" and making your purchase decision. After you have made your purchase, the matrix will serve as a cost-justification tool for management, and a building block for future evaluations. As your organization gains sophistication in using the product you have chosen, add "wish list" features to the matrix and send them to the developer as helpful input into the features subsequent versions of the software must have to be successful in your organization.

Finally, add elements to the matrix that directly target the peculiar characteristics of your network environment. How much packet traffic does a specific application generate? Have you noticed any network irregularities that were not there before you introduced the new application? A key part of your evaluation relates to nonfeature issues such as network performance degradation, driver incompatibilities, and other infrastructure details.

THE COST JUSTIFICATION FOR WORKGROUP APPLICATIONS

Now that you know what you're buying, and what you're paying, you need to take a closer look at what you're getting for all that money. To extend the generic example of forms routing, one way of doing this might be as follows:

Number of users	1000
Cost per user	$324
Total projected cost @ 1000 seats	$324,000
Average # forms per day per person	7
Average fully burdened cost per form	$20
Forms cost per day at current rate	$140,000
Average cost per form with XYZ product	$3
Savings per form	$17
Break-even analysis/# forms	20,000
Time to break even	2.857 days!

I have exaggerated this example to illustrate two principles:

1. Software that may seem expensive at $324 per seat may actually be a terrific bargain.

2. To justify a purchase to upper management, the first question you must be prepared to answer is "time to break even."

Usually, the payback period for a workgroup application is approximately 2 years. It takes that long to evaluate, buy, roll out, train, gain widespread expertise, and finally realize tangible competitive benefits. It is unlikely that any new workgroup tool will help you make next quarter's revenue goal, but the tool *could* be of pivotal value in helping you achieve 3-year operating plan results.

A PRODUCT EVALUATION IS ALSO A COMPANY EVALUATION

Before you buy workgroup software from any vendor, call their support hot line several times during your evaluation and ask the hardest questions you can think of about the product.

What to look for in a product support organization:

- **True support.** Not a sales organization masquerading as support
- **Prompt response.** Same-day call-back; worst case should be 24-hour turnaround
- You should not be put through an interrogation every time you call
- **Technical expertise.** If you know more than they do, you're in trouble!
- **Patience.** Taking the time to organize your problems is helpful, but should not be required
- **Courtesy/resiliency.** Someone who is a pleasure to deal with even when you are in your worst mood

The vendor's sales representatives do not need be highly technical, but they should be good presenters, since you may need their help in training users. They should also possess thorough knowledge of pricing, provide constant updates on upcoming products, and be willing to connect you with other people in their organizations, if necessary. A great salesperson will be focused on establishing a mutually profitable long-term relationship with you. A bad salesperson will always be preoccupied with getting you to take the next hundred seats.

SECURITY

With new workgroup technology, you can move time-critical information around your company—or around the world—in minutes. This information is the most valuable asset in your company. How do you keep it safe? This topic deserves an entire chapter of its own, but let us at least outline the three main security issues you must address when buying workgroup software.

User identity. How do you know users are who they say they are? Some products have a simple password interface. Others require several levels of authentication, especially when users dial in from remote locations. Several products have a *call-back* verification process that refuses a connection after receiving a valid password until the server dials back to a corresponding number in its directory. A straightforward preventative step you can take, mandated by several government agencies, is requiring users to change their passwords at least once every 30 days. Apply this same rule to any dial-in servers and databases that are under your care.

Levels of access. Not every user will have the same access privileges. Depending on the product you are evaluating, examine the granularity of access control to verify that it meets your needs. In a document management system, for example, can you prevent certain people from opening specific documents? Give others read-only access? Further limit privileges within the documents themselves at the paragraph, word, or even character level? Change privileges along the way?

Safe transport. There are several popular encryption schemes for scrambling *in-transit* data while it moves over the wire. The mathematical concepts behind the increasingly popular systems are a little elusive, but think of the adventure movies you saw as a kid when two spies met and put two halves of the same coin together before speaking and you will get the basic idea. The information you send me cannot be unscrambled until both halves of our *coin* meet. RSA Data Security, of Redwood City, California, is leading the way in this area.

Good security systems are effective but unobtrusive. Do not forget that the main point of buying a workgroup product is to get people to use it. Overly burdensome entry and exit procedures can have the effect of scaring off legitimate users and failing by succeeding (no one breaks into the system, but no one uses it, either).

As a last word, you should be aware that there are clever schemes for defeating each of the categories above, some undertaken largely for intellectual amusement, others employed in actual premeditated crimes. The average corporate computer theft is roughly *half a million dollars*! Sadly, most of these crimes are committed by insiders. That alone should convince you to pay careful attention to this issue, especially if the information you intend to transport around between physical sites is valuable and confidential.

PORTABILITY

If your company has a large percentage of mobile users, the workgroup applications you buy must be portable as well as cross-platform and scalable. Products that force you to connect to a data file on a server before you can use the client application will not be of much use on a 747 bound for Tokyo. Being truly portable means that users can work off-line, and send/receive changes to remote servers at their convenience. Some products allow off-line use, but do not support dial-in access.

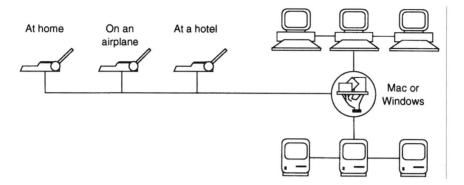

Figure 14.7 Workgroup applications must be portable as well as cross-platform.

During your budget analysis, include the cost of upgrading laptops with modems, as well as additional disk and memory, if users plan to take a workgroup application on the road. Read your software licenses carefully. While many vendors now view "one license" as applying to a single user and whatever machine that person happens to be using, some vendors may charge you for an additional seat.

There are two other trends to keep in mind in portable computing. Size and weight drive this category, so the half-life of any peripherals you buy may be brief. The second trend is that pen-based palmtop machines, sophisticated pagers, combination cell phones/rolodexes, and other new consumer electronics devices will become increasingly important this decade, and the workgroup software you buy should support them. Until hand-held devices have the requisite microprocessors and storage capacity to participate in two-way data exchanges, many will focus on receiving one-way information broadcasts from a network or desktop machine (Figure 14.7).

DO A USER STUDY

Even with all of the preparation you have gone through, you will not really know if the new product has been successful until it has been up and running for several months. You can learn a good deal by polling users on what they like and dislike about a product. Areas to focus on include rate of adoption, frequency of use, overall "comfort level," and user satisfaction.

You may have two groups using the same product on different servers. Group One loves the product. Group Two hates it. Studying the methods

Group One used to spur faster adoption and encourage users to get up to speed may help Group Two's project leaders overcome confusion and resistance. Studying Group Two's problems may alert Group One to issues they were not aware of yet. Compiling such feedback on an ongoing basis will undoubtedly help you fine-tune your training and support systems, and get more incremental value out of the software itself.

In case you have not already thought of this, the easiest way to conduct the survey is through your workgroup product of choice, whether it is e-mail, Notes, Instant Update, Pacer Forum, or some other product specifically designed to share and synthesize feedback.

SUMMARY

Electronic mail alone cannot address all of your workgroup needs.

When evaluating workgroup software, identify specific objectives and organize them in as linear a sequence as possible. Map the product's capabilities to this sequence.

Identify the group decision-makers and agree to a purchase process and specification.

Be ready with quantitative answers when individuals ask, "What's in it for me?"

Modest goals lead to great workgroup products. What the vendor leaves out of a workgroup product is as important as what the vendor puts into it.

To make the right purchase decision for your organization, you must become an information sponge, soaking up knowledge from internal users, trade press reviews, customer referrals, and competitive vendors.

Look for the hidden costs, or "dirty secrets," in the software you are about to buy.

Be rigorous about constructing a complete features evaluation matrix.

Do a cost/benefits analysis, focusing on time to break even.

Know the company you are buying from as well as the product they develop.

Understand and plan around the security implications of the product.

If you have a high percentage of mobile users, the application must be portable.

Develop an internal mechanism for collecting user feedback.

Tremendous advances in networking and distributed database technology will reward forward-thinking companies who adopt the new workgroup tools. The winning products are likely to be clearly defined "friction removers," which remove the drudgery from common tasks like setting up meetings, routing forms, and sharing fast-changing, mission-critical documents and databases. There are many other group-oriented tasks that should be computerized for cross-platform networks; they just have not been effectively automated yet.

ADDITIONAL READING

If you are interested in reading more about workgroup applications and their potential impact on business, here is a brief list of recommend titles:

Books

Shared Minds, by Michael Schrage, published by Random House.

Leading Business Teams, by Robert Johansen, David Sibbet, Suzyn Benson, Alexia Martin, Robert Mittman, and Paul Saffo, published by Addison-Wesley.

Groupware: Computer Support for Business Teams, by Robert Johansen, with contributions by Jeff Charles, Robert Mittman, and Paul Saffo, published by The Free Press, a division of Macmillan, Inc.

Technology for Teams: Enhancing Productivity in Networked Organizations, by Susanna Opper and Henry Fersko-Weiss, published by Van Nostrand Reinhold.

Computer-Supported Cooperative Work: A Book of Readings, by Irene Grief, published by Morgan Kaufmann Publishers, Inc.

Newsletters

Release 1.0, a monthly report by Esther Dyson.

P.C. Letter, a biweekly newsletter, published by Stewart Alsop, edited by David Coursey.

ABOUT THE AUTHOR

Conall Ryan joined ON as vice president of marketing in June 1989 and succeeded Mitchell Kapor as president in September 1990. He is currently chairman of the board.

Before joining ON, Mr. Ryan was a marketing manager at NeXT Computer, Inc., in Palo Alto, California, where he had overall management responsibility for bundled software: Digital Library, Sybase SQL Server, Mathematica, WriteNow, NeXT Mail, Digital Dictionary, Workspace Manager, and various system tools. His other responsibilities included strategic planning and negotiations, competitive hardware analysis, and event marketing.

From 1985 until 1988, Mr. Ryan worked at Lotus Development Coporation in Cambridge, Massachusetts. He was the product manager for Lotus Agenda and Lotus Metro and also had management responsibilities for Lotus HAL and part of 1-2-3. He worked as a project leader at Software Arts until Lotus acquired the company in 1985.

Mr. Ryan is a published author of short fiction, technical articles, and two novels, one a Book-of-the-Month Club Alternate Selection, the other an Edgar Award nominee. His work has been published in the United States and United Kingdom and translated into German and Japanese.

He received a B.A. in English from Boston University.

Index